A PRIDE OF TERRYS

Sarah Ballard Terry
(1817 to 1892)

A PRIDE OF TERRYS

Family Saga

MARGUERITE STEEN

LONGMANS

LONGMANS, GREEN AND CO LTD
48 GROSVENOR STREET, LONDON WI
RAILWAY CRESCENT, CROYDON, VICTORIA, AUSTRALIA
AUCKLAND, KINGSTON (JAMAICA), LAHORE, NAIROBI
LONGMANS SOUTHERN AFRICA (PTY) LTD
THIBAULT HOUSE, THIBAULT SQUARE, CAPE TOWN
JOHANNESBURG, SALISBURY
LONGMANS OF NIGERIA LTD
W. R. INDUSTRIAL ESTATE, IKEJA
LONGMANS OF GHANA LTD
INDUSTRIAL ESTATE, RING ROAD SOUTH, ACCRA
LONGMANS GREEN (FAR EAST) LTD
443 LOCKHART ROAD, HONG KONG
LONGMANS OF MALAYA LTD
44 JALAN AMPANG, KUALA LUMPUR
ORIENT LONGMANS LTD
CALCUTTA, BOMBAY, MADRAS
DELHI, HYDERABAD, DACCA
LONGMANS CANADA LTD
137 BOND STREET, TORONTO 2

© MARGUERITE STEEN 1962

FIRST PUBLISHED 1962

PRINTED IN GREAT BRITAIN BY
THE CAMELOT PRESS LTD., LONDON AND SOUTHAMPTON

To the memory of

SARAH BALLARD TERRY

from her grandchildren,
Olive, daughter of Florence,
&
Phyllis, daughter of Fred
to which dedication the author
humbly subscribes

CONTENTS

Prefatory Note   xi

Sources of Reference   xv

PROLOGUE · Historical

PART I

1 View from Spithead   9

2 'On the Road'   20

3 London   32

4 The Princess's Theatre   51

5 Some Adventures   68

6 Bristol   80

7 'Thunder on the Left'   93

8 Happy (?) Families   116

9 Marriages and Mismarriages   134

FIRST INTERVAL · Historical

PART II

1 Parents and Children   167

2 The Hectic Years   183

3 Turn of the Tide   212

4 Chiaroscuro   227

5 Dark Days   238

6 Fin de Siècle   248

7 Ellen   259

SECOND INTERVAL · Historical

PART III

1	1900—and Onwards	281
2	A Light Goes Out	294
3	Indian Summer	305
4	The First World War	315
5	'Wearin' Awa' to the Land o' the Leal'	331
6	The Younger Generation	348
7	Terry Twilight	375
8	Three Candles and a Cake of Soap	391
	Family Tree	402
	Index	405

PORTRAIT GALLERY

Sarah Ballard Terry (1817 to 1892)   *frontispiece*

facing page

Benjamin Terry, publican of the *Fortune of War*   48

Ben Terry, actor   48

Fred Terry   49

Ben Terry III   49

Charles Terry   49

Photograph by Lewis Carroll of eight members of the family   96

Photographs by Lewis Carroll: Polly and Flossie, Nelly and Flossie, Charlie   97

Kate   112

Polly and Flossie   112

Nelly   112

Three children of Kate Lewis, 1879: Mabel, Lucy, Janet   113
    Elliott & Fry

Edward Godwin   144

Children of Ellen Terry and Edward Godwin: Edy, Ted   144
    Photograph of Ted reproduced by kind permission of the National Trust

Marion Terry   145

Ellen Terry, 1878   160

Florence Morris and her children: Olive, Geoffrey and Jack   160

Fred Terry   161
    Alfred Ellis & Waltery

Julia Neilson   161
    W. & D. Downey

Julia Neilson-Terry and baby Phyllis   208
    H. J. Mendelssohn

Phyllis Neilson-Terry   209
    Vivienne

Dennis Neilson-Terry   209
    E. O. Hoppè

Dennis Neilson-Terry and Mary Glynne 209
 Radio Times Hulton Picture Library

Fred Terry 224
 Bambridge, Gateshead

Julia Neilson 224
 Reproduced from Julia Neilson 'This for Remembrance' by
 permission of Messrs. Hurst & Blackett Ltd.

Ellen Terry 225
 Ridley Studios, Tenterden

Kate Lewis 272
 Elliott & Fry

Marion and Ellen Terry 272

Edward Gordon Craig, Edith Craig and James Carew at the
 funeral of Ellen Terry 273
 Photopress

Phyllis Neilson-Terry 288

Olive Morris 288
 The Gainsborough Studio

Mabel Terry-Lewis 288
 Angus McBean

Val Gielgud 289

John Gielgud 289
 Alec Murray

Gaetano Meo 368

Edward Carrick 368
 Helen Craig

Elena Meo 368
 Helen Craig

Anthony Hawtrey 369

Nicholas Hawtrey 369
 John Brown

Hazel Terry 384

Gemma Hyde 384
 Richard Graydon

Edward Gordon Craig, C.H. 385
 David Lees

PREFATORY NOTE

A Pride of Terrys was first proposed to the writer by Ellen Terry some time in 1921, as a Family Saga.

Ellen Terry had already produced her Autobiography, *The Story of My Life*, first published by Hutchinson, which, after her death, was reissued in America by Putnam and in England by Gollancz, with a brilliant annotation by the late Christopher St John in collaboration with Ellen Terry's daughter, the late Edith Craig, under the title *Ellen Terry's Memoirs*.

I was staying with her at The Farm, Smallhythe (now the Ellen Terry Museum), having known and seen much of her for over four years, when she admitted that she was dissatisfied with and disappointed in her Autobiography, which had not, in her opinion, realized the intention expressed in her own Introduction—

—to tell the truth so far as I know it, to describe things as I see them, to be faithful according to my light, not dreading the abuse of those who might see in my light nothing but darkness.

That was not the fault of Ellen Terry, or of Christopher St John (who ghosted the original work); the convention of the period obliged her to lay a roseate glaze upon certain incidents and relationships. (Much of that glaze was delicately removed by the notes to the *Memoirs*—so delicately as not to damage the basic picture.) Christopher St John, in an unpublished note, referred to the difficulty of getting Ellen Terry to collaborate. Such was not my experience; but it may have been easier for her to talk freely to a girl in her twenties, who was completely disinterested, who had not even then got so far as seriously to regard herself as a writer, and who was actually more than a little taken aback by Ellen Terry's frequent exhortation: 'You must write all this after I'm dead—it's part of the picture. That's what you've got to do: make a picture of all of us.'

Of the imperfection of that picture—in which many will 'see in my light nothing but darkness'—no one is more aware than I. But over the next forty years I had the privilege of close friendships, not only with Ellen Terry, but with her brother Fred, her sister-in-law Julia, her nieces Olive and Phyllis, and many contacts with the Family, including her son and daughter, her friends and acquaintances and distant (or not so distant) relations. It seems possible that she had the Saga in mind when she took me on two or three occasions to visit her sister Kate in the West Cromwell Road (what interest could I have had for Mrs Lewis?). I met Marion Terry at least half a dozen times at Burleigh Mansions—having seen both her and Ellen Terry many times on the stage. I was for three years a (very insignificant) member of the Fred Terry-Julia Neilson Company, and stayed frequently with Fred and Julia Terry at Primrose Hill—even more often than I visited and stayed with Ellen Terry at the King's Road, Chelsea, at Smallhythe and at Burleigh Mansions. Living under a person's roof, one gets to know him (or her) more closely than it is possible to do in the casual exchange of luncheons, tea-parties, dinner-parties—or in the inevitably artificial atmosphere of an 'interview'. I never had an 'interview' with any Terry; they would have laughed their hearty laughter at such an idea.

So when, some forty years after my first meeting with Ellen Terry, I began to think it was time I redeemed my promise to her, I was surprised to discover how many of the family I had known, or met.

I have already said that this does not pretend to be a theatrical record, which anyone can compile with the assistance of a few text-books, but the picture of a great theatrical family, the royalty of the English theatre. When I 'stretched my canvas', I was faced with a problem similar to Frith's, when he began to design his *Derby Day*. On every hand, and fading into the horizon, were Terrys, half-Terrys, quarter-Terrys, pseudo-Terrys and 'perhaps'-Terrys —the majority picturesque and tempting as subjects. I was appalled when I started to contemplate the ramifications of this vast, prolific family, of whom, in the year of Ellen Terry's Jubilee (1906) at least a score had active connections with the theatre; all of whom, whether born on the right or the wrong side of the blanket, were entitled, according to Ellen Terry's project, to figure in 'a picture of us all'.

I was forced to the harsh decision of including, after Ellen Terry's generation (and there were eleven of those) only such members of the Family as had notably contributed to the tradition established by Mr Benjamin Terry and his wife, Miss Sarah Ballard. I have not even fully done justice to all of these, for memories fail, written or printed records are few and dubious, and information to be gained from the contemporary Press is sadly unreliable.

One is bound to write with more authority on people one has known than on those whose names were little more than legend, or a shred of gossip blown about theatre precincts; therefore it is difficult—if not impossible—to preserve a balance.

I did not wish Ellen Terry, nor did she wish herself, to be the heroine of this book, but she proved as irrepressible in history as she was in life; she took the lead as inevitably as she took it at the Lyceum Theatre. And, as the book went on, none measured up to her except her son, Edward Gordon Craig.

My deep gratitude is due to Olive (Morris) Chaplin, daughter of Florence Terry, and to Phyllis (Neilson-Terry) Carvic, daughter of Fred Terry, for their help and encouragement in the compilation of this book.

I am also grateful to Lucy Terry Lewis (daughter of Kate Terry), Minnie Terry (daughter of Charles Terry), Gordon Craig (son of Ellen Terry), Edward Carrick (son of Gordon Craig), John Gielgud and Val Gielgud (grandsons of Kate Terry), Major Sholto-Gray (great-nephew of Kate Terry) and Hazel Terry (granddaughter of Fred Terry, daughter of Dennis Neilson-Terry), for their generous co-operation.

And to many Terrys who, although their claims to relationship did not all, unfortunately, stand up to investigation, were most kind and helpful during my research around Portsmouth.

I wish sincerely to thank the Librarian of the Portsmouth Library, Mr H. Sergeant, and his staff, for invaluable assistance; Mr Frederick K. Challen for disinterested research; Mr Malcolm Morley for notes generously contributed from his own historical research; the British Actors' Equity Association for allowing me to consult their records; and the Trustees of Ellen Terry's Estate. Miss Daphne du Maurier for permission to quote from her grandfather's correspondence; Max Reinhardt for permission to quote from the Terry–Shaw correspondence, and Mrs. Corbett Wallis for holograph letters.

To the late W. Macqueen Pope I am indebted for much good advice.

And, finally, to Mr J. C. Trewin I owe a great debt of gratitude for his kindness and patience in reading an unwieldy typescript; for his generosity with *time* (most valuable of all commodities to the full-time writer); and for his invaluable corrections and contributions to the original text.

SOURCES OF REFERENCE

My primary thanks are due to Mrs Chaplin (Olive Morris), who, as curator of the Ellen Terry Museum, allowed me to work in the library, where I had access to innumerable books from which I snatched, here a line, there a page. Among these were *The Diaries of Macready* and the *History of Covent Garden*, by Alfred Bunn—in addition to Victorian and Edwardian biographies, playbills, contemporary cuttings, personal records, etc. There were the contents of the Museum itself, trophies, portraits, photographs and costumes —covering more than a century of theatrical history.

Mrs Chaplin also kindly put at my disposal the diaries of her mother, Florence (Terry) Morris, and the scrapbooks kept by her father, William Morris—which preserve a vivid, if somewhat disjointed, record of the period—her collection of family photographs, and hundreds of family letters.

Mrs Carvic (Phyllis Neilson-Terry) lent me an invaluable collection of family letters from her grandparents (Ben Terry and Sarah Ballard), her parents (Fred Terry and Julia Neilson), her uncles (Ben and Tom Terry), her aunt (Marion Terry) and her brother (Dennis Neilson-Terry), and many photographs.

Miss Lucy Terry Lewis (daughter of Kate Terry) wrote me long and helpful letters, and contributed photographs.

To these I was able to add my own letters from Ellen, Fred and Julia (Neilson) Terry; my diaries, records of conversations with Ellen Terry (most of them entered briefly into the copy of *The Story of My Life*, for which I saved up my pocket-money, and managed to buy when I was sixteen years old); my collection of playbills, programmes and photographs.

Many books which I consulted proved too inaccurate to be taken seriously as works of reference; but of these the following short list proved worthy:

The Story of My Life.   Ellen Terry
Ellen Terry's Memoirs.   Annotated by Christopher St John
Ellen Terry and Her Secret Self.   Edward Gordon Craig

Ellen Terry and Bernard Shaw: A Correspondence.   Christopher St John
Ellen Terry.   Christopher St John
Ellen Terry and Her Sisters.   Edgar Pemberton

—the last overlaid with contemporary sentimentalism, not wholly reliable, but useful as a signpost to further research. There were altogether too many books on Ellen Terry, and on Henry Irving.

Henry Irving (2 vols.).   Bram Stoker
Henry Irving.   Christopher St John
Henry Irving.   Laurence Irving (grandson)

Edward Gordon Craig.   Janet Leeper
On the Art of the Theatre.   Edward Gordon Craig
The Theatre Advancing.   Edward Gordon Craig
Index to the Story of My Days.   Edward Gordon Craig
The Mask, 1923-29.   Edward Gordon Craig
Edy.   Ed. Eleanor Adlard

This for Remembrance.   Julia Neilson

Early Stages.   John Gielgud
The Years of the Locust.   Val Gielgud
Kate Terry Gielgud.   Kate Terry Gielgud

I also found useful:

My Life in Art.   Constantin Stanislavsky
My Life.   Isadora Duncan
Bernard Shaw and Mrs Patrick Campbell (Letters).   Ed. Alan Dent
Bulwer and Macready.   Charles H. Shattuck
Emigrants in Motley.   Ed. J. M. D. Hardwick
London's Lost Theatres.   Erroll Sherson
The Young George du Maurier.   Daphne du Maurier
The Unconscious Stone.   Dudley Harbron

Who's Who in the Theatre was helpful and accurate for checking dates. (The Terry genealogy is not accurate, but that was no fault of the Editor, who presumably accepted what was supplied to him by the Family—notoriously vague about its antecedents.)

PROLOGUE

Historical

The King is dead, long live the Queen.

It is the year 1837. A buck-toothed little Hanoverian girl with the shot-away jaw and protuberant bluish eyes of her paternal ancestry receives—*en déshabillé*—the homage of her Ministers. She has succeeded to the throne of her uncle William. In due course she is proclaimed. In every shire, city and hamlet of the fair country she is to govern for sixty-two spectacular years, bells ring out in celebration of the accession of Victoria Regina. Excited, proud and blown with her new dignity, little, uncultured Vicky is ignorant of the full richness of her heritage.

The last glow of the Byronic sunset lingers on the horizon (what were a few years to those slow-moving generations?) and Lady Blessington's quill is still active. The D'Orsay tradition survives in masculine elegance. The 'dark, Satanic mills' have yet to destroy the glories of English craftsmanship, and the railways have barely started to fling their poisonous tentacles into the green heart of the English countryside.

At Camilla Cottage, the life of the authoress of *Evelina* is drawing to its close. A Mr Charles Dickens, in spite of puce velvet waistcoats, 'Sheeny' hairdressing and flash jewellery, is taken seriously; he is busy translating into fiction for the Common Reader what a greater man has long been preaching from Cheyne Row. Carlyle has made his name with *The French Revolution*, is lecturing on *Heroes and Hero-Worship*, and preparing his tract on *Chartism*. The pair of them carry a furious torch for the underdog, but for ten who read Carlyle, a hundred read the entertaining Mr Dickens, who has the 'common touch' denied to the Sage of Chelsea.

A Mr William Makepeace Thackeray has attracted notable attention with his *Yellowplush Papers*, and is preferred, by the sophisticated reader, to his rival Mr Dickens. In London lodgings a so far unsuccessful young poet is grieving for the death of his friend and labouring on the first draft of *In Memoriam*. A plain, solemn, young woman in the Midlands is struggling to translate *Leben Jesus*, with the novels that are to make her name famous mere cobwebs in the back of her mind. Three highly-strung girls in a grisly Yorkshire vicarage are scribbling in their little notebooks and doing their best to ignore a drunken brother. The *beau monde* is aware of a wealthy young Mr Browning, who has had flattering notices for his poem *Paracelsus*, and not so flattering a reception for his drama, *Strafford*. A Miss Barrett is perfecting, in Wimpole Street, her role of professional invalid, and a fashionable young lady of the name of Nightingale is suffering qualms of social conscience in the stately home of her family at Romsey.

A young painter called Watts has yet to visit Italy, and become imbued with the burning reds and umbers, the no less stinging blues, of the Venetian school; but he is recognized by the Academy. The forerunner of the breakaway from realism to romanticism, he is already, in a small way, significant to that small section of the public which is intelligently interested in painting. A delicate little boy in Bristol is showing (at the age of four) signs of the talent he is later to devote to architecture and archaeology.

Music—so far as it penetrates the English consciousness—comes from 'abroad'. British soil was not, for some reason, congenial to the growth of musicians, whether composers or executants. Yet one might question whether there has ever been a jollier growth of 'folk' music than in the early nineteenth century; a more assiduous cultivation of traditional tunes and words, a more obstinate weaving of the ancient or contemporary ballad into the life of the people— to such an extent that today, 'Villikins and his Dinah', 'Spanish Ladies' and 'Johnny Shall Buy a Blue Ribbon' are recognizable through the idiom of rock-'n'-roll.

None of these matters to young Victoria, who, like the rest of her ancestors (with the distinguished exception of George IV), is totally indifferent to literature and the arts: an indifference she is to pass down to her descendants. When young Mr Dickens, young Mr Thackeray, young Mr Tennyson and their contemporaries become famous, she is pleased to confer on them her royal patronage. No member of the Royal Family since the first Elizabeth has had sufficient knowledge of, or interest in, the arts to discover, and to help, the artist who is not yet fashionable and expensive.

In 1837 the theatre is at its lowest ebb. The Patent Theatres (their patents conferred by Charles II) have still their stranglehold on artists and managers. Only the Theatres Royal—Covent Garden and Drury Lane—may present a full-length classic drama; at the others—even the Haymarket and the Lyceum—not even a tragedy can be produced unless there are at least five songs or musical divertissements in each act. These mutilated versions of serious plays are called 'burlettas'. The object of this prohibition, in the nineteenth century, is difficult to see: originally it was, of course, a supreme example of royal protection for royal favourites. The 'patented' actors were entitled to wear a special uniform of scarlet and gold and ranked as 'gentlemen of the household'. And that, no doubt, was all very fine when the total population of London was something less than that of the suburb of Croydon today.

But as the population increased, so came the demand for more theatres, and more and more absurd became the monopolies, jealously enforced by proprietors of the patents. Fifty pounds a performance could be (and was) levied against the manager or the individual actor who dared, in one of the upstart or minor theatres, to present the works of William Shakespeare.

So, at the beginning of her reign, the vast majority of Victoria's subjects think of the theatre only in terms of 'hippodramatic spectacles', 'Poses Plastiques' and Planché's mythological extravaganzas, lavishly presented by Lucy Eliza Vestris and her spendthrift young husband in the old slum theatre that Vestris's charm, talent and shrewd estimation of public taste have made fashionable. But while Vestris and Mathews are squandering the vast sums she made at the Olympic on Parma violets and pedigree King Charles spaniels, and devoting her very considerable artistic and archaeological knowledge to extravagant productions of such trivia as *Olympic Revels*, *The Paphian Bower* and *Telemachus: or the Island of Calypso* (in which the lady displayed her lovely singing voice and no less lovely limbs to the ravishment of her audiences), one man is trying 'to establish a theatre worthy of the country, and to have in it the plays of our divine Shakespeare fitly illustrated'.

The Lyceum and the Haymarket, after a determined struggle, have succeeded in getting the Licence, and are setting up a by no means negligible rivalry to the old Theatres Royal. Macready chooses this moment to take over the lease of Covent Garden and announces the fact in a manifesto to the public:

> The decline of the drama, as a branch of English literature, is a matter of public notoriety. The distressed state and direct losses of those whose profession is the stage, if less generally known, are more severely felt.

In this laudable project is involved the famous young author Edward Lytton Bulwer,[1] who has made his name with 3-volume novels (*Eugene Aram, The Last Days of Pompeii* and *Rienzi*) and, encouraged by his friend Macready, is working on a play, *The Lady of Lyons,* which is to be a steady winner for managements and artists up to the end of the century. Radical member for Lincoln, he has just been created a baronet. He is an influential aristocrat, with rooms in Albany and contacts with all the social, literary and artistic world of the period; he is serious about the theatre. His attitude towards the actor, to begin with, is patronizing; instead of going to the theatre, he requests Mr Macready to call upon him; which, somewhat surprisingly, Mr Macready—who does not take kindly to patronage—does. He has detected something of value, of genuine interest, in this grandiose young man, swollen (not unnaturally) with his immense success as a novelist. He is right: for it is Bulwer who in 1843 forces the Act which dissolves the patents, and gives all theatres the right to produce whatever they please, from Shakespeare downwards.

With the death of the glorious Kean, 'yet green in earth', Macready is the only remaining classic actor of stature, the only true heritor of the Kean tradition. To read his diaries is to get, to some degree, the measure of the man: of his artistic probity, his command of theatrical politics, his relationships with his colleagues, and of an egoism which was seldom directed towards his personal advancement, but invariably to the profession he served. The diaries give, unfortunately, little record of individual performances (the only player self-conscious enough to record virtually every breath she drew, every bat of an eyelash, every scrap of acting mechanism —divorced from the intellectual or emotional impetus that prompted it—was Ristori), but something comes through—his own ruthless

[1] Later Sir Edward Bulwer-Lytton, then the Earl of Lytton.

estimation of the 'good' or the 'bad' in his own work—which suggests the *great* artist.

(In 1927, ninety years after this period on which we are embarked, flats stencilled with the name of Macready were stacked in the scene dock at the old Theatre Royal in Bristol. Macready was dust; yet, through that canvas and illegible paint, one could make contact with the passions and pains of a century past.)

At Drury Lane, Charles Kean (educated at Eton, which makes 'a gentleman' of him) is trafficking on the reputation of his father, Edmund. A journeyman actor, archaeology means more to him than acting—which does not prevent his allowing his wife to play Hermione in a crinoline. (Vestris did better; her Carolean beauties and her Mary Queen of Scots would appear, from the record, to have been more conscientiously presented from the archaeological angle than the Kean's *Winter's Tale*.)

In 1841, Macready is to write in his diary:

> It is almost an excuse for expatriation, for anything in the way of *escape* short of suicide, to think one has lived and *had a mind and used it* for so many years, to be *mentioned* at last in the same breath with Mr C. Kean! Particularly offensive!

A man of violent passions, intensely quarrelsome (he beat up his manager, the egregious Mr Alfred Bunn, for some disagreement over the composition of the bill: a somewhat excessive fashion of settling an argument which was, actually, the outcome of a mounting score of dissatisfactions with the then lessee of Covent Garden), Macready's bitterness is reasonable. He is ahead of his age; his attitude to the Throne is in a sense revolutionary. He is righteously, if somewhat unimaginatively, disgusted that the Queen's patronage goes to Van Amburgh's performing lions and to his cheapjack rival at Drury Lane. He is not quite fair to Vicky, who is only in her teens, a commonplace, semi-educated, little girl, she has no cultural tradition whatever to guide her towards the higher branches of the arts. She prefers the Eton-ized sleekness of Mr Charles Kean to the farouche grandeurs of Mr Macready. Having been persuaded by some tactful person to command a performance at Covent Garden, she brushes aside Shakespeare, chooses *The Lady of Lyons* and *Rob Roy*—and only arrives with her mother, the Duchess of Kent, in time for the farce which concludes the bill: in which, needless to say, Mr Macready does not appear.

Mr Macready cannot, in reason, blame Mr Charles Kean for the Queen's bad taste and worse manners. He has a more intimate reason for his resentment. Mr Kean has declined to co-operate in the revival of the drama at Covent Garden. Mr Kean is making big money in the provinces. And Mr Kean has enlisted under his banner an actress who, in Macready's company, made little impression. Given opportunities which did not come her way with Macready, Ellen Tree is now making a name for herself. She and Kean are in love. (They were engaged, but broke it off for family reasons; eventually they are to marry.) According to Hazlitt:

> Without any appearance of art, she played so well that she seemed the character itself, with the ease and simplicity of an innocent schoolgirl. Her figure is very pleasing . . . and she has the handsomest mouth in the world.

It is bitter to Macready, that his rival has secured this promising young artist. He—Macready—is putting up with the moods and tantrums of his own leading lady, Helen Faucit: a good, accomplished, but uninspired actress, not moulded to his own stature. These elements, added to his artistic contempt for the inferior actor, create a friction which, however trying it may be for the protagonists, has a galvanizing effect on the drama. At last the theatre shows signs of coming to life.

This is the artistic climate into which our young heroes, Ben Terry and Sarah Ballard, erupt towards the close of the third decade of the nineteenth century. All those names we have mentioned contribute something to the air they breathe; certain names have particular and permanent significance, others hardly impinge on the consciousness of a girl and youth reared in the provinces in a commercial *milieu*. In the course of their artistic progress they are to become increasingly aware of them.

PART ONE

CHAPTER ONE

View from Spithead

In the year 1837 Portsmouth was still the same uproarious, dangerous and exciting town as it was when Nelson slipped out of the
back-yard of the 'George', and, dodging the crowds that waited to
acclaim him, picked up a row-boat waiting somewhere near the
King's Bastion to take him aboard *Victory*.

There was the same stink of tar and sewage; there were the same
perilous cobbles and malodorous sewage beds, sinister small
courts and alleys that prudent people avoided. The High Street
was still colourful with scarlet and gold lace, with the white
trousers of marines and the bright red coats of policemen. The
Roman bells from the Dover pharos (translated in the reign of
Queen Anne and recast before being hung in the tower of St Thomas
à Becket), still scattered their sweet tune over Spithead to Gosport,
over Portsea and up to Spice Island. The High Street itself—that
noble thoroughfare—ended near the Sally Port at King James's
Gate, with its ball-topped dome and Italianate wings, through which
the venturesome might gain a region dedicated to the mariner, his
practical requirements and his entertainments.

There are various legends, none flattering, as to how Spice Island
—that blunt spur which thrusts out about a quarter of a mile between the harbour mouth and the Camber—got its name. Apart
from the famous Star and Garter Hotel, patronized by the higher
ranks of the Senior Service (including Victoria's uncle William),
and a few marine stores, ships' chandlers and eating houses, its
main trade lay in drinking shops (of which at one time there were
forty-one within five minutes' stroll from the Gate), and brothels,
open round the clock. To call anyone a 'Spice Islander' was to affix
a certain label, unacceptable in polite society.

At a discreet distance from this dubious quarter, and not far
from St Thomas's church,[1] was Crown Street,[2] a neat double row

---

[1] Now Portsmouth Cathedral.
[2] Now demolished, and its site engulfed in the post-war Power Station.

of unpretentious dwellings, one of which was tenanted by a Mr Peter Ballard, builder and Master Sawyer in the Dockyard. He was also a supporter and lay preacher of the Wesleyan meeting, which had not yet acquired its own premises, but collected in rooms loaned, or rented by the 'brethren'.

Ballards regarded themselves as 'superior', the superiority deriving from Mrs Ballard who, before her marriage, was a Miss Copley, descendant of Richard Copley, a Scottish settler in the United States. Richard Copley had two sons, both of whom returned to the British Isles. John Singleton Copley, painter and engraver, achieved the status of Royal Academician, made a small fortune and died in penury. Joseph Copley, the bell founder, married a Miss Sarah Bean, of Dublin, and their daughter married Peter Ballard[1] of Portsmouth.

Ballards were proud of their Copley connections, and of the powerful Scottish blood transmitted to their children, of whom there were three: Sarah, Lizzie (Elizabeth?) and Lou (Louisa?).

There is a pencil sketch of Sarah, in the early eighteen-forties, by Sir Martin Archer Shee: angelically simple, with large, wide-set eyes. In a period when it was every girl's ambition to look tiny and helpless, and by real or assumed fragility to rouse the protective instinct theoretically enclosed within the masculine breast, Sarah's noble height must have been a drawback; yet a more deliciously feminine creature is not to be imagined, from her head of pale, satiny hair (dressed in Jane-Austenish rolls over her ears and lifted into a coil on the crown), her beautifully sculptured eyes and tender mouth, to the springing soles of her feet. She neither 'teetered' nor pattered, according to the fashion of her day, but moved with a natural freedom and grace that disarmed those who professed to find her too tall for a member of 'the weaker sex': a description (as it turned out) singularly inept for Miss Sarah Ballard. And she had a deep, flexible and naturally well-placed voice, which was inherited by her descendants. The famous 'Terry voice' is, actually, the Ballard voice, for Ben Terry, although he took infinite pains

[1] Ballard is a Scottish name and there was, in fact, a Reverend Mr Ballard then living in Portsmouth; but he was a clergyman of the Church of England and there is no evidence of relationship between him and Ballard the builder. The myth of a 'Scotch Presbyterian minister' grandfather, recorded in Edith Craig's notes to Ellen Terry's *Memoirs*, has no factual foundation.

with his diction and gained the approval of Macready and Mrs Charles Kean (a better judge than her husband), had no special vocal endowment.

In the year 1837, Miss Ballard, who, as may well be imagined, had many suitors, was giving concern to her parents by her obstinate addiction to her childhood's playmate, the flashily attractive young Ben Terry who, for many reasons, was the last person they wanted their darling daughter to marry.

Although fellow members of the Wesleyan meeting, which was obligated to Ben's mother, Mrs Catherine Terry, for its premises (the Wesleyan chapel had not yet been built), Terrys and Ballards were not accordant. Before the respective births of Ben and Sarah, they were neighbours in Crown Street; Benjamin Terry I then assisted his brother Edward in the management of a respectable drinking house in High Street, between the Shambles and the Sally Port. There was another brother, James; an agreeable rogue, he married *en deuxième noces* (his first wife was a Miss Bramble, and he had by her three sons, two of whom died in infancy) a Miss Mary Moxon, and on the day his wife was brought to bed of her daughter Mary, was arrested for smuggling. In accordance with contemporary law, all his possessions, down to the bed on which his wife had just been delivered, were impounded, and the shock, not unreasonably, killed her; she died, leaving an infant nine days old, and James was sentenced to seven years at sea.

The ship to which he was committed was lying off the harbour. On the day of Mary Terry's funeral, hearing the bell toll, he went aloft, thinking he might see the cortège as it passed by the Sally Port. He either fell or jumped overboard, and was drowned, leaving his infant daughter and his little son James, who were brought up by their grandmother Terry until she died: the cause of her death being the blowing up of the ancient ship of war, the *Boyne*, in 1795. Old Mrs Terry was standing on a stool, hanging a picture, when the shock of the explosion caused her to fall, and resulted in her death a few months later.

All this, in 1837, was ancient history, but it coloured the attitude of the Ballard parents to young Ben, nephew of James, who had, in their estimation, too much of his uncle in his roistering character. His father, Benjamin, was dead; his mother, Catherine, continued to run the tavern, the Fortune of War[1] (which she and Benjamin took some twenty years earlier), with the assistance of her eldest son Thomas (a tiresome, pompous fellow, over-addicted to the bottle). The other boys—George, Frederick and Ben—lacked paternal control (Frederick was to marry a Miss Maria Stollery, and, in the virile Terry tradition, beget seven children; he also became a publican). There was a girl, Rose, who, because she behaved herself, attracted no adverse attention; she, in due course, married a Mr Morson, and that was the end of her, so far as family interest was concerned. But George! George, for some unknown reason, was given a 'superior' education at Mr Waggett's academy for young gentlemen, and developed a gift for music. And look what George was doing, in 1837; playing the violin in the theatre orchestra! It was George, according to their elder brother Thomas, who led young Ben astray.

To all save a few misanthropes or moralists (among these, the parents of the various young women on whom he scattered the shifting sunlight of his attentions), Ben was irresistible. Invincibly gay, good-humoured and generous, there was a slight favour of the Regency buck about him. He was good-looking, with his reddish-brown hair, his greenish-blue eyes and fresh skin—all of which, if it does not add up to positive handsomeness (contrary to the pious fabrication of his children, Ben was not handsome although, in later years, when he grew his beard, he was a very distinguished-looking old gentleman), makes an agreeable picture. Ben, in his pale, peg-top trousers and nipped-in waist, swaggering into the taverns or giving the girls a treat on Grand Parade, was the local Brummell, but was not well viewed by serious people who had little use for a youth who, into his twenties, had found no steady occupation, and whose whole conception of life appeared to consist in twanging his guitar, airing his pleasant tenor voice at amateur concerts and—here came the rub—hanging about the theatre: a place currently of such ill repute that it had been closed for lack of patronage.

Portsmouth audiences were not squeamish, but what with pick-pocketing, brawls between sailors and their doxies, not to speak of dirt and discomfort—none but inveterate addicts of the drama

---

[1] Just through King James's Gate, on the right of Broad Street, it was demolished in 1844.

risked themselves even in the 'refined' three-and-sixpennies, from which, close as they were to the proscenium, it was often impossible to hear more than a scattered phrase or two through the uproar of the gallery.

In the summer of 1837 the big, gilded, wooden Hand was hung out of the window of the Town Hall, signifying that the Free Mart Fair was on. All down the High Street, from the Shambles to the Sally Port, and along Peacock Street and Penny Street and Oyster Street, ran the stalls with foreign and provincial merchandise. Traders from the Netherlands, Germany and France scattered outlandish vocables on the air.

This was Portsmouth's annual junketing, worth more to it financially than any naval or military event; attracting trade from all over the country, filling inns, crowding taverns, and yielding bounty to the hordes of cripples and beggars that infested the alleys of a great seaport.

Once upon a time, the Free Mart Fair was an honest trading centre; by 1837 it had lost something of its credit. Its side-shows attracted a far from desirable clientèle of mariners, town bloods, Spice Island rabble and their attendant women. Refined young ladies (such as the Misses Ballard of Crown Street) stayed indoors, or did their modest shopping within hail of their parents' dwellings —while gay sparks like Ben Terry of the Fortune of War and his cousin Ned of the Sally Port, larked around the town, ogled the girls and squandered their money in the booths that displayed the Two-headed Woman, the Thibetan Giant and the Performing Fleas.

And the news broke that the theatre was going to be reopened.

The barn-like little building on the corners of High and St Mary's streets, with its handsome classic portico for the box customers, was closed in 1836 'for unseemly and improper conduct' (whether on the part of the audience or the players, does not transpire; more likely the former). It was briefly reopened in March 1837, 'By desire and under the Patronage of Colonel O'Malley and the Officers of the 88th Regiment', for the engagement of 'the most Celebrated Juvenile Actress of the Day, MISS DAVENPORT'.[1] Miss Davenport played Shylock, in scenes from *The Merchant of Venice*, and,

[1] She and her parents had appeared at Covent Garden.

13

in conformity with the monopolies, regaled her public with songs ('The Rose of Lucerne', 'Since Now I'm Doom'd', 'I'm a Brisk and Sprightly Lad just come Home from Sea', 'Poll Dang It, D'y' Go') and danced the Sailor's Hornpipe. She played six characters, male and female, in a piece called *The Manager's Daughter*: all of which suggests that Miss Davenport was a performer of virtuosity, and that the orchestra (including Mr George Terry) had a busy night.

The High Street Theatre (it figured on the bills variously as the Theatre Royal and the Portsmouth Theatre) was one of a group visited by the circuit companies, romantically described as 'strolling players'. Portsmouth was on the Southampton, Winchester, Chichester, Ryde and Newport circuit. It was open for about sixty nights in the year, and its regular season was from February to May, or early June; from then on it was hired for amateur theatricals or concerts—usually by officers of the Fleet, or of local regiments, and their ladies. On these occasions the programmes were printed on fringed satin, and order was kept in the cheap seats by Marines with cutlasses.

The policy of circuit companies was to play towns where there was, for some reason, 'a great concourse of people'—for naval or military manœuvres, a race-meeting or assizes. Ordinarily there would be some kind of diversion for the Free Mart: a nautical melodrama (*Black-Eyed Susan*, featuring Billy Floyer, 'a comedian whose popularity is as wide as his versatility', was a favourite), supplemented by local talent in song and dance.

But this year the theatre, 'under new management', was closed for redecoration, and eventually the *Hampshire Telegraph* came out with an announcement and a warning:

Our theatre is to open in a few days; we hope the new managers will afford somewhat more warmth and company in the house than has hitherto been the case, by excluding the draughts of cold air from the audience part, which last season rendered the boxes almost untenable; that they will alter the arrangement of the gaslights, so that visitors may see with whom they are associated, and that riot and confusion may not take place without any chance of discovery, from the universal gloom in which the upper part of the house has always been shrouded. If these improvements be not effected, we prognosticate that persons will not leave their warm houses, and the speculation will fail, not from want of theatrical feeling, but from the lack of comfortable accommodation.

14

This ultimatum was followed in due course, by a managerial notice:

> The theatre is perfectly aired, large fires having been kept in the boxes, pit, lobbies and on the stage, for several days.

A few words about improved lighting, or the policing of the cheap seats, might have gone farther to restoring public confidence. Respectable people did not care for rubbing shoulders with the town women and their pimps, who infested every part of the house.

Kept *au courant* by brother George, young Ben Terry knew all about the change of management. He had made acquaintance of Mr William Shalders, the new manager; he had ingratiated himself with Mrs, Miss and even the egregious Master Shalders, almost before they had finished unpacking their ramshackle effects. Because his passion for the drama was deep and sincere, he was prepared to seize every opportunity of getting behind the scenes, of making himself useful, with a view to advantages.

Ben had never seen 'great' theatre; when Glorious Kean had his Benefit in 1824, Ben was a child of seven. And that, for about twenty years, was the last 'great' theatre Portsmouth enjoyed. (Otway and Marston—admirable provincial actors—came just too late for Ben to profit by their talents.) But he had seen some garbled versions of Shakespeare that gave him intimations of immortality, or grandiose notions, as you care to look at it. Brothers Thomas and Frederick and sister Rose derided young Ben for adopting the fine manners and fine attitudes of the actors he admired, and for shedding his provincial speech in favour of 'theatrical' English. It was not all façade; Ben had a romantic and chivalric addiction to nobility.

For innumerable nights he leaned his chin on the gallery rail, now and again absently cuffing some obstreperous companion whose noise drowned the words he was straining to hear. Going to the theatre was not, for him, a means of whiling away an empty evening, or creating a rough-house, or fumbling a sly complaisant wench up there in the dark. The small, illuminated proscenium arch was his window on 'faery lands forlorn', inhabited by people who spoke and behaved in a fashion wholly admirable to the boy from Spice Island.

Like most normal youths of his age, he guffawed at and applauded Billy Floyer and grinned at the leg displays of the ladies of the ballet. He delighted in farce and burlesque—but had a distinct perception that it took more than clapping on a red nose to make a comedian.

According to evidence, William Shalders was a good, hard-working theatre craftsman, to whom Mr Charles Dickens, who was obligated to him for the first theatrical production of his work, did scant justice in *Nicholas Nickleby*.

Entering into some agreement too elastic to be called partnership with the previous manager, Shalders bent all his energies to restoring the fortunes and the reputation of the discredited High Street theatre. Nothing was 'beneath' him—were it carpentry, scene painting, mending furniture, making properties. He made himself responsible for billing and box office, for the hiring of cash and check takers, even for such minutiae as candles for the dressing-rooms, coal for the fireplaces, sweeps for the chimneys, and scrub-women for the front of the house. Nor were these the limits of his activities: he wrote pirated versions of London dramas, in which he and his wife and daughter took part, usually in supporting roles to visiting stars. If nothing much as an actor, he was an admirably industrious and conscientious person, and merited praise rather than derision.

Mrs and Miss Shalders contributed their share to theatre economics by supervising and helping with the wardrobe and keeping the scrubwomen up to their work. They also practised their singing and dancing—in those days, important items on the bill. They, too, according to their lights, were dedicated to 'The Profession', and their duty, as they saw it, was to provide the public with honest and well-organized entertainment. Master Shalders probably provided little but nuisance value;[1] in any case, he was at school.

It was amusing, for Ben, to help Mr Shalders repair a throne, daub paint on a damaged flat, remodel a goblet or stick bits of coloured glass in the hilt of a dagger. It was endurable to spend a morning in the office, checking expenses, or to hang around while the gas-fitters did something to the footlights; to loll at the side of the stage while Miss Shalders practised her *battements*, or strum the

---

[1] Two years later at Southampton, Master Shalders was given honourable mention on the bill.

piano for Mrs Shalders's trills and tremolos. But it did not seem to be advancing one much towards being an actor.

There is no record of Ben Terry's acknowledging his indebtedness to the Shalderses, from whom he learned much of the business and the tricks and the trade of acting—as distinct from the art—which, when in his small way he went into management, proved invaluable.

1838 was Coronation year, and the theatre was opening with a bang.

Two years previously, Mr Charles Dickens, a local author, produced a haphazard, untidy pot-boiler called *The Posthumous Papers of the Pickwick Club*, from which emerged one lively character. Mr Shalders, who read *Bentley's Miscellany* and was aware that Dickens had cut a dash with his latest novel (*Oliver Twist*), saw the possibilities in Sam Weller; so he worked out a dramatic version, with parts for himself and all his family. It was sure-fire for Portsmouth in Coronation year: an adaptation of Dickens, the Portsea boy who had made good and, brushing the dust of Portsea off his lacquered boots, was now swaggering around London in his puce waistcoats, a social lion and a person of importance in the literary world.

There was no mention on the playbill—and why should there be?—of an insignificant youth, to be made famous by his descendants, beating a drum in the orchestra.

George had used his influence on behalf of his younger brother. He alone of the family took Ben's addiction to the theatre seriously, and it was he who persuaded the management to take on an extra drummer: Ben's only instrument, apart from the piano, being the guitar.

So Ben and his drum were established under the lip of the tiny stage. (A contemporary watercolour in the Dickens Museum, showing the Portsmouth Theatre as it was *circa* 1830, suggests a puppet show rather than a proscenium within which living actors strutted and ranted in accordance with the convention of their day.) From this advantageous position he feasted his eyes upon the current drama. He had nothing to pay; he himself was actually paid! And night after night he gloated upon the performance and learned, through repetition, something of the art of acting. And told his true-love, Sarah Ballard, all about it.

The Ballards were still hoping that Sarah would get over her fancy for this unstable youth, whose every peccadillo was reported to her by young women jealous of Ben's attachment.

She, having given her heart, that heart which was never to stray to the day of her death, remained calm throughout. She loved him and thought him wonderful; he was so different from her other suitors, with his fine manners and his wit—which was not facetious, in the provincial way, but gay and original. He recited to her, and they read plays together, and she was inevitably infected by his passion for the theatre, and sympathized with the attitude of his family and hers towards what she recognized as Ben's future career. He drew tempting pictures of the player's life and her heart kindled to adventure.

What their respective families appear to have overlooked was that both Ben and Sarah came of age in Coronation year. When he confided in her his determination to join the circuit company whose season was coming to an end, and offered her the dubious prospect of becoming a player's wife, she never hesitated. She was a few months older than he; his birthday fell, actually, on 14 September —and they decided to anticipate it.

Their assets, apart from youth, health and optimism, were negligible. Ben had earned—and squandered—various small sums apart from his drummer's 'salary' (which, considering that an actor's pay was thought good at a pound a week, cannot have amounted to more than a few shillings) by playing his guitar and singing at the various local 'Rooms' and coffee houses and taverns. His mother, the shadowy Mrs Catherine, who idolized him but was in great fear of Thomas, was in his confidence; so were his brother George and his cousin Ned.

Ben, son of Benjamin Terry, publican, and Ned, son of Edward Terry, publican, were baptized on the same day, 17 October 1817, at the church of St Thomas à Becket, and the cradle companionship had persisted. So Ben invited Ned to be his best man at the wedding which, without reference to the Ballards, was planned for 1 September 1838, at St Mary's, Portsea.

Sarah's position was not quite so easy. She had made a confidante of her sister Lizzie, but the two girls were agreed that, so as not to get Lizzie into trouble with their parents, she had better not act as a witness at the wedding. So a Miss Eliza Mitchell was sworn to secrecy, and on the morning of 1 September 1838 Sarah and her friend Eliza walked calmly out of Crown Street, to be met by the groom, with the licence in his pocket.

It was not, in the romantic sense of the word, an 'elopement'; concealing their excitement, Ben and Sarah strolled through familiar streets, exchanging familiar greetings with neighbours and friends. If she was nervous, as indeed she must have been, she did not show it; and everyone was too accustomed to Ben's high spirits to take notice of an access of swagger.

In the presence of Eliza Mitchell and Edward Terry, the Reverend J. V. Stewart married Benjamin Terry, bachelor, to Sarah Ballard, spinster, 'according to the rites and ceremonies of the church'. The bridegroom's father was named as Benjamin Terry, innkeeper, and the bride's as Peter Ballard, builder. Neither was present. As a flourish upon what must have been a somewhat joyless occasion, the bridegroom proceeded in two respects to falsify the register: describing himself, a fortnight before his birthday, as 'of full age', and his Rank or Profession as 'Gentleman'. This touch of *folie de grandeur*, typical of our hero, must be inoffensive to all who knew him in his later years, when the Portsmouth buck had matured into a charming and courtly old gentleman. (The roles of 'ladies' and 'gentlemen' were perfectly supported by all his children, both on and off the stage.)

Immediately after the ceremony, the happy pair set forth on the pilgrimage which was to cover the better part of twenty years. If, as their children were fond of claiming, they left Portsmouth in a post-chaise (it smacks more of one of Ben's bedtime stories to his beloved Nelly), it must have been the last of such 'high class' travel they enjoyed for a long time. Perhaps they picked up the stage coach at the Blue Posts; they may more likely and just as light-heartedly have taken the road on foot, with their new companions, to whom Ben proudly introduced his bride. However it was, they were as gay as larks, and there were no tears in Sarah's eyes for the home she had left behind.

The actor John Coleman, meeting them in Worcester, left a comment on the handsomeness of the pair, Ben Terry and his wife who, for professional occasions, had taken the name of 'Miss Yerret'.

CHAPTER TWO

'On the Road'

To a girl fresh from a conventionally decent lower middle-class home, it was all novel, exciting and, occasionally, disconcerting. Shy, inclined to be reserved and embarrassed by her ignorance of the duties of her new station, Sarah shrank, to begin with, from the hail-fellow-well-met society of her fellow players and was frequently puzzled by their vocabulary; her nonconformist conscience received frequent shocks (although Ben had warned her) from their free behaviour and free language. Scrupulously neat and modest, as she had been taught to be, not only in her person but in household matters, she was dismayed by the conditions of her new life: the lack of privacy, the difficulties of achieving the standards of cleanliness to which she was accustomed, the hurly-burly of men, women and children crowded together, and the primitive accommodation to which they were required to adapt themselves.

Borne, however, on the tide of Ben's endless ebullience, she came to enjoy it all. It was fun, in the glow of autumn dawns or in frosty twilights, to ride on the baggage wagon or to tramp the country roads; to arrive by lamplight at the next station in their pilgrimage —such arrivals not devoid of an element of adventure, for, in certain places where they were known, or the advance publicity had been good, the whole town might turn out to greet them; in others, temporarily under the influence of some itinerant Methodist preacher, the doors of the godly would be closed, and a stone or two, despatched by the more excessively religious, might catch the old wagon-horse in the ribs or land resoundingly on the drum.

Nearly all travel was by road, for the railway, still in its primitive stage, seldom served the smaller circuit towns, and indeed was avoided when possible, for the company exchequer provided (except for the principals) no alternative to the open trucks, smothered in smuts and cinders, that only the roughest and toughest traveller could endure. In bad weather you might, out of your own pocket, scrape up the price of an outside seat on the stage coach; it was, if anything, less comfortable than the wagon, but it was faster, and shortened your exposure to wind, frost or snow.

On arrival, the men's first duty was to lend a hand in unloading the scenery and setting the stage, while the women scattered through the town in search of lodgings, fed the children and got ready a meal. In places where the prejudice against play-actors held good, it was difficult to find accommodation; the men might be obliged to bed-down in a loft or shed, and the women to share pallets in an attic whose roof let in starlight and rain.

Many of the theatres in which they played were little more than barns; such as they were, they often stood for more to the players than the setting of their professional lives. So poor, indeed, was their pay[1] that they were obliged to treat the theatre as their home for all purposes except sleeping, especially in cold weather, when lodging-house keepers refused to provide fires for their impecunious guests. In the daytime they collected in the theatre and pooled their resources of food, heating and clothing. There was at least a fireplace, and, if the management was mean, fuel could be scrounged or bought for a few pence. The women washed and ironed their clothes and cooked meals; thawed their frozen fingers and knitted or mended garments, while the men went round the town distributing playbills and beating up enthusiasm for the evening's performance. Children were taught their alphabet, and to add and spell. Rehearsing and housekeeping went hand in hand; a woman suckled her infant while declaiming, from a chair, the lines of her part in the current drama.

There is a touchingly domestic flavour about strolling players of the mid-nineteenth century, the conditions of whose lives had progressed so little in the course of two centuries that we might well imagine ourselves back in Carolean days. Nor, for another fifty years, was there to be any notable improvement, so far as the lower walks of the profession were concerned. From the point of view of English law, actors were 'rogues and vagabonds', and as such lived their professional lives in cells that would have been condemned as lodgment for animals—damp, verminous, without light,

---

[1] It was dependent on receipts.

heating or sanitation—up to the beginning of the present century.[1]

Little wonder if Miss Ballard missed her warm home, with its scoured and shining floors and polished furniture; the fourposter she shared with sister Lizzie; the cool, coarse linen sheets between which each night she laid her clean limbs and the fresh-smelling bolster on which she laid her tidy head; the well-washed rag rug on which she knelt to say her prayers, and the little basin and ewer of painted china on a thin triangular stand in the corner, from which they splashed their sleep-warmed bodies every morning. She must have missed the orderly routine: bed-making, breakfast, cleaning, baking, shopping, dinner, gossip, sewing, walking, tea-drinking, going to bed, and Sunday meeting, which was the pattern of a well-brought-up girl's life. She must have missed the taste of salt on her lips, and the salty smell of the Solent, and the sound of the bells and the moan of sirens on foggy nights.

Nothing is more evocative than a smell. Slowly Sarah's nostrils adjusted to that smell which is the smell of the theatre down the ages: the amalgam of grease, size, gas, human bodies, and drainage. Not, on the face of it, an attractive mixture, but to anyone who knows and cares about theatre as such, sweeter than the perfumes of Arabia. There is no smell like it in the world.

Animals smell their home. So actors, in whatever country, whatever climate, meeting that smell, relax, expand; say, I am here. I am *home*.

Sarah was gentle, well-mannered and generous, so they forgave her beauty and overlooked her amateurism. Gradually, supported by her popular young husband, she fell into the ways of the troupe and even gained a little confidence in her humble role of 'Walking Lady'.

This, according to Dion Boucicault (who, when Ben and Sarah Terry set forth on their travels, was in his cradle) was the composition of a *first-rate* theatrical company—such as the young Terrys were not to meet for many years:

Leading man, leading juvenile, heavy man—descriptions which speak for themselves. First old man, first low comedian, walking

---

[1] And later. In 1923 the writer shared a verminous dressingroom and an outside privy with 'walking' ladies and gentlemen.

gentleman. Second old man and utility, second low comedian and character, second walking gentleman and utility.

Leading woman, leading juvenile woman, heavy woman. First old woman, first chambermaid, walking lady. Second old woman and utility, second chambermaid and character, second walking lady and utility.

(The delicacy which transmutes leading 'men' and 'women' into 'gentlemen and ladies' in the lower ranks, is typical of the fineness of the relationship between the old-time manager and his employés.)

Plays of the period were written within this strict yet generous compass. The aim of the manager was to assemble around himself a permanent group of actors, each member of which had his separate appeal to some section of the audience, or supplied some 'felt want' in the Company cosmos, and had to be allotted his place so that he was not, artistically or economically, a dead-weight.

Those fascinating terms, 'Heavy', 'Utility' and 'Walking Gentleman' were still current between the two wars; in *The Stage* and *The Era* managers advertised for 'Heavy Man', 'Character and Utility', 'Walking Ladies and Gents'. (In 1928, Bernard Shaw wrote to Mrs Patrick Campbell that she was presumably qualifying for 'matrons, heavies, comedies, character'—a piece of typical Shavian ungraciousness[1] to one who, having 'blazed amazement' from the topmost spars, was sunk so low she could hardly sink lower.)

'Heavies' were actors or actresses who, while not qualifying for leading parts, could contribute strong dramatic support to the principals. 'Characters' masked their faces with wig-paste (to produce a false nose or Cromwellian wart) and crêpe hair; if women, they lined their faces, blacked out a couple of teeth and wore a more or less eccentric wig.

'Utility' meant anything from a footman or gravedigger to 'noises off', and was usually combined with 'Character'.

The lowest form of Company life was the 'Walking Lady or Gentleman', whose business was to 'dress' the stage (i.e. act as figurant), cheek by jowl with the itinerants recruited in every town. Up to the time of the First World War, provincial managements counted on stage-struck youths and maidens to furnish a 'battle

---

[1] It may have been intended as one of his pedestrian jokes; it would assuredly not be accepted as such by the rawly sensitive actress, too conscious of her decline.

scene', or a 'court'. As accredited members of the troupe, 'Walking Ladies and Gentlemen' led the 'crowd', and were expected to make themselves generally useful behind the scenes.

These picturesque terms died out with the death of the big permanent Companies, and their little commonwealths. Sir Frank Benson's Company and those of the Martin Harveys and of Fred Terry, son of Ben, were the last in which they were current. They implied certain social distinctions, ungrateful to the self-consciously 'socialistic' theatre of today.

There were few such hieratic distinctions in the little strolling companies to which Ben and Sarah served their apprenticeship— Ben more successfully than she, for reasons that will presently appear. He had enormous vitality, no bashfulness whatever, and a genuine gift for clowning—which last Sarah secretly and a little humourlessly deplored; proud of his looks, it hurt her wifely pride when he blotted them out under a farcical make-up. He made some small successes and gained locally a bit of *réclame* in the pantomimes which concluded the bill; wielding clown's poker or string of sausages, he dreamed of playing heroes and villains, or young, all-conquering gods in 'mythological extravaganzas'; there is no record of such coming his way. But there is, unfortunately, no record whatever of those first few wandering years, when they went from troupe to troupe, always with the idea of 'bettering' themselves, but always 'in minor capacity'. Sometimes Ben acted as treasurer for the company, and sometimes proud Sarah had the distasteful task of going from door to door selling tickets for somebody's Benefit.

Many a day 'Miss Yerret' in her pattens, with her gown kilted up out of the mud, must have tramped the highroad—'her plaidie to the angry airt'—and in many a chill dawn she must have accepted her feminine fate, and dreaded imparting the tidings to Ben. For whatever mild ambition she may have entertained, or been persuaded into, was soon defeated.

Over twenty-five years, Sarah was almost constantly pregnant. In another walk of life, lacking her Scottish fortitude, she might have taken to invalidism—the stock-in-trade of the Victorian wife, over-taxed or bored with child-bearing. Gallantly trailing in the wake of her indefatigable Ben, there must have been moments when even her stout heart failed; if so, she never betrayed it.

Her first child was born, not in greenroom or dressingroom, as happened to the children of so many strolling players, but in the decent privacy of lodgings. The birth of his son, the third Benjamin Terry, fired Ben's ambitions, and resolved him to break away from the small southern circuits and seek engagement with some of the more important provincial managements. He admittedly had not had much luck so far, but he had gained a lot of experience and felt himself entitled to apply for something better than 'Utility' or 'Walking Gentleman'. As in his drummer-boy days he had goggled across the footlights, ghoulishly hoping one of the actors would drop down dead (when, of course, his place would instantly be taken by Mr Ben Terry, the Portsmouth Roscius—'This day I saw young Terry, like the Sun, usurp the throne of Garrick'—who knew every line of every part in every play he had been privileged to watch), so he maintained his deathless optimism in the face of disappointment.

His granddaughter Olive wrote of him: 'His acting . . . doesn't seem to have been much—I remember him and I think, looking back, he *was* an actor—a *true* one—and had "it" in him—tho' like a good many of his descendants erratic and weak. . . . He had the great gift of being cheerful in adversity.'

It must have seemed like eternity to patient, long-suffering Sarah before the pair of them were engaged to play in *Martin Chuzzlewit* at the Liverpool Theatre Royal. She was given the part of Charity and he played Mark Tapley: a great advance on his previous parts.

The year was 1844. She had had six years of wear and tear on the road and three weary confinements. She had lost two little girls, Kate and Ellen, Kate after his mother and Ellen after hers, and grieved for them. Ben shared her grief—in his fashion; she knew he was thankful to escape from mourning into the work which as time went on absorbed more and more of his mind and his passions. She had no such escape. For her, the bloom of the actor's life had worn away. She was twenty-seven years of age, and looked much older. Up there, in the squalid purlieus of theatrical lodgings, she found herself pregnant again.

Sometimes, looking at her little boy, Sarah was filled with misgiving. What sort of a life was theirs for a child of young Ben's age—bewildered by constant changes of environment, bidden 'be quiet' when he wanted to shout, pushed between greenroom and wardrobe according to the convenience of adults, sleeping one night in lodgings, or, if the landlady were not to be trusted, rolled up in a blanket in the dressingroom and carried 'home' across his father's shoulder in the small hours of the morning? This was the normal life of the children of players, and most of them seemed to flourish on it; but Sarah knew she did not want her bonny bairn to grow up into one of those pale, precocious urchins of the theatre, pushed into acting willy-nilly (Ben's efforts to interest four-year-old Ben in acting had so far proved unavailing; she was sorry for the father and thankful for the child), hearing and seeing things that aged them before their time.

How far were little Ben's naughtiness, his tempers and his bouts of sickness, how far were the deaths of the babies Kate and Ellen attributable to their nomadic existence? A wave of guilt rose in her. She tried to confide something of her doubts to Ben, and met, as she expected, incomprehension in the blue Terry eye, so melting on occasions, on others so glassily absent. A polite uninterest invaded it now.

'I don't understand what you mean.'

'I think—perhaps—I ought to give up acting and look after the children. When the new baby is born.'

The good-looking jaw dropped, the eyes widened with unmistakable dismay.

'But, m'dear, we can't afford it, can we?'

He was right, of course; they could not afford to travel the four of them—counting the new baby—unless she was making her minute contribution to the family exchequer. Lucky as they had been so far, in that they were rarely 'resting'—the actor's euphemism for being out of work—it was not easy, despite Sarah's Scottish providence, to make ends meet.

Ben acted gravity, acted concern, acted serious consideration of the point she had raised. She knew it was acting; it was nearly time to go to the theatre, and his mind was already there. Out of kindness and politeness he was putting on this performance for her benefit. She sat still and looked at her upturned hands, the beautiful fingers scored with coarse sewing, the palms roughened with housework. So this was being an actress.

Ben looked at his watch and rose abruptly.

'It's time we were going. Come along, my boy'—to Ben, playing with his bricks on the hearthrug. 'Be sharp! Get your cap and coat.'

'I don't want to go to the theatre, Papa!' whines Ben.

Sarah cuts in, before his father has time to explode.

'We'll come down in a moment; don't wait—I've got to iron your shirt, the one you brought home last night.'

'Great God, does it take all day to iron a shirt?' Yet her exhausted face brings him compunction. He kisses her tenderly. 'No hurry —you know what a fusser I am! Take your time. And Ben—look after your mother!'

She waits for the slam of the door; but he returns, his face shining with inspiration.

'I believe I've found the answer! You could go and stay with Lizzie for a while.'

Lizzie? Sister Lizzie, now happily married to kind Tom Binsted, the commercial traveller? Her heart leaps up—and sinks again.

'And what about you?'

'I'll be all right!'—with a flourishing gesture. 'We'll talk about it tonight—don't be late,' is his final admonishment as he claps the door behind him.

She picks up the iron, heating on the hob, and begins to press the shirt. Her mind is far from her task. Leave Ben to look after himself, while she goes to stay with Lizzie? No. No. A thousand Noes. She has seen enough and heard enough, and deliberately closed her eyes and her ears. She has been hurt and concealed her pain, frightened and concealed her fear. She loves but no longer trusts her good-looking, swashbuckling Ben.

That night, as usual, she said her prayers. Both of them prayed a lot, in conformity with the training of their childhood. If Ben's prayers were rather part of his conception of 'gentlemanliness' than of any particular conviction that the Lord would concern himself with the affairs of the Terry family, hers were deep and a little desperate. She asked God to deliver her safely and to look after the baby when it was born. She also asked that she might be allowed, for once, to carry it the full time, so that it might not be born in the dour North.

27

Her prayer was answered. In the salty Falmouth air, on a May morning of 1844, a little girl was born and, with an admirable lack of superstition or sentiment, christened Kate. It was a common Victorian practice to christen children by the names of their dead brothers or sisters.

Seeing in the infant Kate a future Faucit, or Siddons, or Abington, Ben's heart leapt up; he indeed beheld a rainbow in the sky. Secretly hurt, though never embittered, by his own want of success, he foresaw fulfilment in a few pounds of fat healthy baby-flesh. If Kate Terry did not grow up to be a great actress, it would be no fault of her father's.

This would seem the moment to examine a legend which clings about the memory of 'Miss Yerret', but was seriously questioned by her son Fred: that she once played Gertrude to Macready's Hamlet and was much praised for her performance.

It is not impossible that on one of his brief provincial appearances Macready descended on a town where the resident Company included Ben and Sarah Terry. (There is the chestnut of Edmund Kean's engagement for a night with some West Country company, arriving too late to rehearse and, requested by the dismayed manager for some instructions to the players who had to support him, snarling, 'Tell them to keep out of my way!')

London stars, on their appearances in the provinces, did not travel their own companies, but accepted such support as the local management offered them.

Not in those days, or for some decades to come, was there in the provincial theatre any equivalent of the 'direction' or 'production' of today. The player was given a handwritten script, more or less illegible, torn, stamped with the finger-prints of former interpreters of the role he was required to memorize within a few hours. (Mrs Siddons is said to have considered forty-eight hours ample time to devote to the 'study' of Lady Macbeth.) 'Study' meant learning the words. So far as interpretation went, all Old Men were the same Old Man, all Heroines the same Heroine, all Villains the same Villain. There was a blue-print for every character, and not to follow it meant not to know your business. Such variations as might appear between Villain A and Villain B were arrived at through change of make-up; accents, movements and gestures were essentially the same.

'Rehearsals' meant the calling together of the company to agree on positions and learn cues. While the Leading Man and Woman and the more important members of the cast dickered for advantage, it was the business of the small-fry to dispose themselves (to the best of their ability) so as not to interfere with the principals, but at the same time to contribute their share to the scene. Quick-wittedness and adaptability were more important for them than acting; the Leading Woman must not be masked, or the Heavy be obliged to direct an important speech upstage. Certain conventions of voice and deportment had to be observed, departures from which were likely to draw a reprimand on the offender.

Only to Leading actors was any kind of originality permitted, the rest being expected at the drop of a hat to fall in with whatever unrehearsed effect was imposed on them by an erratic principal, who might choose to play a scene in a different way, with a different set of positions, forcing his unfortunate fellow-players into un-prepared situations, at each of three successive performances

In its way it was undoubtedly good training, and it may be assumed that the tall, distinguished 'Miss Yerret', with her sin-gularly beautiful voice and fine demeanour, had her blue-print for 'A Queen' well enough established behind her thoughtful brow to give satisfaction when required to play Gertrude to a formidable and difficult Hamlet.

It would seem today that this was the Manchester production of 1849, of which Macready wrote in his diary—'[Played Hamlet] as well as I could; not well, so dreadfully put out by King, Horatio, Ghost, Polonius, etc.' (Three years before, he had made another note on a provincial production of *Hamlet*: 'The rehearsal was one of the most hopeless exhibitions I have almost ever seen. Rested and thought on Hamlet, resolved not to let the inaccuracy and incompetency of these wretches—they are no better!—disturb me.') Did Sarah's beauty and charm blind him to her inexperience as Gertrude? It seems more likely she did not 'get in his way'.

It must be admitted that this biographer has no authority beyond hearsay and the pious myth handed down by her descendants for claiming this notable honour for Sarah Terry.

Forty-seven years later, when her youngest child, Fred—'the Golden Terry'—was on tour, Sarah wrote to him, 'Glasgow is not a lucky place to any of us.' Yet in 1848 they were both billed in the production of *Macbeth* at the Glasgow Theatre Royal: Ben as 'Prince Malcolm—Mr Ben Terry, his first appearance', and Sarah as the '4th Singing Witch—Mrs Terry'. Not 'Miss Yerret'. Perhaps because she had by then another child at her breast.

Her time had come on her again in Coventry, in lodgings— according to her own record 'on the right hand side coming from the market place'. There used to be a controversy about the right or the left. Between the wars one could buy a cheap little souvenir handkerchief at 'Ellen Terry's Birthplace' in Market Street. The bombing of the Second World War nullified argument; left or right, Ellen Terry's birthplace no longer exists.

A midwife, hastily summoned, delivered Sarah by candlelight in a little red-brick tenement of a workers' quarter. The theatre— demolished *circa* 1913—was only a few paces away; one may picture the anxious father rushing back in the intervals of his appearance to know how things were going on.

In some dark hour of the morning of 27 February 1848, his adored Nelly was born; the closest to his heart of all his children, his glory and his despair. She, the Ophelia, the Juliet, the Imogen of all time, was born, very appropriately, within hail of Shakespeare's Stratford.

So, when Sarah was fit to travel, or possibly before, they moved on to Glasgow, with young Ben, and little precocious Kate, and Nelly, a babe in arms. And Ben got his first Shakespearian part, and played Monsieur Fumet, a French waiter, in the farce that followed the mutilated version of *Macbeth*.

Sarah Terry was to give eleven living children to the light—of whom two died; of the number of her miscarriages her daughter Ellen admitted she had only vague recollection—'of Mother being ill and Dad very worried', and Katie and Nelly having to rush around and look after the younger ones.

When one considers the conditions under which she bore those children—before trained midwifery had been heard of, before bacteriology existed as a science, before Lister had discovered the antiseptic properties of common carbolic, before Florence Nightingale had taken up her battle for midwifery as a career for educated women—Sarah's survival, let alone that of her children, might be regarded as a miracle but for one significant fact: that none of the Terry children was born in a hospital. They were never in contact with the infections that accounted for the appalling figures of infant mortality of the mid-nineteenth century. Miss Nightingale herself wrote in the late eighteen-sixties: 'Not a single lying-in woman should ever pass the doors of a general hospital. Is not any risk which can be incurred infinitely smaller?'

Such must have been Sarah's opinion; littering as simply and wholesomely as an animal, she called in the midwife only to perform such offices as she might, at the time, find herself too weak to perform. She knew exactly what to do, what to prepare. She knew what she must suffer without panicking. According to her daughter Ellen, she was never known to complain, whatever discomfort she might be suffering.

Her children, with the exception of Fred, the youngest, inherited her incredible stamina, and with the exception of the hypochondriac Tom, her fortitude. Katie, Nelly, Polly and Floss grew up in an age when 'delicate health' was regarded as a feminine grace; such 'delicate health' as any of them enjoyed was the result of overwork, over-play and (in the cases of Nelly and Floss) their own highly strung temperaments. In her letters to her family and friends Ellen is often 'very ill'; it was an innocent self-deception, which got her out of many boring obligations. They could all feel 'very ill' to order, at the prospect of any distasteful meeting or engagement— and the feeling was perfectly sincere. Wholly governed by their emotions, they died—and rose from their tombs like aureoled Lazaruses when anything diverting offered. This, after all, is the common state of the artist; a form of escapism of which Sarah's integrity never allowed her to avail herself. All of her days she accepted it, without so much as a smile, from her wild, devoted children. They *were* devoted, and she knew it; and when the girls were 'too tired' or 'too ill' to walk a few yards to their parents' door, Sarah understood.

CHAPTER THREE

London

In August 1850 the Charles Keans, in partnership with the Keeleys, entered on a two years' lease of the Princess's Theatre in Oxford Street.

The Princess's had a history of its own. A narrow slip of a theatre, with no façade worth mentioning (it was driven in between a furrier's and a tobacconist's off the Oxford Street pavement), it started under the patronage of George IV as the 'Royal Bazaar, British Diorama and Exhibition of Works of Art' in 1828. As such, in competition with rival houses, it failed, and in 1834 was renamed the Queen's for Queen Adelaide. In 1836 it was converted into a 'regular' theatre, the Court, and four years later again changed its name to the Princess's. In 1843, following the abolition of the monopolies, it was leased by the brilliant actress Annie Keeley and her husband; then came the Vestris management, and after that Macready.

The manager was a Jew, Medec, who called himself Maddox, and one of the backers was a character who could well have come out of Thackeray's *Four Georges*: the drunken, disreputable Duke of Brunswick who, with his unsavoury companions, infested the wings and made nuisances of themselves to the performers. Maddox was glad, in 1850, to sell out to the eminently respectable Mr Charles Kean, whose cheques were not liable to bounce, and under whose direction the ladies of the Company were not likely to suffer from the unwelcome attentions of minor (and dubious) royalty.

The importance of the little Oxford Street theatre derives from its link between the pompous school of Macready and the relatively naturalistic school of Fechter and Boucicault. Between these two falls the Charles Kean régime. As applied to the arts, 'régime' is an unattractive word; it is, however, applicable to the decade of Kean's tenure of the Princess's theatre. (In 1861 and '62 the Keans gave 'farewell' performances at Drury Lane, but as London actors their career finished in 1859, with their spectacular production of *Henry VIII.*)

In 1850, Macready, Charles Kean's overwhelming rival and professional enemy, retired. With a public school education and the outlook rather of a schoolmaster than of an artist, Mr Kean set out to 'revive the drama'. He had the name his father made glorious, a leading lady who could act him off the stage (but had too much tact and affection to do so) and royal patronage. Mr Kean was the Queen's favourite actor—she had an infallible taste for mediocrity. At the beginning of his season at the Princess's, Her Majesty engaged a box, which she retained annually—'and still more satisfactorily marked her approbation of the theatre by constant personal attendance'. During the previous year she had commanded at Windsor two mutilated versions of Shakespeare (*The Merchant of Venice* and *Hamlet*), and some trashy little plays: *Used Up* and *Box and Cox*, by Lee Morton (the pseudonym of Dion Boucicault); Thompson's *The Stranger*, Jerrold's *The Housekeeper*, Oxenford's *Twice Killed* and Kenny's *Sweethearts and Wives*—all presented by schoolmaster Kean in deference to the taste of his Sovereign, which paid off with a diamond ring.

An even more dizzy triumph was his. When Macready received the royal command to appear at Windsor, the great actor had to accept the minor actor's direction. Kean played Antony and Macready Brutus in *Julius Caesar*. Mr Kean sent a message of courtesy to Macready's dressingroom, and Macready replied, 'If Mr Kean has anything to say to me, let him say it through my solicitor.' In spite of which, the performance—in deference to the Throne—went smoothly. But Macready's retirement the following year can hardly have been sweetened by the reflection that his last command was under the direction of one he scorned to acknowledge as his 'rival'.

Physically, there was little striking about Charles Kean; in the more complimentary of his portraits, he appears as a short, thickset man whose chubby features present little if any resemblance to the noble traits of his father. According to contemporary critics, he had an unpleasing, nasal voice, which sounded as though he had closed one nostril with his thumb and was speaking down the other. (Yet Ellen Terry has left it on record that his voice was 'soft and low, yet distinct and clear as a bell', and that when he played

Richard II 'the magical charm of this organ was alone enough to keep the house spell-bound'. Charles Kean's last performance of Richard II was in 1857, a year after Ellen made her début as Mamillius at the age of eight. It would seem rash to accept the impressions of a little girl not yet in her teens and deeply in awe of her first manager.) Having learned fencing at Eton with the renowned Angelo, Charles Kean was a dashing swordsman—indispensable accomplishment for an actor. Devoid of artistic sensibility, he had notable assets: intellectual appreciation of the classics, unlimited self-assurance (some called it conceit), an excellent head for business, and a partner who was not only a very good and intelligent actress, but his loyal and devoted wife. On the debit side, he was a tetchy individual, for ever on the look-out for real or imagined slights, which led him into some stupid quarrels.

In 1850 the youthful charms of the former Miss Ellen Tree had vanished. The lithographs and paintings of her Macready period served only as a sad reminder of the past. She was a formidable 'old' (according to contemporary standards) lady, parrot-beaked and double-chinned, moving solemnly within the periphery of her crinoline. Whether as Beatrice, Hermione or Lady Macbeth, nothing would part Mrs Kean from her crinoline—obscurely bound up with Victorian morality. If there were arguments with the archaeologically minded Charles, Ellen won out—as she won over her coiffure which, regardless of period, was parted in the middle, draped over the ears and swathed round the crown of her head in the fashion made popular by the Queen. As her forehead was very high and the parting very broad, the effect, in such parts as Beatrice and Viola, was grotesque in the extreme. She sedulously refused a wig.

Yet this absurd-looking woman, by virtue of her innate dignity and perfect persuasion of her rightness, commanded the unqualified respect of all who came in contact with her. In her own realm of the theatre she was royal—more royal than her fussy and petulant little husband.

It was twenty years since the death of Mrs Siddons, and thirty-eight since the latter's retirement. On the shoulders of Ellen Tree, known now as Mrs Kean, had fallen—in the estimation of her admirers—the mantle of the actress whom, in a curious way, she physically resembled. She had not the long, swelling throat, the fine arms of Sarah Siddons, nor that majesty of posture; actually, she was short and dumpy, thick-shouldered, and inclined—at least in her later years—to crouch: having accepted the domination of a vain little man who would not have endured a leading lady taller than himself. (The meagre stature of Charles Kean is shown in the well-known photograph with Ellen Terry as Mamillius; the head of the eight-year-old child is only a few inches below Kean's shoulder—and Nelly is relaxed, is dropping her own little head sideways. In all photographs of the Keans together, Mrs Kean is sitting, or kneeling, or bending over.)

Reverting to the Siddons likeness—a comparison between the 'Clemanthe' lithograph by R. J. Lane in the Mander and Mitchenson collection and the Gainsborough in the National Gallery—might easily lead to the conclusion that they are of the same young woman. Ellen Tree, in her twenties, had the aquiline beauty of Sarah Siddons, the large, dark eyes and sensuous mouth, and—so far as one may judge from contemporary criticism—at least a comparable talent. She had also—although this does not appear in the portraits—the same puritan morality.

In 1850 the Keans were at the head of their profession.

If she did not actually believe in her husband's divinity, Ellen Tree was dedicated to his interests and served him with a curiously humble and selfless devotion for so proud and pompous a woman. She had lived down the humiliation of knowing he married her *faute de mieux*. Ever with an eye to the main chance, Charles Kean had previously proposed to Angela Burdett, who inherited from her aunt by marriage, the actress Harriet Mellon, the whole of the fortune of her uncle, Thomas Coutts the banker. Thunderstruck when Miss Burdett Coutts (she added the name Coutts to her patronymic as a condition of her inheritance) rejected him, Charles Kean is said to have rushed back to the theatre and told Ellen Tree, 'If you wish to marry me—tomorrow or never!' She must have been very much in love to sink her pride and accept this graceless proposal from a conceited young actor with little but his father's name to recommend him, for she already had a considerable reputation, not only in London and the provinces but in the United States. The greater part of the capital of £30,000 with which they started their joint career was hers—not comparable with the dowry of a Coutts heiress, but enough to console 'Charlie' for his financial disappointment, and to inspire confidence in the future. They were married in 1842, and Ellen had her only child—Mary Maria—in the following year. Then came a lucrative American tour, followed by the long Macready-Kean rivalry, which culminated in Mr Kean's appointment as manager of theatricals at Windsor Castle. Apart from the emoluments (not over-generous) this meant tremendous prestige for the Keans who, according to their critics, thenceforward became more royal than royalty itself, Mrs Kean in particular founding her every motion on those of her Sovereign, and exacting from all who approached her the dues of her exalted status as 'queen' of the theatre.

Another advantage royal favour brought Mr Kean was to give him virtually the pick of the theatrical profession; so when he and the Keeleys took over the Princess's Theatre, they had the support of a remarkable Company. The Alfred Wigans, and Messrs Meadows, Ryder, Fisher, Cathcart and Addison were experienced actors, with reputations in their own right. Bartley was a famous Falstaff. Flexmore, the clown and dancer, having served his apprenticeship with Grimaldi, was engaged to produce the Christmas Harlequinades and coach the ballet, with an elegant old 'master of deportment', Oscar Byrn. An excellent scenic artist, Thomas Grieves, produced in collaboration with Mr Kean the archaeologically perfect sets for the Shakespearian plays.

Mrs Kean and Mrs Keeley carried the female leads, with the distinguished support of Mrs Alfred Wigan, Mrs Winstanley (a great favourite with London audiences in comedy Old Ladies) and Mrs Daly. To the modern reader these names will mean nothing, and it is difficult among modern talent to select their equivalents. Outside the top six in the theatre today, one might suggest the late Ronald Squire, the late A. E. Matthews, Eric Portman, Michael Redgrave, Margaret Rutherford, Veronica Turleigh, Kay Hammond. A formidable assembly.

There were some attractive young women: Carlotta Leclerq, of a well-known theatrical family, Fanny Ternan, daughter of a Manchester manager and sister of that Ellen who became the mistress of Mr Charles Dickens and bore him an (unacknowledged) son. Fanny Ternan married Anthony Trollope's brother, got infected by literary society and took to writing fiction (some of which was not bad at all). There was Agnes Robertson, ward of the Keans, who presently eloped with Dion Boucicault, and the beautiful Caroline Heath, who married Wilson Barrett and in her later years was appointed reader to the Queen who took a fancy to her rich contralto voice. And there was a lovely, dark, dramatic child, with the shadow of her tragic future already upon her: Clara Denvil died at the age of nineteen of a 'decline' brought on by the disappearance of her lover, Lord Edward Pelham Clinton, to whom she was engaged to be married. These, with Eleanor Bufton, Elizabeth Murray and some others made up the Princess's admired and envied 'beauty chorus'—most of whose members were well capable of carrying important understudies (Miss Heath understudied Mrs Kean) and playing classic parts. There was also a Miss Poole, engaged mainly for her gifts as a singer, who nevertheless was cast by the Keans as the Fool in *King Lear*, made a singing part of it and a notable success. There was no 'dead wood' in the Company at the Princess's, which opened under the new dynasty on 28 September 1850 and played a thirteen months' season, up to 17 October 1851.

The Keans and the Keeleys could not have chosen a better moment to launch their new venture, for 1851 was the year of the first Great Exhibition. London was flooded, not only with provincials, agog at the glories of the Crystal Palace, but also with foreigners attracted by the 'marriage of invention with the humanities, of mechanical progress with ethics, of the sciences with the arts'— for which ambitious programme the handsome, humourless but profoundly intelligent Prince Francis Albert Augustus Charles Emanuel of Saxe-Coburg-Gotha was responsible.

Never had the drama had such a boost. Nineteen theatres, exclusive of the two Italian operas and the St James's (devoted entirely to French tragedy and comedy), were open: a triumph for Bulwer. This list does not include the hippodromes, casinos, 'Grecian saloons' and innumerable 'irregulars' which flourished in every corner of the city and suburbs. Every house was packed out, not only with the aborigines, but with the French-speaking, Dutch-speaking, Italian-speaking, German-speaking visitors to the world-wonder in Hyde Park.

It would be pleasant to relate that the Kean-Keeley management availed itself of this unprecedented opportunity to feature the English classics. In the thirteen months of their first season there were only ninety-two presentations of Shakespeare (*Hamlet* fourteen, *Twelfth Night* forty, *As You Like It* four, *Merchant of Venice* twelve, *Henry the Fourth, Part I* twenty-two); the rest was melodrama, farce and burlesque. The Keans chose *The Gamester* and *Honeymoon* for their benefit; the former had already been damned by contemporary critics as 'obsolete, old-fashioned, commonplace, vapid, prosy and out of date'. Victorian morality reinstated it. 'To us', wrote J. W. Cole, Kean's biographer, in 1859, '*The Gamester* has always appeared a moral lesson worthy of the pulpit.' As such, it would have a powerful appeal to Mr and Mrs Kean, who were both addicted to sermonizing. In Mr and Mrs Beverley it provided them with two excellent parts, and it had a sentimental connotation: they had played it on their wedding-day in Dublin, nine years previously.

They made a profit of £7,000 on that opening season, at the end of which the Keeleys pulled out, leaving Mr Kean as the sole manager of the Princess's Theatre. According to Cole, they remained members of the Company; Mrs Keeley (formerly Miss Annie Gowan) was a valuable comedienne, and Keeley a good, sound actor.

And towards the close of the season, Mr Kean's attention was drawn to a brilliant little girl out in the provinces, whose performance of Prince Arthur, in a stock season in Edinburgh, had been so highly praised by the critics that it might be worth his while to give her an audition.

A brown, provincial fog loaded with factory smoke presses on the window and leaks into the stuffy room whose furnishings have absorbed the grime of so many Lancashire winters that they have lost colour and character.

They were lucky, that week, to have found a landlady who allowed them a fire in their room. Usually they shared the kitchen; a private sittingroom was not to be had for thirty-five shillings inclusive, for six lodgers. In average theatrical lodgings actors were not supposed to be in, except for meals; their place was the theatre and they were expected to stay there. That week fortune favoured them in the shape of a kind landlady who, for an extra shilling, filled the coal-scuttle and gave them the warmth and privacy they seldom enjoyed.

There was the big double bed and the girls' narrow one in a corner. Ben's pallet, which they travelled, renewing the hay with which it was stuffed from time to time, was bundled in the daytime under the big bed. Even so, it did not leave much room, with a chair or two and a table, for three active young people and the infant George who, mummified in a shawl, fenced in by a bolster, slumbered against the bed-rail.

A sullen, handsome schoolboy, hands in pockets, rocked on the back legs of his chair in front of the fire. A leggy, yellow-haired child alternately breathed on the window-panes and smeared out the steam with her little chapped hand, to stare down at the colourless street, at the dismal houses across the way and at the few passers-by: women whose dingy petticoats scooped up the puddles, men whose trousers were crusted to the knee with slime from the cobbles. A stench of fish stalls and breweries percolated through the ill-fitting window frames and, with the miserable whoop of a ship's siren, reminded Sarah that they were again in Liverpool.

Sometimes, in the deadness of winter afternoons, she forgot which town they had reached, for to the strolling player all towns were the same town: a sooty street in the theatre precincts, a lodgings card in the window, a nearby tavern flanked by an old-clothes exchange and naphtha lamps flaring over the costers' barrows. It was always raining, or raw cold nipped the children's fingers; their little bare hands she filled with hot chestnuts, to comfort them.

At the street market she bought a fourpenny rabbit, a twopenny haddock, parsley at a penny a bunch, root vegetables or greens, according to the season: anything cheap and wholesome that her Scots economy could translate into a tasty meal for the family. An egg was a treat; meat was the odds and ends from the butcher's slab which could be made, with the addition of an onion, a turnip and a few potatoes, into a stew or a hot-pot. On these shopping expeditions the baby was rolled up in her arms; Ben, when not at school, slouched reluctantly in her wake; Nelly shrank from the discomfort and boredom of Mama's shopping, and Katie had her invariable excuse: a rehearsal. Katie, at eight years old, was already very much aware of herself as a 'coming' actress.

Into Kate, her father, Ben Terry, put all the experience he had gained over his long, frustrating years on the road. At two, this precocious imp was learning to sing and dance, to recite and play the piano. At three she was an accredited member of the troupe, and Ben fatuous over the achievements of his diminutive daughter. He taught her to speak distinctly, without mouthing the words, and so to pitch her childish voice that she was audible from pit to gallery. He taught her the finesse of bows and curtsys, and the simple mechanics of the stage. She was soon hopping about in ballet, or figuring as an attendant nymph or fairy in extravaganzas.

In bonnet and shawl, piping the words and executing with assurance the steps and gestures in which her father coached her, Kate had her own number—'I'm Ninety-five'—which, with unsophisticated provincial audiences, brought the house down. And at Saturday noon, when 'the ghost walked' (for nearly another half-century, actors received their salaries on Saturday, instead of on Friday night, as in the present day), Miss Kate Terry's name was on the pay-roll.

In 1851 she was an experienced and self-assured young lady, who would have been something less than human if public acclaim, the encouragement of a doting father, and the sight of her own name on playbills had not gone to her head. To Sarah, no less doting but more far-seeing than Ben, she was 'poor little conceited Kate'. She was a beloved child who had come by success (that Prince Arthur in Edinburgh) earlier than was good for her.

Nelly might be pretty some day; not yet, with her puffy apple cheeks, in which were imbedded the aquamarine splinters of her eyes. She had the lankiness of a foal, and its unconscious grace; some sort of wildness of a breeze, or of barley rocking on its long, pale stalk. She would be tall, like her mother's people. (Kate, though dainty, was a squat little thing, like her Terry grandmother.) Nelly was not, like her elder sister, 'a good child'; she did not willingly help to darn her father's and brother's woollens, or feed the baby its pap. Moody, and constantly spoilt by her father, she was not yet to be trusted to behave herself in the theatre, not to get in the way, or pester the property man, or torment the overworked wardrobe mistress. But how lovely and beguiling she was, and how hard it was to be strict with her!

'Draw the curtains, Nelly.'

'I'm watching for the lamplighter, Mama.'

'Draw the curtains; it's getting cold.'

'He'll be here any minute——'

'Do as I tell you, Nelly.'

'Oh, *Mama!*' But she recognized the note of authority and jerked the dingy baize across the window. 'There's nothing to look at and nothing to do!' exploded Nelly, and launched a kick at the leg of her brother's chair.

Ben's shout as he heeled over backwards anticipated his mother's exclamation. He flung himself at Nelly, to kick her shins and pummel her with his fists; she set her teeth and clutched his straw-blond hair, that matched her own. Their conflict woke the infant George and sent him into a screaming fit; Sarah snatched him up and ordered the combatants apart. They obeyed, from habit: Nelly smiling like an angel out of the corners of her eyes, Ben with crimson cheeks, jutting jaw and set teeth, glaring at his own clenched fists. At a word from his mother, his loving heart would melt away in tears; she knew it, and knew that, for his sake, she must not speak that word. She had too often been accused of making a milksop of her eldest son.

A heavy, handsome child, going on for five when his sister Kate was born, Benjy[1] was a very affectionate little boy, yearning towards the gay, jolly father who was affronted that a child of his should show no interest in the theatre. Benjy could not help not caring about the theatre, and was too honest to pretend, even for the sake of gaining his father's favour. So inevitably he was drawn more and more closely to the tender and loving mother, whose heart often ached for her handsome and headstrong lad, by now hopelessly at odds with his father. Benjy was the true grandson of Benjamin the publican and Peter the builder. Benjy, thirteen years old, was Sarah's most painful problem.

There was laughter outside: warm, gay, masculine laughter and a silvery, childish peal. They rushed in—father Ben and Kate—on a puff of fog, ravenous from rehearsal. While Ben embraced his Nelly, gave his eldest son a pat and lifted baby George on his knee, Sarah pulled the boots off Kate's little frozen feet, rolled her in a

---

[1] I do not know that Benjy was ever so called in the family, but to avoid confusion with his father, I have christened him thus.

shawl and tucked her up on the big bed; she was so tired she fell asleep immediately, regardless of hunger.

While Sarah was in the kitchen, preparing the meal (at six shillings a head, one not only catered but cooked for oneself), Nelly curled into her father's arm, the object of his fondest attention.

' "Come unto these yellow sands——" '

' "Sands", not "thandth"; make it hiss-ss, like a snake.'

Nelly giggled and plunged her hand in the pocket of her apron. 'Thut your eyeth and hold out your hand, Papa; I've kept it for you! '

Ben gaped at a little pearl dropped in his palm.

'That'th my 'eth tooth!'

They went off into whoops of laughter. ' "Curtthied while you have, and kitht, the wild waveth witht' ", reduced them to hysteria. Nelly rolled on the hearthrug; the loss of her 's' tooth provided them with mirth for months. Sarah, coming in to say the meal was ready, envied the pair their inextinguishable spirits. Like creatures from 'an uninhabited island', they wove their magic in the air, they shared a divine madness to which sober little Kate and literal Ben held no clue.

" 'I hear,' " chanted Nelly, " 'the thtrain of thtrutting chanti-cleer——' "

'Hush, hush, dear; don't disturb Katie.'

Like long-married couples, they talked in ellipses. It was after midnight; the girls, spoonwise on their narrow bed, were fast asleep, and Benjy snoring on his hay-bag. The baby George, a warm cocoon, was within reach of Sarah's hand.

'She can't go by herself', says Sarah, into the darkness.

'No, no; that's impossible', comes sleepily from Ben.

The letter from Mr Charles Kean was addressed, very properly, to Mr Ben Terry, offering his clever little daughter an audition at the Princess's Theatre. It was Katie's opportunity, at eight years old, to break away from the rough-and-ready provincial circuits, and place herself under the discipline and direction of a great London management. So far, she herself knew nothing about it, but neither Ben nor Sarah thought of rejecting it. To Ben it was the realization of a dream: the fulfilment, through his little girl, of all he had hoped for himself, all as the slow, unrewarding years went on he had resigned. He was too intelligent not to realize that he lacked the magic spark; that it was not enough to speak beautifully, to move beautifully, to know every trick of the stage, to be handsome and attractive and popular with his colleagues. The spark denied to him had kindled in his daughter.

To Sarah it meant more than Kate's professional advancement. There were two sons to be educated; there might, as time went on, be others. They might eventually drift on to the stage, in the wake of their parents and sister, but they ought to have the advantages of good schooling. If Katie got an engagement with the Keans, it would mean a much-needed addition to the family exchequer. Sarah was typical of her generation in considering that schooling for the little girls was not important; Ben taught them to read, write, spell and do sums. She taught them the simple economics of housekeeping, how to make their beds, keep a room clean and cook a meal. Nelly, at four, could make the breakfast porridge, roast a joint and wash up after the meal.

But Sarah longed—passionately she longed—for a stable *home*, a place they could truly call their own. Through Katie she could envisage it. She and Katie had much in common; they shared the *bourgeois* streak which—oddly—had evaded Ben. Over fourteen years of the provincial theatre she had been deeply disillusioned. Deathlessly loyal to her husband, prepared to make any personal sacrifice for his sake and that of the children—'Miss Yerret' had lost sight of herself as an actress. She had never seriously taken herself as such.

'It's all right; Nelly'll make my breakfast.'

She told herself it was bound to happen. It entailed for her the biggest sacrifice she had been called upon to make, and it never occurred to her not to make it; but it would have helped if Ben recognized that it was, on her part, a sacrifice. Ben had the Liverpool engagement and was bound to play it out. That meant, if she took Katie to London, they were to be separated for the first time since their marriage. Sarah had no illusions; she knew exactly what that separation would mean.

Miss Yerret—who had almost forgotten her stage name, so little opportunity had she had of using it—stitched her fine fingers to the bone on Katie's wardrobe, and tried to put a few elementary ideas on 'looking after Dad' into Nelly's fair, heedless head. Those two were birds of a feather, and would probably make out in their own fashion.

Miss Yerret took gallantly off into the unknown world of London, with excited little Kate, a boy too young to be of comfort to his mother, and a babe in arms—for the good, not only of Katie, but of many Terrys to come. Ben put them into a coach and, through tear-dimmed eyes, she watched the pair of them—Ben and Nelly—waving her off through the steam and smoke of the railway station.

The seats were hard. Smoke and soot penetrated the ill-fitting windows. Within an hour the boys were filthy. Kate, in her little crinoline, her bonnet askew on her tired head, her white stockings reduced to dull grey, was fretful: no longer the important Miss Terry, but a weary child whose head dropped against her mother's shoulder. Sarah's arm slid round her elder daughter; poor little conceited Kate!—so sure of herself; able, at eight years old, to handle a tricky audience, turn a ribald laugh to advantage, manœuvre herself about stages of different sizes; who had had a great deal more flattery than was good for her, and was inclined to put on airs. An endless maternal patience rose in Sarah's heart—and a prayer for the future.

The luxury of first-class travel was not for the theatrical family Terry, and only first-class trains went straight through to London. This meant that certainly at Crewe, and possibly another station, they all had to tumble out, with their innumerable pieces of baggage, which it was Katie's duty to count, while Benjy galloped off to find the booking office and buy tickets for the next stage of their journey; second-class passengers were not allowed the privilege of booking straight through to their destination except on short journeys. Poor Benjy—with moisture matting the blond hair on his brow—trying to memorize what the clerk told him: that if they wanted to continue their journey second class they would have to wait several hours, and the alternative was to go on by the third-class train which happened to be waiting at the platform; rushing back to ask Mama what to do, and Mama, with her divine calm, saying, 'We'll go straight on'—the infant George in her mind. One

can picture it all: and Sarah's regal ascent into a third-class coach—
not so primitive as a few years before: the seats were wooden and
there was hardly any space for their bags and baskets, but at least
it was enclosed; their fellow travellers, if vulgar, were friendly.

For a young woman travelling for the first time without the
support of her husband, the arrival in London was formidable. She
had been told exactly what to do, and had the address of a theatrical
lodging house from one of the members of the Liverpool Company;
Benjy also had his instructions from his father—to find a porter
and tell him to find a cab. All the way from Liverpool Benjy had
been fingering the sixpence he was to tip the porter, in fear of losing
it. Sixpence to a porter seemed very grand; the Terrys were cutting
a dash!

Long before the train ran into Euston Station, Sarah had got the
children cleaned up, brushed their hair, changed Katie's stockings
and pinched up the ribbons on her bonnet. Her beautiful, handsome
children! In the little hand-mirror she took out of her reticule she
looked at her own jaded face, which had once been lovely: now thin,
lined and sallow; the nose too big, the jaw-line puckered. It did
not matter. All that mattered, for the moment, was Katie: pink,
plump, and self-assured. It stopped Sarah's heart to think that on
that little girl, vain and physically frail (Katie's quinsies were one
of the anxieties of their winters), rested, in all probability, the whole
of the Terry future. Was Katie really as good as the provincial
critics—not to speak of her doting father—proclaimed her? If, in
the estimation of the great Mr and Mrs Charles Kean, she was not,
it meant back to the provincial routine: the trailing around from
town to town, which was all right for the girls, but ruinous to the
boys' characters and education. Distracted for her sons, Sarah, at
that moment, a little under-estimated her daughter Katie's qualities.

It must have been an awe-inspiring encounter—that first with
the Keans. Sarah and Kate put on their best clothes; they walked
all the way down, through the buffeting traffic, from Camden
Town to Oxford Street. They were dazed with the sound of foreign
languages (according to Cole, a conscientious chronicler of the
period, 'You met two foreigners, as you perambulated the streets,
for one indigenous child of the soil'); after the small ale of the
provinces, London was like champagne.

They were ushered into The Presence, and dropped their curtsys. (Was Benjy keeping his eye on George, as he had promised? worried Sarah. Was Nelly remembering to send her Dad's shirts to the washerwoman, and not letting the breakfast porridge burn?)

Katie had her separate interview with Mr Kean, recited something and gave satisfaction. She was engaged—not for the Shakespearian parts she had been playing in the provinces, but for the Christmas pantomime which was already in rehearsal: Sala's *Harlequin Bill Taylor*, billed as a 'Grand Operatico, Tragico, Serio-Pastoralico, Nautico, Demoniaco, Cabalistico Original Christmas Pantomime, *Harlequin Billy Taylor*; or the Flying Dutchman and the King of Raritongo'.

There were scores of these pantomimes, first introduced to London by Rich, lessee of Covent Garden, in 1717. Elaborations of the Commedia dell' Arte, they took in the classic characters of Clown, Harlequin, Pantaloon and Columbine, and added many more. They were first and foremost spectacles, but the original 'Harlequin Sorcerer', played by Rich in dumb show, was interpreted as a speaking part by Garrick in the seventeen-thirties. Slapstick and metamorphoses, fable and fancy were their ingredients; they ended always with a Grand Transformation scene.

Miss Kate Terry stood on the deck of a battleship, while *Rule Britannia* was sung amid bursts of coloured fire. She then sedately descended to stage level and, waving her wand, conjured up the Transformation. It sounds simple to the point of inanity; it actually required more command of the stage than most little girls of her age, whether or not brought up in the theatre, were capable of. Miss Terry was a success; so much so that within a few weeks of her London début she was auditioned by Mr and Mrs Kean for the part of Prince Arthur in the forthcoming production of *King John*.

According to her sister Ellen's *Memoirs*, Ben and Nelly remained in the provinces for two years. Apart from the extreme unlikelihood of Sarah's leaving her husband and younger daughter by themselves for so long, the name of Ben Terry, as 'A gamekeeper' in a piece called *A Roland for an Oliver*, appears in the Princess's bill for 18 September 1852, and figures in every season up to 1859. Over fourteen years, Ben had built up his own small reputation as a well-spoken and reliable actor; he supported Macready on the same occasion that Sarah (presumably) played Gertrude, and along the mysterious grapevine of the theatre the Keans had heard of him and offered him an engagement, at the same time as they sent for Kate. Ben had to finish out the Liverpool season before joining his family in town. He had to make sure that Kate had made good, before pulling up his provincial roots, and taking the tremendous gamble (for a small-part actor) of coming to London.

By the end of the '51-'52 season, Kate had fulfilled his fondest hopes; her success as Prince Arthur established her as an accredited member of the Princess's Company. It was grievous that he was unable to be present at her London début in so important a part, knowing how much he had contributed to his little daughter's success: the hours he had spent in coaching her in every nuance, every inflection of the delicate part of Arthur. By the time he arrived in town—having worked out his Liverpool contract—Kate was slapped back into the minor role of Piccolo, a Page, in the burlesque (*Whittikind and His Brothers*) that followed the Shakespearian production, and was too good a little trouper to resent the loss of prestige.

Meanwhile, she had had the fabulous experience of appearing by Royal Command at Windsor Castle: an awesome event for a young provincial actress. All the members of the cast were given a drilling in deportment and etiquette in preparation for this great occasion; Katie's heart beat fast under her little braided bodice when they came in sight of the Castle itself. Its history, of which she knew next to nothing, gave her no thrill, but oh! supposing—just supposing— she, Miss Kate Terry, were presented to the Queen? A shock went through her; playing Prince Arthur, ought she to bow or to curtsy to her Sovereign? Why, oh why, hadn't she remembered to ask Mrs Kean!—who now, alas, was unavailable, withdrawn as royalty itself into her private coach and into her role of Constance.

This horrid problem so occupied Katie while she was dressing and up to the moment of her first entrance that it is by no means surprising that she made little if any impression on her distinguished audience. When the Keans and one or two members of the Company were privately informed that Her Majesty was pleased to receive them after the fall of the curtain, Miss Kate Terry received no summons. Deeply mortified, pride controlled her tears. She appeared in two more Command Performances at the Castle— *King Henry IV*, as Robin, and *King Henry V*, as the Boy—in inferior roles to her Prince Arthur; she was never among the elect, which taught her, probably, a necessary lesson in humility. A soberer and more modest little girl approached the grey towers of Windsor on her second and third visits. She had muffed her big chance—Arthur was a *real* part—and the Queen was not likely to be interested in Servants! She hardly bothered, in Mr Byrn's classes, to pay attention to the technique of bows and curtsys; in any case, she knew it all already, from Dad. For Dad's sake, she was sorry she had no opportunity to make her obeisance to the Queen and her very handsome—but, thought Katie privately, rather dull—Consort.

Ben came up to town with his long-legged, irrepressible Nelly, and beguiled every moment of the journey by showing her off to the other occupants of their compartment. Used to being called upon at any moment, in any company, to recite her bit of poetry, her fable or her speech from Shakespeare, Nelly played up admirably —though wild with excitement at the prospect of London and reunion with Mama, Katie and the boys. She was a happy child, had never heard of shyness, yet had none of the disagreeable precocity of the average children of players: Ben and Sarah had seen to that. They loved their children enough to be stern with them. They did not spare—if not the rod, the slipper. So all the Terry children had beautiful manners, and even Nelly knew she could go so far, and no farther. She could go a little farther than the others, because she was her father's favourite. Romping and roaring and gay as a bird, she was not at all a typical Victorian child. But neither were Ben and Sarah typical Victorian parents. Actually, they were an odd mixture of the prudery of their Wesleyan upbringing and the laxity of their profession. On Ben's side the prudery was superficial, and kept up largely in deference to Sarah. Women were supposed to be innocent, and Ben cherished Sarah's innocence; it paid him to do so. He never appreciated her deep, quiet sagacity. It would have been too uncomfortable to admit it.

Carried away by the grandeurs and glories of the capital city, in which he had never previously set foot, and by the honour of

Benjamin Terry, publican
of the *Fortune of War*

Ben Terry, actor

Fred Terry

Ben Terry III

Charles Terry

belonging to a great London Company, Ben characteristically overlooked the fact that on his small salary and Kate's it was going to
be difficult to make ends meet, with lodgings and provisions and
clothing and the common necessities of existence costing nearly
double what they cost in the provinces.

There was nothing for 'Miss Yerret'—even as 'walking lady'—
in the Kean Company; her worn beauty could not compete with
the attractions of much younger women, with London experience
which enabled them to carry understudies—no casual matter under
Mr Kean's direction. So Ben's *folie de grandeur* sustained a rude blow
when Sarah informed him that she had accepted the humble
situation of a wardrobe woman, so as to contribute a few more
shillings to their meagre exchequer. She had arranged this with
Mrs Kean.

Profoundly kind, under her veneer of pomposity, Ellen Kean had
not forgotten her struggling years. Her guarded heart went out to
this jaded, sometime beautiful young woman, with a charming,
irresponsible husband, four children and another—by the look of
things—on the way. Undoubtedly she respected Sarah Terry for her
willingness to accept a menial position in the theatre, for the
benefit of her husband and children.

Why, demanded Sarah, *vis-à-vis* with Ben's resentment—why, if
Mrs Kean did not consider it beneath her dignity to mend her
husband's tights, or even to stitch up the hem of a tunic worn by
some careless member of the Company, should she, Sarah, mind
helping in the wardrobe? She and Ben had served their apprenticeship in the provinces, where even leading men and women did
their own packing and unpacking, laid out their make-up and dressed
themselves, so far as they were able, without assistance; where
younger members of the Companies were happy to show respect
by lacing a bodice or holding a candle close to a speckled looking-
glass. The youth who played a Page took it as part of his business
to rush out for a mug of beer, to carry a message, act as doorman.
dogsbody or whipping-boy; the Chambermaid, between her
entrances, looked after the babies tucked up in the greenroom,
emptied slops or gave a touch of the goffering iron to a crumpled
frill. Was there anything to suggest that Mrs Siddons' Lady Macbeth lost anything by its interpreter's spending her time between

E

49

acts in patching a petticoat, stitching tapes on a chemise or cleaning stage jewellery?

Helping in the wardrobe meant being in the theatre all the time, to keep an eye on Kate and Nelly, and seeing the latter behaved herself.

There was the rent to pay, and Benjy's schooling. The girls were growing out of everything—it didn't matter about Nelly; she could make do for a few more years with Katie's cast-offs. But Benjy must not, with shabbiness, invite the derision of his schoolfellows, and Ben must not appear at a disadvantage in the well-dressed Company of a great London theatre. And they all six—presently there would be seven—must eat!

CHAPTER FOUR

The Princess's Theatre

'I do hope, Mama, that Nelly will *behave*', was Kate's anxious observation to her mother.

She need have had no misgivings on that score. Unthinking, idle, wild and gay, Nelly, at four, had the fine sensibilities of the artist. She was deeply impressed by the discipline that controlled those long rehearsals, starting at ten in the morning and often going on without a break up to midnight. She who knew nothing of schooling apart from what she gleaned from her brother's accounts, felt in an awed fashion that it must be something like school, and was fascinated by the novelty of it.

From his seat in the stalls, Mr Kean furiously rang a handbell each time something displeased him on the stage; from her chair at the side Mrs Kean, propelled by her crinoline, majestically swept on the delinquent, demonstrated his or her error, then graciously retired, to await her next summons. Mrs Kean's stern benevolence to all the children in the Company quickly won Nelly's devotion. Mrs Kean knew everything—but everything!—about acting; even more—though this might be heresy—than Dad.

From greenroom or wardrobe the clang of the bell was audible, and kept everyone conscious of what was happening on the stage. In the greenroom the children learned to keep out of the way of somebody who, striding up and down, was memorizing his lines, or practising some trick of timing or gesture. They curled up in the window-seat overlooking the scene dock, and watched the rats, horridly fulminating over timber and canvas. Sometimes old Mr Byrn collected the children for an impromptu dancing-class; he played his little fiddle—called a 'kit'—and they pranced and pointed their toes and bowed and curtsied in time to the thin, sweet music, and hoped they might be chosen for the burlesques or pantomimes. Nelly became very earnest about all this, and rather envious of sister Kate who, since playing Arthur, was an important member of the Comapany.

Sometimes she crept out, and, dodging behind a flat, watched the rehearsal; or, tired and fretful, she climbed the stairs to the wardrobe, where Mama sat stitching or starching, with George crawling round her feet. She was hungry; she dipped chunks of bread into the thick Scotch broth that simmered perpetually on the hearth. She was sleepy, and was tucked up in a dress basket. At dusk or dark, her arm linked into Mama's, she tramped back to their lodgings, climbed three or four flights of stairs, and helped Mama make supper for Dad and Katie, hungry Ben, baby George and the latest baby, Mary Ann Betsy, Polly to the family. She learnt to scrape potatoes, and what went into a stew.

Benjy was at day-school. Intelligent, disastrously handsome and out of tune with the family—his termly reports were not gratifying. It was not easy for the proud, spirited boy to accept the patronage of his five-years-younger sister Kate, sedate and smug in her assured position as a seeded member of the Charles Kean Company. (Later—much later—he was to be proud of her, and prouder still of Nelly, who was closer to him in temperament than any of his sisters.) There was nothing of the artist in Benjy; he was a throwback to the commercial Terrys, with a certain wildness deriving, not improbably, from great-uncle James.

George, a fat, sedate, good baby, healthy and obedient, hardly counted in the family cosmos; and even less the infant Polly.

Both Ben and Sarah, in their different fashions, were very strict with the children; their morals and their manners were equally strictly supervised. The wild young man from Spice Island had turned into the typical Victorian father: which is to say that Ben, discreet almost to the point of smugness in the bosom of the family, found plenty of outlet on the side for his abounding high spirits and his superabundant virility. Whatever Sarah knew, or guessed, she closed her beautiful eyes to. She knew she had lost her looks, that she was thin, haggard, and often misshapen; she sometimes wondered that Ben continued her lover. Which he most certainly did, and left the pledge of it too frequently—according to modern ideas. Proudly and gallantly she carried her annual burden—and, unconsciously, was beautified by it.

They were still living on a top floor in Gower Street: Benjy, Kate, Nelly, George, Polly, and presently Charles and the adorable Flossie (Florence), most lovely and beloved of all the Terry girls. Kate and Nelly were used to the routine arrival of a new little brother or sister. Katie, playing Fairy Queen or Preciosa in the pantomime, Duke of York in *Richard III* (with Dad as the Lord Mayor) and a Lady-in-Waiting in *Henry VIII* (Dad as the Surveyor), had to rush home and help Mama and Nelly to bath the babies.

The season 1855-56 included the production, on 28 April, of *The Winter's Tale*. Ben was cast as An Attendant, and Kate as Servant to the Old Shepherd. Out of a clutter of young aspirants, including Clara Denvil, Nelly was chosen by Mrs Kean for the part of Mamillius. That shrewd eye had been on the tiresome, tomboyish child who took, like a fish to water, to Mr Byrn's dancing classes; who could speak lines distinctly, with intelligence, and shared with her sister Kate a genuine sense of the theatre. Katie was generously gratified by her little sister's success, and Ben, needless to say, enraptured. Sarah set to work on the little red and silver tunic Nelly was to wear, and Nelly herself was sobered by being allowed, for the first time, as a member of the Company, to watch the tremendous preparations of a Kean production.

In his usual fashion, Charles Kean was devoting as much—if not more—time to research than to the study of his part as Leontes. In the '52-'53 season he had instituted his 'Fly-Leaves': lengthy additions to the playbill, in which he set forth academically the fruits of his intellectual labours. It would be interesting to know what percentage of his public cared about the historical accuracy of Mr Kean's productions. His revival of Byron's *Sardanapalus* in his fourth season (1854) was the talk of the town and set the teeth of insurance companies on edge. The public adored red ruin, fire and slaughter; did they really care that Leontes's robe was printed with an authentic Greek design, that Hermione's gown was faithfully copied from a statue and that the child's go-cart could be verified on a vase in the British Museum?

The schoolmaster in Charles Kean insisted on impressing these matters on his audiences. It was partly a show-off, and partly a form of compensation for the genius he had not inherited. He found for his wife a beautifully draped robe which she proceeded to ruin by the addition of innumerable petticoats, and for himself authentic patterns which were hand-painted on to his chiton and the chlamys that covered it. Like his wife, unable to leave well alone, he unfortunately added to his costume a kind of May-Day garland, which not only enlarged his over-large head, but reduced his height. A pity; for without that wreath Kean as Leontes could have cut a fine figure.

Each member of the cast was tricked out in admirably historical costume, to which Victorian prudery unfortunately added undergarments and bright pink tights. Nelly's tights were awful; a size too large for her, they were badly adjusted by the dresser (the wife of Grieve the scene-painter, known to the children as 'Peter Grieveus') and bagged round her immature knees.

Slowly the production built up; the Company watched the assembly of sets and properties; of Grieve's impressive back-cloths. Rehearsals went on to four and five in the morning; in the clasp of her father's arm, little Mamillius nodded and waked, nodded and waked at the back of the dress circle, where all of the Company not immediately required on the stage were assembled. Katie, trying to be grown-up, grey as wax with fatigue, forced her lids not to fall over her exhausted eyes; she was only twelve, but had had four years of Kean discipline, and four more of professional experience; it was up to her to show an example to Nelly.

28 April 1856 was a momentous date for Terrys. Before an audience that included the Queen and the Prince Consort, Ben, Kate and Ellen made their united appearance in *The Winter's Tale*. Discounting the 'Mustard Pot' episode in Scotland, later claimed by both sisters,[1] it was Ellen's début. Ben and Kate, in their respective modest parts, made no impression; Nelly, in an access of zeal falling flat over the handle of her Greek go-cart and bawling with mortification, got a big hand, and commendation from Mrs Kean.

Insignificant among the fashionable audience was a young tutor from Christ Church, Oxford, within ten years to be famous as Lewis Carroll, and brilliantly, with his camera, to record the Terry family.

All but unconscious with exhaustion and excitement, clinging to their father's arms, Katie and Nelly staggered home to tell Mama

[1] *cf.* Ellen Terry's *Memoirs*.

all about it. Ben and George, Polly and Tom and Floss were fast asleep—Floss only just over eight months old. Sarah, not fully recovered from the birth of her last baby, stretched her loving arms and, kissing Nelly's flushed apple cheeks, accepted the fact that she had lost another daughter to the stage.

The top floor in Gower Street shrank round the increasing family, and it was Katie who, devoted to her mother, suggested they ought to move. It was an effort for Sarah to carry or pull the little ones up and down the four flights of stairs, and although the rooms— being so high up—were airy and clean, the unavoidable over-crowding was not good for any of them. There were Katie's quinsies, and the common cold which ran like wildfire at intervals through the family. Ben complained of 'shortness of breath', not yet to be identified as 'the Terry heart', which persisted down the generations. He was as gay and optimistic as ever—increasingly so, since Nelly started to contribute lustre to the name.

Nelly, as a follow-up to her Mamillius, was chosen for Puck in the autumn's production of *A Midsummer Night's Dream*, and Katie, who was thinning down and had beautiful auburn hair past her waist, was given the understudy of Miss Leclerq's Titania and was to play the Fairy—'Over hill, over dale, Thorough bush, thorough brier. . . .'

'It shouldn't be "thorough", should it? "Through", it means "through",' objected Nelly, inviting from her father a lesson in scansion.

It was just beginning to dawn on Nelly that the profession was not (to use a contemporary term) all beer and skittles. She was wakened up at all hours to recite her lines; Ben, lovingly relentless, was determined she should make a sensation in her first big part. It seems not unlikely that the early failure of Ellen Terry's memory and the painful difficulty she, Marion and Fred, at the height of their careers, had in memorizing lines, went back to the pressure put on them in childhood by an eager and ambitious father.

'At breakfast,' wrote Ellen, in *The Story of My Life*, 'father would begin the day's coaching. Often I had to lay down my fork and say my lines. He would conduct these extra rehearsals anywhere—in the street, in the 'bus—we were never safe! I vividly remember going into a chemist's shop and being stood upon a stool to say my part to the chemist!'

(Today the young actress goes to a Berkeley Square hairdresser and emerges from a *plissée* nylon robe with a fashionable hair set, and what that does for her heaven itself may possibly know.)

On a less hearty and healthy child this could have had a shattering effect; Nelly flourished under it. Blithe as a cock sparrow, with her blonde hair chopped short for the part, she looked—according to her own description, 'a sight'. Grease paint had not been invented; the only make-up was powder and rouge, and 'liners' for eyebrows and wrinkles. In a modern make-up, Nelly could have been lovely; with a chill bloom of rice-powder (which she wore to the end) and the hare's foot dabbed vaguely over her fat cheekbones, she was, according to contemporary photographs, grotesque.

Her salary of fifteen shillings was doubled because she nobly finished the play with her big toe caught in the trap through which Puck rose at the end of the last act. That night Katie was playing her understudy—Titania; she lent moral and physical support to her suffering sister. Nelly's toe was broken. 'Oh, Katie, Katie!' 'Oh, Nelly, Nelly!'[1] It was a *tour de force* of fortitude for a little girl of eight, and Ben had reason to be proud of his daughter. To his manager he wrote one of his courteous letters:

Dear Sir,
   I am much obliged to you for your kind consideration of my dear Nelly. Accept my best thanks, and believe me to remain

Dear Sir,
Yours truly
Ben Terry.

C. Kean, Esqre.

One night in the audience there was a young architect who, as a hobby, had started to take a serious interest in the theatre. Innocent and gay, Nelly capered, as Puck, in front of her future lover.

The increase in Nelly's salary justified the removal to Kentish Town—no longer 'a small village on the way to Highgate', but a fairly recently developed project of neat red-brick streets and terraced houses at economical rents, designed to appeal to families

[1] Ellen Terry's *Memoirs*.

of limited income but genteel pretensions. London smoke having as yet laid but a faint patina on the brickwork, it was considered a 'healthy and salubrious district'; even a few trees of the original village survived, and—oddly interspersed among the modern architecture—here and there a 'gentleman's dwelling', still kept up by its obstinate owner, who, in spite of the encroachment of 'modern' building, maintained his staff of indoor and outdoor servants, his carriage and pair, and lent something of style to the neighbourhood.

So humble a little house—the hall, which could be called a lobby, not wide enough for the passage, side by side, of two people; the steep stairs barely wide enough for one—certainly not wide enough for the descent of a coffin, which, fortunately, during the Terry tenancy, was not requisitioned. To modern ideas (1960) it is rather pretty, with its little iron balconies overhanging the area; it is 'condemned', like the majority of houses in Stanhope Street, whose place has been taken by soaring modern apartment houses. Today, like its small neighbours, it has a melancholy air; to the Terrys, who had never had a whole house of their own, it was a palace. It is flanked today, as it must have been a hundred years ago, by a tavern and a pawnbroker's—the latter with the all but legendary three golden balls. It is a pity no plaque can be set up —for the little house is shortly to be pulled down—to mark 92 Stanhope Street as the original home of the Theatrical Terrys.

A house of their own, after all those nomadic years! One can picture the boys, tomboy Nelly and little Polly, thundering up and down the uncarpeted stairs—'shushed' by Sarah ('Darlings don't, or the neighbours will complain'). There was even a garden!—actually a little paved yard at the back, with borders and a brick wall trailed with ivy. Overlooking the 'garden' was a narrow balcony, on to which opened, through French doors, the drawingroom; the first drawingroom the Terrys had ever possessed.

While the children and their father romped and raged round the empty rooms, Katie and her mother tried to go soberly into ways and means. Rent and rates had to be covered, and something set aside for theatre vacations. There would have to be beds, and chairs, and a table or two; a little furniture and some carpet to make the drawingroom—where they would receive their friends—presentable.

Ellen Terry remembered going with her Mama to a secondhand

dealer's somewhere in Camden Town and haggling over a little chest of drawers, for which the dealer wanted three-and-sixpence. They got it eventually for something over two shillings, and threepence for the man who delivered it in a handcart. Slowly a heterogeneous collection of furniture—most of it from secondhand shops and market stalls—was assembled; few pieces matched and all were shabby. There were no cupboards or wardrobes; the boys spent their time hammering in nails on which the girls hung their dresses, and covered them with old sheets or bedspreads.

As theatre people went, in those days, the Terrys were moderately prosperous, but, with an ever-increasing family, the strain on their resources augmented. The father was extravagant, far too good a 'mixer' and invariably paid while others fumbled. There were the boys' school fees, their clothing and their healthy appetites —not to mention the appetites of their parents and five more lively brothers and sisters—to be catered for, out of Ben's salary, and Katie's, and Nelly's, and Sarah's pittance in the wardrobe. It was no small problem, even in those days, when the pound was worth ten times its value today, to furnish a house, to equip it with even the bare necessities of housekeeping, and at the same time to keep up the kind of façade Sarah was determined for the sake of her daughters to maintain.

All the best bits of furniture were pushed into the drawingroom —to which Ben's contribution was a piano he got for five pounds in an auction. For once, Sarah did not reproach him with extravagance; the piano, in the eighteen-sixties, was a *sine qua non* of gentility; self-taught, he himself played it charmingly, and taught his children. If the worst came to the worst, they could take in a couple of lodgers. In defence of her hard-earned home, there was nothing Sarah was not prepared to do. Her hopes, like Ben's, were fixed on Katie, in whom Mr and Mrs Kean believed as firmly (so it appeared) as Katie's father. For Katie, Sarah performed miracles of dressmaking: creating a 'model' from a length of stuff bought from a coster's barrow, or bits and pieces from the theatre wardrobe. Her patient fingers stitched scores of yards of velvet ribbon, *soutache* or fringe on to the girls' bodices, their voluminous skirts. Midnight found her ironing the babies' clothes, Ben's shirts, the girls' pantalettes. Sitting up in bed, she stitched by candlelight, a curtain, a stool-cover, or patched the boys' breeches. To this came 'Miss Yerret', one-time Queen Gertrude to Macready's Hamlet: and never made moan.

The theatre closed for approximately four months during the summer, when the fashionable world went out of town, and the actors had to shift for themselves. Some got engagements on the provincial circuits; some—not a few—suffered for their improvidence.

Ben Terry, with his Portsmouth connections, was lucky; for several summer seasons he rented the little old bug-ridden theatre at Ryde, and put on farces that the great comedian Robson and the Keeleys had popularized in London. He had the opportunity to put into practice all he had learned with Shalders of management and booking, of making the best of odds and ends of scenery and properties remaining from former leases. He could cut a great dash as 'a London actor', and enjoy at the same time the kudos of the 'local boy who made good': for the Fortune of War was nearly as well known 'across the water' as it was on The Point (no longer spoken of as 'Spice Island'). Apart from his own experience, his principal assets were two brilliant little daughters: Katie, who melted all hearts in romantic pieces, and Nelly, a joyous buffoon, who 'brought the house down' (coached by her father) as Jacob Earwig in *Boots at the Swan*. She was only eight; it is not possible that she could realize the qualities of the great original, Robson— 'the passionate cry, the wail of misery, the bright tears and, before they were dry, prancing about, the comic mountebank'. But to the simple Ryde audiences, who had never seen, and many of whom had never heard of Robson, Nelly was 'a wonder'! Rumours of her performance even attracted a few ardent theatregoers from the mainland—not, it may be added, her aunt Rose or her aunt Lou; wedded to the Wesleyan meeting even more closely than to their lawful husbands, neither wished anything to do with sinful theatre folk, or had any interest in their nephews and nieces—a tune which changed later on, when Kate and Ellen became famous.

They were living in a cottage rented to Sarah by sister Lizzie (born Ballard, now Binsted); originally Rose Cottage, it was rechristened, towards the end of the century, Belle Vue. It was in

Clay Lane, leading down to the beach. It was the nearest thing to a holiday Sarah had ever enjoyed; the boys and the babies scuffling round in the sand, while Katie and Nelly endlessly rehearsed with their father, she looked across the Solent to the home of her youth. How far had her life departed from those distant, carefree days; she was surprised to find that she had no great desire to renew the contacts of her girlhood. Her parents were dead, her sisters Lizzie and Lou married—she had never had much *rapport* with Lou, who now (so Lizzie told her) was living in Portsea, and dear, lovely Lizzie was living very happily, somewhere in the North.

No, she did not want to go over to Portsmouth, although Ben offered to take her. He, on the contrary, took his few opportunities of revisiting his glimpses of the moon. Proud of his handsome boys, he showed them the scenes of his youth; took them on Sunday morning to watch the troops on the Grand Parade: the whirling sticks in the hands of the leopard-skinned drummer, the buttons and colours and feathers, the march up the High Street in which the crowds—including the little Terry boys—joined, keeping step with the Redcoats, following them to Cambridge, Victoria or Anglesea barracks.

To Ben Terry, Portsmouth of the 'fifties, in comparison with Portsmouth of the 'thirties, seemed singularly sedate. He learned with a shock that the Free Mart Fair, which had flourished for six hundred years, was abolished by Act of Parliament in 1847.

He took the boys to the Sally Port, where the little, dark, unhappy bride of Charles II landed nearly two hundred years before; and showed them King James's Gate and the old Star and Garter from which Franklin sailed, with *Erebus* and *Terror*, to seek the North-West Passage, and never returned. Young Ben could remember that; but he was too young to be suitably impressed by the initials 'H.N.' scratched on a seaward window, between 'Dot' and 'Flora', Nelson's last record on his last visit to the famous inn.

The theatre was closed for the vacation, but they went all over it. The climax of their tour was a visit to the Fortune of War, where Mrs Catherine Terry, old and dim, but astonishingly like her grandchild Katie (whom she was never to meet), embraced her favourite son, and the little boys of whom the elder vividly recalled her husband Benjamin. The handsome boy, just in his teens, delighted his grandmother and was himself delighted by the ambience of the old tavern. He would a lot rather be an innkeeper than an actor! He would rather spend a night rattling round Portsmouth than return to Rose Cottage, Mama and the children.

And so—back to London and 92 Stanhope Street. The Ryde season had been a success, their expenses were small, and there was a little money to spend on the house—on curtains and fripperies, on renewing shabby upholstery. The girls still made the beds, dusted and polished, helped to prepare the meals, but there was a scrubwoman for 'the rough'; for cleaning grates, washing floors and carrying coals, and a washwoman who, once a week, came in and lit a fire under the 'copper' in the scullery and boiled all the household linen and the body linen; and Katie's ambition for a girl 'to answer the door' was soon to be fulfilled.

The Princess's Theatre opened with *The Tempest*, Katie as Ariel. She looked lovely, and played it as well as any very down-to-earth little girl could be expected to interpret a fantastical part. ('She shone most', Charles Reade was presently to write, 'in modern characters.')

Nelly, unbearably cocky after her *succès fou* at Ryde, was playing Fairy Goldenstar to her sister's lead in the *White Cat* pantomime, and Karl in a burlesque of *Faust*. Flaming with energy and well aware she was her father's idol, the only person who could keep Nelly in order was Mrs Kean, to whom the younger Miss Terry had the sense to pay suitable deference. All the men in the Company took Nelly as an enormous joke, and most of the women could not abide her. To her sister Kate she was a constant source of anxiety and embarrassment.

Kate, at fourteen, was a grown-up young lady, pretty, sedate, responsible and imbued with respect for her elders and betters; above all, eager to learn. She had already caught the discerning eye of Charles Reade, the playwright and critic (who in that same year had consolidated his reputation with a comedy, *Masks and Faces*, at the Haymarket) and of his friend and collaborateur, Tom Taylor, then Secretary to the Board of Health, author or adapter of numerous plays, and free-lance journalist.

Graduates respectively of Oxford and Cambridge, elected Fellows of their respective colleges of Magdalen and Trinity (Reade was

Vice-President of Magdalen in 1851 and Taylor held the Chair of English at University College, London; both studied for and were called to the Bar), they were by no means representative of journalistic bohemia. Reade, as the son of an Oxfordshire squire, had social connections; Taylor, who hailed from a middle-class Sunderland family, was well placed in intellectual circles. They both had the valuable thing called 'influence' which meant much to a struggling young actress.

These two distinguished, youngish men exercised a beneficent avuncularism over Kate and Ellen Terry. Tom Taylor, with a handsome house and grounds in the then elegant Lavender Sweep, was married to a stern, intelligent woman who cherished her vague, short-sighted little husband, gave him a son called Wicliffe, and was an admirable hostess to his innumerable guests. A Haymarket actress, Laura Seymour, kept house for the bachelor Reade, and the pair of them contrived, in the teeth of Victorian morality, to convince society of the purity of their association. Never, never would Katie and Nelly Terry have been allowed to visit the Reades if there had been anything even faintly equivocal about that ménage. Charles Reade was an influential man, and Laura Seymour a very discreet woman; the truth will never be known about their attachment.

At the Tom Taylors' and at Charles Reade's the two little Terry girls contacted a society which would never have come in their way as children of humble players living in the mediocre district of Kentish Town. They met critics, painters, playwrights, the great names in contemporary journalism, and an occasional visitant from *le beau monde*. They got invitations to grand houses. In her *Memoirs* Ellen Terry wrote of a Christmas party in Half Moon Street, when she danced with the Duke of Cambridge. Most of these invitations came through the great Charles Reade, the humanitarian writer, dedicated to the exposure of social abuses—coffin ships, victimization of trade unionists and the scandal of the private lunatic asylums. Katie and Nelly could not have cared less about coffin ships or mad-houses; Mr Reade wrote for and about the stage, and introduced them to lovely rich people, in some way connected with the theatre, who could help them to get parts and plaster their names in the Press.

Up to now, the relationship between the Terrys and their management was of the warmest, and reflects much credit on the Keans. Kate wrote in her thin, spikey script to her manageress—

My dear Mrs Kean,

I cannot sufficiently thank you for the wine which was left for me at home by your orders.

You must please excuse my adding more as my hand is still very painful. With kind love to Mr Kean and yourself

I remain

Yours sincerely,

Kate Terry

And Ben:

Dear Sir,

The introduction of my daughter Kate to the public as Ariel, I feel assured will be most valuable to her.

Will you accept my sincere thanks for this proof of your kindness? I should have preferred to have personally thanked you but (under circumstances) regret to believe that this method of expressing my obligations will be more acceptable to you.

Allow me to take this opportunity of sincerely thanking you for your kind enquiries and generous consideration of me during my illness.

Believe me, Dear Sir,

Yours truly obliged

Ben Terry

C. Kean Esqre.

The significance of this letter lies in the third paragraph. Ben Terry and his manager were not on good terms. They preserved—on Ben's side—a superficial courtesy, wholly for Katie's and Nelly's sakes. They avoided, whenever possible, personal contacts. Ben Terry was not the only member of the Company who detested Mr Kean; the leader of the anti-Kean faction was the excellent old actor Ryder, of whom Ellen Terry gave the admirable description that he was 'like an old tree that has been struck by lightning, or a greenless, barren rock'. The root of the dislike would appear to have been a very natural and human resentment of a man who, with negligible equipment, took precedence of many superior actors by virtue of money and royal favour. Old Ryder and old Harley could have acted Charles Kean off the stage. Ben Terry did not come into that category, and the coolness between him and Kean was certainly not the outcome of jealousy on Ben's part—jealousy being, in fact, a vice of which he was incapable.

It was a matter of deep incompatibility between two forceful characters, possibly spiked on Kean's side by subconscious resentment of Ben's fine appearance on the stage, to which his courtly manners both on and off lent emphasis. Ben certainly had elegant manners, and too sharp a sense of theatre politics wilfully to annoy his manager. He had another quality, less acceptable to the tetchy little man: an unbounded sense of humour, expressing itself perhaps too frequently in that rich, uproarious laugh which his son Fred was admirably to reproduce in after years. That laugh, ringing from greenroom to wings, may have carried derisory echoes to the sensitive ears of Kean, and disinclined him towards a dashing young man who was too obviously furnished with qualities in which he —Kean—was deficient.

No mention has so far been made of the Terry Temper, to which justice can only be done by one who has suffered from it. It was unpredictable, spectacular and bore no relationship to justice, or even ordinary commonsense. Its finest exponent was Ben's youngest son Fred (unborn at the time of which we are speaking), who rarely on the stage produced anything that could compare with his private explosions. All the children inherited this uproarious temper, so violent as to be funny, except to hypersensitive people. It was invariably followed by the tenderest compunction.

There is no verbal or written record of the drama which drew from Katie this pathetic little note to her manageress:

My dear Mrs Kean,
    I have been and am very unhappy to hear that my Papa has offended Mr Kean, so much as to cause my dear sister Nelly to be removed from the theatre.
    I hope it will not occasion you to withdraw your kindliness and good wishes toward me, which I have been, and always shall be, most grateful for.
    With kind love to Mr Kean and yourself

Believe me
Yours sincerely
Kate Terry

Prudent little Kate, disassociating herself from Papa's indiscretions. What 'dear sister Nelly' had been up to, history does not relate; she had probably made a mischievous nuisance of herself and, furious with Ben, Charles Kean felt 'a pox on all these Terrys!' Kate begged her mother to bring Dad to his right mind, and the outcome was the following letter, written from 7 Harrington Street:[1]

Dear Sir,
I deeply regret the circumstances of yesterday. I was wrong in making the observation I did to Mrs Lambert in the Treasury. It was done most foolishly, although never intended for your hearing. From a conversation I have had with Colonel Bruce (who has on many occasions advised me) it appears that both Mrs Kean and yourself are much displeased with me. He has pointed out and convinced me of the error I have committed, but I hope for my daughter Kate's sake if not for my own, you will permit me to withdraw the uncourteous observations I used, and that you will not allow the circumstance of my having done so to interfere with your kind feelings towards my children whose interest I will leave entirely in your hands

I remain Dr Sir,
yrs faithfully
Ben Terry

Charles Kean Esqr.

There is abundant proof in surviving scraps of Kean-Terry correspondence of the Keans' generosity to members of their Company. In 1855 (the date on the postmark is illegible; Terrys seldom, if ever, dated their letters) Ben was writing,

Dear Sir,
I take the earliest opportunity to acknowledge the liberality and kindness you last week exercised towards me and mine, and to express my best thanks for same.

The nature of the 'liberality' may be guessed from a letter from Kate in the following year—the year of the great cholera epidemic:

My dear Mrs Kean,
I am happy to say I am very much better but still very weak. I hope however soon to resume my duties in the Theatre.
Will you kindly give my love and thanks to Mr Kean for the continuance of my salary and with love and many thanks for your kind enquiries

Believe me
Yours sincerely
Kate Terry

[1] The address of the Colonel Bruce mentioned in the letter.

The standard theatrical contract of those days contained the clause that if actors were 'off', for whatever reason, they forfeited their salary. This harsh clause appears never to have been enforced by the Keans in cases of illness, and its cancellation is undoubtedly the 'liberality' to which Ben refers. The coolness between him and his manager continued, however, to the end of their association; like the elephant, Kean never forgot and Ben's explosion in the Treasury (whatever it was over) cost him favour which his talents as an actor were insufficient to regain for him.

Katie, however, continued to bask in managerial sunlight; she was well behaved, hard-working and something more, which was confirmed when Mr Kean, partly on his wife's advice, cast her as Cordelia, and, at the age of fourteen, she leapt to stardom overnight. (That production of *King Lear* was also notable for its 'singing Fool'—Miss Poole, who had made her début in 1831; special music was written for the occasion by Hatton, an able, if not particularly inspired contemporary composer.) Caroline Heath played Goneril and Eleanor Bufton Regan; Ryder played Edgar and Walter Lacy Edmund. It was what, today, would be called an 'all-star cast', and was hailed as such, even by the anti-Kean faction, and the critics (headed, of course, by Reade and Taylor) were lyrical over the charms of Cordelia. Katie received a gold brooch as a mark of favour from Mrs Kean.

It was a deeply moving occasion for Ben, who had done so much to build his little girl towards this outstanding success.

Katie wrote one of her modest letters to her manager:

My dear Mr Kean,

I received last night with great pleasure your kind note for which accept my most sincere thanks not only for your present kindness but also for giving me the opportunity of trying to please you by casting me in such parts as 'Cordelia' and 'Ariel'—It is almost needless to say that I shall always endeavour to the utmost of my power to merit your appreciation.

The kind addition to my salary is one of the many proofs you have already afforded me of the interest you take in my welfare—Hoping that both yourself and Mrs Kean will accept my very best thanks

Believe me

My dear Mr Kean

Yours very sincerely

Kate Terry

Never to fall short in graciousness, Ben wrote:

Dear Sir,

I beg most sincerely to thank you for your kind and liberal appreciation of my daughter Kate's performance of Cordelia.

If on any former occasion I have failed to express my thanks for your estimation of her general conduct and attention I beg to assure you that it has been an error of the head and not of the heart.

Again thanking you for this additional favour, believe me

Dear Sir
Yours truly
Ben Terry

Kate's success as Cordelia may be said to have changed the whole 'complexion'—social as well as artistic—of the Terry family.

CHAPTER FIVE

Some Adventures

For One Night Only
Tuesday Evening, March 13th, 1860

MISS KATE TERRY

and

MISS ELLEN TERRY

The original representatives[1] *of* Ariel, Cordelia, Arthur, Puck, etc.

With this Crummles-like announcement Ben Terry proudly
presented his first essay in London management.

Spectacular as had been Charles Kean's success in the 1858
season with *King Lear*, the play was a financial failure. The theatre
was too small, the prices too low and the extravagance of the production out of all proportion to receipts. The Keans lost £4,000
and the lease of the Princess's was running out. On the credit side,
Mr Kean had consolidated his professional reputation and collected
a Fellowship of the Society of Antiquaries—which gave him in-
ordinate satisfaction; no actor had previously received such an
honour. (On the other hand, no actor previous to Mr Kean had
endeavoured to combine acting with serious archaeology; 'one thing
at a time, and that done well' was a catchword of the day.)

Before the curtain fell on the last performance of *King Lear* the
Company grapevine was humming with the news: the 1858-59
season was to be the Farewell. No specific statement was issued
to the Company before the Keans took off for their holiday in
Italy (where Mrs Kean bribed her way into the Vatican and managed
to get the exact measurements of a cardinal's robe, so that Charles
should play his final Wolsey in a perfect replica of the original).

---

[1] The italics are mine.—M. S.

68

The Princess's was given over to the painters and cleaners, and Grieve was labouring over his scenery—having been handed a formidable list of forthcoming revivals.

The Terrys left town, as usual, for the Isle of Wight, but this time the venture was not so lightsome. They had seriously to consider the future. All of the shrewd commercial side rose in Ben, as he agreed with Sarah that, having managed to establish domicile in London, it would be a mistake again to drift into the provinces. Rumour had it that the Keans were planning a farewell tour; it was unlikely that the Terrys would be invited to take part in that. Apart from Ben's continued unpopularity with his manager, the Keans were loaded with dependants, one of whom, Patty Chapman (Mrs Kean's niece), was already crowding Kate, and had been given the part of Jessica in the revival of *The Merchant of Venice* with which the season was planned to open. None of the Terrys was cast in this.

That Farewell season was a formidable one, not only for the actors but for all the personnel of the big, expensive Company. At the end of a fortnight *The Merchant* (Kean as an indifferent Shylock and Mrs Kean as a grisly Portia) was taken off and *King John* put on. Ben played the King of France and Kate played Blanche of Spain. Nelly was cast in Kate's former part of Prince Arthur and incurred Mrs Kean's severest criticism; it was the first time she, the spoilt darling, had come up *hard* against the relentless discipline of the theatre. She was not the 'small miracle' she had been encouraged to think herself, but a heedless little girl who knew a few theatre tricks and thought they were good enough! Ellen Kean hammered her into realization of the deep and touching implications of her part, with the result that she and Ryder (the Hubert) created a furore: too much of a furore for jealous little Charles. A notice was put up that no curtain calls would be allowed at the end of a scene; but public demand defeated jealousy. The pair of them were obliged to take the call—Nelly galloping in the wake of Ryder's 'archaeological' strides.

In *Macbeth*, which, a fortnight later, followed *King John*, Ben played Seward and Nelly a lazy, careless little Fleance. Her carelessness may have accounted for the fact that, in the revival of *A Midsummer Night's Dream* which followed the Christmas pantomime, she was not again cast as Puck. Or had she grown too long and lanky? She was taller than Katie, who played Titania.

There is a discrepancy between the records of Malcolm Morley and of Edgar Pemberton in regard to the latter half of the Farewell season; Morley claims a day-to-day diary of the Charles Kean lease of the Princess's Theatre, yet makes no mention of the revival of *Henry V* on 28 March 1859 for the Keans' Benefit; Mrs Kean played the Katherine and it ran 84 nights. Pemberton, with typical indifference, gives no dates, but quotes the *Athenaeum*, a distinguished journal of the period, on Kate's performance of the Boy: 'There was in it an intelligible indication of the wonderful daring by which the battle of Agincourt was won. To men who were once such lads as he nothing was impossible. . . . That little bit of acting, in regard to its completeness, was the gem of the performance.' Katie may have had no gift for fantasy; she had a strong, earthy perception of human verities, which endeared her to her growing public. This curiously underlay her Victorian 'gentility'—of which Nelly had no scrap. Nelly was a tomboy and a romp, a perpetual humiliation to her genteel elder sister, and showed, as yet, no glimmer of the undoubted genius which, in Kate's case, forced itself through that brittle Victorian shell of 'behaviour' and 'manners' for which the mother was responsible.

On 29 August 1859 Charles Kean presented, as his actual Farewell, the most spectacular of all his productions, *Henry VIII*. Ben Terry played the Duke of Norfolk, and there were no parts for the girls.

Mr Kean's farewell speech must have set up a record for such, and could more fitly have been delivered by a university don to an audience of undergraduates, but the Victorian audience would appear, according to *The Times*, to have accepted its lecture with becoming humility and applause. Little Charles patted himself on the back for his historical exploits, and they applauded respectfully. When, however, he turned to the subject of finance, there was 'extraordinary excitement'. That they could all understand! That Mr Kean had spent £50,000 in a single season and given weekly employment to nearly 550 persons, which, including the upkeep of their families, might be reckoned four times as many, went right home to a British audience—slightly awed, but fundamentally unmoved, by references to Latin MSS and Greek research. They applauded him to the echo.

Ben, Nelly and Katie stood in the wings, with the rest of the Company, listening to that tremendous speech. To the girls, it was the end of a great epoch; Katie was in tears—like the rest of the women in the Company—and Nelly awed. Neither was conscious of the education she had received—apart from her professional training—while with the Charles Kean management. Shreds and orts of that education were to haunt Nelly throughout her professional life, and to condition her approach to the *vie de Bohème* which she alone, of Ben's children, ever achieved. She had mopped up, like a little sponge, the love and regard for historical beauty that the Keans brought to their productions. She wasn't even aware of it; it was there, in her, part of her. It disposed her, a few years later, towards the person who, according to her family, was Nelly's 'downfall': according to her, her pride and her pain.

Ben had got it all planned out. As soon as the Kean engagement ended, he and Sarah and the girls, and a young man called Sydney Naylor, who played the piano, were going into the Royal Colosseum at Regent's Park, with what was billed as 'A Drawingroom Entertainment'. Shrewd Ben, with his Nonconformist upbringing behind him, knew that there was a considerable public which, although it would consider it 'sinful' to go to the theatre, would enthusiastically patronize an 'entertainment' in the innocent exhibition hall in the park, with its bogus stalactite caverns and its concert room with a little stage, just the right size for the pieces he planned to present with the girls.

Even so modest a project, however, required capital, and, for the first time in his life, Ben had a little capital. Mrs Catherine of the Fortune of War had died and left Ben (according to his son Fred) 'a few thousand pounds'.[1] The 'few thousand', to Ben, was a fortune; it came along at exactly the right moment to finance his small gamble—which, considering Katie's reputation and Nelly's charm, was hardly to be regarded as a gamble, but as an investment. It enabled them to pay a servant—a nurserymaid or housekeeper—

[1] More likely a few hundreds. In 1859 a thousand pounds would have been a fortune to anyone in Ben Terry's position.

to look after the children, Ben, George, Polly, Flossie and, by now, the baby Charlie, while Sarah, at the Colosseum, chaperoned her wage-earning daughters, kept a tight (and necessary) hand on Nelly and supervised the back-stage, while Ben looked after the box office, front of the house and stage-management.

The two little plays that made up the 'Entertainment' were called, respectively, *Distant Relations* and *Home for the Holidays*, and the second, with Katie in two parts, a girl in her teens and a starchy old maid, and Nelly as a fly-by-night, cigar-smoking schoolboy, brought down the house. In thirty nights more than thirty thousand people paid for admission. Nelly's arm linked into her father's and Katie's into her mother's, the four of them walked back through the blue-green gloom of the park, across Albany Street, with its dubious purlieus, through Park Village East into Stanhope Street; a long walk for two tired little girls, but always enlivened by the gaiety of the father, whose irrepressible spirits devised endless diversion for each weary block they traversed.

Late as it was when they got in, there were often people to supper: Reade and Taylor and their friends—whom, for Katie's sake, the parents encouraged. Sarah ran upstairs to make sure that the boys were indoors and the little ones tucked up in their cribs. She ran down to the basement to preside over the meal, at which all the talk was of Katie and her future, and Nelly and what might be her future, and the little tour Ben was planning to fill in the gap between the end of their lease of the Colosseum and the opening of the London season. He had already booked one-night stands at Croydon (the Lecture Hall) and several suburban houses; he aspired to a short provincial tour—after which Katie was booked in at the St James's Theatre, with Mr and Mrs Alfred Wigan, the beautiful Miss Herbert (who later took over the management) and an able company that included Sam Emery and Frank Dewar; and Nelly's name was put down on an agent's books.

It did not occur to Ben, of course, that this scattering of the family provided Sarah with a new set of problems, although, the financial position being a little easier, she was better able to deal with them than she would have been a few years earlier.

That madonna-face, that face of sorrows—the 'face without a frown', which had yet mislaid its smile! There was a singular aristocracy in that face—which Lewis Carroll, in his amateur photographs, was presently so singularly to distort as to leave one seriously in doubt that it is indeed Sarah, were it not for the family grouped around her. That face carries the record of the torments and disillusionments of twenty years of married life. The devotion of her children must have made up for some of them; they all adored her, as indeed they should have done.

'I have been faithful to thee in my fashion' may be said fairly to cover Ben's attitude to his wife. It was perhaps asking too much—total fidelity from a man in his thirties, virile, exuberant and so plentifully endowed with what a century later was called 'sex appeal' that women never let him alone. He suffered from the illusion—common to errant husbands—that Sarah knew nothing about it. Actually, being no fool and deeply sensitive, she took shock after shock, and drew consolation from the pledge of Ben's affection which proved itself year after year in a new little son or daughter. Year after year she carried her weary load, and shouldered her maternal duties without complaining: saw her beauty fading, and recaptured some of its delight through her bonny Kate, her incalculable Nelly, Polly at seven the image of herself and entrancing little five-year-old Flossie.

But Benjy?—and George?—and Charlie, at three, a vision of beauty? Charlie was just a charming baby; George a stuffy little well-behaved boy; Benjy . . . If only Ben would take some interest in the boys. She had tried so often to talk to him about Benjy's future. The lad had consistently bad reports from school: so far as his work was concerned, he was apparently intelligent, no more idle than the average schoolboy and smart on the playing-fields; but unamenable to discipline and given to playing truant. What, during his hours of truancy, was Benjy doing? She, whom he dearly loved, had failed to gain his confidence. Oddly enough, Benjy was on better terms with his father than he had been as a little boy. His Spice Island days, probably, in his mind, Ben had a taste for a handsome, rakish son—but, for the love of heaven, could Ben not see that there was a difference between playing the rake round Spice Island, and mixing with the flash youths who were quick to profit by acquaintanceship with a bold sprig with (apparently) unlimited cash in his pockets and no aversion to spending or lending it? Innocent as she was, Sarah was no fool; when her eldest son came in with blue stains under his eyes and tobacco yellow on his fingers and beer on his breath, her heart stood still. A job must be found for Benjy—and quickly.

A marked silence engulfs Terry records of Benjy and George. Kate and Marion brushed aside any references to their brothers, excepting the lovable Charlie, and the 'Golden Terry', Fred. Benjy, George and Tom were never to be mentioned: as was never to be mentioned the girls' secret generosity to the brothers of whom they were snobbishly self-conscious. Ellen had no such snobbism; such little as she knew, she told—but even she could not remember to what trade her brother Ben was apprenticed. She could remember his sweet and loving nature, to which his letters from Mandalay in the 1870s, '80s and '90s bear witness.

Sarah did not want to go out on that tour of a few weeks that Ben was planning. She did not want Benjy and George to come back from school to a house which, lacking a mother, was not a 'home', and Polly, Floss and Charlie to be left to the care of a paid house-keeper or to casual caretakers. She was torn in two—for neither could she endure the idea of Katie and Nelly going out on tour without her chaperonage. And the girls' clothes had to be seen to; long, lanky Nelly could no longer be fitted with Katie's cast-offs, and Katie, as a juvenile lead at the St James's, must be suitably equipped. Sarah was tired of carrying her sewing basket from lodgings to wardrobe and back again, of packing and unpacking, mending and laundering. She was in many respects so sensible a mother that it seems surprising that Katie at fifteen and Nelly at twelve were not made to look after their own clothes; to do their own mending and washing and ironing. They were supposed to, but—in Nelly's case at least—it usually stopped at 'supposing'.

She and Ben had one of their few quarrels, in which, as usual, Ben won. Ben and Sarah, Katie, Nelly and Sydney Naylor went out on a brief lucrative tour with the 'Drawingroom Entertainment'.

They travelled, according to Ellen, in a carriage, and, on one occasion, tramped from Bristol to Exeter. That must have recalled their early days to Ben and Sarah! Along the dusty highroads did their hands touch, their eyes meet, to exchange recollections of the past? It was great fun for the girls, and for young Sydney

Naylor; not quite so much fun for Sarah, carrying another child.

It was the girls' first sight of the pastoral heart of England, and may have disposed Ellen towards the country life she was later to know intimately and, with a few reservations, to love. For a little girl just entering her teens, a little girl who had grown up in smoke and bricks and mortar, 'the country' was an adventure. Nelly was the only one of the Terry children of her generation, who loved *with understanding* the simplicity of the English countryside, divorced from the grandeurs of 'seats' and 'places', of retinues of domestics and gardeners and grooms, and whose love persisted to the day she died in her Kentish cottage. To her last years Ellen Terry held in her nostrils the scent of those West Country lanes and on her lips the tenderness of hedgerow flowers.

> I know a bank whereon the wild thyme blows,
> Where oxlips and the nodding violet grows,
> Quite over-canopied with lush woodbine,
> With sweet musk roses and with eglantine.

How often, from the dusty wings, had she listened to those lines, which 'came alive' for the first time during that little tour of one-night stands.

They arrived at an inn, where Sarah promptly put the girls to bed, drew the blinds to invite sleep, and went down to the hall or lecture-room where Ben was setting the stage, making the best of whatever properties were available, and using his ingenuity as a carpenter to invent others. Sydney was tuning the piano. Sarah looked for an ironing board to press Katie's dresses as Sister Letty and Miss Terrorbody, and Nelly's checked pants and smock. There was never a proper dressingroom or wardrobe, because the 'Drawing-room Entertainment' was never given in a theatre. In any town where they stayed over the Sunday, the pretty Miss Terrys, escorted by their handsome father and their dignified mother, attended the Wesleyan meeting, or, failing that, evensong in the local Protestant church: which made a favourable impression on the local audience—accustomed to regard actors as 'loose folk'—and had advantageous effect on the Monday-night receipts.

According to Ellen, their little divertissement pulled in from ten to fifteen pounds a performance, which supposing they played only four or five nights in the week, meant a minimum of fifty pounds, when the pound stood for real money. At the end of the tour they had not made a fortune, but when expenses were paid there was a considerable profit—for which the upkeep of the house in London, the boys' school fees and domestic wear and tear speedily accounted; the inroad into their little capital, however, was negligible, and would shortly be recouped when Ben and Katie opened with the Wigans and Nelly found a job.

The Terrys got back to Stanhope Street in time for rehearsals at the St James's, and, summoned by her agent, Nelly borrowed Katie's best bonnet—pink silk with black lace—and went off to an audition.

Madame Albina de Rhona was a Parisienne actress and dancer who, having had some success in Paris and St Petersburg, was determined to conquer London. At the St James's and Drury Lane theatres she had got good notices, which encouraged her to lease the Royal Soho Theatre, which she proceeded to rechristen the Royalty. It was (architecturally) an elegant little theatre, with a long tradition: not distinguished but woven into the history of the London stage.

She took a look at the long-legged girl with 'harvest-coloured' hair (Charles Reade's description), with aquamarine eyes, big hands and big feet and the coltish ungracefulness of her years, and engaged her on the spot. (Nelly was convinced that it was Katie's bonnet that had done it.) Madame de Rhona may be credited with being the first to discern the dramatic genius somnolent beneath those ungainly movements and those romantic eyes, that irregular, adolescent beauty which, alone of her descendants, Ellen's great-niece Hazel reproduced. Hazel's jaw was a shade heavier, her mouth a little more crooked; she was in a sense a caricature of her lovely great-aunt; yet the undeniable 'glory' was there.

A lot of nonsense was written by contemporary biographers and critics about the 'beautiful' Miss Kate Terry. Katie was never 'beautiful', she was bonny and very attractive. The only 'beauty' in the family was Polly, who blossomed from an exceptionally plain childhood into the image of her mother. And as for Nelly—

> Her hair was long, her step was light,
> And her eyes were wild.

76

While Kate was playing small parts under the distinguished Wigan management at the St James's, Nelly was shrieking her lungs out in Sue melodrama at the Royalty. For each it was a salutary experience. Katie profited by the easy pace of the St James's productions, the meticulous direction of the Wigans. Ambitious for his eldest daughter, Ben was less contented than Katie when she continued to be cast for understudies and insignificant parts which only procured her small print in the bills. He was not placated when, at twenty-four hours' notice, Katie picked up her understudy and became 'famous' overnight.

The piece was an adaptation of Sardou's *Nos Intimes*, called *Friends or Foes*, which was later, as *Peril*, to be one of the Bancrofts' *pièces de résistance*, and to hold the stage for at least half a century. Katie had a walk-on, and understudied Miss Herbert, who played the Lady Ormonde of the piece. The excitement at Stanhope Street may be imagined when Katie and Ben rushed home after the fall of the curtain—to tell the family that Miss Herbert was ill and Katie had to be down at the theatre early for a run-through with the Company and have her dresses fitted in the wardrobe.

Two at least of the great contemporary critics were in the theatre on that memorable night, and let fly a fanfaronade in the Press: Tom Taylor in *The Times* hailed Kate Terry as the genius of the age, and Clement Scott wrote more soberly: 'No one knew that we had amongst us a young actress of so much beauty, talent and ... dramatic power, for the temptation scene wants acting, and not the kind of trifling that we see in these modern and amateurish days.'

At the fall of the curtain, Nelly rushed from the Royalty to the St James's, to fling her arms round her sister's neck. News had been brought to the little Soho theatre of Kate's overwhelming success. Both the girls had been taught never to leave the theatre in their stage make-up—which was an ordinary custom of the time; in the hackney cab Sarah used the old maternal trick of a saliva-wetted handkerchief to remove the more garish evidences of Nelly's profession, like a cat cleaning up its kitten.

Such an occasion today would be celebrated with supper at the Savoy; Ben, Sarah and the girls treated themselves to a cab-ride back to Stanhope Street, ate their simple supper and retired to bed. (I am sure it was supplemented for once with a bottle of wine!)

Long after the girls were asleep, Ben and Sarah sat discussing the next move for Katie. It was typical of Ben's extreme good sense and shrewdness in the conduct of his daughters' careers that, at the height of his excitement and joy over Kate's triumph, there was no question in his mind of allowing his brilliant girl to rest on her laurels, to sit back and wait for offers. Great and unquestionable as had been her success, Kate's theatrical education was not, in the opinion of her father, complete. But the sensation she had made in Miss Herbert's part would not endear her to her manageress when that lady recovered from her indisposition; she was unlikely, in that Company, to gain advancement.

It is not to be doubted that Kate Terry, after her triumph at the St James's, could have got an engagement with any London management as a leading actress. She would have been received with open arms at the Princess's—now under the management of Augustus Harris (father of 'Druriolanus'); she would have had the immense advantage of playing with Phelps and Fechter;[1] in the pantomimes she would have been associated with Leon Espinosa, lineal descendant of Taglioni and Petitpas. She would have been welcome at the Lane, the Lyceum, the Haymarket and the Strand. (At the Princess's she would have had the dubious honour of playing with a conceited young man who called himself Henry Irving: his patronymic being Brodribb and his nearest claim to distinction being his connection with the Welsh family of Davies, which produced a finer poet than ever young Brodribb was an actor.)

None of these prospects appealed to level-headed Ben for his daughter. What did appeal to him was an offer from Mr J. H. Chute, who was running a stock Company at the Bristol Theatre Royal. Cunning Ben; his own experience had taught him the value of those old stock Companies and the training they gave their young members, who were expected to play burlesque, burletta, farce and low comedy, yet to support a London star in a 'special engagement'.

'Little conceited Katie' had turned into little modest Kate. Her great success had disposed her more humbly to accept the advice of her father. It is difficult to imagine the young star of today taking off quietly into the provinces, to play whatever she was handed in

[1] Before her retirement Kate did play with Fechter, see p. 88.

one of the repertory Companies which are the nearest approach to the Stock Company of the past.

Ben got, without difficulty, a minor engagement with the Chutes. Sarah stayed in London, to keep her eye on Nelly—entranced with Madame de Rhona's gallicism, her tempers and tantrums, and her undoubted gifts as a dancer. Nelly was playing joyous rubbish—attuned to her age and her temperament; was peeking into green-room supper-parties and getting her ears boxed by Sarah; was making a 'screaming' success of her part in *Atar Gull* and getting her first taste of stage fright in *The Governor's Wife*. All the plays put on under the de Rhona management were (theatrically speaking) garbage, and none ran more than a few nights. For Nelly it was enormous fun. Her real education in the theatre only began when she and Mama joined Dad and Katie in Bristol in the autumn of 1861.

When would they all be peacefully collected together in Stanhope Street? was Sarah's thought when she and Nelly arrived, with their small baggage, at the rooms Ben had found for them in Queen Square.

It was a comfort again to be united with Katie: so good, so responsible, so unspoiled by her success. 'Darling Mama!'—and Katie's arms round her neck. 'Darling Mama' came freely from the other children and did not mean quite the same. It was only to Katie that Sarah could confide her ambition that the little ones, Polly and Charlie and Floss, should have a proper education, should go to good schools and be brought up in 'upper class' fashion. Only to Katie could Sarah confide her misery about Benjy and her anxiety about George. Perhaps it was not fair to lay on those young shoulders so intolerable a burden. Yet—where otherwise could she turn? And there was a certain hardness in Katie that was capable of carrying the load.

CHAPTER SIX
Bristol

What a change from the Princess's to the beautiful little old Theatre Royal in King Street, off the Bristol Backs! Whichever way you walked you came to water, and the slow ships drifting up under naked shrouds into the heart of the town. Nearly opposite the theatre was the Llandoger Trow tavern; according to legend there was a secret passage between them, along which, before and after Abolition, slaves were dragged to auction in the Trow. The girls were shown the passage; Katie was shocked and Nelly thrilled. Nelly was fascinated, too, by that curious piece of building, like the underside of a mushroom, that supported the auditorium, from which the circular passages broke away—on one side towards the Trow and on the other to the waterfront. She felt she could act, or at any rate rehearse down there, as, in the stalactite caverns of the Regent's Park Colosseum, she had studied Juliet: 'How if, when I am laid into the tomb, I wake before the time that Romeo come to redeem me?'

Practical Kate was exercised about her dressingroom: with how many people would she be sharing it, how much space would there be for her costumes, and what sort of attendance would she be able to command? It was not vanity, but the anxiety of the artist to procure the best possible conditions for her work. She was shown the dressingroom dedicated by tradition to Sarah Siddons. Ah, if she could have had that! But Kate Terry was only one of a Company that included Henrietta Hodson (later Mrs Labouchère), Madge Robertson (later Mrs Kendal), Marie Wilton (later Mrs Bancroft), Coghlan, the Rignolds and many other distinguished young actors. She was engaged as juvenile lead, and had too much good sense to imagine this gave her superiority over her seniors in the Company.

Chute seems to have had the gift of attracting the best of the theatrical youth of his day: a great achievement for a provincial management, far removed from the great London theatres which then, as frequently now, chose the fashionable in preference to the talented. It was a feather in Chute's cap to have contracted the Terry girls, an advantage to them, and a great tribute to their impresario, who happened, incidentally, to be their father.

It must have been a shock to Edward Godwin to meet the chubby Puck he had extolled in his 'Jottings', transformed into a lovely, lanky girl, wildly innocent and gay, playing Nerissa and Hero to her famous sister's Portia and Beatrice.

Edward William Godwin was an odd product for a mercantile city, whose great men—unlike their Liverpool rivals—were uninterested in the arts. The Pre-Raphaelites—in particular Holman Hunt, Rossetti and Ford Madox Brown—owed much to the patronage of the 'Liverpool princes'. An exhibition of 'Industrial and Ornamental Art' presented at the Bristol Fine Arts Academy in 1861 attracted only 24,000 persons at sixpence a head in the course of three months. Even the historian Latimer—always anxious to present the Bristol picture from its most becoming angle—records the 'great apathy' of the public.

Godwin came of interesting stock. His father, William, currier and leather-worker, piled up a small but sufficient fortune, retired while young enough to enjoy his profits, and bought a house called Earl's Mead on the banks of the Frome, where he loaded his considerable garden with odd bits of masonry—mainly from derelict churches—and created a romantic atmosphere for his three children (two boys and a girl) to which Edward, the younger boy, was susceptible. Edward was passionately interested in those bits of carved stone; he had what today is called a 'sense of period'. He wanted to know not only how they came to be carved that way, but what the workmen were like who carved them; what tools they used, what was their vocabulary—even what clothes they wore. He had a mania for costume; he was always copying old prints and drawings, colouring and cutting them out as figurines in imaginary dramas.

In 1862, when the Terrys came to Bristol, he was very much the established young architect. He had helped to illustrate a book— *The Architectural Antiquities of Bristol and Neighbourhood*—which brought him and his associates considerable *réclame*, and been chosen from eight competitors to design and build the Northampton Town Hall.

He was married to a Miss Sarah Yonge, daughter of a Henley-on-Thames parson, and had set up house at Number 21 Portland Square—then a fashionable quarter of Bristol, now (1959) derelict, and the Godwin corner house virtually in ruins. Into his new, imposing house he had built an organ—the organ being one of his hobbies. His other hobby was the theatre; Mr and Mrs Godwin attended every first night at the Theatre Royal, and Mr Godwin recorded the performance for the Press in his 'Jottings'—making profit out of pleasure.

He was, according to the taste of the day, a romantic figure: tall, elegantly slight. His eyes were brown, his weak chin (inherited by his son) was masked by a silky beard. He had a fine, down-tilted nose, slightly aquiline. Women were crazy about him, and he found them irresistible. He had boundless assurance (on a visit to London he wrote to Charles Kean, criticizing some small archaeological error in the current production).

At 21 Portland Square he conducted a congeries of kindred spirits who shared his taste for Shakespeare, for books, plays and costume. As a Fellow of the Bristol Architectural Society, as Honorary Secretary and Librarian, and as delegate to the Architectural Alliance in Conduit Street, London, he could command what he pleased of artistic and intellectual society. An invitation to Portland Square was a compliment to a young actress. Or so it was represented to Sarah Terry, who was not carried away by her first meeting with Mr Godwin.

She was not having an easy time with Kate and Nelly: both of them demure and well behaved, but besieged by youths who fell in love with them across the footlights. Every night the stage door was jammed with besotted young men; every night the short journey to their lodgings in Queen Square was made intolerable by their insistent escort. The girls followed Mama's instructions, pulled their hoods over their faces and clung to her arms.

An anonymous contributor to Edgar Pemberton's *Ellen Terry and Her Sisters* furnishes this picture:

> I recollect one poor lad who was an assistant in a large drapery establishment in Wine Street, Bristol. He was infatuated with the beautiful Kate Terry, though he had never spoken to her, and probably he never ever saw her off the stage. But he left bouquets and gifts addressed to

her at the stage door, and as there was nothing to indicate who the donor was, or where he lived, she could not send them back. Some time after this young fellow was arrested for embezzlement. He had taken his employer's money, partly in order to gratify a passion for the theatre, and partly to enable him to buy presents for the divinity he worshipped from afar.

Sarah was well aware of this heady adulation that surrounded her daughters. She was 'not amused' when a silky-bearded, willowy, young married man presented himself, proposing that Kate and Nelly should join 'a reading party' at his house in Portland Square. The invitation, from her point of view, should have come from Mrs Godwin. But she consulted Mrs Chute, according to whom the invitation was *convenable*; the Godwins were accredited members of the audience, and important people in Bristol; it would be to the girls' advantage to visit Portland Square.

So in their best crinolines (the Bristol Press, which had little room to spare for an exhibition of art, devoted a column to an amusing controversy on the right of way of crinolined ladies), Kate and Nelly set out on the long walk by Narrow Wine Street, and Merchant Street, and Rosemary Street, and Milk Street—names that entranced Nelly. Katie was more exercised about keeping her boots and stockings clean.

They had never seen anything like it before: the pale lofty rooms hung with Japanese prints, the polished floors sparsely scattered with Persian rugs, the few carefully chosen pieces of furniture which their limited education did not allow them to identify as antiques. It was Nelly's first conscious encounter with beauty as applied to the domestic scene, and it made an indelible impression on her; she was never again to be contented with the plush-and-bobbles, the over-stuffed furniture and deep carpets that stood for prosperity in the mid-Victorian age.

Besides Mr and Mrs Godwin, the company included Hine, Godwin's collaborator in *Architectural Antiquities*, and two other architects, Burges and Crisp. The evening's entertainment consisted of a reading of *A Midsummer Night's Dream*, with which Mr Chute was proposing to reopen the Theatre Royal, Bath (burnt down at the beginning of the year, and in process of rebuilding) with Nelly as Titania. The Miss Terrys read their parts beautifully, and their hosts were enraptured: Godwin fascinated by the wildly lovely child Nelly, whose long limbs adumbrated all he had dreamed of in designing his costumes. (Nelly does not appear to have paid much attention to Mr Godwin; her big, pale eyes reflected faint pine trees and birds, polished floors and the peach-glow of rugs.)

'It was very agreeable,' reported Kate, on their return. 'But I don't think Mr and Mrs Godwin can be very well off; they've got no carpets and hardly any furniture!'

'It was wonderful', sighed Nelly.

A few days later Mr Godwin called at Queen Square, to conduct the girls to Westbury-on-Trym, where his friend, Henry Crisp, had a picturesque cottage. Gripping the handrail, Nelly leapt from the upper to the lower landing in a bound, followed by Kate, sedately floating on her crinoline from step to step. Both of the men were entranced by the lovely, happy romp.

After *The Merchant of Venice* and *Much Ado About Nothing* came a series of burlesques. In the Broughs' *Endymion* Henrietta Hodson played the title-role, Kate Diana and Nelly (with immense brio) Cupid. Two factions developed—pro-Terry and pro-Hodson—and free fights broke out every night in the cheap seats, very profitable to Mr Chute. Nelly, in a brief tunic which today would seem excessive for the part of Cupid, was considered slightly scandalous by the provincial audience, and scored a big personal success. In a second burlesque, Miss Hodson played Perseus and Kate Andromeda, and Nelly got a lot of fun out of her relatively small part as Dictys; she was still billed as 'Miss Nelly Terry', and her every appearance drew roars of applause from pit and gallery.

They were both so popular and so well known to the public that their few excursions about the town and neighbourhood began, to Sarah's annoyance, to assume something of the air of a royal progress. The news that the Miss Terrys were shopping was enough to crowd the emporium they favoured with women struggling to glimpse the attractive pair. They were 'bunched' and flattered and seem to have been very little spoilt by their adulation. On one occasion Nelly got slapped for winking across her shoulder at one of her bolder swains; the slap hurt less than Katie's accusation of 'vulgarity'. Miss Kate Terry was invariably genteel and took herself very seriously. But sometimes the gentility broke down—she was not quite out of her teens—when the girls giggled over their (often misspelt) love-letters, which they dutifully showed to Mama. To autograph-hunters they were allowed to reply politely, on their tiny letter paper—Kate in her neat, spiky hand, Nelly in the sprawling flourish of her youth, which was later to mature into a bold, beautiful script.

In one respect Sarah was adamant: they were allowed to accept no presents, other than flowers. If an address was enclosed, the gift was returned to its sender with a courteous note from Mr or Mrs Ben Terry. What became of anonymous offerings history does not relate; certainly the girls did not profit by them.

They made a few friends in Bristol, of whom the principals were the Godwins. Mr and Mrs Godwin appear to have given the girls the freedom of their home—which they were allowed to accept, although Sarah continued not to care for Mr Godwin. It must have been an 'I do not like thee, Doctor Fell', for there was nothing about the attractive, good-looking, intelligent and well-informed young man to inspire dislike. Or it could have been some deep-rooted, maternal instinct that disposed Sarah against one destined to have so fatal an influence, not only on Nelly, but on all the family. It was very kind of the Godwins, Ben and Sarah agreed, to interest themselves in the girls, and a great privilege for Katie and Nelly to be received in cultured society.

Godwin himself proposed to design the Titania costume for Nelly's appearance at Bath. It must be purely Greek in inspiration.

'Like our clothes in *Winter's Tale*?' naïvely proposed Nelly, and was told, 'No, not at all like that.'

A long piece of silk was procured; she watched Mr Godwin cut out the chiton. A few stitches, and Nelly proposed to put it on— over her petticoats, in the Kean tradition. Godwin showed her drawings to prove that that was not the way the chiton was intended to be worn; it must be worn over nothing but a thin slip. She gasped when he plunged it into water, wrung it out, and ordered her to bind it from neck to hem with cotton, and leave it to dry. From that dated what, to the writer, she described as her 'clothes-conscience'. 'I could not play a part if I had to wear something that was *wrong*.'

Neither Ben nor Katie had parts in the *Dream*. Nelly's crinkled silk Titania dress, moulding her long adolescent limbs, was much admired—and scandalized not a few.

Back to Stanhope Street, just in time—again—for Sarah. In the middle of midday dinner, Benjy was sent flying for the nurse to Charlotte Street, and Tom was born in the afternoon: Thomas Walter—a whining, self-pitying baby, least Terry of all the Terrys, yet adored by his sisters and brothers as all the babies were.

Benjy by now was a lanky youth in stiff collars, with wrists and ankles sadly protruding from the clothes he had outgrown. He had left school and was 'in business'—what the 'business' was his sisters, forty years later, professed not to know, or chose to forget. Even his youngest brother, Fred, guiltless of snobbery, had no idea what 'old Ben' was doing, before they sent him abroad. He thought it might have been 'something to do with the wine and spirits trade'.

Poor Benjy, with his handsomeness and charm, was born, like not a few of the Terrys, to trouble as the sparks fly upward. He was certainly a rake, never a rogue, like his brother Tom. Deeply affectionate, he was beloved by his brothers and sisters, over whom he occasionally tried to exert—as if in compunction for his own misdoings—some mild degree of moral suasion. His letter to Polly and Floss, on their confirmation, is a pattern of brotherly rectitude; a birthday letter to Tom is full of grave reminders of the latter's duty to the family and 'little Fred'.

Love and loyalty have suppressed the records of those misdemeanours which were serious enough to result in Benjy's being packed off to Australia—the classic Victorian solution of the problem of troublesome sons. His farewell letter to his parents is full of love and compunction:

My ever dearest Papa & Mama!
  It's a long lane that has no turning and I may almost compare myself with this lane, but with one difference. I have been going on and on and have at last found a turning. Yes, dearest ones, I have played the fool long enough, have been wicked enough to cause you both a great deal of pain and anxiety but at last dear ones I feel in myself that I shall be an altered chap. The Colonies have turned out many a smart lad and I

pray God I shall not come to grief. I am now nearly 21 years of age; a man in fact; but before many years are past I hope to be a *man* in a very different sense of the word, with God's help & my own hands and head.

Grieve not for me dearest mother, best of mothers for you gave me life with pain and trouble and altho I have been nothing but a trouble to you ever since, you have still been the all-caring, all-loving mother to me and us all.

I pray the other boys may be more dutiful.

You dear father who ought in a few years to be sitting in your chair & your boys striving and working for you and their dear mother, have still to work for the family; I also from this day forward will strive to work & gain, that I may add to your earnings.

George seems a good hard working fellow & I have no doubt will soon be able partly to keep himself. God bless him & you all. Don't think this promise I have made to myself are idle words. I mean it.

You have both forgiven my past conduct and I thank you very much, more than I can express here. Live happily together surrounded by the children who will I hope be an easier task for you than has been your son Ben.

Every night ere I sleep, to see you all again in health and happiness will be the prayer to God of your still affectionate son

Ben.

Goodbye—God bless you all. Thousands of kisses.

A heartbreak of a letter for them all. It was many years before they were to see handsome Ben III again, and only for brief spaces in his wandering life was he to know the contentment of British domicile. Working now for the South Indian Railway, now for a company of brewers and distillers in Mandalay, the third Ben Terry was always a rolling stone, always industrious, and always a little unlucky. Not that he ever complained; he left the whining to his hypochondriac brother Tom.

Baby Tom in her arms, Sarah reviewed her family: George, sensible and a little smug (he had yet to petrify the family by turning Roman Catholic). Charles, too beautiful—almost—to be true! Polly, shy, reserved and sensitive; at this moment she was very plain, with sallow skin and lanky hair, showing no promise of the beauty into which, later, she blossomed. Her whole life was wrapped up in her little sister Floss.

In all the many photographs of Florence Terry as a child, one gets the impression of an adored and adoring little girl. Her head droops lovingly towards a supporting shoulder, her little hand comes to rest, like a homing pigeon, on a knee or a wrist. Famous Katie looks fondly up at the lovely little thing; self-centred, tragic Nelly is comforted by the contact of the childish body; Polly and Flossy nestle together like a couple of turtle-doves. Inevitably encouraged and coached by their doting father, they were as much disposed towards the theatre as their elder sisters at the same age; but Sarah had different ideas—in which she was supported by Katie. Polly and Floss were to have a genteel education, before (and if?) they took to the stage.

Although faithful 'in her fashion' to The Profession (she observed and to her last years supported her children in strict conformity with the discipline of the theatre), she was not besotted, as was Ben, with the limelight. She had endured much and she knew, only too well, the chanciness of an actor's life. On behalf of her children, her mind was turning otherwise.

Kate was Fechter's leading lady at the Lyceum.

Fechter was a superb *capa y spada* actor of the school later glorified by Lewis Waller. Affecting to be a Frenchman (he made his début in Paris), he was actually a Londoner, born in Hanway Yard off Oxford Street, then part of 'the foreign quarter'. His mother was English, his father German or Flemish. He always repudiated German blood, and pronounced the *ch* in his name as *sh*: *Feshter*. Brought up in France, with French as his native language (which called forth some rude comments from the English Press when he presented his *Hamlet* in London), he was the original Armand in *La Dame aux Camélias*, and the original Fabien and Louis dei Franchi in *The Corsican Brothers*. The first Augustus Harris 'discovered' him in Paris, brought him to London and put him on at the Princess's in *Ruy Blas*: a piece admirably calculated to display the talents and charms of the brilliant young 'foreign' actor. And when, with the backing of Charles Dickens and some others, he went into management at the Lyceum Theatre, he was well advised to engage Miss Kate Terry as his leading lady.

The success of the venture was a foregone conclusion. The theatre had been newly and elegantly decorated. Fechter was supported by an exceptional cast. They opened with *The Duke's Motto*, an adaptation of one of Paul Feval's novels. Dickens, dropping in on a midnight rehearsal, on the stripped stage and stark lights of a bare theatre, on all the business-like din and disorder of production, recorded Kate's Blanche de Nevers as 'the very best piece of womanly tenderness he had ever seen on the stage'. Whatever qualifications Mr Dickens may or may not have had as a theatre critic, his word carried with the public, and he sang Kate's praises high and low. When Fechter revived his sensational *Hamlet*—partly sensational because, for the first time in theatre records, he played the gloomy Dane in a blond wig—Katie as Ophelia created a furore.

Nelly was not so happily established at the Haymarket. She had arrived at the 'difficult' age. A cocky little girl, thoroughly spoilt, and protected by her parents from the cold blasts of criticism, of practical joking, of the rough-and-tumble of theatre freemasonry, she did not get on with her manager, Buckstone, and detested the fascinating Sothern—then a public idol—who, from her own account, teased her unendurably. (Later on, Ellen Terry regarded her engagement at the Haymarket as 'one of her lost opportunities', which she 'would have given much to have over again'.) With the Chippendales, Compton and Farren in the cast, she was introduced to the finesses of old-comedy acting, for which, at fifteen, she was unprepared. She simply was not interested. The Bristol interlude had done Nelly no good; she was *détraquée*, temporarily in revolt against the simple, tough, crude world of the theatre. More sensitive than Katie, she existed in a dream-world of people 'with quiet voices and elegant manners', who cared about music and painting. She suffered the disturbances of all young people who, without sympathy or encouragement from those nearest to them, have 'intimations of immortality' beyond their personal achievements. Nelly, in fact, was all set for the tragedy that followed in due course.

Her happiest times were the Sundays when they took the horse bus over to Lavender Sweep, to sit on the Taylors' green lawns under their lilacs and chestnuts and syringa, perhaps to play croquet with boys and girls of her own age, but far removed from the tawdry and tinselly world of which she was sickened. Charles Reade (she called him 'Daddy') was always there, with Laura Seymour; in affectionate conspiracy with Tom Taylor for the advancement of the young Terrys, he often brought 'important people'—critics and writers and painters and poets. In the big drawingroom, filled with the translucent green of the chestnut trees, Clara Schumann played the piano and sang; there were readings and recitations and much discussion of the arts, none of the greenroom gossip and scandal that bored Nelly to death. (She had not enhanced her popularity with the Haymarket Company by her dramatic exit—'Ladies and gentlemen, I leave my character behind me!'—a piece of impudence from a chit who, at the time, was *not* distinguishing herself as Julia in *The Rivals*).

Sarah and Tom Taylor had reached an understanding. She liked little untidy Tom, with his spectacles tied on with string, his social clumsiness and absence of mind, which masked a basic shrewdness which Sarah respected. Under cover of the music or of conversation, they murmured together in a corner of the drawingroom. Tom understood better than Ben the problems that beset her. Ben was content, playing small parts in small theatres and boasting, in a modest fashion, about his brilliant daughters. It never occurred to Ben that his brilliant daughters were now of an age to fall, hook, line and sinker, for the first attractive young detrimental who happened to cross their paths. Ben would have taken it for granted that Katie and Nelly, if they fell in love, would fall in love with actors, and marry into the Profession.

Not even to Tom Taylor did Sarah give tacit expression to her aversion—based on observation—to 'theatrical' marriages for her daughters. Not wholly mercenary, she desired for them what she herself had never known: security. Through his cock-eyed spectacles, Tom blinked understanding. Security meant money, but money by itself was not enough; there must be some kind of distinction. If Katie was not to be wasted on any of the enamoured young suitors who, since she came of marriageable age, had never ceased to pester her, she was equally not to be allowed to squander her charms on a husband incapable of appreciating her rare quality. Fortunately, Katie was co-operative in this matter, she was quite wily and worldly enough not to commit herself to any of her admirers, although open to a conventional flirtation. There was a youth called Arthur Montague—he died a few years later in America—who seriously tested her common-sense. He was what

the twentieth century described as a 'matinée idol', and there is
evidence that Kate Terry considered him as her husband. But before
she was committed, Tom Taylor and her mother swept in.

Tom knew everybody, including the fashionable portraitist
George Frederick Watts, who, having seen Kate with Fechter at the
Lyceum and with Henry Neville at the Olympic, regarded her, with
her blonde, English charm, as the perfect subject for his brush. No
doubt he was influenced by her theatrical fame; if he had been only
in search of a model, any village could have produced the superior,
in looks, to dumpy little Kate, whose exquisite complexion was her
only claim to beauty. She was a pure throwback to her grandmother
Catherine, of the Fortune of War. But she was Blanche de Nevers,
she was Ophelia, and she was half a dozen characters in the little
old Wych Street theatre (the Olympic), as leading lady to Henry
Neville—a charmer in his day—and as such she had caught the eye
of a spoilt, neurotic, middle-aged man, surrounded by a court of
fashionable women who addressed him as 'Signor'.

Three of the Miss Pattles (there were seven in all), daughters of
a wealthy Bengal Civil Servant and his French wife, made good
marriages: one (known as 'Dash') became Mrs Thoby Prinsep,
another ('Beauty') Lady Somers, and the third ('Talent') Mrs
Cameron. 'Dash' took a grip on her husband's sick friend, George
Watts, the painter, and firmly established him in a studio annex to
their home, Little Holland House. A domineering woman, of
immense social ambition, she recognized the potentialities in
Watts and had some appreciation of his quality as a painter. She
liked to regard herself as a 'Bohemian', the bohemianism, according
to Mrs Prinsep, consisting in the maintenance of an eminent
painter and the entertainment of his distinguished friends, or of
the celebrities who arrived to be painted by Watts and photographed
by her sister, Julia Cameron. Watts, who arrived for a few days,
and stayed thirty years, was treated *en prince*, his every whim and
fancy being given precedence of the convenience of the household.
His court of ladies waited on him hand and foot, and accepted
his smallest utterances as law.

Had Sarah known all this, she might not so easily have accepted
Tom Taylor's proposition: that Katie should sit for Watts, and

that the sittings might very well lead to a more permanent relationship. Neither of them took seriously Kate's dalliance with young Montague.

The time for the sittings was arranged, but, according to the convention of the day, Kate could not go, unchaperoned, to the studio even of so distinguished and respectable a painter as Mr Watts. Polly and Flossy and Charlie and Tom could not be left by themselves. So Nelly, not at all reluctantly, agreed to accompany Kate. They took the omnibus to Hyde Park Corner and walked on their sturdy legs the two miles to Holland Park. It was pure country, all elm trees and sweeping pastures, with grazing cattle and smocked labourers, who pulled their forelocks soberly to the two young actresses who asked the way to Little Holland House. They found it eventually, by way of a farm; it was actually the dower house on Lord Holland's estate. A manservant conducted them to the presence of the châtelaine, who, after making some fuss of the famous Kate Terry, ushered them into the studio.

Blinded with beauty, Nelly was hardly aware of the short, thin, bearded man who, with finikin gestures, directed Katie to the dais on which was placed the model's chair. Nelly's great pale eyes took in tapestries, light and colour; her spirit imbibed an atmosphere in which it was at home.

Watts started on his *croquis* of Kate, and as the work went on, became more and more distracted by the 'mystical, ideal and mediaeval beauty' (Clement Scott's description) of the younger girl; the beauty into which, in a few short years, she had matured from lanky, apple-cheeked childhood. So the portrait of Kate Terry became 'The Sisters'; Ellen leaning on Kate's shoulder, Kate, madonnaish, even maternal, dropping her cheek towards Nelly's fair head. Watts already saw Nelly as his ideal model for the romantic subjects towards which his mind was directed.

CHAPTER SEVEN

'Thunder on the Left'

If Watts had expressed a fancy for a slice of the moon, it is safe to say that Mrs Prinsep would have done all in her power to supply, if not the object itself, the most acceptable substitute. It was part of her policy of possession, of her determination to bind the painter to her with hoops of steel. Out of a welter of gossip and conjecture emerges the indubitable fact that it was she who—on Watts's side —organized his marriage to Ellen Terry.

She had for some time been uneasily aware of fleeting attachments to beautiful (and well-born) sitters. According to contemporary gossip, there was such a one on the *tapis* at the time of the Terry girls' introduction to the painter. Not that it was likely to come to anything without her, Mrs Prinsep's, active encouragement. All the same, the Signor was approaching the 'dangerous age', and it was policy to get him 'settled'.

There is no suggestion, at any time, of any amatory attachment between Mrs Prinsep and Watts. She was satisfactorily married. There is something curiously cold-blooded in her patronage of a 'rising' artist, whom she backed very much as one might back a horse. Her pay-off was not in cash—of which she had no need—but in prestige. She and her husband eagerly lent themselves to Tom Taylor's innocent plot to marry Watts to the famous young actress Kate Terry. Such a marriage would in no way challenge Mrs Prinsep's authority. Kate Terry would, of course, retire from the stage and live in her husband's shadow: posing for him when he wished, and humbly accepting the direction of their patroness in all domestic and social matters. What could a young woman, born and brought up in the greenroom, know of the distinguished world in which the Prinseps and their *protégé* moved?

From the moment of setting eyes on Katie, her ideas received a rude shock. This pretty, well-mannered young woman was no puppet to be manœuvred to her convenience. Miss Kate Terry had an admirable aplomb, a sense of dignity and a will of her own. Mrs Prinsep was no fool; she recognized—belatedly—that Kate Terry could hardly have arrived at theatrical eminence without these inconvenient qualities. Her well-laid plot had gone agley. So it was with considerable relief that she perceived that the Signor's errant fancy had lighted on the younger sister. Her practised and worldly eye recognized in Nelly the material she had hoped for in Kate: innocence and ignorance and a disposition to hero-worship; humility, nice behaviour, but no sort of 'style' or self-assurance.

Perfectly recognizing the pusillanimity of Watts, and the unlikelihood of his nerving himself to action without her strong support, she set to work to expedite the marriage.

The attitude of Ben and Sarah to the projected match can only be conjectured. Hers was the more practical. Nelly was restless, and making no conspicuous success at the Haymarket. She had not—apparently—the *cœur au métier* of her sister Kate, and marriage might 'steady' her.

A deeply loving mother, Sarah must have had misgivings about the marriage of her gay Nelly—only sixteen years old—to a man of forty-seven, pampered and 'old for his age'. ('He was nervous about his health, and always teetering about in goloshes,' said Ellen Terry: not an attractive proposition for a high-spirited girl, bursting with mischief and energy.) But such doubts as she may have entertained were overborne by the enthusiasm of Tom Taylor. It was 'a wonderful match' for Nelly; 'a most advantageous connection for the Terrys'—*et patati et patata*.

About the theatre Sarah was disillusioned. She was an eager playgoer and (according to her children) an astute critic; but her whole life was not, like Ben's, 'the theatre'. Proud of her brilliant girls, rejoicing in their successes, at the back of her mind was one permanent ambition: to marry them well—and 'well', according to Sarah, was away from the incalculable theatre with its chanciness and its heartbreaks. There was also in Sarah—and she passed it down to the girls—an innocent kind of snobbism. She had come a long way from the little terrace house in Portsmouth; thanks to Reade and Taylor, and to Katie's eminence in the Profession, she had contacted a society which would hardly have come in the way of Miss Ballard, the builder's daughter, and which proudly reminded her of her Copley connections. She was well on her way to being the 'aristocratic' old lady she eventually became.

Ben kept his mouth shut: which is not to say he had no feelings about the marriage of his adored Nelly to a middle-aged, pampered and prosperous painter. There were harsh words between the Taylors and Charles Reade, who regarded themselves as sponsors for the Terry girls, and a lot of 'voices off', before the news was broken to Nelly that Mr Watts requested her hand in marriage. She uttered a stunned 'Yes'.

She was bored with the theatre and envisaged a dream existence in a world of beauty she had glimpsed at the Godwins' house in Bristol. She could imagine no greater rapture than to serve Mr Watts as model, to live in a lovely house and, as its châtelaine (she had no notion of what the office entailed), to entertain the great artistic and literary figures who frequented the Signor's studio. Green as grass, she looked to Mrs Prinsep (who made a great fuss of her) to befriend and advise her. And Katie, who had seen through Mrs Prinsep at a glance, as the latter had seen through her, gave her no warning.

Sarah had just had the last of her babies, Fred, 'the Golden Terry': the lucky, gifted, lovely one. On her wedding morning Nelly performed her last act of devotion to her beloved Mama: she bathed the little ones—Floss, Charlie, Tom, and the baby—and brushed out their flaxen hair. Then, hurriedly and carelessly, she flung on her brown silk wedding dress. It was designed by Holman Hunt, as a tribute to his friend Watts,[1] she departed on her father's arm to the church of St Barnabas, Kensington.

It was a dreary January morning; the church, like the out-of-doors, was grey, dismal, icy-cold. No flowers, no music. Watts was self-conscious—as well he might be—about his marriage to a girl young enough to be his daughter, whose father looked considerably younger and much more sprightly and handsome than the shivering bridegroom. Was Nelly conscious of the contrast? After the gloomy little ceremony she panicked and wept, and was told by her husband to stop crying—'It makes your nose swell.' Apart from her

---

[1] Who may have been apprehensive that Nelly would turn up in white satin at the altar. 'It was a very pretty dress,' said Ellen, 'but rather staid for a bride of sixteen!'

father, the bride had no support; there were a few hand-picked friends of the groom. Where were Sarah, Kate and George? Nobody knows. Where were Reade and Taylor—her avowed friends?

Watts's own misgivings are clearly indicated in a letter to his friend, Lady Constance Leslie, shortly before the marriage:

> To make the poor child what I wish her to be will take a long time, and most likely cost a great deal of trouble, and I shall want the sympathy of all my friends.

That he could ever imagine that either 'time' or 'trouble' would alter his child-bride suggests, on the side of Watts, a high degree of imperceptivity and of egoism; there is something pasha-like about his attitude to the 'poor child', and something more than a little craven in his anxiety in advance to range his friends on his side, and, by implication, against Nelly. It is a fair assumption that Watts, at the eleventh hour, had qualms—but they were all for himself; so far as the writer has been able to ascertain, there is no indication of his showing any solicitude for the future happiness of Nelly.

There was no honeymoon. The ill-matched pair went back to Little Holland House. On her marriage night Nelly was discovered, crying bitterly, on the staircase outside the nuptial chamber. Her initiation, at the hands of a fumbling and neurotic lover, was a sad one.

Even so, it might have worked out if Watts had been man enough to claim for his young bride the position that was rightfully hers: if he had removed her from proximity with a jealous, possessive woman who regarded the little actress only as an accessory to the Signor's comfort and convenience. That was not Watts's way; his personal comfort came before everything, and he was incapable of love, except as a form of self-indulgence.

Sweet-natured and resilient, Nelly recovered from the shock of her wedding night. She was proud of her ring—so proud that she wanted to show it to everybody she met: casual acquaintances, tradesfolk, the hangers-on of the Prinsep ménage. 'See—I'm married!' She was thrilled to be presented as 'Mrs Watts' to her husband's friends, of whom the principal was the poet Tennyson (whose boys became her playmates), and all the fashionable habitués

Photograph by Lewis Carroll of eight members
of the family

                  Nelly   Kate   Polly

Ben   Flossie   Charlie   Sarah

Tom

Polly and Flossie   Nelly and Flossie

Charlie

Photographs by Lewis Carroll

of the studio. She sat for hours—swooning with fatigue—for the Signor; she modelled for him in armour, as 'Sir Galahad' and 'The Watchman' and lay along a willow bole as 'Ophelia'. She sat for the 'Head of a Young Girl' (later called 'Choosing') and for the portrait in profile, with clasped hands, which is the truest record Watts left of his young wife.

In the studio she was herself, and rapturously happy. It was a different story when she was required to play her humble part in the fashionable hospitality of Little Holland House: the false *vie de Bohème* which Mrs Prinsep created round 'the Signor', who in velvet *déshabillé*, lolled on a sofa, languidly accepting the tributes of his admirers. In view of what eventually transpired, the comment of a young painter, half French, half English, educated in France, privileged to be accepted in such company, is of interest:

'Somehow in the very delightful atmosphere of this house', wrote George du Maurier to his friend Tom Armstrong, 'I seem to perceive a slight element of looseness, hein! which I don't sympathize with—when I say delightful, it isn't enormously so to me but could be if I were a "gay" young bachelor.'

That was written before Nelly's marriage. Innocent and ignorant as the dawn, she may well have been at a loss when she encountered this 'slight element of looseness', for which nothing in her life had prepared her. There was nothing in her of the *intrigante*; she was incapable of imagining the female jealousy with which she was surrounded. She liked Mrs Prinsep's big, handsome son Val, and thought he liked her (which indeed he did, but was too conscious of his mother to risk any display of even friendly preference), and she liked the Tennyson boys and found them fun. She was altogether too gay, too simple and too energetic for her pampered, elderly husband.

On her frequent visits to Stanhope Street, all of her life at Little Holland House was represented as *couleur de rose*. There was never a word of the humiliations and slights to which she was continually subjected. To the end of her days, Ellen Terry never broke her loyal silence, or spoke a malicious or resentful word about the woman who made her first marriage all but intolerable. But there were eye-witnesses and ear-witnesses whose indignation, after the *débâcle*, loosened their tongues; who remembered, and passed on their recollections.

'I met her in Holland Park Road, thin as paper and white as a ghost, with drowned eyes. She didn't even hear my greeting; she brushed past me like a broken-winged bird.'

'She was abominably treated and snubbed into silence whenever important people were present. Sometimes she was ordered not to appear at all.'

'Watts was not man enough to give her the support she needed.'

Forty-odd years ago I carelessly jotted down these comments. Through frequenting Leighton House and, later, the private gallery in which she presented her sister's work, I had become a young friend—it might be more accurate to say protégée—of Mrs (Wilhelmina) Stirling, sister of Evelyn Pickering de Morgan who was named by Watts as 'the greatest of the Pre-Raphaelites'. Whether or not Mrs de Morgan merited the description, the two Pickering girls were constantly in and out of Little Holland House, and were therefore well placed to draw conclusions. But they must at the time of which we speak have been very young, and I cannot remember whether the stories Mrs Stirling repeated to me were hearsay or personal observation. She was extremely scrupulous and accurate, and would have been unlikely to pass on anything of whose truth she herself was not convinced.

It was a far cry from Little Holland House to the comfortable shabbiness, the homely table, the smell and sound of small children which was Stanhope Street. Once a week, or oftener, young Mrs Watts sank into the familiar *milieu*, where she was not criticized (except for her untidiness and her aversion to the needle) and never repressed.

Yet she was sufficiently beglamoured by her new home gladly to return to it. And her great friend, Mr Godwin, had left Bristol and established himself at 23 Baker Street, and was a frequent and welcome guest at Little Holland House.

His wife was dead—the beautiful, artistic and sensitive Sarah Godwin; legend has it that she died to the strains of a Bach fugue which she asked her husband to play on the organ while the brokers were in possession of their house in Apsley Place, Clifton. There was no good reason for the brokers to have come in; the firm of Godwin and Crisp, Architects, was not only solvent but solid. Godwin, however, was indifferent to the practical conduct of a household. Bills came in, were left to pile up and never paid, while the partners were pursuing their various lucrative projects. (Among other awards, they received first, second and third prizes for designs for the Bristol Assize Courts, although, for some unknown reason, they failed to get the commission. But they had enormous local prestige and were never short of money.) The peace of mind of a delicate and ailing wife never entered into Godwin's calculations; for her delectation he would play the organ by the hour, but could not bring himself to sign a simple cheque.

After Sarah Godwin's death he moved to London, to work with Burgess on designs for the new Law Courts (these, like the Assize Courts at Bristol, came to nothing, although, according to a contemporary critic, they were by far the best tendered). The fascinating and handsome Mr Godwin was speedily *persona grata* at Little Holland House, and, as he and Mrs Watts were friends of long standing, it was hardly possible to exclude her from the scene. He got on very well with the Signor, and when the three of them were relieved of the intrusive presence of the mistress of the house they were wholly accordant, and Nelly as gay as a lark. Used to being snubbed and thrust into the background, she joyously welcomed someone with whom she could chatter about the carefree past, and be simple and gay and passionate about the things that matter to a girl of seventeen—of which not the least was clothes!

Godwin did not give a fig for 'fashion', but cared deeply and knowledgeably about beautiful materials, colours and what today is known as 'line'. The eighteen-sixties were the apogee of the crinoline, and were dominated by the first of the great man-designers, Worth. To Godwin, the styles worn by Mrs Prinsep and her smart friends were not merely ugly but also ludicrous. He was dedicated to the pure lines of the Greek, the mediaeval and the Japanese. Her Bristol lessons in the back of her mind, Nelly eagerly adopted his views—although several years were to elapse before, under his tutorship, she put them into practice.

He also cared genuinely about the theatre—for which, now she was away from it, Nelly discovered nostalgic yearnings—and about

Shakespeare, and about music, painting and sculpture: to all of which she responded rapturously. It never occurred to her that her 'friend' was falling in love with her; she was sufficiently Sarah's daughter to have been shocked if anyone had pointed out the fact. She was devoted to the Signor, believed in him as the greatest painter of the age, and considered herself privileged to serve him. A less sweet-natured girl might well have turned sullen, as he never took her side or defended her in any way, but she was more or less contented, learning 'French and German and a little Latin' from her husband. Relieved of a marital relationship in which she had experienced more embarrassment and discomfort than pleasure, she honestly believed that she and Mr Watts (true to Victorian tradition, her husband was always 'Mr Watts' to Nelly) were 'good friends'.

Incapable of falsity, she would not have believed, had she been warned of it, what was going on behind her innocent back: that Watts's brief infatuation was over; that, having painted and drawn her innumerable times, and been irritated by her high spirits and *sans gêne* towards his pompous and important friends, he had in effect gone over to the Prinsep side. Encouraged by his patroness, Watts was complaining that his wife 'exhausted' him, and that, after twelve months, she seemed to have little idea of adapting herself to the society into which she had married.

This was exactly what Mrs Prinsep was waiting for. She had laid the sacrifice on the altar, and now the god rejected it. All that remained was to dispose of it in the most tactful and inconspicuous fashion. In all simplicity, Nelly herself thwarted this project of inconspicuous disposal.

She and Watts had frequently called on Godwin in his rooms over the office in Baker Street. During her lonely walks (the young Terrys were great walkers) she sometimes dropped in to see her friend, to hear theatre gossip, to look at drawings, costume designs or whatever at the moment was occupying Godwin's far-ranging interest. She never made a secret of these visits, and Watts— whether out of indifference or trust—made nothing of them. In any case, the pair were never alone; clerks, students, occasionally his partner Crisp (still domiciled in Bristol) and sometimes Burgess, relieved the tête-à-tête.

But a day came when Nelly, calling unexpectedly at dusk, found Godwin in bed, a very sick man. Used to Katie's quinsies and the children's whooping coughs and chicken-pox, it never occurred to her not to stay and look after him. She slept on a bamboo couch in the studio and got up at intervals to renew poultices and supply drinks to the invalid. In the morning he was better. Worn by her night watch, she took a cab to Little Holland House. Mrs Prinsep would be furious, but the Signor was bound to understand.

Too tired to talk sense, she walked slap into a reception committee: not only the Prinseps (Watts had absented himself) but Dad and Mama had been convened to this sorry meeting. 'There do exist', Ellen Terry wrote charitably in her *Memoirs*, 'such things as honest misunderstanding.' There was little honesty about this one. The unsophisticated little goose, Nelly, had played straight into her enemy's hands, and the enemy had profited by the occasion. It would have been easy for anyone who cared to go over to Baker Street and companion her through her vigil. A message to Stanhope Street, and Sarah, or Katie, or both, would have hurried from Camden Town. Deliberately that message was withheld, until the following morning, by which time Nelly had 'compromised' herself.

True to masculine morality, Ben (who was in no position to cast a pebble, let alone a stone, at his darling daughter) took the more aggressive attitude. Sarah was plain heartbroken. Her original distrust and distaste for Mr Godwin justified (in her own opinion), she made no attempt to stand up for her errant child. Humiliated and sick at heart, the Terry parents went back to Stanhope Street, leaving Nelly temporarily at the mercy of her husband, who vowed he would never speak to her again.

Watts's views were negligible; he thought as he was ordered to think by his patroness. All the Pattle women gathered around to strengthen him in his resolution. Still Nelly—in her innocence —could not believe that the Signor would not forgive her, and take her back to his heart. And Edward Godwin—that poor knight!— prudently withdrew from the picture. He would marry Nelly if she got a divorce—the very word unspeakable in the Terry family, and to Watts unthinkable. His mind was set on a knighthood (at least), and that or any other honour from the Victorian Throne was not to be conferred on anyone involved (however innocently) in a divorce.

Ostracized in the Prinsep household, Nelly begged at last to come home. She had not given up hope of reconciliation with her husband, but she had no idea of the powerful forces ranged against her. Over Mrs Prinsep's dead body would a reconciliation have been arranged, and neither Watts nor Nelly was consulted over the terms of the separation, which was agreed on grounds of 'incompatibility', after long argument and delay.

Ellen was given a room of her own at Stanhope Street: bobbles and plush, and an outlook over the little brick-enclosed yard—euphemistically called garden. No more the sunlit flower beds, the sweep of lawns, copper beeches and elms. No more the colour and light of the studio, the gracious draperies, the casts—which she had just learned to distinguish from sculptures—of Greek and Roman heads, of a shoulder or an arm or a torso, the delicate charcoal sketch, the primed canvas on its easel. Plush sofas and chairs, 'ornaments', oleographs—nothing beautiful, as Nelly had learned to recognize beauty. She hated it all.

The children were baffled. Why had Nelly come home? What had happened to Mr Watts? Why was Nelly so bad tempered—she who always loved the little ones and was loved by them? (Fred Terry never forgave his sister Ellen because, in some uncontrollable moment of nervous irritation, she shut him up in a dark cupboard and left him to bawl his head off with terror. In his sixties, with out-thrust jaw and narrowed eyes, he declared, 'I hated Nell ever after.' The hatred faded out in a loving reconciliation only a few months before Ellen Terry died.)

The one to suffer most was Kate—established at the Olympic as Henry Neville's leading lady and receiving at least one proposal of marriage a week: all of which that level-headed young lady had the sense to turn down. Very conventional and socially ambitious, when Nelly's marriage broke up she was being courted seriously by a rich young man of commercial stock, who was also an amateur of the arts.

Between 1790 and 1800, a young Welsh draper and haberdasher came to London and opened a small drapery business in Upper

Regent Street. Stephen Lewis's brave venture so prospered that he was soon looking for more capital, with a view to expansion, and offered a partnership to his friend Allenby, who was able to put up the money required to enlarge the business and employ more staff. (Their head assistant was a young man called Swan, who left them in 1812 or 1813 to start up independently, and eventually took a partner called Edgar.) Lewis & Allenby, Ltd., were appointed Silk Mercers to the Queen, and held the Royal Warrant, a great prize in those days, and on the high tide of prosperity Lewis married, acquired a handsome house known as The Rookery in Roehampton Lane, S.W., and begat seven children, two boys and five girls. The elder son, Stephen, succeeded his father, when the latter retired from the business. The younger, Arthur, was sent at the age of eleven to learn French in Geneva, returned to office-boy work in the shop, but at fifteen was promoted as courier and interpreter to Mr Allenby on the latter's continental journeys as buyer for the firm. Child of a wealthy, commercial and puritanical family, there was something more in Arthur than the yardstick and cash-box and chapel which shaped the fortunes of his family.

He was a youth of rare conscience and character, successfully combining, as time went on, devotion to the business with his private interests, which lay all in the direction of the arts—in particular, painting and music. It may be taken for granted that on his trips abroad with Mr Allenby he had profited by the opportunities which came his way for the cultivation of the arts. He handled silks, and, in Italian galleries, identified them with portraits of *condottieri* and calm-browed women with pearls in their hair. He heard opera in Milan, and made acquaintance of the artists of the Renaissance.

He gained advancement in the business, and presently rented a commodious bachelor apartment in Jermyn Street, where he was able to entertain in the grand manner the artists he admired, and whose friendship he had gained. His peculiarly attractive personality and total lack of pretension rapidly made him *persona grata* in the society he most wished to cultivate. A tall, attractive, intelligent and sensitive young man, he was affectionately known as 'Lewis the Linendraper', and young George du Maurier wrote in one of his letters to his mother, 'He is certainly a princely fellow'.

By the year 1862, Lewis's 'Evenings' were established, and it was monstrously flattering to be one of his guests. In that year, George du Maurier proudly wrote to his mama:

Lewises [*sic*] evenings have begun. I'm going tonight and was there last Saturday week—very jolly as usual, such splendid glee-singing . . . the gorgeous Leighton was there & the divine Millais & the noble Watts, who's one of the stunningest fellows out. The presence of Lord Gerald Fitzgerald made the wax candles unnecessary and added considerably to the smoke. I've no doubt there were lots of other Lords besides, for Lord G. wasn't the worst dressed man in the room.

In the following year he wrote:

Lewis has just established a splendid bachelor's paradise in Campden Hill—ah *che casa! che giardino!* All kinds of manly sports on the Sunday afternoon, including claret cup & a jolly supper at eight, 20 fellows sat down to it last Sunday, and by Jove the number increased to 40 in no time.

And two years after that:

Tonight I am going to Lewis's, whose evenings are getting more and more gorgeous; half the peerage will be there tonight and very likely the Prince of Wales.

In the interim between the last two letters, the United Arts (later The Arts) Club had taken shape in a series of sessions at Moray Lodge (Lewis's bachelor paradise), and was domiciled at Number 17, Hanover Square; the entrance fee and subscription were alike modest—five guineas entrance, five guineas subscription. Most of the foundation members could have afforded three times the amount, and probably some donated more. Lewis did not wish his club to be a resort of 'gilded bohemia', but a place where men with mutual interests could gather, regardless of wealth or social status. In establishing the United Arts he made a notable and permanent contribution to the intellectual and artistic world—not only of his period, but of ages to follow; not only painters and musicians, but the élite of the journalistic and writing world gathered there. It was an advantageous thing for the young practitioner of literature, music or the graphic arts to be a member of Lewis's club: as young du Maurier recognized, when he scraped up, with difficulty, the ten guineas for his entrance and subscription.

Handsome and kindly, wealthy and influential, Arthur Lewis was emphatically a *parti*—even for a theatrical star of the magnitude of young Kate Terry. He was deeply and truly in love with her, and by far the most eligible of her many swains.

Nothing could have been more unfortunate, from Kate's point of view, than Nelly's descent on the household, trailing her tears and her tragedies: a young wife cast off by her famous husband and accused of the unspeakable in Victorian society.

They had got on well enough as children; as they grew up, Nelly's lightsome temperament clashed with the rather starchy one of Kate. There was no glimmer of bohemianism in Katie; she liked rich, successful, fashionable people, and took little interest in any of the arts apart from her own, of which indeed she was past mistress, and the most famous young actress of her epoch. Later, under her husband's tuition, she developed her small talent for music and (presumably for love of him: Arthur Lewis was a 'Sunday painter') interested herself, so far as she was able, in painting. The prospect of marriage to an attractive, wealthy and infatuated young man was alluring, but Katie wanted to play it at her own tempo. It may have been coquetry or disinclination immediately to forfeit her public status. Whatever it was, Nelly did not fit into the picture—Nelly, whose 'shame' was likely to brush off, like charcoal, on the rest of the family.

Nelly, upstairs, darned (very badly) the children's stockings, while Katie, down below, thrashed Beethoven (nearly as badly) out of the parlour upright. They were barely on speaking terms. Little Floss, beloved by both, pattered between the two, bewildered, unable to imagine what was the matter. Nobody seems to have noticed that plain, sensitive Polly, was taking it all in, and was painfully conscious of the division in the formerly close-knit pattern of the family.

In 1864, the year of Nelly's marriage to Watts, a young man arrived at Stanhope Street with a note of introduction from the indefatigable Tom Taylor. Mr Dodgson (not yet famous as Lewis Carroll) was an enthusiastic amateur of photography and, needless to say, an admirer of Miss Kate Terry. A don of Christ Church, Oxford, he had had about ten years of experiment in the new collodion process; among his distinguished sitters were the Rossettis and the Tennysons, but his mania was for children—especially little girls—whom he liked to dress up in fanciful costumes and pose in unlikely attitudes against oddments of 'scenery'. His essays in the new art were approved by Mrs (Julia) Cameron, herself highly accomplished, and, although technically not the equal of young Mr Dodgson, more of an artist. She was one of the Pattles, a sister of Mrs Prinsep; so Dodgson had a double line of approach.

He showed Mrs Terry a good, unaffected study of Tom Taylor on the porch at Lavender Sweep, and a funny one of little Wicliff, Tom's boy, with a spear and helmet, against a striped curtain. Not to be outdone, Sarah presented him with studio photographs of Kate (as Ophelia), Polly, Floss, Charlie and Tom. He hinted he could improve on them, and it was agreed that he should return in October to take pictures of the whole family, 'including Mrs Watts'.

In October there was too much rain and mist; the sittings were postponed to April 1865; but though Mr Dodgson (by then famous as Lewis Carroll, *Alice in Wonderland* having created a small furore in the previous autumn) came along to view the house and garden, as backgrounds for his photographs, it was not until July that he got down to work.

He spent three days at Stanhope Street, and on the first—which was rainy most of the time—took the tragic and beautiful half-lengths of Nelly, and the tender little study of Nelly with Floss. He took Polly in a mob-cap, lolling in an armchair, looking three times her age, which was thirteen.

The naïveté of those photographs has to be seen to be believed: the girls, with their hair well brushed out, pose against the brick wall of the yard in costumes an amateur dramatic society would reject today. The full glare of common daylight provides all there is of lighting. Like good little actresses, they are taking their ordeal with perfect seriousness. The neighbours, crowded at their windows, are peering through their muslin curtains; what do Katie and Marion and Flossie care? They are getting 'for free' photographs which might be (actually, they never were) professionally useful. And they all (Flossie, his favourite, in particular) love Mr Dodgson, who calls himself Lewis Carroll, and has written their favourite book.

His *chef d'œuvre* was the family group he took on the third day:

tall, slim Nelly and plump Kate gazing with actresses' smiles respectively towards cherubic Charlie and their mother. Polly stands with her hand on Sarah's shoulder, smileless, aloof, sad, if not sullen: a little girl in the uncomfortable standing water of adolescence. On the left, Ben looks out of the corners of his eyes, his right hand steadying little Tom's restless head—Tom who, incidentally, looks much more like a girl than a boy, with his long locks and his contemporary frock. Floss, with downcast eyes, drapes herself across her father's shoulder. Young Ben was, unfortunately, still in exile, and George in his workshop; the baby 'Tops' (Fred) for some reason does not appear. A delicate child, he may have been sick, or had one of his screaming outbursts of temper. Nothing less could account for his exclusion from this important record.

Kate was playing out her contract with Henry Neville, in various rubbishy pieces by Tom Taylor and in a version of *Twelfth Night*, in which she doubled Viola and Sebastian. Her father continued to act as her adviser and impresario, and the acceptance by this famous young woman of his guidance ('Dad knows best') speaks volumes for them both. At the close of the Olympic season he got her a short engagement at the Prince's, Manchester, to play in Dion Boucicault's *Hunted Down*, with an unknown provincial actor, who called himself Henry Irving, as her leading man: an association which left no agreeable impression on Kate, whose utmost experience and skill were required to cover up the uncouthness of her stage partner. She came back to the Adelphi, where she created a sensation in Charles Reade's dramatized version of Tennyson's poem *Dora*.

But not all of Ben's attention was given to his brilliant eldest daughter. He was still plodding away on the road, and, under a cover labelled in Ben Terry's hand 'Letters from my Dear Children, God bless them', a letter from the two younger girls shows that Nelly, with Polly as her companion and chaperon, was not (as one might gather from Ellen Terry's *Memoirs*) entirely left to languish in Stanhope Street after the break-up of her marriage. The year was 1866; what the town or what the play we do not know.

My dear Mamma,
We have arrived all safe and sound. The first thing we did was to take a cab to the Theatre and enquire about Lodgings, but we did not

107

succeed. Then Papa thought he would go to the George an Hotel we slept there one night. The next morning Papa looked for Lodgings and did succeed that time luckily.

We went to see the Hidden Hand on Friday Oh it was something awful tell Kate I did not think it would be played at all well but Papa Nelly and I did not think it could be played like it was.

They had both seen *The Hidden Hand*, an adaptation of *L'Aieulle*, at the Olympic, with a cast including Henry Neville, Kate Terry, Lydia Foote, and Nellie Farren in the lead. True to her Terry blood, thirteen-year-old Polly was shocked by the provincial production.

Oh you should see Nelly's Clement Austin he is like . . . I don't know what he is like I must finish my letter now because Nelly says I can't have any more paper to do the copy so give my love and kisses and thousands to Tops. Tell George Flo Charlie Tom and Tops that I will not forget them if they are good

> believe me my dear Mamma
> your ever affectionate
> Daughter Polly.

On which Nelly claimed the pen:

Poor old Polly was as nervous as either of us I believe. She helped me with my change (for which there was loads of time!) & 'felt so relieved when you had *done* your fall Nell'!

Pa played the Major *very well indeed*. He was very nervous & will I feel sure act better tonight than last night.

He lacked what I possessed & I lacked what he possessed. I was *too fast*—he was too *slow*.

Then follows a passage which, added to other evidence, must dispose of the fiction of 'estrangement' between Ellen Terry and her family propagated by her daughter Edith Craig:

Read this to yr self!!!

To finish up the night in a pleasant manner, I went to bed and dreamed not of the Theatre (isn't that strange?) but of Mr Watts!

I dreamed he was dying, & I woke up in the greatest grief—crying!

This is the 20th of the month! my Wedding day! Married 2 years ago today! & it is such a day. *Pouring* with rain! & altogether wretched!!

Oh! . . . with all thy faults, I love thee still!

It is inconceivable that an 'estranged' daughter should write in such touching and intimate terms to her mother.

In that same year, 1866, Nelly played Helen to Kate's Julia

in *The Hunchback*, at the Olympic. She was photographed in a *décolletage* that 'made Mama very angry'! A more innocent *décolletage* is unimaginable; there is the mere hint, within a narrow neck-line, of a young, swelling breast; there is no coquetry in the young, thoughtful face, the fair hair lifted and swept back from an intelligent brow.[1] But Sarah's Puritan-Wesleyanism was outraged—on Katie's account.

Kate was not having a wholly easy time. Her engagement to Arthur Lewis was announced in 1867. It was a wounding time for Nelly—all that joy and excitement and thrill over Katie's retirement, which none but Ben appears to have regretted. Kate's own emotions were locked into her young, secretive heart. There is no evidence that she entertained misgivings, having once made her choice between a brilliant public life and a life less sparkling but distinguished and secure, as mistress of Moray Lodge. She was twenty-three, strong and sure of herself, sure, above all, of what she wanted: a stable background, a devoted and wealthy husband who could 'place' her in the society towards which she had always had ambitions. Twenty years of the stage had destroyed her illusions. For all her genius, there was in her none of the passion that illuminated Ben, and was presently to kindle in her sister Nelly. She abandoned without qualms her great career.

But there were obstacles, of which the chief was an antagonistic mother-in-law to be. Mrs Jane Lewis, domiciled at Roehampton, was all against her son's marriage to an actress, and it took all of Kate's pretty, prim manners, her conventional outlook and her share of the Terry charm, to convince her that marriage into a theatrical family did not spell ruin for the Lewises. Both Sarah and Kate were afraid that the scandal about Nelly might reach Mrs Lewis.

Arthur Lewis, meanwhile, was endearing himself to his future brothers- and sisters-in-law by his kindness and generosity. He devised endless treats for the children: strawberry parties and hay parties at Moray Lodge, drawingroom theatricals, indoor and outdoor games, visits to circuses, and the like. He 'got on' with the parents; he was a very lovable young man, with a strongly philoprogenitive streak.

[1] See photograph facing p. 112.

He mounted sad Nelly on one of his hacks (according to a photograph, it was a graceless but good-natured beast) and taught her to ride—so well that the pair of them figured sedately in the Row, in the wake of Kate, whose royal progress was acclaimed by innumerable admirers who recognized the young star of the Olympic and the Adelphi. Few took notice of the willowy girl, pale and tragic-eyed, who made the third of the little *cortège*. Nelly was playing small parts at the Queen's, where Mrs Wigan was concentrating on the gifted, undisciplined young actress all of her long experience in the theatre. And Nelly was deadly bored.

Kate's final season at the Adelphi drew hysterical adulation from her public. As Juliet she made her London farewell. The curtain fell on the classic scene—the young star retiring, pale and dishevelled, her arms full of flowers—and rose on the farce, of which the audience was having none. They continued to roar for Kate Terry. At last she came on, dressed to leave the theatre. She spoke a 'few faltering words', and motioned to the stage manager to bring down the curtain—which he did. Rejecting the farce which was billed to follow, the whole audience poured out and milled outside the stage door in Maiden Lane, while Kate, panic-stricken and tearful, clutching Sarah and Polly, shot out through the front of the house into Arthur Lewis's brougham, which was waiting in the Strand.

It was not, actually, her final appearance. On 4 October, she opened in Manchester in a trivial piece called *Plot and Passion*. At the Queen's, in London, they were rehearsing a piece called *A Double Marriage*, by Charles Reade: a dramatization of his novel, *White Lies*.

The Queen's was a new theatre, of which the nominal lessee was Alfred Wigan;[1] it was lavishly decorated by the painter Albert Moore.[2] Built on the site of the old St Martin's Hall in Long Acre, it was the largest theatre in London, except the two opera houses and Drury Lane. For Nelly, an all but unknown young actress, to have secured an engagement with the Wigan Company

[1] The actual lessee was Henry Labouchère, of *Truth*, who eventually bought the theatre from Lionel Lawson of the *Daily Telegraph* and used it to exploit the talent of his wife, Henrietta Hodson.

[2] Mainly known for his grouping of young women in pseudo-Greek costumes, cuddling sprays of apple blossom on chilly marble benches.

was a feather in the Terry cap, and derived from her brief engagement with the Keans. Other members of the Company were Charles Wyndham, Lionel Brough and Fanny Addison: all destined to achieve fame in later years.

Nelly and Wyndham were released for a few days to support Kate in Manchester; Wyndham took the male lead, and Nelly was there to play propriety to her sister, for Arthur Lewis had gone North, to be present at the last public appearances of his future bride. When the curtain fell, he clasped on her arm a gold bracelet, inscribed on its inner curve with the titles of a hundred plays in which she had appeared, and the parts she had acted in them. On the outer curve it bore the inscription: 'To Kate Terry on her retirement from the stage, from him for whom she leaves it.'

Some ten years later, Charles Reade wrote into his diary as clear an impression of the art of Kate Terry as any writer may hope to leave of the fleeting art of the stage:

> The sweetest, tenderest and most intelligent actress of the day. Young in years but old in experience, and fuller of talent than ever an egg was of meat. She shone most, to my mind, in modern characters, and her forte lay in the pathetic.

Wise as he was in the theatre, Reade seems to have overlooked that fact that 'pathos' is or was the forte of virtually every young and talented actress. It is in no sense to belittle the achievements of Kate Terry that we make the suggestion that no small part of her success derived from the fact that from 'the moment she stepped on the stage, the manly breast took a keen interest in her', according to Reade.

'She represented with great truth all feminine sorrows'—and the contemporary manly breast was very susceptible to the dramatization of feminine sorrows, if less sensitive to them on the domestic hearth.

> Aged thirteen, she played Joliquet in *The Courrier* of Lyons, and Dora in my poetical drama was her last creation. She played the two parts to absolute perfection. In *Dora* she sang 'The Brook' to her dying lover; broke down in the middle of the words 'For men may come and men may go'; shed real tears and then by an effort finished the song.

> She had little voice but by dint of brains far out-sang the operatic singers—

Her face was not remarkably pretty in absolute repose, but beautiful under the illumination of expression.

Dora, terrified by her uncle's violence, swoons away at last. Miss Terry did this with such absolute truth in all the details that I went behind the scene one night to watch her more closely. But if I had gone with a microscope, this *honest and careful artist*[1] would have borne the test— it was quite indistinguishable from a real faint, and the little hysterical sobs with which she came to, and then the gentle weeping, and the dove-like way she said 'His harsh words frightened me so,' was infinitely feminine and lovable.

She was an actress who never whined. Now, the women all whine on the stage.

(So, in 1839, Bulwer had written to Macready:

May I beg you to implore Miss Faucit to say 'I love AND I am a woman,' and with as much majestic swelling as she can. Tonight she says, 'I love *but* I am a woman,' which is nonsense, and she whined it into the bargain.

No child of Ben Terry's would have been permitted to 'whine' on the stage.)

It is impossible today to estimate how 'great' Kate Terry was as an actress. She made an immense appeal to the theatre-going public of her epoch, which accepted the pattern of femininity set by Thackeray and Dickens; she was technically perfect, having mastered every trick of the trade from her childhood. But she was never tested in full-length Shakespearian tragedy,[2] in the comedies of Sheridan or in Restoration drama. That was not her fault; such plays were not in vogue. Her art was perfectly adapted to the shallow or sentimental rubbish that Taylor and Reade ground out, and to bowdlerized translations of French plays. She made gold out of dross, bricks without straw, because she was an excellent young actress, incapable of putting a foot wrong on her native heath— the stage. It is questionable that she had a glimmer of the divine afflatus that illuminated her sister Nelly and, from time to time, kindled in her sister Polly.

At twenty-three, Katie, the 'sweet and tender' Dora, was as

---

[1] The italics are the author's. M. S.
[2] The Shakespeare she played—her Ophelia and her Juliet—were perversions.

Kate

Polly and Flossie

Nelly

Mabel

Lucy

Janet

Three children of Kate Lewis, 1879

formidable a proposition as she was fifty years later, an old lady in West Cromwell Road. Having acted the fine lady in many plays and been trained by her mother in the simple economics of house-keeping, she had no faintest misgiving about her ability to assume the role she was now offered: mistress of an important house and a staff of experienced servants, hostess to her husband's distinguished guests.

She was married a fortnight after her Manchester farewell. It was a rapturous occasion for the children—Polly, Floss, Charlie and Tom (Tops—Fred—was too young to profit from the cele-brations). Sarah, serene and beautiful, was contented by the reali-zation of her hopes for her eldest daughter, and George was very happy that Katie had married so nice a chap as Arthur Lewis— with lots of money!—of whom he could boast to his friends at Maple's furniture store, to which he was now apprenticed as a cabinet maker.

There were two sad figures at the wedding: Ben and Nelly. Ben's was the deep disappointment of one who, having put most of his eggs into one basket, saw the basket crumble. He had staked much on Katie, had put into her all he had of experience and love of the profession to which he was dedicated. He grieved that Katie, whose successes had made up to him for all his personal failures, had quitted the stage. He held Nelly's hand. Her sadness was her own affair; incapable of envy, she just felt how wonderful it would be to be as happily established as Katie, with someone to be loved by, and to love.

Kate went off on her honeymoon and Nelly, horribly bored, returned to the Queen's Theatre—to Rose de Beaurepaire in *The Double Marriage*. All her affection for her 'stage Papa', Charles Reade, could not blind her to the essential worthlessness of the parts that were forced on her. She went from bad to worse, as Mrs Mildmay in a revival of *Still Waters Run Deep*; as Katherine in a perversion of *The Taming of the Shrew*—and reached her limit as Kitty in *The Household Fairy*. She was furious at being billed as 'Mrs G. F. Watts', instead of by the name she had worked to establish.

The one person she regarded as her friend had not come forward to comfort her in her need. She was not in love with Godwin, as he, belatedly and ineffectively, appears to have been in love with her.

(Actually, he was as little capable as Watts of truly loving a woman. Completely egoistical, obsessed with his mediaeval castles—he had just then a commission from the Earl of Limerick, to design a castle at Dromore with a banqueting hall fifty-six feet long, thirty feet wide and thirty-six feet high—he was romantically attached to Nelly, but blind to her sensitivity, and quite incapable of imagining what, at this time, she was suffering of personal humiliation and artistic frustration. Nelly needed comforting, and this was the last thing Godwin, soaked in his own interests, could offer her.)

'I can no more.'

During the run of *The Household Fairy*, Nelly bolted. She was met in Long Acre by a friend who described her as 'radiantly beautiful, with holes in the tips of her cotton gloves'.

'Let me take you home, Nelly.'

She refused, with evident embarrassment, and went straight from the theatre to her dilatory lover.

In the panic of Nelly's disappearance, it would appear that it occurred to no one to get in touch with Godwin who, at his Baker Street office, was certainly accessible. This suggests two things: that Nelly had been discreet, not to say secretive, about her continued association with Godwin, and that the parents were terrified of starting a scandal. In these days, the disappearance of a well-known young actress would be plastered throughout the national Press. All of her known friends were contacted—even her old enemy at Little Holland House, whose single preoccupation was to spare the Signor the 'shock'. What a mercy this had not occurred while Nelly was domiciled with her husband.

The police were at last alerted, and a morning came when Ben Terry was summoned to identify the body of a girl fished out of the Thames. Crazy with grief, it is not surprising that he identified the tall blonde young woman as his adored Nelly. But Sarah was not so easily persuaded. Having nerved herself to follow Ben to the mortuary, she declared positively that it was not her daughter, who had a strawberry mark on her left arm.[1] The corpse was eventually identified as the young wife of a commercial traveller, who had committed suicide more than a week after Nelly's disappearance.

[1] It was actually on her hip.

Somebody told Nelly of this distressing incident, and she rushed to town from Hertfordshire to reassure her grief-stricken family. She was received with joy, love and forgiveness. There was no 'turning out into the snow' of the dishonoured child—as later implied by her daughter. Nelly had behaved thoughtlessly and selfishly, had caused untold anguish to her parents, but love endured.

Yet it was impossible—and Nelly herself realized it—in those mid-Victorian days for a young woman who had 'lost her character' to be received under the roof that sheltered her innocent brothers and sisters. That was all right by Nelly—content in her country hide-out.

In 1868 Kate's first child, christened Kate, was born in a thunderstorm. Katie had everything a young mother could desire: a devoted husband—'so tall and upright, with such bright, sweet eyes'—a luxurious home, unlimited domestic service and every advantage medical skill could bring to her confinement. The baby was born on 5 July, and within a few months Kate was again pregnant.

The gates of Moray Lodge were flung wide to the parents, to the girls and the boys, but young Mrs Lewis made it abundantly plain that her disgraced sister Nell could not claim the hospitality of the house on Campden Hill. It was the last thing Nelly herself would have desired. She and Katie were never accordant—though in their old age they patched up a limited friendship; Ellen was amusingly tolerant about 'old Kate'.

CHAPTER EIGHT

Happy (?) Families

Polly and Floss had been sent to boarding school, to be modelled into 'young ladies'. Sarah and Kate were agreed upon this, and Kate, out of her handsome salary, had undertaken to foot the bill. Advised by Mrs Tom Taylor, Sarah chose Sunnyside, Knight's Park, Kingston-on-Thames: a refined establishment 'for the Daughters of Gentlemen'.

Confirmation was part of the high-class ritual of Sunnyside, and this was another step up for Polly and Floss. They were no longer little Nonconformists, but little Church of Englanders. None of the other children had been confirmed, although they occasionally went to church, which was then considered more genteel than chapel.

In 1869, the year when Kate's second child and Nelly's first were born, Sarah wrote to her daughters:

Your dresses will reach you tomorrow evening my darlings I have not enclosed the belts they will be sent in an envelope as they were at Katie's. I have been waiting to see her as she told me she would buy your veils. I have sent you some I had, if Kitty sends you better wear *them* darlings.

I hope you are well my pets and quite prepared for your confirmation. Wear your high petticoat bodys and make small shawls of your Plaids to put on in the Cab. I hope please God you will not catch cold the weather is very severe here.

With fondest love
believe me my own darlings
your ever affec
Mother.

To this she added an anxious postscript:

Hearing Katie has not sent your belts my darlings I bought new and send them with some white shawls they ought to be delivered tonight Tuesday

God bless you my dear ones
ever yours
Mamma.

Inside the envelope Ben scribbled:

Best love and kisses from your affectionate Daddy.

To one member of the family, the girls' confirmation was something more than 'a production'. Newly returned from Australia,
their brother Ben wrote:

My dear Polly and Flo!
... I hope you will have every blessing at your confirmation & that
you both know what a real responsibility you take upon yourselves ...

It is curious, how frequently the so-called 'reprobate' Ben came
up with serious, and unquestionably sincere, admonitions to his
younger brothers and sisters. A few years later he was writing to
Tom:

I need hardly tell you old boy that when Charlie goes to business
you will be the eldest one at school—so work well. I am quite certain you
will look after little Fred ... *learn* all you can. Not learning so that
you will forget half an hour after you've said your lesson to your master.

For the first time in years, Sarah had liberty to devote some
attention to her sons. Ben, returned from Australia (over the
Australian episode posterity drew a veil, which has not been lifted
to the present day), was, in the intervals of 'doing something in the
wine and spirit trade' (his brother Fred's vague description),
getting himself again into plenty of trouble, for which his charm
was largely responsible. 'The wine and spirit trade' was at this
period much favoured as a career for young men of the middle (and
upper middle) classes whose parents were not in a position to subsidize them, or whose personal qualifications were not such as to
procure them the entrée to the professions, or to entitle them to
commissions in the Army. The word 'trade', damning in Society,
was beginning to be associated with a Society of its own, of which
the leaders were the City merchants. In the wine trade, above all, a
personable youth like young Ben Terry, with a brother-in-law
who entertained the *crème de la crème* had opportunities of contacting
on terms of equality a class of customer to whom Grandfather
Benjamin and Grandmother Catherine, of the Fortune of War,
would have been deferential: young, spendthrift 'bloods', who,
recognizing in the gay young spark behind the counter a bird of

their own feather, speedily introduced Young Ben to a world for which neither his means nor his experience prepared him.

Devoted to his parents, his brothers and sisters, he embarked on a mildly Jekyll and Hyde career: was in great demand as an escort to the girls and in great favour for his fine Terry manners and bonhomie at Moray Lodge. He had a touch of his father's magnificence: he could not resist grandly tipping his younger brothers, George and Tom. 'George £5', 'Tom £5' figure in one of his sporadic attempts at keeping accounts. George, already a respected young apprentice to cabinet-making, trying hard, but not very successfully, to arrive at some sort of independence, deserved the five pounds—which he spent on tools for his trade; the whining schoolboy Tom was not worth five pence—but Ben had to play the 'big brother'.

He was an inveterate gambler. For the settlement of his 'debts of honour' he had frequent recourse to his generous sister Kate and —in moments of desperation—to Mama. (Certain items in his little account book suggest that he was trying to repay these loans: 'Mother £1.0.0. Mother £.16.8. Mother 1.6'—this last surely for a cab fare. Five dinners—10s. 8d. for the five, including the tip, 4s. 6d. for oysters, 4s. 0d. for ties, a pound for cabs and £6 15s. to the tailor hardly indicate a riotous scale of living; but they plainly belong to one of young Ben's periods of reform —probably following a row with his father or a serious talking-to from his brother-in-law, of whom he was fond. Such periods— there never was a better-hearted boy—were frequent, but, as time went on, of shorter and shorter duration. They could come only to one end; although, rollicking along his primrose path, he never heard it, already the bell was tolling for poor young Ben.)

Tom, according to his sister Ellen, was 'a fascinating wretch'; I have not been able to find confirmation of the description from any-one who ever knew him. He had, no doubt, his share of the 'Terry charm'; he was not very strong, which led to his spoiling at home. His brothers and sisters somehow built up a barricade of loyalty around him. From one who had something more than a passing acquaintance with him I had the description: 'He was the sort of man who must have been the sort of boy who cheated at games and cheated in the classroom and cheated himself out of any mess into which his dishonesty landed him.' He grew up with a chip on his shoulder—it is difficult to see why, surrounded as he was with patience and lovingkindness; perhaps his one-year-older brother Charlie had something to do with it—Charlie who was a bright boy in school, a universal favourite and, of the four boys, the favourite of his father, of whom, on a smaller, finer scale, he was 'the spitten image'.

It is easy to understand Ben Terry's preference for his son Charlie. Charlie alone of the three elder boys cared about the theatre, yet Ben, in his hard-won wisdom, could not believe in him as an actor. Charlie was sensitive, loving and gentle; in temperament very much akin to his sister Floss. He had none of that hard core of self-interest, a necessary ingredient of success, which was in Kate, Ellen and—already wise Ben detected it—in Polly Ann. He was in every respect the antithesis of his younger brother Tom; he was born with the fatal gift of so endearing himself not only to his family but to everyone with whom he came in contact that, according to his brother Fred, 'Old Charlie always got away with murder!' It was a very mild form of 'murder': extravagance, addiction to 'the ladies', and generosity—for which last, it must be admitted, someone else usually had to pay.

Two people were unfailingly kind and understanding to the beatnik Tom: his brother Ben and his sister Polly Ann. But Polly Ann loved, indiscriminately, the whole of the family. She, who died a virgin at the age of seventy-seven, was the most deeply warm-hearted and maternal of the four girls. It would have surprised some who were inclined to take this cool, fashionable and seemingly aloof young woman (even in her teens Polly was a little formidable, except to her few intimates) at face value, to discover how deeply she was beloved not only by her brothers and sisters but also by the younger generation.

The 'baby', darling Tops (Fred), was roaring his head off with temper, as well he might, in a Fauntleroy suit. Mrs Hodgson Burnett's classic had not yet appeared to blight the life of little boys and expose them to the ribaldry of their contemporaries. But Tennyson's boy Hallam and George Macdonald's boy Greville had been photographed by Lewis Carroll with long hair and in fancy dress. So a very masculine, pugilistic, little Terry was put by his doting mama and sisters into some velvet anticry, and his curling blond hair was allowed to grow down to his shoulders. So far as looks went, darling Tops could well have been the original of the egregious Ceddie Erroll. His temper matched his father's. It is not difficult, for one who knew Fred in his later years, to imagine the wealth of Ben's vocabulary when his youngest was presented to him in this unspeakable get-up. It was just one of the absurd, the drivelling things that added a millimetre to the growing gap between Ben and Sarah.

They were, it is sad to say, no longer in accord, and for this neither can be called 'to blame'. It was rather the inevitable growing-apart of a married couple who, having reached middle life, find themselves no longer in full sympathy with each other's plans and projects. Sarah had long closed her wise eyes to Ben's many light-hearted departures from the strait path of strict conjugal fidelity, because, in the depths of her faithful heart, she knew he was faithful to her in his fashion. But there were moments when Ben wondered if Sarah had forgotten 'Miss Yerret' and the good old strolling days, and Ben sleeping on his hay-bag, and the camaraderie of poor players, and the old horse pulling the baggage wagon, and little old candlelit theatres and the stewpot bubbling over the fire in the wardrobe. She appeared not to care for reminders of these, or of the shabby, kindly company that had made her welcome when she bravely took off, with her young husband, into the incalculable world of the theatre.

Ben was a dedicated actor of what was already the Old School. His spiritual home was the plain, hard-working theatre, with no fashionable varnish: the theatre in which the men were 'Ol' boy' and the women 'M'dear', and the rendezvous for men and women the tavern nearest to the stage door. The grander his wife and daughters became, the more—privately—he reverted to the simplicities of The Profession. He had faced and accepted the fact that he had not in him the makings of a great actor, but the smell and the sound of the theatre were to him the breath of life.

Not that he was averse from grandeur. He went to his son-in-law's fine parties at Moray Lodge and mingled with the aristocracy of the arts as to the manner born, charming all with his 'style', his courtesy and his wit. It is a little more difficult to see him at Divach, Arthur Lewis's shooting lodge near Glenurquhart, where

Kate, having perfected her role as a London hostess, was tackling the much more tricky one of 'mistress of the manse'. Never having had a gun—apart from a property one—in his hand, it is doubtful that Ben appreciated the hospitality of the Highlands; unlike Sarah, whose Scotch blood was roused by the glens. He was never sorry to return to London, to the company of his own kind, with whom he could talk theatre over a glass of ale.

He was seldom, if ever, out of work. Now and again he got a part in a suburban or provincial production, but he preferred to take utilities in town, in the small, now forgotten theatres such as the Alexandra—almost on his Camden Town doorstep—the King's Cross (known successively as the Panharmonium—inevitably translated to 'Pandemonium' Regent—Cabinet and Argyll) and the Marylebone. He enjoyed considerable prestige as the father of Kate and of Ellen.

He had had two deep disappointments: the disinclination of his elder sons towards the theatre and Kate's retirement. And one shocking blow: the withdrawal of his beloved Nelly—she in whom he saw, reflected as in a mirror, all he had ever hoped to do and to be. Intent on the material and social advancement of her younger daughters, Sarah was not in sympathy, though she was fully prepared, on their leaving school, for them to follow their elder sisters on to the stage; she recognized, as Ben did, the talent latent in Polly and Floss, and went so far as to encourage it. During their school holidays she read poetry and plays with them, in her beautiful voice that never exaggerated or falsified a syllable. The favourite plays were the *Dream* and *The Tempest*; sometimes the boys took part —Charlie eagerly and Tom *faute de mieux*. Darling Tops, still in the CAT SAT ON A MAT stage, could not take part in the readings, but he had a memory like the elephant's for anything that interested him, an impeccable ear, and a gift—like his father's—for mimicry which would have made him a valuable member of the Drawingroom Entertainment of the family's humble past. Thanks to these readings with their mother, Polly and Floss grew up with a perfect pronunciation of the English tongue and a fine perception of (spoken) dramatic values. Although they had few direct contacts with the theatre (such not being regarded as desirable for the young ladies of Sunnyside), it was more or less taken for granted they would go on the stage and graduate thence (this was Sarah's idea) into happy, successful marriages—like Katie's—within a year or two.

Nelly was living happily in the depths of the Hertfordshire countryside, and swelling out with her first baby. According to her own account, she was looking after goats, ducks and hens, lighting fires and scrubbing floors—all of which she did, no doubt, in her own sweet way at her own sweet time. She groomed the pony and tramped across the common to fetch the evening milk.

The morning milk was delivered by a boy called Fred. To the local peasantry he was 'Fred' and she was 'Nelly'; the future Ellen Terry and Fred Archer were just plain folk in Mackery End.[1]

She knew nothing of country living, and romanticized it wildly; it took her quite a while to realize that a goat was not to be milked three or four times a day—according to her convenience; that fowls needed—and expected—regular feeding; and that a pony was not to be stuffed and immediately allowed to blow itself out with unlimited water.

Sister Kate was ordering out the landau or the brougham, driving her phaeton, commanding her household, entertaining—with the support of a lavish staff—innumerable guests, playing Lady Bountiful to the family in Stanhope Street and stitching cambric, lawn and lace in anticipation of her second baby. Kate was an admirable housewife; she had inherited all of Sarah's gift for economy. No shopkeeper could take advantage of young Mrs Arthur Lewis, who knew all the best cuts of meat and *l'art de s'accommoder les restes*. Her servants respected a mistress who went closely over the books and was sharp to question any unauthorized expenditure. The tradesfolk respected a customer who spent lavishly, but saw to it that she received value for money. Whether it were foodstuffs, shoe-leather or woollen underwear, Katie knew exactly what the price should be for the best quality. She knew exactly what should be going on, at every hour of the day, in kitchen, servants' hall or nursery. She regulated her own life no less strictly than she regulated that of her staff: an hour for needlework, an hour for the piano, an hour for baby Katie, an hour for conference with the cook,

[1] They kept up their friendship; Fred Archer gave her the fox terrier Fussie, which she later gave to Henry Irving.

butler and parlourmaid, an hour for rest—so that when Arthur
came home from his office in Conduit Street he found a smiling
soignée young wife, prepared to entertain or be entertained, to go to
'the play', with perhaps a supper party to follow, or enjoy 'a little
music' at home with a few chosen friends.

Sister Nelly, also heavy with child, cooked abominable meals
for her lover, invariably forgetting some essential ingredient, or
letting the dish burn while she petted the animals, or wandered
along the hedgerows, gathering autumn leaves and berries, which
she was idly arranging while Godwin craved for his supper. For
'staff' she had a rough girl who knew as little as herself about
cookery, and was equally forgetful. There would be no fuel, or no
oil in the lamps; no water drawn from the pump, and a litter of
lifeless ash on the hearth. And upon this joyless scene would arrive
a tired, chilled, nervous man, having made the journey from London
in an unheated third-class carriage. Nelly would sit up to all hours,
making tracings and transcriptions from his current notes. Was
Godwin to be blamed if he longed at moments for a buxom, brainless
mistress who would produce a blazing fire and a succulent steak
and leave him, in the long night watches, to get on with his own
work? Like many of his kind, he wanted to eat his cake and have it.
He wanted the inspiration of Nelly's beauty, her iridescent presence,
and expected her at the same time to minister to his (admittedly not
exigent) material needs.

Wholly self-centred, he took it for granted that his young,
beautiful and gifted companion would devote herself to his interests,
be grateful for the favours he bestowed (at his convenience) upon her,
and act round the clock as his housekeeper, cook, amanuensis, and
partner of his bed. He never recognized the crying need in Nelly,
after her disastrous marriage, of tenderness and care. Of both he
was incapable. He was, according to his lights, 'in love' with her;
but love, to Godwin, carried none of the connotations it implied
to a romantic and sensitive girl. A monumental egoist, taking feminine adulation for granted, his increasing professional prestige
gradually took precedence of his attachment to Nelly.

He was, by this time, a Fellow and a member of the Council
of the Royal Institute of British Architects, and an active member
of the Architectural Association. He had moved his office from

Baker Street to Albany Street, and spent much of his time there. His commitments to the Archaeological Society took him all over the country, and for days at a time left Nelly lonely at Mackery End.

When he did not come home, he did not trouble to let her know what he was doing. He would appear never to have given a thought to the anxious girl, waiting at the railway halt with the pony cart. The train comes in; a mailbag is thrown out on the platform; her eyes strain past the glimmer of lamplight as the train pulls out— with never a living soul but the old porter, who drags the mail into his office. So she drives back alone under the ghostly moon, to a whooping of owls, an empty house and some food she has no heart, in solitude, to eat.

It never occurred to Godwin that Nelly, unused to country silence, might be frightened, might imagine an accident, or wonder whether her lover was deceiving her with one of his numerous flames.

In October 1869 Kate's second daughter, Janet, was born, with panoply of doctors and nurses; with a devoted husband and a loving mother to supply all a young wife could desire of attention and support through her ordeal.

On a December night of the same year, no such comforts surrounded the birth of a little girl at Mackery End. Godwin—who must have known the birth was imminent—was away. Fortunately for Nelly, she had made acquaintance with a local doctor and his wife. She engaged Doctor Rumball for her lying-in.

Eldest but two of nine brothers and sisters, Nelly was too accustomed to the ritual of childbirth to panic. It was a bitter night. When her pains began, towards dusk, she got the girl to help her pull a mattress downstairs in front of the livingroom fire, then sent the girl for Doctor Rumball, who was out when the message came. But he was there in time to help the baby, Edith Terry, into the world.

Godwin eventually got down to building the house he had promised, on the edge of Harpenden Common. They called it Fallows Green, after the plot on which it was established. It had a long, sloping roof and a lych gate. It was there, intact, half a century later, when Harpenden was still an innocent country town, not the 'dormitory' it became between the two wars.

Nelly had no desire ever to return to the theatre. She accepted without question the dogmatism of Godwin, whose precepts governed her to the end of her days. Ellen Terry never wore a 'fashionable' dress; she preferred linen and flax to silks (except the so-called 'Tyrian' silk of Liberty, which, with its crinkles, no doubt reminded her of the wring-and-dry tunic Godwin fashioned for her at Bristol). She chose pottery, rather than porcelain, for her table, but made an exception of a willow pattern service given to her by Godwin's friend Whistler.[1] She associated herself with Godwin's revolt from the tasteless and over-decorated standards of the Victorian age, and with his addiction to the pure line and colour of the Greek and the Japanese.

Pregnant with her second child, Nelly was struggling to harness the pony, to drive Godwin to the station. He caught her at it and exploded with puerile rage.

'Haven't you cost me enough money already, without obliging me to fetch a doctor to you?'

'I nearly left him then', Ellen Terry told me. 'It was an unforgivable thing to say to a woman carrying a child.'

It is fair to say that Nelly was no easy proposition for a neurotic man in his late thirties, ambitious, overladen with work, and unpractical. She was untidy, unpunctual and extravagant, and alone of the four girls never profited by Sarah's teaching and example. 'Unthinking, idle, wild and gay', she managed always to evade her share of domestic responsibility—of which, as Mrs Watts, she had had none whatever. She had never ordered, let alone prepared, a formal meal; never seen a butcher's or baker's bill. Coming home, tired out and hungry, Godwin would find that Nelly had not only not started to cook supper, but had nothing in the larder. 'You didn't leave me any money and the butcher won't send anything until his bill's paid,' blithely said Nelly, who, woman-like, was content to live on milk, eggs and garden produce.

[1] She liked a horrid 'butcher-blue' linen, crudely stitched, for cushion covers and table mats.

By the time the second child, a boy, Edward, was born, the pair of them were on edge.

On a holiday in France—Nelly's first glimpse of 'abroad'—they patched things up. It was a blissful time for both—perhaps the first unadulterated bliss she had known since her attachment to Godwin. She had no responsibilities: the children, who accompanied them, were taken off her hands by a nursemaid, known as 'Bo' (she was a relative of Doctor Rumball's widow—called 'Boo'—who moved in as a kind of companion housekeeper to Nelly at Fallows Green, and remained with Ellen Terry for over thirty years). She had only to drift in her lover's wake round cathedrals and cathedral towns, inebriated with their beauty, confirming the glories he had described to her in the long nights when she acted as his secretary, as his clerk. The professional side of Godwin was stimulated by the earnest attention of his lovely companion; their love quickened in surroundings where Nelly's domestic inadequacy did not bring an element of irritation into their relationship.

There was not then, or ever, anything of the student in Ellen Terry, but throughout her life her intelligence and deep sensitivity towards all forms of the arts endeared her to the painters, poets and musicians who became her closest friends. She had a strong power of so absorbing beauty into herself that a delicate line, a subtlety of phrasing, a fine-woven textile, a nuance of colouring all became part of her. Those who deplored her first marriage and lowered holy eyelids on the Godwin interlude might have done better to reflect on how much those two men, Watts and Godwin, contributed to the genius which was presently to burst upon the theatre and reduce every contemporary star to a rushlight.

Three little Lewis girls—Lucy Maud was born in 1871; Mabel Gwynedd, the only one of the four to inherit the talent of her mother, had not yet been 'given to the light'—were growing up in muslin frocks, silken stockings, bronze sandals and coral necklaces. They were beautifully brought up, by carefully chosen nurses and governesses. They had one of the first kindergartens in England and learned riding on their own Shetland pony. They knelt down every morning when Mama read family prayers to the household (Kate, like her sisters Polly and Floss, had gravitated from nonconformity to the Church of England) and were taken in the brougham to visit their paralysed Lewis grandmother at Roehampton. They doted on their Terry grandparents, on their pretty aunts Polly and Floss and their handsome young uncles (golden-haired Fred only three years older than his niece Katie).

It was an age of elaborate and formal hospitalities, for the grown-ups endless dinner parties, conversaziones, soirées, musical evenings and amateur theatricals; for the children, indoor and outdoor junketings, games, parties, 'acting' in nursery or school-room—of which all the little Lewises' young friends and relatives partook. No invitations, however, came in the way of two little illegitimate cousins down in Hertfordshire.

Had Edith and Edward Terry been born fifty years earlier, on the tail-end of an epoch which took bastardy in its stride: had they been born fifty years later, when Victorian hypocrisy was on the wane— the situation might have resolved itself painlessly for all. Kate Lewis was not to be blamed for setting her chubby face against the sister with whom she had never been in close sympathy; and whose life was so much at odds with her protected and prosperous one. Her first duty was to her little girls, and the inclusion of an unauthorized niece and nephew in Moray Lodge parties would certainly have been regarded as an affront by the parents and nannies of children born on the right side of the blanket, and could seriously have prejudiced the social futures of Katie, Janet, Lucy and Mabel.

Nor is it certain that Nelly, under Godwin's influence, would have appreciated any kindly overtures. The well-disciplined, well-brought-up little Lewises would have had little in common with *farouche* Edy and spoilt Ted, whose mother's conscience for putting them into a censorious world expressed itself in the form of an idolatry which, when they were hardly out of diapers, gave them a monstrously overblown idea of their own importance. They referred to themselves invariably as 'Miss' Edy and 'Master' Teddy—which may have started as a joke and been encouraged by Boo and Bo. Joke or not, they appear to have been a couple of intolerable children, whose father had neither time nor inclination to keep them in order, and whose mother was incapable of making them behave, because everything they did was miraculous in her eyes.

None who knew her in ugly-duckling childhood could have foreseen the beauty into which Polly blossomed in her teens. She had heavy, russet hair and the most exquisitely modelled eyes—her mother's—varying between hazel and light brown.

As a child she was very quiet, with none of the high spirits that normally go with the dramatic temperament, and she loved music. Her tastes were all for the classic; from her own account, she played Beethoven and Bach with such facility that it was considered she might become a pianist, for which career she admitted she had much more addiction than for acting. She was an interesting girl, very discreet and reserved, but deeply affectionate to the few she entrusted with her friendship. There was no kind of bohemianism, of camaraderie about Polly. She did not care for the slap-happy theatre folk she met occasionally in school holidays; she preferred the society to which she was introduced at Lavender Sweep and at Moray Lodge, where she frequently stayed, the favourite of her sister Kate. She liked formality, and famous people, and social elegance.

And yet—The Germ was there.

In the year 1910 Marion Terry contributed to a series of articles called *My First Appearance* in *The Sketch*.

> As a matter of fact, it was through my playing the piano that I really came to go on the stage at all. . . . One day . . . Mrs Taylor was playing some duets with me. I got greatly excited over the music and I appeared anything but the quiet, demure, young damsel they were accustomed to see. Mr and Mrs Taylor began talking about me and they came to the conclusion that perhaps, after all, I might be able to do something on the stage.

The year after her confirmation, 1870, Polly—no longer Mary Ann Betsy,[1] but Miss Marion Terry—made her début in Leeds, in Tom Taylor's perversion of *Hamlet*. Sarah and Floss went down with her. She played Ophelia in white flannel—as Ellen was later to play it at the Lyceum. She had never appeared even on the amateur stage.

A statement of singular fatuity was made thirty years later in a biography of *Ellen Terry and Her Sisters*, to the effect that Marion

[1] She always disliked her simple Christian names, but kept to the B. for Betsy at any rate on her luggage, 'M.B.T.'

and Florence Terry, when they took to the profession, were 'quite unaccustomed to the stage'. How should this be of the children of Ben and Sarah? Theatre was in the air they breathed; they knew stage doors, greenrooms, dressingrooms and wings from babyhood. They watched rehearsals. They were coached by their mother in the great scenes and great speeches of Shakespearian drama. All the conversation at home was theatrical 'shop'. They were precociously critical of productions and individual performances.

So when Marion dried up in the Mad Scene (there was no prompter at Leeds), she went on playing with her flowers and presently got up, went over to the actor who was playing Laertes and, dropping her head on his shoulder, whispered, 'Tell me what I say next.' He gave her the line, and she went back and played the rest of the scene tranquilly. Tom Taylor was in front, and noticed what had happened; at the fall of the curtain he went round and patted her head. 'You'll do all right; you've got the making of a real actress in you.'

They played Leeds two nights and—thanks to Taylor's connection with the production—got notices in the London papers. The Ophelia was singled out for special commendation, and when, on the third night, they opened in Manchester there was a telegram for Miss Marion Terry from Henry Neville, lessee and manager of the Olympic Theatre.

Son of an actor-manager known as 'Handsome Jack' Neville, Henry Neville was the Lewis Waller of his epoch, the *jeune premier* (a title he continued to carry long after he was entitled to it) and the idol of every sentimental feminine playgoer of the 'seventies and 'eighties. He had the bonhomie of William Terriss, the sex-appeal of Waller, and the robust charm of Robert Loraine. He happened also to be a very fine actor. It sheds a curious light upon the incalculability of the public memory that his name is unknown save to a handful of serious students of theatrical history today, and prompts the inquiry, would Terriss (not so good an actor as Neville) be remembered if he had not been murdered at the stage door of the Adelphi and left a daughter who made a name of her own in light comedy?

Neville had made a sensation in *The Ticket of Leave Man* (one of Tom Taylor's adaptations from the French), which ran the all but unprecedented number of four hundred nights on its original production. In this good old stand-by of the drama, he played the hero, Bob Brierly, more than two thousand times. He had taken over the management of the Olympic from the Wigans and preserved the best traditions of romantic drama, playing among other parts Claude Melnotte to the Pauline of Kate Saville. He had an assured public and the favour of the critics. It was no small achievement for a young actress to get into his Company, where she was sure of catching—for good or ill—the public eye.

The magic of the Terry name must have had something to do with Neville's offer of an engagement to two inexperienced young actresses. Granted, it was not much of a part; the piece was a cheap one-act, called *Love in Humble Life*, in which, on alternate nights, Polly and Floss—now Miss Marion and Miss Florence Terry —played Christine, the female lead.

Kate drove over from Moray Lodge to coach them at their rehearsals; Sarah resumed her all-but-forgotten role as chaperon, as dresser, as general factotum to the girls; and Ben was in the seventh heaven. Two more young Terrys had taken to the theatre like ducklings to water—but wise Ben did not forget that at Marion's age Kate was already a leading lady, and at Florence's Nelly had more than ten years of experience behind her. Neither Polly nor Floss had gone through the toughening process that brought the best out of Kate, and left Nelly—so far—something of an unknown quantity. (Actually, Ben's belief in his Nelly had never faltered, and was soon to be confirmed.)

So his first consideration was to make sure that neither of these comparatively sensitive plants was forced.

The most unexpected development of the Olympic engagement was Florence's triumph in her trivial role. Marion had not Florence's gay approach, her lightsome charm, which captivated audiences and shrivelled the roots of adverse criticism. Something of Marion's private reserve pursued her on to the stage and was not appreciated by the public which, like the daughter of the horse-leech, cries, 'Give, give!' 'Darling Floss' instantly became 'Darling Florence' to her audiences—a fact of which rival managements were speedily aware. She was offered a tiny part at the Adelphi, in an English version of *Le Malade Imaginaire*, in which she acquitted herself so well that she was engaged, in November of the same year, to play the title role in *Little Nell*, Andrew Halliday's adaptation of *The Old Curiosity Shop*, and endeared herself to an even larger public than she had played to at the Olympic. Professionally, she had outstripped her elder sister Marion—which could partly account for the claim by some theatrical historians that Florence made her début four years before Marion Terry.

It speaks well for a young actress who had earned some measure of easy success that Marion accepted her father's guidance, and turned down some tempting offers that came her way. Ben had proved that the best training for a novice lay out in the provinces, where her successes and possibly her failures attracted little attention, and she could learn the business unbedazzled by the fierce light that beat upon the London stage. (Reade and Taylor are said to have disagreed with him: to have urged him to profit by the name of Terry, which Kate had glorified before her retirement. Ben was not to be budged from the line he had taken up in regard to his daughters, and presently Florence was to follow Marion 'on the road'.)

At the conclusion of her Olympic engagement, Marion went out to get experience in minor parts in bad little plays; the nearest she came to town for three years was the Crystal Palace, where she repeated her Ophelia to Steele Mackaye's Hamlet: a production which drew little attention from the critics and flopped in the provinces. A very few people recognized in Marion Terry the makings of a great actress.

For the first time, with all of the family—with the exception of schoolboys Tom and Fred—earning, the Terrys tasted comparative affluence. Relieved of pecuniary strain, Sarah began to recover something of her former beauty, lost her haggard look and, encouraged by her devoted daughters, took an interest in her own appearance. She was fully occupied in chaperoning her pretty and popular girls. It was lucky for slim Marion and slimmer Florence that Kate was getting fatter and fatter, and that their sister's beautiful cast-off gowns could, with the critical help of Mama and the practical assistance of a sewing woman, be remodelled to their young forms. The elaborate gowns of the period were not within the scope of the home dressmaker, even so skilled a one as Sarah. The crinoline had flattened down in front, only to elongate itself behind; it was draped and trimmed like a chimney-piece; it took acres of material and leagues of fringe, passementerie, buttons and bows; it was preparing its next phase of horror—the bustle.

Miss Marion and Miss Florence Terry had to be dressed in the height of fashion, to grace the many functions to which they were invited. Their brothers, often in request as escort, were proud of the elegant girls.

Charlie was apprenticed to a firm of wine merchants, with affiliations in Bordeaux. Everyone liked Charlie. On the Terry name, he had freedom of box office, wings and dressingrooms; all his spare time was spent round stage doors, gloating on a forbidden world. It was hard on one who longed to be an actor. But he was too young and too gentle to rebel. He had inherited all of his father's most lovable qualities and some of his talent, without the driving power.

Growing up in the shadow of their gifted sisters, life cannot have been easy for the boys. To read the numerous Terry biographies and autobiographies is to gain the impression that, with the notable exception of the youngest, Fred, Ben's sons were such complete nonentities that they did not rate a line of print. This is not true. Ben and George were manly youths, devoted sons and brothers, whose only 'crime' was their want of active subscription to the family religion of the theatre. The affectionate generosity of their sisters, far from mitigating, contributed to a state of mind for which the Freudian cliché had not then been invented.

Young Ben's rakishness, George's lethargy, Charlie's weakness and lack of concentration and Tom's want of principle may be checked back to the years when they were made to feel their inferiority to their successful sisters. Ben, George and Tom were throwbacks to Spice Island, the Fortune of War and the Terry grandparents none of them could remember.

In 1874 Marion had her first notable success, when she played Hero in Henry Neville's excellent production of *Much Ado About Nothing* at the Olympic. Florence understudied her. The production owed much of its *réclame* to Neville's sparkling performance as Benedick, which was never equalled until Fred Terry played the part in 1911, and never surpassed until Fred's nephew, John

Gielgud, played it in 1931. Neville was as popular with his colleagues as with his audiences. It was a happy engagement for Marion and Florence; Marion profited by it, and to her father's delight, got better notices than usually fall to the share of a supporting actress.

That was the year Nelly chose to explode back on the theatre she had deserted for her six-year-long interlude with Godwin.

CHAPTER NINE

Marriages and Mismarriages

In the Godwin *ménage* history was repeating itself. Mainly because its master's mind was too loftily occupied with the mediaeval to attend to such mundane trifles as settling bills or keeping up the mortgage payments, the bailiff's men moved in on Fallows End. Godwin's, however, was not all the blame. He gave Nelly money from time to time, and took it not unreasonably for granted that she and Boo between them would look after the tradesmen. Boo was not actually much better a business woman than Nelly; she had made a botch of running the mental home established by the good Doctor Rumball with the view of providing his wife with a competence for the rest of her days. And, like most other people, she was beglamoured by Nelly, whose least wish, to Boo, was law. So it may be taken for granted that few of those sovereigns Godwin flung carelessly from his pocket found their way to the butcher, baker or candlestick maker; they were more likely frittered on presents for the children, on a gown for Boo or a trinket for Bo. Ellen Terry herself left it on record that her servant went to church in silk and the mistress of the house in cotton. Little if any of Nelly's squandering went on herself, but throughout her life *giving*, with her, was a vice, of which few of her friends attempted to cure her.

The day inevitably came when the effect of Nelly's angelic smile failed on people who had their own expenses to meet and required a more substantial form of coinage than the honey-gold of her hair. It is doubtful that she blamed herself, even then, or recognized her own share of responsibility for the financial disaster. But the hard-headed Terry streak proved itself in her manner of dealing with the solution which dropped into her strong, capable hands.

It could have been one of the contemporary dramas which, stretching credulity to its breaking-point, were nevertheless rapturously accepted by Victorian audiences. In an age of materialism, the theatre provided the outlet for the sneaking, half-ashamed romantic that formed the soft core of the national character.

The golden-haired Heroine is driving her pony-cart down a lane, when a wheel comes off. The children scream; the Heroine calms them (wondering what to do next), when over a hedge flashes, in the pink of the local hunt, the Long-Lost Lover, unmet for years.

Actually, and unlikely as it must appear, it was Charles Reade, Nelly's 'stage Papa', who had never set eyes on her since she bolted from the Queen's Theatre in 1868, and who, as it happened, was about to put on a new piece at that very theatre. It was not actually a new piece: *The Wandering Heir*, Reade's current piece of theatrical trash, founded on the Tichborne Case, had been a failure in the provinces, but Reade stubbornly insisted on bringing it to town, and had gone so far, at the time of his momentous encounter with Nelly, as to engage as his leading lady an actress who was anxious enough to make a come-back to the London stage as to overlook the far from promising reception the play had had in the North. Regardless, however, of his commitment to Mrs John Wood—the Old Friend offers the Heroine the leading role in his new play. To which, thinking of home and children, she, in the best traditions of melodrama, replies 'Never!'

Having 'taken in' the broken-down pony-cart, the gingham gown, the two gaping children, he flings at her the one word 'Fool!' . . . and Nelly, remembering the bailiffs, the undependability of her lover, her own insecure future and that of the children, does a quick double-take.

All the egoism which lay only paper-deep under that tender and yielding surface rose to brandish itself in the face of Charles Reade's challenge. The big, pale eyes concentrated. She would think of it, said Nelly, for forty pounds a week.

This gave Reade pause. He had always shared Ben Terry's belief in Nelly, but forty pounds was a star's salary, and more than he was proposing to pay Mrs John Wood. The memory of the public is notoriously short, and Nelly had made no notable impression during her season at the Queen's. Coming to his senses, he told her she would not be opening in town, but would be taking over from an actress who had agreed only to a limited engagement. The name of Mrs John Wood—in spite of her unfortunate performance in *Barnaby Rudge*, which had made her the laughing stock of the critics—still stood for more to the general public than that of Ellen Terry. Nelly batted her mermaid's eyes, and, with the utmost sweetness, reiterated her insistance on forty pounds a week. Reade looked at the young face, the young limbs that Watts had celebrated; remembered the flashes of genius both he and Taylor had marked in her earlier performances—and capitulated.

In the winter of 1873-74, a thin young woman in absurd clothes moved herself and her family up to a small house in Taviton Street, off Gordon Square. There were six of them: Godwin, Nelly, the children, Boo and Bo. In a period when every woman was blown out with horsehair and tight-laced to the limit of breathing, and children wore dreadful little imitations of grown-up people's clothes, Edy and Teddy, in their Japanese kimonos[1] and Nelly in her Viollet-le-Duc tabards must have been antic figures in Bloomsbury.

Her sole preoccupation was with her children. It was on their account that, to fill in time until she took up her engagement at the Queen's, she accepted a short engagement in Liverpool, leaving Godwin to get on with the domestic arrangements in Taviton Street. 'You cannot go on caring about somebody in whom you no longer have faith', she said in later years. Her experience at Fallows End had jolted her out of her irresponsible youth; she perceived that, so far as the children's future was concerned, all depended on her.

She had long, whining letters from Godwin:

Another wet day and I dread going out. Thin trousers and so cold. How I have wanted my umbrella. I wouldn't buy another. Hope you got it out of the Museum all right.

He had engaged a charwoman (so he said) and a cook; there were Japan-paper curtains for the diningroom; Nelly was not to make a bedroom out of the back drawingroom for the present. Their two small brass bedsteads were to be put up in the bedroom, but in the dressingroom there was a chair-bed, which he could use, so as not to disturb Nelly. What were her views of this belated consideration are only to be conjectured.

[1] A present from Godwin's friend Whistler.

He had papered both floors to the whole height of the wall, as it saved time and money, and, after these labours, he was naturally exhausted. He begged Ellen, when she came home, to 'keep the chicks and Boo away from me except at meals, and give yourself to me altogether as a martyr for a day or two'.

In such ways he tried, belatedly, to make up for his neglect of his young lover; he may even, by then, have discovered something of the meaning of love. He may have been disturbed by Nelly's sudden independence. On her side, 'When love has turned to kindliness . . .' would seem to cover the situation.

On 28 February 1874, the day after her twenty-sixth birthday, Ellen Terry took up the part of Philippa Chester in Charles Reade's drama *The Wandering Heir*. It was the beginning of a valuable relationship for a young actress who, though possessed of unquestionable genius, had yet much to learn. Reade was a mediocre playwright; as a theatrical coach he was well-nigh impeccable. He flattered and encouraged her; he was ruthless in condemning her technical shortcomings—which were many. He 'saw through' her: describing her in his diary as 'hysterical, sentimental, hard as a nail in money matters but velvet on the surface. A creature born to please and to deceive.'

He detested Godwin—which helped to drive the wedge between Ellen Terry and her lover; he recognized the falsification of Ellen's character which had come about through her attachment to one who, incapable of appreciating her quality, sought only to remodel her in the image of himself—a project defeated, fortunately for the English stage, by the powerful egoism of his subject.

None of her own family was present at her first night. Those who subscribed to the legend of Nelly's 'neglect' by her parents, brothers and sisters, found no doubt, in this, proof of their contention. Ben was working and the girls rehearsing (in those days, rehearsals did not stop in time for the actors to go on to a cocktail party, a show and supper to follow), with Sarah looking after them. For all one knows, the boys may have been there—at any rate, George and Charlie—unregarded.

There were many—more than either she or Charles Reade expected—who remembered Ellen Terry, and warmly welcomed her back to the stage. She had a great reception, and the notices were lyrical. They were read emotionally in Stanhope Street. They were read at Moray Lodge, and young Mrs Lewis was proud of her sister's success. They cannot fail to have been read at Little Holland House, although Mrs Prinsep may have tried to suppress them in deference to the sensibilities of the Signor. But Watts was not quite so weak a character as his patroness would have liked to consider him; as an artist, he could not withhold his tribute to an artist.

The enthusiasm of the critics for the new leading lady did not extend to the play: 'It would be almost wearying to sit it out, even if every actor in it were equal to Miss Terry.' It ran one hundred and thirty nights and was taken off and replaced by Reade's ancient pot-boiler, *It's Never Too Late to Mend* (with Ellen again in the lead). Even Nelly's charm could not triumph over this claptrap, and Reade, who, like the majority of playwrights, never blamed himself, but the imperceptivity of his public, for his failures, promptly took *The Wandering Heir*, with the entire London cast, out on the road.

Godwin remained in Taviton Street, with the children, Boo and Bo. His offspring, according to their own reminiscences, must have seen very little of him, and that was hardly his fault. An aggressive girl, a spoilt and conceited boy, offered little in the way of companionship to a depressed and nervous man whose work, temporarily, had petered out. For want, presumably, of more serious occupation, he espoused a movement started by the editress of *Women and Work*, Miss Emily Faithful, in support of women's future as architects. In earnest of his theories he took on a young lady student, a Miss Beatrice Philip—who was one of the surprises Ellen faced on her return from the provinces.

Another, to which she was hardened, was the presence of the brokers' men. There was not much of value for them to carry away: the straw-coloured matting, the wicker furniture, the grey-blue draperies and the full-size cast of the Venus de Milo, perpetually wreathed in blue smoke from a brazier: these in the drawingroom. Upstairs little but the beds, the children's cots, and valueless oddments. For obvious reasons, most of the better furniture had been left behind in the country, back to which Ellen now packed the children, in charge of Boo and Bo. Godwin would appear to have arrived at an agreement with his creditors in

Hertfordshire, and the first thing that Ellen felt should be tackled was to remove Edy and Ted out of range of their father's exacerbated nerves. A good, broad vein of practical common sense ran through the quicksilver of her character and took temporary charge of a situation with which Godwin appeared incapable of coping. While the brokers removed everything but the matting and the Venus, she tried to get to grips with the future and brought her glowing enthusiasm to bear on Godwin's all but completed book on *The Architecture and Costume of Shakespeare's Plays*, the fruits of his long research into the drama.

She had made very little out of her tour; as on its original journey round the provinces, the public's opinion of *The Wandering Heir* by no means came up to its author's. Her contracted forty pounds a week had been whittled down—hard-headed as she was, in one way, about money, it was either accept a salary cut or close down, and she had nothing in view.

So the unexpected offer from the Bancrofts to play Portia in the production of *The Merchant of Venice* at the Prince of Wales's Theatre in Tottenham Street, came as a godsend. The brilliant little actress Marie Wilton, who had made her name in Strand burlesque, who was associated in the public mind with principal boys and the lightest of light comedy, could obviously not take up a major Shakespearian role, even under her husband's aegis. Her elegance, her humorous little face, her pouter pigeon figure (Marie Tempest, in her youth, bore a striking likeness to Marie Wilton) were good for a burst of applause and laughter as soon as she stepped out of the shadow of the wings. 'By my troth, Nerissa, my little body is a-weary of this great world', Portia's opening lines, would have brought the house down, and turned the scene into a romp.

If Ellen Terry had any mental reservations (which is more than unlikely) over accepting the offer, they were dispelled by the codicil to Mrs Bancroft's proposal—which took place in the shadow of the towering Venus, in an otherwise empty room: an antic setting for the fashionable little actress, a perfect background for the tall, slender young woman whose tabard made Mrs Bancroft widen her diamond-shaped eyes. 'And Mr Godwin will be asked to control the artistic direction.'

It was the first great theatrical opportunity which had ever come in the way either of Ellen or of Godwin.

Money appeared to be no object;[1] Godwin despatched the scene-painter, Gordon, to Venice, to get 'local colour'. With the exception of his friend Whistler, most of his fellow-members of the Arts Club—which, let it be recalled, was founded in 1863 by Arthur Lewis, and established in a handsome Georgian house, number 17, Hanover Square—deplored his excursus into the theatre: he was deserting his architectural colleagues. Be that as it may, the production of *The Merchant of Venice* displayed, as none of his previous achievements had done, the wide range of Edward Godwin's artistic genius. It was not only a masterpiece of archaeology, but a perfect welding together of the arts of the actor and the designer. It was, above all, the perfect setting for Ellen Terry—at whose casket scene, in her almond-blossom gown, the house rose. Never had been seen such a Portia.

Many who saw it could remember Mrs Kean's Portia—in Victorian hair-style and blown-out petticoats. Ellen, with her 'front hair in massive curls, carried down in smaller curls to the ears' and lifted at the back; her high-necked Venetian gown, with stiffened lace collar 'reaching as high as the poll'—nothing of its kind had ever been seen before. Only a tall, slender, young woman could have carried it. Oscar Wilde burst into a sonnet, and Ellen Terry became in a night the tutelary goddess of the Aesthetes.

A miserable Shylock—Charles Coghlan—robbed the production of the success to which it was entitled. To put on *The Merchant of Venice* without the Jew was equivalent to putting on *Hamlet* without the Dane. The play ran only a few weeks—but long enough to establish Ellen Terry at the head of her profession.

Not for forty years was she to know what it meant to be out of work—'resting' as it was euphemistically known in The Profession. Her great *réclame* as Portia, its emotional impact on the artistic and poetic world, had 'placed' her. Whistler, Swinburne, Watts-Dunton, Wilde, Alfred Gilbert—everyone who could paint, sculp, or make music out of words, was at her feet. Her star had

---

[1] Ellen's salary was £20, but Bancroft, lavish in expenses of production, was notoriously mean on salaries, and she was too wise to try the bluff she had successfully pulled on Reade.

risen at exactly the right moment: that moment of artistic renaissance of which the Pre-Raphaelites and the Aesthetes were the prophets.

This would seem the place to kill the false and cruel story that Ellen Terry was not received back into the bosom of her family until she became famous. There is no word of truth in it. What made it possible for her to resume the easy come and go between her home and Fallows Green was Godwin's desertion. It was not so easy, even then, because of the children: but Marion and Florence, meeting their sister, were not obliged to accept their sister's lover, and the little Lewis girls were not liable to be 'contaminated' by contacts with their aunt Ellen's paramour.

It seems unlikely that, even if Watts had given her a divorce, Godwin would eventually have married Ellen Terry, or, if he had proposed it, that she would have accepted. They were both egoists, on a monumental scale. The inevitable happened. The young student, Beatrice Philip, who accepted Godwin as *cher maître*, was what he really wanted; she was a short, plump, brown girl, an amateur of the arts, addicted to hero-worship. Such artistic qualities as she possessed in no way challenged those of her master. So he left Ellen Terry and married Beatrice Philip.

This was what made it possible for Ellen to return to the family which had never ceased to love her. After the (financial) failure of *The Merchant of Venice*, she played Clara Douglas in Bulwer's *Money*; Mabel Vane in Reade and Taylor's *Masks and Faces*; Blanche Haye in Robertson's *Ours*. All rubbish; all waste of her genius, said some of her admirers, but not the most devoted of them all. Ben's beloved Nelly had much time to make up, and the main thing was to go on acting, regardless of the material she was offered by her management. Ellen Terry agreed with her father—not wholly on aesthetic grounds; although her salary had risen steadily she was always in trouble over money: she had the expenses of a household on her hands, Boo and Bo to keep, and the children's education on her mind. They were intelligent children—as how should they not be, with such parentage; and Ellen was determined they should enjoy all the privileges she, as a child, had lacked. She also knew—none better—the value of the guidance and discipline she was receiving from two devoted friends, Reade and Taylor, who dedicated themselves not only to her personal interests but to those of the whole of her family. Taylor, as dramatic and art critic for *The Times*, editor of *Punch*, and an indefatigable playwright, was immensely influential. When he died, 'I lost a friend the like of whom I never had again', wrote Ellen Terry in her *Memoirs*. And a friend she needed at the Prince of Wales's, where, after her Portia, she played second fiddle to Marie Bancroft with all the good grace in the world. But it was not entirely a happy association; the indiscriminate enthusiasm of Ellen Terry's admirers, who applauded to the echo her every moment, was not calculated to sweeten the relationship with the wife of her manager. Incapable, herself, of jealousy and a sincere admirer of Mrs Bancroft, she was embarrassed by these untimely demonstrations. It is perhaps not surprising that Mrs Bancroft's very genuine admiration of Ellen Terry was faintly adulterated (to the end of the former's professional life) with a touch of reminiscent acrimony.

1876 was the year of the Queen's proclamation as Empress of India; an event of uninterest to Terrys, whose Empire was the theatre. Important things were Ellen's engagement at the Prince of Wales's, and Marion's at the Strand; Florence was on tour— the indefatigable Tom Taylor had got her the engagement—as Lady Betty in a reprehensible piece called *Lady Clancarty*.

At the Lyceum—home of Fechter, Celeste, Vestris—a very striking actor called Henry Irving was in partnership with Mrs Bateman, the lessee and leading lady of most of the Lyceum productions. Irving had come up 'the hard way'; had been hissed by audiences and slated by critics. He had stage-managed and acted at the St James's Theatre, and had three years of experience at the Edinburgh Theatre Royal. At the St James's he made no favourable impression, but when Miss Herbert (the lessee) took the Company on tour, including *The Rivals* in her repertory, Irving, as Captain Absolute, received notice as 'a painstaking and respectable artist'.

He progressed from *The Bells*, in 1871, to *Charles I*, *Eugene Aram*, *Richelieu*, *Hamlet* and *Macbeth*, to *Othello* and *Queen Mary* in 1876; and in that year, Coghlan, Ellen Terry's disastrous Shylock, but still her colleague at the Prince of Wales's, and her friend, invited her to see Irving's King Philip—of which, later, she wrote, 'he never did anything better to the day of his death'.

She had seen him before: in 1874 she had gone with Tom Taylor to the Lyceum first night of *Hamlet*—the 'one and only Hamlet of her life'. In 1878 she saw that Hamlet again: when he played it for her in Birmingham, having engaged her as his Ophelia—and was 'swept away'. Her description of his performance is a classic in stage literature.[1] Ellen Terry alone of the Terrys of her generation, had the gift of words; her great-nephew, John Gielgud, has it today, and his mother Katie had it to a lesser degree. These three have left a picture, not only of the contemporary theatre, but of contemporary life, that remains as a permanent record of their separate generations.

1876 was a significant year for Terrys. Ellen, 'trailing clouds of glory', exchanged the Bancroft management for that of John Hare, at the Court, Sloane Square. At this theatre she made a blazing success as Olivia in W. G. Wills's adaptation of *The Vicar of Wakefield*, and got her divorce from Watts: of which she proceeded to make the most unfortunate possible use.

In September of that same year, Marion—so far shadowed by her elder sister—had her first notable opportunity in a play called *Dan'l Druce, Blacksmith*, by W. S. Gilbert, at the Haymarket Theatre. She had had some success at the Strand in trivial comedies, but had never had a part to 'get her teeth into' until she played Dorothy. In the cast at the Haymarket were Hermann Vezin, Henry Howe, Odell and Johnston Forbes-Robertson—the last deeply in love with her sister Ellen.

It was little Katie Lewis's first visit to the theatre. Of it, she left in her autobiography an enchanting impression. Kate was ill ('I think Mother must have had a quinsy'), and Sarah took her granddaughter. They sat in a box—the beautiful, ageing lady with the weight of her experience behind her: the sometime strolling player who now, in a great London theatre, assisted at her daughter's success. Two generations and a whole range of disparate experience separated her from excited little Katie, at whose age—just eight years old—her mother and her aunt Nell, children of the stage, took for granted all the hardships and discipline of the player's life: none of which Katie and her sisters, with their governesses, nurses and nursemaids, their lessons in French and German, their

---

[1] See *The Story of My Life*, Ellen Terry.

hand-picked companions and cosy, cocoon-like routine of 'little gentlewomen' would ever know. Those four beautifully mannered little girls stood to Sarah for confirmation of something towards which she had struggled through long, harsh years. Answering Katie's excited questions, watching her lovely Polly with the dove-like voice in the dove-coloured gown, and glorying in her triumph, did Sarah Terry hope that her daughters Marion and Florence would soon, like Kate, find rich, kind, understanding husbands, who would remove them from the precarious world of the theatre and 'place' them in a society for which she had a somewhat exaggerated respect? It does not seem unlikely.

Yet—*désenchantée* as she may have been—Sarah preserved her loyalty to The Profession. Ellen Terry had a story that, on a fogbound London day, her mother said it was impossible for her to get to the Lyceum. When this story came to his ears, Fred Terry exploded with rage. 'It could *never* have been mother. It must have been Boo. Mother would have said, "You must get to the theatre if you walk all the way!"' (Which, actually, she did; she was then living in Barkston Gardens. The tap of a blind man's stick sounded on the pavement, and Ellen rushed down the steps. 'Do you know the way to the Lyceum?' He did, and, clinging to his arm, Irving's leading Lady was delivered in safety to the stage door.)

It is perhaps of interest that while her aunt Marion's performance in *Dan'l Druce* made an ineradicable impression on small Katie, she remembered nothing of her aunt Ellen in *New Men and Old Acres* at the Court in the same year. Kate Lewis—later Kate Terry Gielgud—was one of a by no means negligible section of the playgoing public who placed Marion above her sister Ellen as an actress. There was no prejudice about it; it was the considered judgement of a very intelligent woman who, no actress herself, had a cultural background which entitled her to opinions sometimes at odds with those of the average critic.

Among Ellen Terry's colleagues at the Court was Charles Kelly, a hearty young actor whose patronymic was Wardell. He was the son of a parson, and had fought through the Crimean War. Among her innumerable suitors he was 'on the short list'; the most favoured at the moment was Johnston Forbes-Robertson, and no

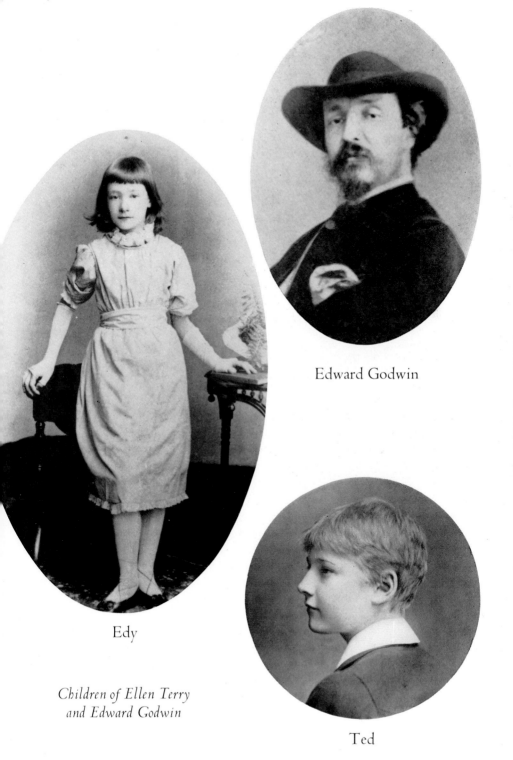

Edward Godwin

Edy

*Children of Ellen Terry
and Edward Godwin*

Ted

Marion Terry

two men could have presented a greater contrast, Kelly *l'homme moyen sensuel* and Forbes-Robertson the romantic. Each in his different way was a good sound artist; each was in love with Ellen, and apparently prepared to take on, in addition to a beautiful and exigent wife, two stepchildren.

More than a lover, she needed at that moment a husband to help and advise her in handling those spoilt and headstrong children, those little gods of her idolatry, whom she had encouraged in every way to consider themselves exceptional: 'My poor children!' she still called them, when she was in her seventies and they in their fifties. She never lived down the Victorian sense of guilt that threaded its morbid streak through the golden web of her bohemianism.

So she decided that she would get married, and give Edy and Ted a father and a name they could call their own.

There is an admittedly apocryphal flavour about the circumstances of her marriage to Charles Kelly: yet it was vouched for in later years by her brother Fred, whose memory was no sharper than his regard for the plain truth. Fred was twelve years old when his sister Nell made up her mind for the second time to get married: but who to choose from those many suitors?—with none of whom she was seriously in love. The story goes that she wrote all their names down on strips of paper, which she dropped into a hat; Fred held the hat and shook it up, and Ellen, with closed eyes, drew out the fatal ticket—or, according to another version, Fred did the drawing.

Ellen Terry married Charles Kelly 'secretly' during the run of *The Vicar of Wakefield*. His triumph over his rivals went to Kelly's head; that night he was drunk in the wings. Forbes-Robertson, the poet, the idealist, came in from the Haymarket after his love-scene with Marion, took in the situation with horror, and said to Ellen, 'You *couldn't* marry a man like that!' And she, turning her pale eyes on him: 'You're too late; I was married to him this morning.'

Ben Terry, to whom his Nelly had admitted her *tendresse* for Charles Kelly, had warned her of Kelly's addiction to 'the bottle'; to which she blithesomely replied, 'Oh, but I shall reform him!' She, most beloved of his children, had already cut him to the quick, first in her desertion of the stage, and then by her liaison with Godwin; his comment on her second marriage was, 'It's a princess' (one of his pet-names for her was 'duchess') 'marrying a cellarman.'

It was hardly a fair comment on Charles Kelly, who came of a good family, and was, within his limited range, a good actor; who was *bon viveur* but not drunkard, and, though violent tempered and inclined to be jealous, essentially kind, and affectionate to his stepchildren—who now were called Wardell. Edy liked him (she had disliked her own father); pig-headed little Ted got a wrong idea of him. . . . 'I suppose my mother objected to Charles Kelly flourishing his hunting crop at us in the Lord of the Manor style, when we made a beastly noise in the morning.' This, according to Edith Craig, was an invention; it could easily be. Both of Ellen's children were addicted to invention: not to deliberate lying, but to the presentation of facts in a becoming or advantageous light to themselves, or to anyone they happened to favour.

So the second of Ellen's luckless marriages took place—and lasted just five years. She created no notable sensation as Lady Teazle in 1877—the year of Marion's triumph as Belinda Treherne in W. S. Gilbert's farcical comedy, *Engaged*, when she proved herself an exquisite comedienne, of a finesse that at first a little baffled audiences accustomed to the broader methods of her contemporaries and rivals: to Mrs Bancroft, signalling with a *moue*, a lift of the eyebrows or a gesture that a laugh was coming. For a few nights, Marion's dead-pan dropping of one of her excruciating lines (Gilbert's dialogue was at its worst Lytton Bulwer, at its best Victorian chit-chat) missed fire: then, warmed up by her love-scenes with Forbes-Robertson, the audiences gradually caught on to a type of humour of which Marion Terry may fairly be said to have been a pioneer, the throwaway, the deliberate understatement. ('If I had allowed my face to express those absurd lines,' she said in later years, 'I'd have burst out laughing; and the comedian who laughs at himself is lost.') So the house rocked when Marion smilelessly uttered, 'I am glad, sir, that you are pleased with my modesty. It has often been admired.'

Kate Lewis went often to rehearsals, criticizing and coaching her sister's performance; Ben and Sarah, at home, were lovingly ruthless about words and lines. Charlie Terry, who was present at many of those fireside coachings, said latterly, 'Polly wasn't capable of going wrong on timing'—perhaps the most valuable of all qualities for the actress. Poor Charlie, watching and envying—and wondering if he had got his accounts right at the office, and if that last shipment he had seen through Customs was up to standard, and if his current girl friend was entertaining one of his rivals, while he and Tom sat on the parental hearth, stoking the fire, and Polly was put relentlessly through her elocutionary paces by Dad and Mama.

The domestic scene was not yet broken up—although young Ben was away in India, and George had married and, to the distress of his parents, had become a Catholic (his wife's religion). The three younger boys were at home, so was Marion, and, when not in the provinces, so was Florence. Kate and her family were in close call, and Ellen, now Mrs Wardell in Longridge Road, was within easy walk of Moray Lodge on the other side of Kensington High Street. It was on Longridge Road, Earl's Court—whose reputation in the 1870s was higher than today—that Henry Irving descended from the relative grandeur of Grafton Street,[1] to engage Ellen Terry as his leading lady in his forthcoming production of *Hamlet* at the Lyceum, of which he had just become sole lessee.

With characteristic ruthlessness he had bought out and disposed of his former fellow-lessee, Isabella Bateman, who had played an admirable Queen Mary to his Philip II. With characteristic arrogance he had not put himself out to see Ellen Terry's Olivia, in the Wills version of *The Vicar of Wakefield*, which was the talk of the town. For the first time since she left the Bancroft management she had a part built to her measure—Hare had commissioned it for her—and sensational support: Hermann Vezin as the Vicar, William Terriss as Thornhill—and Charles Kelly ought to have played Burchell; he had given excellent performances as Mr Brown in *New Men and Old Acres*, and as the farmer in Reade's adaptation of Tennyson's *Dora*. His successes had gone a little to his head; he was offended at not being offered the Vicar, and took himself out of the cast. (But up to the time of their separation he played lead to Ellen Terry in all her provincial tours that filled in the Lyceum vacations, and was, according to her account—with which

[1] The house carries a commemorative tablet over the side entrance of Asprey's.

contemporary critics agreed—a 'splendid' Benedick to her Beatrice).
Young Norman Forbes (half-brother of Johnston Forbes-Robertson)
played Moses in the Court production of *Olivia*, and Edy and Ted
walked on.

To anyone unacquainted with Irving's egoism it must seem incredible that he never troubled to see this Olivia which made the
kind of sensation in the 'seventies that Peggy Ashcroft in *Rosmersholm* made nearly a century later. But Irving never had the slightest
interest in the work of any of his great contemporaries; or, one
wonders, could it be that, in the long night watches, he had salutary
doubts of his own pre-eminence, and preferred not to have his self-
assurance shaken by some involuntary, private comparison with
such artists as Coquelin, Bernhardt and Guitry *ainé*, whose performances in London he always took pains to avoid? That, if it
were so, would be a sign of grace. But it is unlikely; he was already,
when he came to Longridge Road in 1878, the tutelary god of the
Lyceum, taking adulation for granted, somewhat carried away—
as was not unnatural—by his rise from *nothing* to theatrical and
social eminence.

The exquisite Olivia at the Court had been represented to him
by people on whose judgement he relied, as a good investment: a
suitable artistic consort for one who already saw himself as what,
eventually, he became: the Majesty of the English stage.

At that first meeting he was struck by her beauty—and by something more. From her girlhood Nelly Terry had had that disposition
to reverence which betrayed her into her first disastrous marriage
and into her association with Godwin. She had seen, and been
deeply affected by, Irving's Hamlet and his King Philip. It is
unlikely that their first meeting was not coloured by her impressions
of these, and that Irving was not aware of it. The situation might
well be summed up in the words of Dickens:

> Whose Knowledge of the World
> Though somewhat extensive
> Never brought him acquainted with
> A SPIRIT
> More capable of
> Looking Up To Him.

The inscription on the tomb of Ethelinda, Reverential Wife of

Mr Thomas Sapsea, admirably applies not only to Ellen Terry's approach to Henry Irving, but to his attitude to her. Even when, as inevitably happened, he fell in love with her, it is questionable that Irving ever recognized the genius of Ellen Terry, except as an accessory to his own. A natural actor, he had no intellectuality; was never known to read a book unless it had direct bearing on the part he was studying. He never shared her wide-ranging interest in the development of the theatre, in painting or poetry—save in so far as these could serve his professional interests.

Carried away by his prestige, his personality and his looks (which latter, to any artist, were overwhelming—Godwin's friend Whistler had painted a full-length study of Irving as Philip II which Irving did not like: in his estimation it was not sufficiently flattering), Ellen Terry accepted her first contract, Ophelia to Irving's Hamlet, at the Lyceum. He insisted that she should come down to Birmingham to see the performance. Meek as a lamb, down she went, to learn what was expected of her from her actor-manager. It was a new sort of meekness for Ellen Terry; it did not quite fit in with her relationship with her new husband, Charles Kelly.

In regard to this period, Marion was drily to say, 'Nobody seems to remember that there was a time when *I* was the Terry of the age!' Marion, unfortunately, had no Irving to lift her to glory. Yet, on her own merits, she had a great following: there was almost as much fury between the respective supporters of Ellen and Marion Terry as there had been, in old Bristol days, between the supporters of Kate Terry and Henrietta Hodson. Ellen, with her fabulous, as one of her admirers wrote, her 'mystical' beauty, and her appeal to both sexes and to all classes of audience, 'got away with murder': with lines imperfectly memorized, business that might vary according to her mood (a heinous offence in The Profession which, in the course of twenty years, had formalized itself) and eccentricities which alternately maddened and bedazzled her authors and producers.[1] (At that period the terms were largely synonymous.)

Those under Ellen's deathless spell were unlikely to appreciate the serious, the deeply conscientious work, of Marion, who, although

[1] The term 'producer' has now been replaced in the theatre by 'director', but it is used in its original sense throughout the first two parts of this book.

study came hard to her, was never satisfied unless word-perfect, unless she had realized to her intellectual utmost the part she was playing.

Ellen acted as a lark sang. It is not to say she had the joyous irresponsibility of a lark. To the last of her performances, she suffered torment on her first nights; was physically and mentally wracked—as all players are. According to her own descriptions, all first nights were hell (every actress would say the same), but afterwards the lark soared. 'Cast care aside, Lean on thy Guide, His boundless mercy Will provide!'—as grandparents Terry and Ballard must often have sung in the meeting.

Marion never 'cast care aside', never soared, to that degree. But the naked partisanship of Kate Terry Gielgud for her aunt Marion, as against her aunt Ellen, is not wholly a matter of prejudice. Marion Terry was already, at the end of the eighth decade of the nineteenth century, a great actress: a beautiful, elegant, accomplished young actress, who went from strength to strength; whose light was a little dimmed by her sister Ellen's *fata morgana*, but whose quality was recognized by those whose judgement of the art of the theatre was not blinded by their emotional reaction to Ellen's charm.

And Florence—'darling Floss'?

She was shedding her light on the provinces; playing leads in Manchester, Liverpool, Edinburgh and Glasgow, in plays her sisters made famous in town. She played Marion's Dorothy in *Dan'l Druce*, Ellen's Olivia, as well as the part Tom Taylor had written for her in *Lady Clancarty* (which never came to town). The name of Terry was good for a lead anywhere in the North. None of her Press notices seems to have survived; sweet, gay Florence, who had so much of her father in her, does not appear to have taken herself seriously as an actress—although others did. She would hardly have been offered the part of Nerissa to her sister Ellen's Portia at the Lyceum if she had been no more than a charming amateur; nor is it credible that Irving, even for Ellen's sake, would have lent himself to the Farewell performance of a mediocre actress.

She came back from the provinces to play the lead in a piece of claptrap called *Ellen; or Love's Cunning*, at the Haymarket, and when this came off, went out with her brother-in-law Charles Kelly, as Lilian Vavasour (Ellen's creation) in *New Men and Old Acres*.

Florence Terry never had the privilege of creating a part; it was her lot always to follow or understudy her famous sisters. She had no envy and, it would appear, little ambition. In her beautiful, confused description of the Lyceum *Merchant of Venice*, 1880, Ellen makes no mention of her sister's Nerissa. According to Edgar Pemberton (no very reliable authority), Florence was 'a very pretty and engaging Nerissa'. The play ran two hundred and fifty nights (the longest run ever known for *The Merchant*), and Florence was offered the part of Lady Ellen in *The Iron Chest*, which followed it. (Irving had meant to put on *The Iron Chest* before *The Merchant of Venice*, but, having been taken on a cruise to the Levant by his patroness, the Baroness Burdett Coutts—that same whom Charles Kean, twenty years earlier, had aspired to marry—was infected by the Levantine atmosphere; and there was nothing in Colman's drama for Ellen Terry.)

So 'darling Floss' played out her engagement at the Lyceum, and thereafter appears to have taken little serious interest in the professional theatre. Her love for acting was happily fulfilled in amateur performances (notably at Whistler's White House); amateur theatricals had an immense vogue in the mid-nineteenth century, and actors and actresses of rank and fashion delighted in showing off their talents (whatever these amounted to) in private houses, of which the most charming and well equipped was Campden House with its romantic gardens and its Hanoverian atmosphere, and the most curious Mr Charles Dickens's miniature theatre at Tavistock House in Bloomsbury. The White House was very 'fashionable', with indulgent private audiences and supper to follow.

It is interesting that around this period both Marion and Florence are frequently 'seedy' or 'not the thing', and both visiting the famous Dr (Morell) Mackenzie. It is hardly surprising, for, apart from their professional engagements, they were leading a hectic social life. Florence's diary becomes a record of balls, dances, 'crushes' and private views. At home she read Hazlitt and Henry James; arranged flowers, kept her room in order and spent much time with Nell. A significant name appears in her diary—'Willie' —usually followed by two exclamation marks. 'Willie comes in the evening! No *doubt*. V.nice!' 'Letter from Willie!!' 'Gilbert's At Home, 5-12, was very jolly indeed. Willie Fred & Polly were there(!!)' 'Willie' was a very wealthy young lawyer, William Morris, of the firm Ashurst, Morris and Crisp, which, specializing in Company law, had a reputation not confined to London, but also in high esteem 'abroad'. Over the next thirty years, William Morris's affairs were to knit themselves closely into those of the Terry family.

William Morris was tall, dark, austere and handsome, with brown eyes and thick black hair (he went to a fancy dress ball in Turkish costume, and looked more Eastern than any pasha): a type to appeal to small, romantic Floss. In some ways he was a typical lawyer, but under a veneer of ice he was (according to his daughter Olive) 'mysterious and kindly'.

On 3 January 1882, Florence wrote in her little black cloth diary (later it was of red leather, initialled F.M. in gilt) the one word 'Engaged'.

That was the year and the month when the Terry girls implemented their long-discussed project of moving the family from Camden Town to the more genteel purlieus of Earl's Court. 57 Cathcart Road was almost within a stone's throw of Ellen who, in Longridge Road, cheek by jowl with such famous, or about to become famous characters as D. S. MacColl, George Macdonald and Marie Corelli, was, as usual, living far beyond her income, what with the children, Boo, Bo, domestic service and the hired brougham which conveyed her to and from the Lyceum. Cathcart Road was also within walking distance of Moray Lodge, and of Campden House Road, where William and Florence were presently to set up house. In the following year, when Tom Terry married his first wife, known to the family as 'Edie Tom', he settled in Earl's Court, at 24 Fopstone Road—an address which has now vanished from the directory. So, although the home was broken up, the tribal spirit persisted.

Marion went to stay with Kate over the removal from Camden Town, and Florence to Longridge Road, where, in Ellen's absence (she was playing in Brighton), she had the care of her nephew and niece, Ted and Edy, to whom she always showed angelic forbearance and affection. In the midst of getting her own home ready, of buying furniture at Shoolbred's and ordering her trousseau, she looked after Ellen's children as she was presently to look after

Minnie, Charles's child prodigy daughter—though, by then, she had children of her own to care about. The most selfless and generous of Sarah's four daughters, 'darling Floss' may well be her epitaph.

On the eve of Flossie's marriage there was a minor disaster. She wore her beautiful hair, at night, in two long thick plaits. What drama, on the wedding morning, to find one of them missing! Enough to send any bride into hysterics, to finger that patch of stubble, where once had been the silken braid. But not light-hearted Floss. She coiled the surviving locks underneath her veil and went serenely to the altar. It was not until the end of the honeymoon that the mystery was solved.

Among the oddments she then collected from Cathcart Road was the hatbox in which she kept her riding topper. Back in her new home in Campden House Road, she—or her maid—lifted the lid, and there coiled round the brim of the hat, was the shining plait which, in her last virginal sleep, she had cut off, and, climbing on a chair to reach the top of the wardrobe, had laid as a wreath round the crown of the hat which she had worn on so many happy occasions of her girlhood.

FIRST INTERVAL
Historical

During the eighth and ninth decades of the nineteenth century the Theatre underwent vast changes; structural, artistic, moral and social. The opening within four years of no fewer than nine new theatres reflects the mood of the times. A wealthy aristocracy, unplagued by Income Tax and Death Duties, a prosperous bourgeoisie with grandeurs and snobisms of its own, and lower classes which, in spite of poverty unimaginable today, contrived to indulge in their own jollifications, of which the Theatre was outstanding, brought a resurgence of enthusiasm for the Drama reminiscent of the palmy days of the first Elizabeth, although unfortunately there was no Shakespeare to embody it, and no direction from the Throne.

With the death of George IV aesthetic twilight had descended on the Court. Stubbornly submerged in mourning for her blameless Consort, the Widow of Windsor had, in any case, no taste for the serious theatre; when, in her old age, she revived command performances at the Castle, her preference was for farce, or for anything with 'a good, clear plot' which she, Victoria, could see through and, turning to her ladies, commend with, 'There! You didn't expect that, did you?'—the inference being that Majesty's omniscient eye had foreseen it from the start.

The Queen did not care to have about her people whose taste and education were superior to her own, so, although it is not to be questioned that there were many such in her entourage, all found it politic to conceal their talents—with the result that High Society no longer acted as cultural leaders to society at large, and the lightest of light entertainment came into vogue, such as would attract without overstraining the fashionable harebrains who escaped the ponderous solemnity of the Court.

To satisfy a moneyed clientèle, managers proceeded to re-style their houses; 'voluptuous comfort for the playgoer' was a primary consideration, and in this minor revolution the crinoline played no small part, the ladies requiring space for their spreading petticoats.

The old-fashioned pit benches were replaced by *fauteuils*, the cramped little boxes by open tiers supported on pillars rooted in what were to become the stalls. A few *avant-garde* managers abolished the pillars (which obstructed the view of ground-floor patrons) and installed a shallow circle, backed by small open boxes, pre-dating the modern cantilever. Floors and stairs were carpeted in tune with the Victorian mystique, to which physical comfort was of the first importance. No such improvements came in the way of the players, who continued to occupy their small, ill-lit, ill-ventilated and inconvenient loose-boxes behind the stage; but it will be remembered that dressingrooms still fulfilled only a strictly utilitarian purpose; for their relaxation and for the waits between their entrances actors and actresses used the greenroom, where they could receive privileged friends and, on receiving their calls, could touch up their make-up and costumes at the large and well-lit mirrors before going into the wings. Few dressingrooms in those days had more than a small square of looking-glass, just big enough to reflect the head and shoulders of the artist.

The most important innovation, from the point of view of actors and audience, was the lighting. The spermaceti candles and oil-lamps had long been replaced by gas—with disastrous results. According to an article in *The Builder* in 1856 'The fate of a theatre is to be burned. It seems simply a question of time.' Gas had been installed, partially or throughout, between 1817 and 1827, and during that decade theatre fires more than doubled their numbers.

To begin with, its use was mainly confined to the auditorium. When tried on the stage, its effect was generally considered inferior to that of candles and lamps. Dutton Cook wrote that, since the time of Garrick, little had been done except to increase the *quantity* of light. That would seem likely, for the delicate illusion of wax and oil was not to be captured by the new form of lighting. Gas added to the dangers and discomforts of the players who, dazzled by the glare of the floats, felt a loss of contact with audiences whose faces became nothing but rows of pale bubbles beyond a hissing yellow barrier. When forced downstage, they complained that the roaring heat of the jets melted their make-up and dissolved their false beards and moustaches off their faces; it was not uncommon for a minor member of the Company (principals spent most of their time well upstage) to start a scene fully hirsute and end it with a jowl as clean as a baby's. And it did not contribute to the charm of the ladies when, advancing towards the audience, their complexions were seen to be running in rivulets into their bosoms. Apart from what may be described as occupational disasters, a much more serious result of 'the gas-light's glitter' was the blindness from which, in their old age, many players suffered.

Experience, however, disposed of much of the crudity of the original gas-lighting. Henry Irving, at the Lyceum, achieved with primitive materials effects unheard of in the Theatre of ten years before, using coloured scrim over wire guards to produce gradations of lighting—a method which must have chilled the blood of insurance companies and fire chiefs. Irving was not the first to use scrim and wire, but he was the first to break his floats up into blocks of various colours, independently controlled, so that changes of lighting could take place while the scene was actually in progress.

Gas was followed by 'limelight' which created some magical effects through the blending and crossing of different-coloured beams and had yet, as 'the spot', to be abused as a means of concentrating the audience's attention on the principal actor. Elder playgoers may recall Messrs Beerbohm Tree and Arthur Bourchier dickering for the spot in a melodrama called *The Right to Kill* at His Majesty's Theatre, during the First World War; their artfulness being received with roars of glee from the gallery; and Lady Bancroft is said to have protested that in a scene with Irving she had never caught a glimpse of her husband except the lower part of his legs.

And so—Electricity.

It had already been tried on façades, foyers and staircases. In 1860 the Paris Opera, in a production called *Mosè in Egitto*, tried it for the first time on the stage, in a primitive form of arc-light.

The first English theatre to be lit throughout with electricity was the Savoy, built in 1881 by D'Oyly Carte for Gilbert and Sullivan opera. 'This will be the first time', trumpeted *The Times*, 'that any theatre or public building will have been illuminated in every part by electricity alone.'

Change of lighting was followed, inevitably, by change of makeup. The old, dry *maquillage*, with fuller's earth, rice powder, powdered antimony, dry rouge and burnt cork as its main ingredients, could not stand up to the scorching heat of gas-light, which sucked it into the pores. Cursory cleaning with a greasy towel was not effective, and the mark—off-stage—of the 'professional' was a coarse, un-healthy skin.

Grease-paints, the invention of a Bavarian opera singer, Ludwig Leichner, came on the market, and revolutionized the art of make-up. Feeding, instead of impoverishing, the skin, they had a kind of luminosity, exquisitely becoming to women—although the latter, disliking their oiliness, were slower than men in taking to them. But the superiority of grease over dry colour, its durability and the natural effect it produced, quickly brought it into common use with both sexes—although the die-hards[1] clung to their familiar make-up, regardless of the skin diseases, the blood poisonings and the occasional death (white lead, common cosmetic of Georgian beauties, was still in use at the time of which we are speaking) that followed their use.

It would be pleasant to record that these advances in what might be termed the common mechanics of the theatre were matched in the quality of the fare offered to audiences of the 'seventies and 'eighties.

In 1871 the Philharmonic Theatre—currently known as the Spittoon—having already presented to its customers a bowdlerized version of the can-can, boldly staged Offenbach's *Gèneviéve de Brabant*, with Soldene and Dolly Dolaro as its principal attractions and, for good measure, a bevy of easy-going beauty in the bar: and created a furore. Opera bouffe hit the town and, for the next eleven or twelve years, carried all before it.

Opera bouffe was French, it was naughty, it was the antithesis of Victorian prunes and prisms, against which, it now appeared, the bulk of the public was in rebellion. Seasoned with burlesque and absurdity, opera bouffe titillated the jaded palate of the con-temporary playgoer and offered an escape from contemporary hypocrisy. Bored with dramas and melodramas in which virtue

---

[1] Ellen Terry used dry make-up to the end; but nature had endowed her and most of her family with a magnolia-like skin, of so radiant a pallor that it needed the mere touch of the hare's foot to kindle it into beauty that 'outburned Canopus'.

triumphed and vice was punished, in which the heroine was the 'pretty maid of seventeen', the hero a cross between Lancelot and Galahad and the villain 'black as the Earl of Hell's riding boots', audiences turned with relief towards a fresh convention. The heroine was no longer the wife or sweetheart, but the mistress; love-making was conducted with the tongue in the cheek; the climax was not happy marriage but successful seduction. A link between Restoration comedy and twentieth-century revue, the humour of opera bouffe was *un peu faisandé*, its situations off-beat and its dialogue not such as would have got by at Windsor Castle.

The works of Offenbach, Suppé, Lecocq, Hervé and Strauss went through the country like a prolonged epidemic—and their production was not confined to the 'light' theatres. The managements of (among others) the Strand, Globe and the St. James's used opera bouffe to recoup their losses on drama. Needless to say, the new style in entertainment was not patronized by the virtuous bourgeoisie; fathers did not take their families, or young men their fiancées or sisters. It was considered 'fast' for an unmarried woman to be seen at a performance of *La Cigale, La Vie Parisienne* or *Vert-Vert*—to pick at random three current titles; but opera bouffe played consistently to full houses, subsidized managements and made possible the engagement (for limited seasons) of such expensive artists as the Kendals (she, when Madge Robertson, had been Kate Terry's rival at the Bristol Theatre Royal), Mrs Bernard Beere[1] (ex-barmaid at the Alhambra, described by Sarah Bernhardt as 'a superb actress' in the part of Lena Despard in *As In a Looking Glass*) and, shall we add, Miss Marion Terry.

It was said by Oscar Wilde that tragedy flourishes when a race or a country is at the zenith of its power. Such was emphatically not the case in those prosperous, mid-Victorian years. The lightest of light entertainment, varied by genteel domestic comedy and an occasional old-fashioned melodrama, was good enough for our great-grandparents, although a certain sober element showed appreciation for serious theatre. Plays like Gilbert's *Dan'l Druce*, in which Marion

---

[1] Mrs Bernard Beere came of respected parentage. Her father (Frank White-head) was a minor painter, but his early death and the subsequent poverty of his widow and daughter obliged the latter to earn her living 'in any way within the scope of virtue'.

Terry made her first outstanding success, following it up by an exquisite performance as the blind girl in a ranting melodrama called (in its English version) *The Two Orphans*, and by the title-role in *Gretchen*, Gilbert's adaptation of *Faust*, attracted a limited public and had short runs. (Of the last the critic Edgar Pemberton wrote that 'if the piece failed to draw the multitude, it was no fault of the author'.) A wooden young actor at the Lyceum was bombarding managements with a series of plays that ranged from farce to drama, and was soon known to the public as Arthur Wing Pinero, and another young man who (his detractors said) was inclined to mistake the stage for the pulpit, was nevertheless making headway; his name was Henry Arthur Jones. He had nothing like the versatility of Pinero and his dialogue was clumsy and lacking in the realism of his rival's, but these two young dramatists, limited as was their horizon, helped to advance the art of playwriting something beyond the mediocre and artificial standards which Lytton and Boucicault (among others) had imposed on the theatre. Pinero was to write at least one play which, more than half a century later, is still in the repertory of every leading actress: *The Second Mrs Tanqueray*. *The Notorious Mrs Ebbsmith* and *The Gay Lord Quex* (Pinero had a flair for titles), though probably unacceptable today, were good examples of his ripening talent.

It was not until the beginning of the final decade of the century that Ibsen (introduced to London by the Dutch visionary, J. T. Grein) put gunpowder under the accepted notions of dramatics with *The Doll's House*; that Oscar Wilde redeemed the innate banality of his pastiches of Society by the brilliance of his dialogue (and wrote one immortal comedy, *The Importance of Being Earnest*, which, in the opinion of at least one critic, the undergraduate Edward Marsh, was 'the greatest thing since Sheridan'); that Shaw (endeavouring to imitate Ibsen) presented *Widowers' Houses*.

Meanwhile, the great talents of contemporary actors were frittered away on the lath-and-plaster inventions of contemporary playwrights, whose one (subconscious) object seems to have been to avoid approach to human realities.

Only two theatres, the Lyceum and the Haymarket, stood consistently for 'high quality' entertainment: the former, dominated by the overwhelming personality of Irving, the latter, under the

Bancroft management, its closest rival. (In order to maintain the standard he set himself, Bancroft, in 1880, abolished the Pit, provoking first-night riots in the cheaper parts of the house.)

There was more than a little in common between the two actors: astute men of business, flamboyant personalities, consummate showmen and past masters in the exploitation of their individual talents. Highly picturesque, immensely vain and dedicated to the upholding of the dignity of The Profession, neither had a glimmer of the intellectual and humanitarian possibilities implicit in their art. Their notion of production was 'situations', no matter how false or exaggerated in sentiment, that would draw cheers from the gallery; a 'banger' to bring down the curtain. Irving swaggered about the town with long hair, a 'wide-awake' and a fur-collared overcoat; Bancroft swaggered about with a top-hat, an eyeglass and a cane.[1] Neither of them ever ceased acting, on the stage or off. In days before 'publicity' was commercialized, each was his own best publicity agent.

If Irving, of the two, was taken more seriously as an actor, it was because he presented Shakespeare. He also rated as a tragedian, which was regarded as superior, in the hierarchy of the theatre, to the exponent of comedy or farce. It is difficult to see why; almost any novice can make an impression in a tragic role, but it takes long acquaintance with tragedy and apprenticeship to the pure technique of acting to produce a comedian. All the great comedians, from Deburau to Chaplin, owe their *maîtrise* to the tragic *fond*. No tragedian is complete without that comic awareness—which, in Irving, was lacking; which he strove to replace by satire, a quality ungrateful to the British character. What he possessed, *in excelsis*, was the power of imposing his own personality on the public, to such a degree that, even before Ellen Terry became his leading lady, the Great Irving Myth was already established. He had a kind of personal grandeur.

He was unaware of any essential difference between the plays of Shakespeare and the cheap dramas that alternated with them at

---

[1] I remember Squire Bancroft in the nineteen-twenties, then known as the Ghost of Piccadilly, a magnificent white-haired, black-browed, monocled old gentleman, sallying forth from Albany on his weekly visit to his bank, where he scrupulously checked his current account.

Ellen Terry 1878

Florence Morris and her
children: Olive, Geoffrey
and Jack

Fred Terry

Julia Neilson

the Lyceum;[1] his touchstone, so far as plays were concerned was, What did they offer *him* in the way of parts, of dressing up, of verbal fireworks, hairbreadth escapes or heroic dénouement?

It has already been said that Irving was never known to read a book unless it had some bearing on his current or projected production. His private collection of pictures and drawings, sold at Christie's in 1905, indicates no appreciation of art, as apart from the theatre. Yet he had the acumen to employ such artists as Alma Tadema, Seymour Lucas, Ford Madox Brown, Burne-Jones and Hawes Craven for his scenery and costumes—names which carry no weight today but were respected in their time. And once at least he reached into the future, when he commissioned a poster from J. and W. Beggarstaff, the *nom de guerre* of two unknown young artists, William Nicholson and James Pryde, who were revolutionizing the art of the poster. By that time (1894) he had learned something—although he would not have admitted it—from Ellen Terry. That the fine Don Quixote poster never reached the hoardings was no fault of the Beggarstaffs; the play was never produced, and of it no record remains except the poster, which Ellen Terry treasured at Smallhythe.

There were some who considered Irving the greater artist of the two, and others who tolerated him only for the sake of his enchanting partner.

From all I have read and heard from his contemporaries (including Ellen Terry), it would not appear that Irving, as an actor, had the qualities of immortality. In comparison with Garrick, he seems too stylized, too inflexible, too egotistical, too shallow. But his imprint on the Theatre of his epoch is indelible. A hero-worship unknown since the days of Garrick built up round the actor-manager of the Lyceum, and was shrewdly fostered by Irving himself. He had learned the value of those eccentricities of gait and enunciation for which, in the past, critics berated him, and used them deliberately to his advantage. He became the apotheosis of what, in the twentieth century, was known as 'The Old Actorr'. As recently as the nineteen-twenties there survived, up and down the Strand and in the purlieus of Leicester Square and Charing Cross Road, prototypes,

---

[1] His outlook was wholly commercial; to an American colleague he is recorded to have said that Shakespeare 'spelt ruin'.

in all but accomplishment, of Henry Irving. The long hair, the spacious gestures and mannered speech evoked the derision of the younger generation; yet those old ghosts, in their pride not only of being but of looking like actors, adumbrated the nobility of Irving's theatre.

In 1881 *Punch* carried a cartoon of three young ladies, holding forth on their ambitions to the new governess.

> *Lady Gwendoline*: Papa says *I'm* to be a great Artist and exhibit at the Royal Academy!
> *Lady Yseult*: And Papa says *I'm* to be a great Pianist and play at the Monday Pops!
> *Lady Edelgitha*: And *I'm* going to be a famous Actress and act Ophelia and cut out Miss Ellen Terry. Papa says I may—that is, if I can, you know!

—to which the new governess suitably expresses her horror, that ladies should practise the arts 'for hire'. Evidently, the aspirations of the younger generation were more leniently viewed by the aristocracy than by the 'genteel' classes.

The mania for amateur theatricals that swept Society during the 'seventies and 'eighties led to a development which might well have been foreseen. Girls who made a *succès fou* in London drawing-rooms yearned to extend the orbit of their triumphs. Impassioned for Ellen Terry, they made the Lyceum their Mecca. It was not difficult, through friends or relations, to make acquaintance of the divine Miss Terry (herself, by then, a figure in Society) and, through her, to get a walk-on at the Lyceum—to the disgust of young women dependent on such work for their livelihood. According to an old actress,[1] the wings 'stank of debs and Debrett', and the patience of authentic members of the Company was much tested by these frivolous invaders, on whom it was impossible to impose the discipline of the theatre.

It offended and surprised many that Ellen Terry, so truly professional in her approach to her work, encouraged these amateurs, but those who accused her of snobbery mistook the innocence of her intent. Undoubtedly, in those early Lyceum days, she was often taken in by young women whose enthusiasm for acting was only a cover for vanity, or for the desire to be close to the goddess of their

[1] The late Kate Phillips, long a member of Irving's Company.

idolatry; who boasted of being her 'ladies-in-waiting' both on and off the stage, and had no faintest intention of taking The Profession seriously, or of sacrificing their social lives to the exigencies of the theatre. She learned in time.

Meanwhile—the Lyceum was the first of the theatres to open its door to the fashionable amateur, an example quickly followed by others, swift to see the advantages of attracting the admirers of the Honourable This or Lady That, whose five minutes' appearance in the 'crowd' was good for a block of stalls or two or three boxes most nights in the week. Miss This and Lady That were gradually permitted to mutter a line or two, and the lot of the professional actress became progressively harder, as the invasion of the stage by amateurs went on. Certain managements became notorious for preferring to engage 'ladies'—ostensibly because their superior education and familiarity with social usage equipped them for parts outside the scope of professionals, but actually because they were indifferent to salaries, and could afford to dress themselves better than the average young actress could do. In all provincial and suburban theatres, and some West End ones, the actress was required to provide her own wardrobe.[1] Many were skilled in making their own costumes, but these could not compete with a gown from a fashionable *couturier*.

It was the thin end of the wedge. Many years elapsed before the unequal competition between amateur and professional was levelled out by the contract which included the provision of costume. (Even then, 'accessories', which included gloves, stockings, shoes and jewellery, took a bite out of small salaries.)

Up to the time of the First World War, only full evening dress was permitted in stalls and dress circle; at matinées (known to The Profession as 'morning performances') ladies wore—and, at the rise of the curtain, removed—their hats or bonnets. The system of queueing had disposed for good of the often dangerous and violent milling for the cheap seats.

The actors—knowing their business—did not avail themselves of artificial means (i.e. the microphone) to project their voices into the auditorium; the cry of 'Speak up!' from pit or gallery reflected disgracefully on the player who evoked it.

[1] Not in all; Julia Neilson's contracts with Tree specify 'Costumes' as well as salary.

PART TWO

PART TWO

CHAPTER ONE

Parents and Children

Earl's Court of the 'seventies and 'eighties had not wholly lost its rural character. There were patches of market garden, from which, before dawn, the wagons set out for Covent Garden Market, and to which local greengrocers went for their supplies, or careful house-wives for apples, pears, plums, a bunch of flowers or a potted plant for the *jardinière*. The little owls came whooping down from Holland Park; on summer evenings the nightingale sang in The Boltons. The stench of petrol and smoke had not yet obliterated the scent of lilac, laburnum and syringa.

The southern boundary line of upper-class cosmogony was generally taken to be the Brompton Road, below which social eminence gradually petered out in the direction of the Chelsea slums; but in the middle of the century the intervening mile be-tween the Brompton and King's Roads (the latter with its many handsome old houses and squares) became a recognized settlement of the prosperous or modestly well-to-do middle classes.

Cathcart Road was a fairly broad street of tall, narrow houses, and, if not aristocratic, was a good-class conventional address and a distinct advance on Stanhope Street, which, with surrounding property, was rapidly deteriorating as rows of jerry-building crowded in upon it. Many of the larger houses had been turned into lodging houses, for a not wholly desirable class of boarder—and the old home where the four youngest Terrys were born was inconvenient for an ageing couple, as their children one after another flew the coop.

Number 57 was on the south side of the road (the north side was considered the better); a steep flight of half a dozen steps, spanning the area, led up to the door which opened into a narrow hall, with, at its farther end, an even steeper and narrower flight of stairs. Counting its basement, 57 Cathcart Road was built on five floors, with a room and a 'slip' on each—which today would be considered an undesirable proposition for elderly people, but which Ben (in spite of shortness of breath) and Sarah (slowed down by time and increasing weight) seem to have taken in their stride. In comparison with 92 Stanhope Street it was rather 'grand', according to Victorian ideas. It was actually not nearly so pretty or well proportioned.

The neighbours were sedate and self-contained behind their polished door-knockers and their Nottingham lace-draped windows. Each house had its servant, some had two, and a 'girl' who scrubbed the steps and shone the brass and the boots; where there were children there was usually a nursemaid. The husbands, mainly 'in business', a discreet formula used to cover both retail and wholesale trade, departed each morning, top-hatted and umbrellaed, to catch the horse-bus for the City. Some of the wives aped their betters with At Home days, but for the most part the ladies of Cathcart Road were content with tea parties, or, once in a long while, entertaining their husbands' business friends to a midday meal on Sunday. None of which artless occupations interested Mr and Mrs Ben Terry, or roused their curiosity about their neighbours.

But when a handsome elderly gentleman took to appearing, shortly before noon, on the steps of Number 57, and strode down the street with a remarkably elastic movement for a person of his years, the curiosity of Cathcart Street quivered behind the lace curtains. What could be the profession of one who went out at so odd an hour, and appeared to come back at any hour of the afternoon, evening or, presumably, night? He might of course be a retired lawyer's clerk, or tradesman, or Civil Servant: but the description, applied to the dashing person with his long beard, swaggering gait and twirling walking-stick was unconvincing, even to the simple residents of Cathcart Road.

The solution of the mystery came of course from the grapevine of the areas; the Terry's servant gossiped to her neighbour, who rushed to tell her gaping mistress that they were actually living next door to an actor: to Mr Ben Terry, the father, no less, of the famous Ellen Terry. Think of it: an actor in Cathcart Road!

The first shock having subsided, it was generally conceded that Mr Terry was extremely gentlemanly, for an actor—a concession which held good even when the lively Ben was observed to have something more than a roving eye for anything in petticoats. Winking at a pretty servant girl, assuming the grand manner to offer his escort to a young lady crossing the traffic, whistling at an infant in a perambulator to attract the nursemaid's attention— Cathcart Road agreed, for the sake of Mr Terry's famous daughter, to overlook these indiscretions.

But when it came to the arrival of a constant succession of stylish equipages before the steps of Number 57; when rumour had it that these broughams and barouches, drawn by spanking animals, with liveried coachmen and grooms, were kept by the daughters of Mr and Mrs Terry, scandal leapt sky-high. Ellen Terry herself never called on her parents, did she? No; pure as the driven snow, beautiful as an angel, you'd only got to see her at the Lyceum to know her incapable of any baseness. (Ellen's rare visits, in a shabby hackney cab, her swift rush up the steps with one of her pieces of drapery round her head, seem to have escaped the notice of the spies. Pestered by her admirers, she had learned to make her comings and goings as inconspicuous as possible.)

Unaware of, as she would have been indifferent to, gossip, had she known of it—although she would have been very angry at any aspersions cast on the girls—Sarah had aged into beauty. Something of the tragic mask had withdrawn from her calm face, strangely unwrinkled. She still carried herself like a queen. A stranger, meeting her for the first time, might have described her as a serene old lady who had translated all the disturbances and sorrows of her youth into a philosophy which lay like sunshine on her twilight years. One of the blessings of age is said to be a diminution of sensibility; another is forgetfulness. She had forgotten a good deal, and this no doubt contributed to the impression of tranquillity she gave to those who did not know her well. But what she had developed down the years was not a philosophy—she had no philosophical leanings— but a tower of reserve, to which she had learned to retreat in time of need. Through the hooded windows of that tower sometimes the true Sarah looked out with sorrowful penetration.

She had much to be thankful for: her good home, her freedom from pecuniary cares, the devotion of her children. Yet . . .

There were times when the house seemed as empty and silent as a deserted nest.[1] There was time to be lonely, to think and to grieve, although few days passed without proof of the girls' thought for her. If Kate had not time to drive her phaeton, one of the Lewis carriages arrived with a note or a little present (young Mrs Lewis's presents were always practical: some fish, a bottle of wine for Papa, or a discarded bonnet); or it might be the four prim Lewis girls, chaperoned by their French governess, who were sent by Mama to inquire after Grandmama's cough. Of the four, Sarah's favourite was Janet. Katie and Lucy, although sweet girls, were 'just a little too good to be true'. Janet was handsome, bold, spirited and mischievous, always incurring the disapproval of her elder sister. Mabel was a nice child, although nothing much yet in looks or character.

Or it might be darling Floss, arriving from Campden House Road, radiantly pregnant, bubbling over with love and laughter, with accounts of the parties she had been to, and others she was planning; with rapturous descriptions of her baby Olive, and now, very soon, there would be another. How fortunate she was, and how blessed. Sarah listened, and concealed her misgivings. Flossie was so gay and restless—although evidently as happy as a bird. But surely she was doing too much, leading too active a social life? She laughed at warnings: 'Darling Mama! When did you make a fuss of yourself over any of us!' which was unanswerable.

Nelly was always scribbling little notes and sending them round by Bo, of which the burthen was frequently that she was 'so tired', or 'so unwell', but she'd 'soon' come and see her dear Dad and Mama. Sarah was not deceived; she knew without telling that Nell was in trouble again, that the Kelly marriage was on the rocks and Nell infatuated with her new manager; that in spite of her good and steady salary at the Lyceum, she was hard up. She was trying to pay off all the money she had borrowed and the debts she had contracted during the years with Godwin. And now she had the children's education to pay for—they were at Mrs Cole's co-educational school in Earl's Court, but for their own good must soon be sent to boarding school and eventually 'finished' abroad. The

[1] For some years after the move to Cathcart Road, Marion and Fred continued to live with their parents, but their work often took them away from home. And Fred got married.

dedicated actress at last, Ellen's every moment was taken up with her work, with study, rehearsals—and Irving. Such time as she was able to spend in her home she was 'resting': saving herself up for study, rehearsals—and Irving. There was no bitterness in Sarah's heart because she saw less of her daughter Nell—within ten minutes' walk of her parents' home—than of Katie and Floss, north of the Park.

Dear, sensible, dignified Polly, who should, like her sisters, by now have found a husband, was always on tour between her short London engagements.

One of the most interesting parts she was called upon to play was Bathsheba, in Comyns Carr's adaptation of *Far From the Madding Crowd*; both Kate and Florence went up for the production at Liverpool, of which Florence records in her diary that 'Polly played Bathsheba beautifully'. It was very nearly a 'great' part, and perhaps the young actress was not yet ripe for it, for when the play came to town Mrs Bernard Beere was given the lead—a disappointment for Marion and the family. This was on 22 March 1882—the year of Florence's marriage. A week later, Ben, Sarah and Florence went to the first night of *Romeo and Juliet* at the Lyceum, of which Floss wrote sternly, that '*all* the acting except Juliet and the Nurse might be better', and young Katie Lewis lyrically: she fancied herself as a critic, but was actually in a state of hectic enthusiasm for theatre. (The Lewis girls were not allowed to see *Far From the Madding Crowd* when it came to London; Hardy was not *pour les jeunes filles*—any more than Ouida, George Moore and Miss Braddon. The deprivation, for Katie, was not great, since her aunt Marion was not playing.)

There was something about Marion—for ever Polly to her family—that held at bay her innumerable admirers. Too fastidious, too reserved, too demanding in personal relationships, she expected an impossible standard of conduct from the few she favoured with her confidence. Had Polly, her parents wondered, secretly given her heart in some forbidden quarter? If so, no one, least of all the object of her affections, would ever know. And no one knows, to the present day, why this enchanting young woman, warm-hearted, maternal and kind beneath a somewhat freezing exterior towards all but her nearest and dearest, never married. There is the impression of a soul more sensitive than that of any of her brothers and sisters: of an idealism which, in her youth, perhaps received a shock from which it never recovered.

In her sittingroom upstairs the furniture was shrouded, the piano locked, the flower-vases empty. No one arranged flowers like Polly. But no week went by without one or two of her loving letters. As perfectly domesticated as her sisters Kate and Florence, Polly never caused her parents an anxious thought.

After Floss's marriage, only Polly and Fred remained at home: climbing those steep steps, welcoming their friends in the narrow hall. Polly's visitors would find it difficult to believe that their elegant young hostess had spent the afternoon in collecting Fred's washing, and telling the laundress 'not to put any blue' in his theatrical body-linen![1]

Sarah, on the girls' insistence, occasionally took a few days' 'rest' at Moray Lodge or Campden House Road. But what need had she, nowadays, for rest?—an old woman, sitting alone in a silent house. No meals to be rushed on, costumes hurriedly improvised, lines to be heard. No washing, ironing or mending—except an occasional button or patch, a darn in Ben's socks or pants. No need to keep an eye on the clock. No clatter of impatient feet and voices. No disorder to be cleared up. Sometimes no one to speak to from breakfast to supper, except the servant, or the tradesmen's boys delivering at the area door.

After the fullness of her life, did her thoughts go back to the night she played Gertrude to Macready's Hamlet, and he was pleased to approve of her because (according to his own account) 'unlike the run of women, she didn't wear hairpins'? It does not seem likely; she had long said Good-bye to all that. She preferred to let her mind dwell on Nell, starring at the Lyceum, on Polly, enchanting her audiences at the Royalty or St James's, on Fred, earning good notices out in the provinces, and on the most recent Terry recruit to The Profession, Charlie's little Minnie, making a name for herself at the Haymarket. And on Katie and Floss, established in domestic bliss and magnificence on Campden Hill.

Ben and she, by imperceptible degrees, had drawn so far apart that their communications were little more than polite acknowledgements of each other's existence. Every morning he stepped

[1] *Cf.* Sarah Terry's correspondence.

smartly out to join his cronies at the stage doors and in the pubs of
the Strand and Charing Cross Road—where there might be a
chance of 'picking up something'; but for all his courage, his
cheeriness and his popularity, engagements never seemed to come
his way. There were more old actors than there were parts for them
in contemporary plays, and Ben's apprenticeship to provincial drama
was a drawback rather than an asset. Experienced as he was, his
style was too old-fashioned, even for the suburban theatres. The
fact that Lyceum nepotism, which was extended to two of the
Terry boys, as well as to the children of Ellen, did not include their
father would confirm the impression that Ben Terry had more
goodwill than accomplishment.[1]

For all his gay bravado, Ben was finding it hard to make ends
meet. He would have found it equally hard if he had had a pension
of a thousand a year, for money melted through his fingers—which
is almost certainly the reason why his daughters did not make him
a sufficient allowance to secure his independence of the theatre.
They all contributed, according to their means and (in the case of
Ellen and Marion) the fluctuation of their circumstances, but they
were shrewd enough to realize that the people who would mainly
benefit by their generosity would be, not their parents, but Ben's
impecunious friends, his boon companions of the bars: and also
their brothers, who found Papa 'an easy touch' for a pound or two.

A little note from Ellen Terry throws light on Ben's pecuniary
situation:

Dear Dad,
    I don't know whether these odds and ends might perhaps be able to
save your better things in dull weather—if not maybe you know someone to give them to!

Were the 'odds and ends' some of Kelly's leavings? At all events,
cast-off clothing was grateful to the father of the successful (and,
by implication, wealthy) Miss Terrys. 'Surely' (one hears the
shocked voices of some of the critics who eagerly pounce upon the
foibles of the famous) 'Ellen Terry, with all she was earning,
could have afforded to buy her father a new suit!' Perhaps she could;

[1] Henry Irving was particularly fond of engaging 'The Old Actorr' who knew
his business, and on whom he could depend for support.

but she saw no point in giving him a suit for the boys to 'borrow' and wear out.

> I feel very strange at getting no letters from anyone at home. . . .
> Try & write dear a line or two. If unable ask someone at home to drop
> me a line & say all's well.

> I've not had a line from anyone *this year*. Mother dear used to be a
> regular correspondent! But the last I received from her was on Xmas
> Day '83.

Re-reading these letters from her firstborn, Sarah's conscience may have pricked her. But with the failure of her sight and the increasing lassitude that arose less from physical debility than from the want of occupation, the effort of writing those long letters for which poor young Ben craved seemed to be beyond her power, and the longer she put it off the more impossible the task became.

All of her sons except Fred were now married and scattered. About young Ben's marriage no reliable information is available; none of the older generation seemed to remember whom he married, or when. He refers in one of his letters to 'Vic'—who 'has never any sickness to talk of', and in a birthday letter to his Father sends 'Best love from us both', the inference being that 'Vic' was his wife. Ben remembered all his parents' and sisters' birthdays, and wrote with passionate affection and interest of all their doings (which he was left to glean from occasional newspapers or magazines) and, with nostalgia, of the past.

It is hard to imagine the reason for their neglect of their eldest son and brother, for Ben was making an honest living—although he admitted that his lack of advancement was no one's fault but his own. Among various posts he had filled to the apparent satisfaction of his employers were four and a half years (his longest billet) in the Police, Acting Superintendent of Railways, and Contractor on the construction of a new State Railway, but in the autumn of 1884 he was writing from Allahabad:

> That I am restless and soon get tired of a good job to get into another
> not nearly so good is true . . . and that is one part of my composition
> that I can't make out. It is more likely so, but I see so much crawling,
> toadying etc and am disgusted with it all.

This strikes a rare note of pessimism; the letters are for the most part full of courage and jocularity, giving the brightest possible picture of a life which, reading between the lines, must often have been very lonely and dispiriting for home-loving Ben. Whatever were the 'crimes' that accounted in the first place for his exile, it is plain that he repented, and was expiating them to the best of his ability.

George (according to his brother 'the illustrious old G') had settled at Wimbledon, taking himself, his marriage and his carpentry with his usual solemnity. Dull, steady and honest, 'illustrious old G', thanks to his sister Nell, had got himself into the Lyceum as Master Carpenter—and actually went out with the Company on the first American tour. The Georges were not *persona grata* at Cathcart Road; Ben and Sarah did not care for his wife, whom they considered 'ordinary' (a term of mild opprobrium they also applied to the wives of Charlie and Tom), and found her Roman Catholicism offensive. George's ultimate apostasy cut them to the heart and made a breach between him and his parents which was never fully bridged.

The Toms lived inconveniently close, in Fopstone Road, and were for ever in trouble over money, Edie-Tom (as she was known to the family) coming round tearfully to say they had nothing with which to pay the rent, the Gas, Light & Coke, the butcher and baker or the doctor, when the children (they had two: a boy and a girl) were ill. Eventually Tom 'got into trouble' (a Victorian euphemism that might stretch from larceny to embezzlement, or to bigamy, but was always understood to involve the police) and, according to hearsay, his wise and wealthy brothers-in-law came to the conclusion that the more he was apart from his long-suffering family, the better all would be. They all deplored Tom and avoided references to him but, blood being thicker than water, Marion and Florence made him small remittances and Ellen occasionally sent little cheques to Edie-Tom, who became, as time went on, one of the most persistent of her many pensioners. The black sheep of the family is said always to be his mother's favourite, and there is proof in Tom's letters that Sarah was writing to him frequently and sending money he did not always trouble to acknowledge, and that she left him a little money in her will.

In one of Tom's whining letters from Launceston, Tasmania, occurs the ambiguous sentence:

> My dear Father, no one is more alive [than I] to the 'objections' to my domicile in England.

The 'objections' are easily imagined: one would have been the obligation to support his wife and children, or, in the event of divorce, to pay alimony.

Tom Terry's is a squalid story which may be disposed of briefly.

> I have employment for a time at least and I trust it will lead to something better. Should nothing unpleasant transpire—*nothing of the past I mean*[1]—I am almost certain to go to the Chicago Exhibition. . . .

'Something unpleasant' apparently transpired, for he did not get the appointment, which involved the handling of accounts. In the autumn of the same year (1892) he was living the life of a hobo around Sydney, chopping wood or doing odd jobs ('sometimes I get 1/-, sometimes a meal'), pawning his clothes, sleeping in verminous barracks provided for the unemployed, or in the open parks. He applied in vain for State Relief and borrowed money to cable home for help, which of course was immediately forthcoming—*et patati et patata*. Even Nell's easy good-nature broke down eventually and she wrote to her Father not to go on worrying about Tom—'the poor old chap is such a liar!' But of course they all 'went on worrying', and continuing to subsidize the scapegrace to his last sorry day.

And so to Charles, his father's favourite son. When he fell in love with a Miss Margaret Pratt of Tooting, it occurred to him that it was about time he found himself the kind of job which would enable him to get married and support a family. Miss Pratt appears to have been the first of his loves to give him these intimations of responsibility, upon which he acted with admirable promptitude. Through his London employers he obtained an excellent appointment to a firm of wine-merchants in Bordeaux, which had the advantage, among many others, of enabling him to extricate himself all but painlessly from his varied amatory entanglements round and about London.

[1] The italics are the author's.

They got married and went happily off to the lovely town on the banks of the Garonne, in the heart of the wine country (Bordeaux was also reputed then to have the best *cuisine* of all the French provincial towns), where they lived in princely fashion on extraordinarily little money, and all, according to his letters home, went as sweetly as wedding bells. Presently he was writing lyrically about the birth of his little daughter Minnie who, modelled in his own image, rapidly grew into a most beguiling and precocious child, already, towards the end of her second year, showing unmistakable proof of her Terry ancestry. Charles doted on her and seized every opportunity of drawing attention to her intelligence and talent—he behaved, in fact, exactly as his father (to whom Minnie's delicate, sharp little features and large bright eyes bore strong resemblance) had behaved over the infants Kate and Ellen. At three Minnie was dancing, singing and acting with the utmost aplomb and, his attention riveted on this future fulfilment of his own ambitions, Charles was inclined to overlook the fact that his wife had meanwhile presented him with a beautiful little red-headed son, whom they christened Horace (and who was also, briefly, to become an actor).

Horace's birth was followed by the first signs of a rift within the lute. Minnie Terry was later to say that her mother was a nagger (Minnie herself bolted from home at the earliest opportunity), but it could be that Margaret had something to nag about. It may have been hard for a young wife to find her husband riveting all his attention on his infant prodigy daughter, and not giving (in the wife's opinion) sufficient attention to his son, not to mention his wife. It may have been difficult to keep up non-stop enthusiasm for Charles's endless enthusiasm for Minnie's future—especially as there was by then another baby on the way.

Sweet-natured but high-spirited, Charles was quick to resent the tartness of Margaret's tongue; her criticisms and complaints got on his nerves. Shortly before the birth of the third baby, Beatrice (who was eventually well known as an actress in the States), he discovered he was bored, not only with matrimony, but with the wine trade. Saying something about 'an offer' from Paris, he left Margaret and the children in Bordeaux, went to Paris and there proceeded to turn down the finest (pecuniary) proposition that had ever come his way. For a very small sum he could have bought himself a partnership in the store now well-known as Old England. If he had taken that chance, he and the children would not have known another care in their lives. He could have launched his precious Minnie against a background of security, educated the children and provided for his wife.

Years later, his refusal to avail himself of this offer was referred to by his youngest brother as 'Old Charlie's crowning folly'. Yet there is another side to the picture. Like his father, Charlie had one true love, the Theatre, and to that love he was now faithful. He went back to Bordeaux, told his wife the deal had not come off and, ignoring her reproaches (it was not for some years that she found out actually what the deal amounted to, and what it would have meant to her and the children, and told a friend that she would never forgive Charlie), concluded his arrangements for returning to England. The sea-voyage was long, Margaret and little Horace were very ill and Minnie, once over her sea-sickness, wild with excitement.

They had nowhere to go; it was a miserable homecoming. But Charlie found them lodgings. For the first and probably the last time in his life, he seems to have acted with a ruthlessness so alien to his nature that it appeared not to be himself but some outsider who was doing and saying things hardly premeditated. With the ruthlessness of desperation—for now, although he did not find courage immediately to tell her so, he knew he would never live with his wife again—he made two announcements: he was going to Dublin, to act as business manager for Michael Gunn at the Theatre Royal. And as for Minnie—he had made an appointment for her and himself with Miss Fortescue, who was putting on *Frou-Frou* at the Standard Theatre and needed a child actress for a small part.

There is no record of Margaret Terry's reception of this news; but the following morning, Minnie Terry, clasping her father's hand, went down in a bus to the old Standard in Shoreditch (one of the three Standards run by a Crummles-type manager named Douglass), on whose vast stage—it was nearly the size of Drury Lane—the not yet four-year-old girl was put through her paces, and, to the delight of her anxious Papa, was given her first engagement. There was little about the part but a few gestures and movements, which the child performed with such charm and assurance that she made an instant conquest of her manageress.

And so, for Charlie, to Dublin—back to the Land! Care fell from him, as he breathed the familiar air of the Theatre again. How had he existed four years on the routine of a wine-merchant's office? He lost his head a little, proceeding to fall in love with an Irish lady, who fell in love with him, and to whom he was faithful—in his fashion—for many years, and—more unfortunately—giving up his small but steady salary with Michael Gunn for the hazards of a tour with the Compton Comedy Company. Charlie just *had* to go on the stage.

It took a series of failures to persuade him that love alone is not enough to make an actor. A resounding flop in Mrs Edward Baker's Company, and empty pockets, took Charlie back to London, where he made a notable success of box office management at the Lyceum, during Mary Anderson's season, selling four hundred seats (a record) in one day.

It is not usual for front-of-the-house executives to rate an interview in the Press, but in 1883 *Topical Times* gave Charlie a spread, and summarized his (not notably distinguished) career. There was the name of Terry, of course, and the charm that brought him many offers for touring management; there was reflected glory as father of the greatest child actress of the age; and he had formed his own little troupe—The Holiday Entertainment Company, 'a superior drawingroom entertainment', with which he toured the south-coast resorts and made money—enough at least to pay for trips to Ireland and visits to his lady-love. In this small venture his father, as may be imagined, took passionate interest, and supported his favourite Charlie with (much) advice and (a very little) capital.

Remained only 'darling Tops'—young Fred; the idol of his sister Polly, the beautiful boy with blond, silken hair, the nature of an angel and the temper of a fiend. No one but his sister Nell (whom he detested accordingly) had ever tried to discipline Fred in the home.

It was sister Polly who, when Fred was fourteen, insisted on Fred's being educated abroad. Their father disagreed; his idea was to put Fred—who showed no disposition for the stage—into apprenticeship with Lewis & Allenby, his brother-in-law Arthur Lewis sponsoring him. Marion protested strongly, and professed herself ready to undertake the cost of sending Fred to school in Switzerland; she did not approve of turning her little brother into a shop assistant!

Marion had none of the spendthrift tendencies of her brothers and her sister Ellen; cool, choosy about parts and adamant over salaries, she had the reputation of being 'careful' over money; some people called it mean. Yet she was already contributing to the upkeep of 57 Cathcart Road, paying for the education of her niece Minnie, sending small but regular sums to her brother Tom, opening her pocket to Charlie's not infrequent borrowing (which he always intended to pay back), and eventually helping young Fred with his gambling debts. Meanness is a matter of values; the level-headed Marion chose to use her money for the good of her family, rather than squander it in lavish presents or entertaining. (She had her few private extravagances, of which the principal one was dress, but that was an essential of her profession.)[1]

So Fred went to Paris and Geneva and came back, speaking beautiful French. He was sixteen, tall, handsome, merry and

---

[1] In regard to Marion's reputed carefulness, it is curious to find that she had no banking account until the year 1888. In that year her father wrote:

My dear Polly,

I have opened an account for you, and paid in to your credit, Ten pounds at the London and Westminster Bank, Stratford Place, as you will perceive on reference to the accompanying 'Paying In Book'. I have also sent you a cheque book —and whenever you pay your cheque always be sure and 'cross' it thus /& Co/. Keep your cheque book under lock and key and nothing else remains for me to add, except that in all money transactions do nothing *hurriedly*, and always cast your eye over your cheque and assure yourself it is correct and that it agrees with the adverse side. . . . The corresponding detached slip dated Sept. 10th has been left with your Baker that is I mean your Banker.

(This is signed, with a drawing, 'Mournful Tommy', and concludes with 'A faithful pen and ink sketch of what I yam and what I were.')

So it would appear that up to this date Marion Terry was paying cash for all her purchases—the reason for which is hard to imagine in so prudent a person. Did she keep a cash box, or had she some secret hiding place for the considerable sums which must from time to time have been in her possession? On Friday, after the ghost walked, what did she do with her fifty or sixty pounds?—tuck them under her mattress? And if, as is more probable, her salary was paid by cheque, someone must have cashed it for her, as she had no banker.

It is amusing to find careless Ben giving such good advice to his cautious daughter.

sociable; he had the looks, presence and showmanship of the actor—but still no inclination towards The Profession. To fill in time he agreed, good-humouredly enough, to go into the shop, but it became speedily apparent that commerce was no more his *métier* than it was Charlie's.

A meeting, through his sister Ellen, with the Bancrofts suggested to Fred that the stage, after all, offered a more agreeable way of earning one's living than that presented by Lewis & Allenby. He got a walk-on as a 'Club Member' in the drama *Money*.

The night of Fred's début as a Walking Gentleman, at a guinea a week, was the exciting one of the Old Prices riots at the Haymarket Theatre.

The first real acting part he got was with Ellen and Charles Kelly, in a morning performance of *New Men and Old Acres*, at the Crystal Palace. Fred played Bertie FitzUrse to Ellen's Lilian Vavasour, and an incident occurred which did not sweeten the relationship between brother and sister. In a scene with Ellen, Fred's voice cracked, and she, quick to seize upon the comedy possibilities of the mishap, started to imitate him—to the rapture of the audience, which rolled in its seats, and the misery of Fred who, purple in the face, floundered, dried up and at the fall of the curtain was not on speaking terms with his sister, with whom, he vowed, nothing would ever induce him to play again.

Acting on Bancroft's advice, he got an audition with the Chippendales and, borrowing two pounds from his mother, set out on an eighteen-months' tour of the provinces. It was very hard work, and big and vigorous though he appeared, Fred was not as strong as the rest of his family. Like Kate, he suffered from quinsies, against which he fought manfully. He had the great good fortune to be given small parts and understudies in Shakespeare and Sheridan, and took to these as a duck to water. It was soon evident that young Terry had more than his looks to recommend him. When, at the end of the tour, he came back to town, to be auditioned by Irving (Ellen arranged this, perhaps in compunction for the *débâcle* at the Crystal Palace), he had played every male part in *Romeo and Juliet* except Romeo, the Apothecary and the Friar, all the male parts in *Much Ado About Nothing* except Benedick and the low comedy characters, and all in *The School for Scandal* except Sir Peter, Sir

Oliver and Moses: an honourable list for a young actor not yet turned twenty. According to the provincial notices, he had acquitted himself creditably in them all.

To do honour to the Actor-Manager of the Lyceum, 'Fred got himself up to kill': silk hat, cane, lavender gloves and a flower in his buttonhole, and stood modestly in the wings, awaiting his summons.

'What *is* it? What *is* it?' hissed Irving.

'That's Miss Terry's brother, guv'nor,' he was informed by Bram Stoker.[1] 'You told us to send him a call.'

'My Gad,' said Irving. 'My Gad.'

It took Fred long to recover from this unfortunate reception of his well-meant gesture—every word of which the admirable acoustics of the Lyceum carried to his ear. But the Eye had penetrated the dude outfit, and seen, through Fred's burning blush, the fantastic physical likeness to his sister Ellen. He had nothing immediately to offer the courtly young man (Irving was preparing his first American tour), but young Terry might well fit into future projects.

Something of this was conveyed to young Terry who, withdrawing himself from The Presence, went off to tell his friends the Easts all about his contact with Immortality. The East brothers (John and Charles) were sharing a dressingroom at the Adelphi with a couple of 'utilities': G. P. Huntley and Archer Prince, an embittered man who was later to murder William Terriss at the Adelphi stage-door. The play was *In the Ranks*, the management A. & S. Gatti. Dining at the Royal Adelaide Galleries in the Strand, Charles East introduced Fred to the Gatti brothers, who booked them both to tour with *In the Ranks*, Henry George playing the lead and Mary Rorke in the cast. It was Fred's introduction to modern comedy. (*A Pair of Wings* in which he played with brother-in-law Charles Kelly was a flop after a few performances—although Kelly, according to Fred, was excellent in his part.)

[1] Irving's business manager.

CHAPTER TWO

The Hectic Years

I

Between 1878, when she joined the Company at the Lyceum, and 1883, the date of her first visit to America, Ellen Terry played Ophelia, Lady Anne, Desdemona and Juliet (in that order), Camma, in Tennyson's 'great little play', *The Cup*, and Letitia Hardy in *The Belle's Stratagem*—the last two, in the same bill, constituting something of a *tour de force,* and enrapturing her public: even those who contended she was not as 'great' an actress as Irving was an actor could scarce forbear to cheer. On the first night of *Hamlet* she felt she had failed, and fled to the Embankment intending to drown herself; there was no Ophelia to accept the rapturous applause at the fall of the curtain. With affectionate intuition, Boo followed her and took her back to her lodgings in Longridge Road—where, after midnight, Irving came to her: and this was the beginning, according to Ellen, of their attachment of going on twenty years.[1]

The rest of the work she did during the '78-'83 period was largely in the nature of support to Irving. 'We must have no more of these second-fiddle parts for you, Duchess!' her father shocked her by telling her. Ophelias and Desdemonas were 'second-fiddle parts' in Ben's estimation. That is a matter of opinion: but it is impossible to imagine a modern leading lady accepting such trivial parts as Ruth Meadowes in *Eugene Aram* and Jeanette in *The Lyons Mail*: parts overshadowed by the overwhelming personality of Irving. She undertook them in the way of duty to her manager and the Company. Utterly without personal vanity, her training in stock companies stood her in good stead.

Even to those who only saw Ellen Terry in old age, it was evident

[1] Ellen Terry's account to the author, recorded at the time in my copy of her *Story of My Life* (the original title of the *Memoirs*).

that Ellen in her prime had not only a beauty which was (almost literally) 'out of this world', but a purely magical quality in her acting which defied analysis. To this quality the art of Godwin gave fit setting, for he continued to design her costumes, of which the Greek draperies she wore as Camma were in colour, pattern and shape an unforgettable example of his gift for wedding archaeological perfection with an exquisite sense of theatrical fitness.

But physical beauty, that which for want of a better word may be called 'magic', and a superb costumier are not, alone, enough to make an actress of the calibre of Ellen Terry. Her diaries and prompt-books bear witness to the profound study she brought to her parts —study she scattered so lightly, with such starlight effect, over her performances, that it has been said, by persons who should have known better, that the secret of Ellen's charm was the 'spontaneity' of her acting. These fools took no account of the laborious hours on which the apparent 'spontaneity' was built.

She regulated her life with conscious care, always with regard to the demands of her profession—which, under an exigent manager, were many, and, in times when two hundred and fifty performances were considered a long run, meant the constant memorizing and rehearsing of new parts. Already the strain of this was beginning to tell on a memory which had been overloaded since childhood.

She was indeed in an enviable position as leading lady to the leading actor-manager of the leading theatre in London. But those first five years at the Lyceum took it out of her. In 1883 she was as thin as paper, in spite of eating heartily, usually sleeping well, and rarely ailing. Veering constantly between the wildest of high spirits and deep depression, she would, in the present day, be said to be heading for a breakdown. In addition to her almost continuous work in the theatre she had the nervous and emotional disturbances of her private life, of which the first was her relationship with Henry Irving; to this we will return.

The first year of her engagement at the Lyceum had seen the break-up of her marriage to Charles Kelly, of which, although she was relieved to be free from him, she was so ashamed that she could not bear to speak of it, even to her family. An affectionate husband and a good stepfather to the children, he had developed the unforgivable vice of jealousy. He had always been touchy about his

position as an actor, to which unfortunate sentiment he gave
expression when he foolishly walked out of the cast of *Olivia*; but
now, watching the progress of his wife's friendship with Irving,
he gave way to a much more reasonable fury—although Ellen did
not choose to see it in that light. During their tour, when he played
Benedick to her Beatrice, they quarrelled frequently and, on their
return to town, Kelly proposed a divorce. Ellen was horrified;
surely he could see the impossibility, for her, of going through that
again? (From her own point of view there was nothing to be gained
by it, since Irving was married to a woman who, although they had
been separated for some years, had declared she would never
divorce him.)

So, shrugging his shoulders, Kelly went his way, and in 1881 a
judicial separation was arranged. They might have spared themselves
the trouble; four years later Ellen Terry was called to his deathbed
by the girl with whom he was then living, a Miss Hunt (or Hunter?).
'I thanked her for all she had done for him', said Ellen Terry. 'When
I went upstairs I could not feel it was Charles, but I had the strangest
wish to rehearse Juliet there by the bed on which he was lying!'

There are still some (including Irving's grandson Laurence and
Ellen Terry's niece Olive) who incline to the opinion that Irving
and Ellen Terry were never lovers. To this controversy one can but
contribute the testimony of the latter's word, given shortly after
the First World War, when I had been for several years much in her
company. The conversation had turned on some troublesome affair
of my own, and led to my asking Ellen point-blank whether she
had ever been Irving's mistress. She answered without hesitation.

'Of course I was. We were terribly in love for a while. Then,
later on, when it didn't matter so much to me, he wanted us to go
on, and so I did, because I was very, very fond of him and he said
he needed me.'

She was then in her late sixties, and to her all that past was very
far away; so far that she did not mind answering the over-bold
question of a girl in her early twenties.

She then went on to say that after they had agreed to love each
other, she was overwhelmed with embarrassment every time they
acted a love-scene on the stage: 'I felt stiff and self-conscious and

found myself blushing from head to foot—which was very difficult for Henry!'

On another occasion she recounted how, after long consideration, she made up her mind to explain to her daughter Edy, then in her early 'teens but wise beyond her years, 'something of the relationship' between herself and Irving. Edy, who like all young people, adored Irving, listened with her hands in her pockets, and, after a long silence through which her mother listened to the beating of her own heart, said, 'I think you've been very badly treated, and I'm glad about you and Henry.'

The only other time Ellen Terry referred to the subject was when I was staying with her in Bath for the unveiling of the Siddons Memorial in 1921. I found in a secondhand bookshop a volume which I knew was not in Ellen Terry's collection of Irving biographies, and took it back to the hotel with the glee of a puppy bringing a bone to its mistress. Ellen Terry glanced at the title and the name of the author and laid the book quietly aside.

'Thank you, my dear. . . . Henry left me for Mrs Aria.'

After twenty years, that wound still ached.

These three pieces of evidence would appear to confirm the relationship between Henry Irving and Ellen Terry, which lasted —perhaps?—until the break-up of their artistic partnership.

In these days it may appear exaggerated to lay stress upon a situation which is now publicized in every walk of life; when not only artists, but aristocracy, bourgeoisie and the lower classes have no embarrassment when their private aberrations are plastered in what used (fairly) to be called 'the gutter Press', for the entertainment of all and sundry.

It is not to be assumed that Victorian Society was any more moral than its Georgian prototype, but its members were too scared of forfeiting their *entrée* to Court and the royal enclave either publicly to misbehave themselves or to keep company with the less discreet. So came into being what its critics call the Golden Age of Hypocrisy; for which a more euphonious name might be found. 'Taste' is an almost indefinable term, as applied to behaviour and manners, and—in that application—is obsolete today; but the Victorians and Edwardians practised it in regard to the preservation of their privacy, and the dignity of whatever society they happened to belong to. To call it the Golden Age of Behaviour would seem to strike a mean between moral and aesthetic implications; accepting 'behaviour' as a code of conduct inoffensive to any person, regardless of moral or aesthetic persuasions.[1]

Irving and Ellen Terry subscribed to the Victorian code. In their position, they were exposed to a limelight which, admittedly more lambent and less searching than that of the present day, obliged them to exercise a particular discretion. Thanks to their immense *réclame*, they were moving in a Society whose favour they must allow no action of theirs to forfeit.

The Stage, stubbornly and against flagrant proof to the contrary, maintained its reputation for immoral living, against which the notorious domesticity of the Charles Keans, the Kendals, the Bancrofts and their innumerable followers could not prevail. The reason for this is not far to seek; exactly as, up to the time of the Second World War, the female novelist was identified with the characters she portrayed, so playgoers persisted in identifying players with their roles. The villain on stage was bound to be, off stage, the *roué*; the sedate matron who, in the drama, deceived her husband, was a harlot in private life—as was the well-brought-up and well-chaperoned girl who lent her talents to the role of a streetwalker. For this reason, actors and actresses who could afford to pick and choose frequently avoided what were called 'unsympathetic' parts, though these might offer them a better vehicle for their gifts than the heroes and heroines who, in contemporary drama, were invariably blameless. The naïveté of audiences undoubtedly contributed to the low dramatic standard of the day.

It is not to be assumed that the distinguished people who not only lent their patronage to the Lyceum, but accepted and returned Irving's hospitalities, were all so simple as not to recognize the relationship between him and his leading lady—which indeed was a contemporary *on dit*, not only in the theatre but in Society. There were some of broader-minded or slightly bohemian tendencies who would have been pleased to accept it. But they were not called upon to do so. Ellen's innate modesty, her distaste for the mildest form of indelicacy would not have tolerated it.

[1] Dame Marie Tempest said to the author, 'What, after all, are good morals but good manners?'

It is difficult, in these days, to imagine the stress and strain, in Victorian days, of conducting a clandestine love-affair. Presumably they made their opportunities—which cannot have been without difficulty and anxiety for both. Irving had his rooms in Grafton Street, to which (according to her own account) Ellen never went except on formal occasions, as a guest among guests. Ellen was by then established at Barkston Gardens, with her daughter Edy, with Boo and Bo and living-in servants. When Irving bought the house on Brook Green as a place to entertain his friends, he never spent a night there; for some time the bedrooms were not even furnished, except for a few toilet tables and cheval glasses for the convenience of the ladies.

The smallest indiscretion on Ellen's part would have brought down on her the malice of Irving's wife. (This danger was eventually cancelled out by his agreement to pay Mrs Irving an allowance, instantly to be stopped, if by word or action, she brought trouble on Ellen Terry.) Yet—they made their opportunities: one of which was described by an American lady, a dear friend of both (as, later of the author's), who with her husband[1] entertained them frequently on Staten Island.

They trusted her to preserve their secret, which she faithfully kept until both were dead. It is not conceivable that Mrs Alexander Shaw was the only friend to give them joint invitations, or to make convenient arrangements. Her description of Ellen lying on a white bearskin rug in front of the fire, of Irving holding out his hand to lead her up the stairs when midnight struck, is lively in the author's memory.

A deep and bitter struggle added its pangs to Ellen Terry's existence: the struggle between impatient love and devotion to her children, Edy and Ted—still called Wardell, although the one who lent them the protection of his name had departed out of their lives. They knew it was not their own name, and equally that they had no legal name of their own, although they had variously been known as Godwin, as Terry and as Wardell—which appears to have worried their mother more than it did them.

[1] 'Sandy' (Alexander) Shaw took Ellen Terry on explorations of the Bowery and Greenwich Village.

There are two slightly different versions of how the children came by the name of Craig. Ellen Terry's was that the three of them, with Irving, were on holiday in Scotland and went sailing round the islands, to one of which Edy pointed and asked what it was called. Told it was Ailsa Craig, she said, 'What a pretty name; why can't I be Ailsa Craig?'

Edith Craig's version, which would appear to be the more reliable of the two—because when Ellen Terry gave me hers her memory was failing and many discrepancies appear in her accounts, at the time, of incidents and people—is that Edy herself was not present, and her mother and brother were not on holiday but on tour with Irving; that Ellen Terry said, 'What a good stage name! A pity you can't have it, Ted. I shall give it to Edy.'

It is a minor point, and of little importance, save that it helps to fix the time of the christening, which could not have been, as stated in the Notes by Christopher St John to Ellen Terry's *Memoirs*, in the early 'eighties, but between the first two American tours; prior to which there was no tour in Scotland.

Edy was given the names Edith Ailsa Geraldine, and Ted, Edward Henry Gordon. The godparents were Henry Irving for both, Lady Gordon for Ted and Mrs Stephen Coleridge for Edy. The name Craig was added, and confirmed by deed poll. The children were no longer nameless. This, at the time, meant more to Ellen Terry than it did to them.

Yet she was tormented by the future. Always her 'poor children' (she was still calling them that in her seventies, although, spoiled and surfeited in every sentimental and material sense, no less appropriate adjective could at any moment in their lives have applied to them) must come before everything. Her unquiet heart told her that Irving would not long be content to take second place, and she . . . she knew her own weakness.

So love and compunction flung her into a frenzy of solicitude for the children—who returned her devotion in their own fashion. Edy, a precociously intelligent girl of fourteen, with her father's dark eyes, and original features—wide, thin mouth and rather a clumsy nose which did not belong to either side of the family—hid her mother-worship under an attitude of cool and often critical detachment. She may have developed this Cordelia-like attitude as a form

189

of silent protest against the sickly adulation of which she saw her mother a victim. Child though she was, she was intelligent enough to sense the meretriciousness of such demonstrations, and deplored the ease with which Ellen Terry lent herself to them. Yet, if any person other than herself dared in her opinion to slight or criticize Ellen, Edy was instant and savage in reprisal. The rare depth and quality of her character were recognized by few, for her approach to strangers was defensive, not to say *farouche*, and the tenderness of her heart was suspected only by those (they were not a few) who profited by it.

The antithesis of his sister in looks and character, Ted was pretty and babyish (the latter when it advantaged him), a little gilt serpent of guile and, as he well knew, the idol of his mother, whom he could twist round his finger. He got his own way with everybody except Edy, who despised him for his cowardice (he was a great cry-baby), hit him over the head and exhorted him to be a woman! (She was already a feminist, and became more of one when she went to her boarding school in Gloucestershire, kept by Mrs Malleson, one of the pioneers of Women's Suffrage.)

According to one account, Ellen Terry was 'guiltless of spoiling her children', but it is unlikely either of them was popular at school, for they had both been encouraged to regard themselves as something exceptional and superior to what they were pleased to call 'ordinary' people. The blame for that rests, probably, less on Ellen Terry than on those who sought to please her by making a fuss of the children. Ted's vanity was so pronounced that when he missed the train that took him to school—he was a fat and physically lazy boy—he demanded it should be called back. 'I'm the son of Miss Ellen Terry!' Incredibly, the train was called back.

In her arduous life she had little time to give them, but that little she gave passionately; read poetry and Shakespeare with them, encouraged Ted's drawing and Edy's music, and taught them beautiful manners, which Ted instantly adopted as part of his battery of charm and Edy reserved for the people she cared about, treating others to a brand of boorishness peculiarly her own.

Irving's toleration (it grew later into deep affection and respect for Edy and grimly humorous appreciation of Ted) of these two difficult children was no doubt, to begin with, part of his policy of pleasing Ellen. They were allowed (at home) to call him Henry, their interruptions and arguments were not reproved, but laughed at, and they were given the run of the Lyceum,[1] which privilege they were shrewd enough not to abuse. So they adored Irving, and by their adoration completed Ellen's surrender.

They knew very little, at this time, of their Terry relations, apart from uncle Charlie, gay, swaggering uncle Fred (only three years older than Edy), aunt Marion (a passing acquaintance; she was kind, in an absent fashion and had a disconcerting way of looking deeply into the eyes of the person she was talking to, under her own lowered lids), and aunt Flossie who was sweet and full of laughter and swept them off sometimes to her big house on Campden Hill. She had a little girl called Olive and was expecting another baby. They had some other baby cousins whom they had never seen and whose names they did not even know. As the prohibition on Moray Lodge still held good, they never met any of the Lewises. This would not appear to be a loss on either side; emphatically the young Craigs would not have fitted into the 'bun teas', the lawn tennis parties, the vast, formal receptions on whose smooth waters the four little Lewis girls glided as expertly as ducklings.

To get the full flavour of life at Moray Lodge at that period one must read Kate Terry Gielgud's autobiography, an unequalled 'period piece' which should be in the hands of anyone attempting in fiction or drama to reconstruct the atmosphere of the 1880s and '90s. The receptions to which more than three hundred guests were invited, the great summer garden party which was an event of the season, and had to be arranged so as not to clash with the Chelsea Flower Show, the meets of the Coaching Club, racing at Sandown, polo at Ranelagh, or Henley Regatta: at which children were welcome and had their own special buffet and kindergarten tables—these belong to a way of living unimaginable to the majority today. The band which played amid laughter and the hum of voices and 'the well-dressed crowd in its trailing skirts and big hats . . .

---

[1] Within limits. E. T. wrote in rather injured terms to Edy, in Germany, that it was 'silly' not to allow her whiteheaded boy to stand in the wings, making drawings.

fichus and feather boas'[1]—it is probable that the parade of high fashion on their aunt Kate's lawns would have been considered 'vulgar'[2] by Edy Craig, whose mother draped her long, lithe limbs in falling folds that bore no relationship to the mode of the day, never wore a corset and pushed her short pale gold hair into a careless fringe that came softly down to her beautiful darkened brows. Edy would have had some right to her opinion, for the 1880s were not distinguished for elegance, although a vast improvement on the previous decade; the bustle had gone, but there was still a plethora of meaningless drapery on skirts, and the plain bodices with high necks and 'tuckers' were very unbecoming to all but the slenderest figures.

The young Craigs would have had nothing in common with their fashionable cousins (although Edy eventually, after they were both grown up, got on terms with Janet, born in the same year as herself, and the most independent and individual of the four), but it seems a pity that they were deprived of early acquaintance with their kind and charming uncle Arthur Lewis, lover and patron of the arts, and that it was years before they heard the matchless voice of their aunt Kate, whose readings of Shakespeare were a feature of evenings at Moray Lodge.

Their closest approach to 'conventional' society was at Campden House Road—the adjective in inverted commas because there was so little in their aunt Florence that was conventional in more than a superficial sense. Certainly she was an accomplished hostess and a scrupulous housewife, giving out the household stores once a week, personally supervising her linen cupboard, butler's pantry, stillroom and all the personnel of her big household (there were parlourmaid, housemaids, cook, kitchenmaids, butler and groom, as well as nurse and under-nurse for the babies). Like her sister Kate— and no doubt with much advice from her—Florence had perfectly assimilated the duties of her enhanced position. It seems astonishing that those two girls, brought up in the utmost simplicity, adapted themselves with so much grace and skill to a scale of living for which they had little preparation beyond the natural

[1] Kate Gielgud's memory would appear to have betrayed her here; the feather boa did not come in until the late 'nineties.

[2] Her epithet for a doll in a pink satin dress which she was given as a child.

quickness of their wits and their talent for observation. There must, to begin with, have been *gaffes*, but they were quickly covered up, and never repeated. Kate put her (by now) vast experience at her younger sister's disposal—and one can imagine Florence accepting it light-heartedly, and weaving it into her thousand interests.

Little wonder she was adored by young people. Her parties were no less brilliant, but less staid than sister Katie's; protocol was less severe—in spite of the formality on which her husband insisted. One of the many proofs she gave of the sweetness of her disposition was the smiling patience with which she endured Willie Morris's reading aloud to her when she was 'resting'. She, a most beautiful reader, bore this, as she bore other trials he inflicted—from the best motives—upon her, with angelic grace. But it was surely unfortunate for 'darling Floss', that she had married a man who was very fond of the sound of his own voice.

Her married state qualifying her for chaperonage, she was the favourite of her spirited niece Janet, the pair of them aiding and abetting each other in all kinds of mischief—to the disapproval of Katie, her mother's 'amenable daughter'. In the midst of a hectic social life—'rinking', dancing, theatre-going, endless 'calling' and entertaining and 'treats' for the children, all recorded in her diaries—drops a cool little note of reminder: '*Lend Edie-Tom for housepapering £1. Purse 19/6. B.(?) 15/6.*' What 'Purse' means, or who 'B' was no one knows. Like her sisters Kate and Marion, Florence was careful; she can never have expected to get back that pound from Edie-Tom, but she put it down, for the record.

II

Twelfth Night, with which Irving opened on his return from the first American tour, was, from the beginning to its premature end, a chapter of accidents. For some reason Irving's usually impeccable instinct for casting deserted him; Terriss as Orsino looked 'all wrong',[1] and convinced neither himself nor anyone else as the lovesick Duke; Rose Leclercq, specially engaged to play Olivia, could have been Orsino's mother and her stiff *grande dame* performance made nonsense of the scenes with Viola. Too old and too

[1] Ellen Terry.

stylized for the part—she had been a member of Charles Kean's Company when Ellen Terry made her début as Mamillius!—she had for some time given up romantic parts for aristocratic dowagers. It is to be supposed she could not resist Irving's offer, although she would have been wiser to refuse it, but what induced him to make it will never be known.

The comedy scenes were dull, lacking in humour or inspiration —which was not surprising; Irving had as little talent for producing comedy as he had for acting it. He could, when required, produce a saturnine brand of humour peculiarly his own, but he lacked both the inventiveness and the imagination of the 'comic'. Rehearsals went on through broiling summer weather, while the actors lost confidence in themselves and their parts and everybody but Irving, possibly Ellen Terry (who spent much of her time in the country, getting her lines: it was Irving's custom at this time to postpone rehearsing her until the play was more or less set) and the dashing young Sebastian, Fred Terry, felt they were in for a 'flop'. As it would have been heresy, even among themselves, to voice such an opinion, they continued loyally to back up 'the Guv'nor', but rehearsals got slower and slower, the comics lost pace and, as continual changes were made in their business, became bogged down in contradictory instructions.

Whether Irving was over-exhausted, and his perception consequently dimmed, after the American tour, it was painfully clear before the first night that *Twelfth Night* was not his play and Malvolio was not his part. All, then, must rest on Ellen Terry and on young Fred, the likeness between the pair of them forming the *clou* of the production. And, for the only time in her life, Ellen failed him.

She came back from her cottage (it was now in Kingston Vale: it had a little Regency verandah, a monkey-puzzle tree just inside the iron railings that fenced it from the road, and an old, gnarled vine which gave it its name and still produced a few clusters of grapes) with her arm in a sling and her face fever-white. She thought it was a whitlow; actually, she had been bitten by a horse-fly. On the first night, almost fainting with the pain of her swollen arm, she played most of her scenes sitting down. It needed but that to condemn the play.

In her *Memoirs*, Ellen Terry ascribed the hostile demonstration that followed the fall of the curtain to the resentment of a certain element in the audience of Irving's reservation of the pit. Contemporary notices make it plain enough that Irving's dreary Malvolio and the colourlessness of the comedy scenes robbed the production of most of its character. One performance the critics were unanimous in commending: that of Mr Fred Terry, whose fortuitous likeness to his sister Ellen only underlined the excellence of his performance in the small but vital part of Sebastian. As for Ellen Terry, she was so *au-dessous de ses forces* that only her magic accounted for the few meagre bouquets the Press awarded her. It was the only time, under Irving's management, that booing was heard at the Lyceum.

Irving was foolish enough to lose his temper. In his speech at the end of the play he berated the audience, which, after all, had only exercised its right to signify its opinion of a performance which fell below the standard it had come to expect of the Lyceum. He himself had created that standard and might have appreciated the point of view of a public he had helped to educate. Some years later, when contemplating a production of *The Tempest*, which he rightly rejected, he acknowledged his error over *Twelfth Night*: he should have engaged three great comedians. Possibly that one conspicuous failure, coming on top of the heady adulation of the American tour, was good for him.

Within a few nights of the opening, Ellen collapsed with blood-poisoning; her arm was the size of a bolster and there was question of amputation. Fortunately, the ever-dependable Marion was 'resting' after a succession of domestic comedies and farces. A polished and beautiful young actress, her apprenticeship to Gilbert had imposed upon her exactly the form of discipline suited to her art and her temperament. Every word, every gesture, every position had to be strictly memorized; there must be no departure by so much as an inflection or the flick of an eyelash from the part as set by an inexorable author. Yet, within this strait compass, the essentially subtle and delicate genius of Marion Terry flourished like a fragile plant in a hothouse. Treatment which would have destroyed her sister Ellen, whose art was scattered with so many sweet wild flowers of improvisation, and who was seldom word-perfect, was right for Marion. (It is odd that her vast public, which acclaimed her as the great exponent, on the stage, of the 'good' woman, rarely remembered her as the supreme *blagueuse*, whose solemn air masked resources of humour which often made her audiences wonder why they were laughing.)

At the Lyceum she was not given this strict Gilbertian direction; Irving had had the good sense to allow Ellen to create her parts herself, within the limits of the over-all production. Viola was one of the parts Marion, following her father's advice, had studied, although she had not played it before. Ellen was too ill to coach her, but she got the business from the prompt-book and made a success.

Before the end of the run, Irving had got hold of a rubbishy version of *Faust* and been attracted by the part of Mephistopheles for himself and Marguerite for Ellen. He was invariably drawn to fustian. The accusation of his critics is true: that apart from Shakespeare and three plays by Tennyson (*The Cup, Becket* and *King Arthur*) he never produced a play of the least literary, artistic or intellectual merit. But by the force of his art he transmuted dross into fine metal; he took bits of tinsel and coloured glass, and gave them so superb a setting that even connoisseurs were content to accept them at least as semi-precious stones. (His ardent disciple Fred Terry had also this gift, indispensable to the actor-manager; from the year when he set up in management, Fred never produced a single play that was not, by all standards of art and the drama, pure garbage; but he treated each one as though it were a classic.) In condemning Irving for the rubbish he produced, and imposed upon his infinitely more intelligent leading lady, one must not overlook the fact that among the regular patrons of the Lyceum were all the intellectual, the literary and the artistic *monde* of the day. It was then the player who counted, not the play; theatre audiences, even of the so-called intelligentsia, were less interested in the subject matter than in its interpretation.

Irving was, without question, within the limits of his powerful idiosyncrasy, a great actor, and an even greater director, and it would be both ignorant and futile to belittle the achievements of one who, by precept and example, did so much to elevate the status of the theatre and of the actor. Much of the antagonism he roused during his lifetime was from supporters of Ellen Terry, who rightly deprecated his never (in their opinion) providing her with fit material for the exercise of her genius. Even she, for all her loyalty and, on her own account, incapability of resentment, deplored as time went on his antipathy to dramatic forms in which she longed to experiment. From his own point of view, Irving was right; he had the supreme virtue of recognizing his own limitations, and had little or no *rapport* with advancing schools of thought, as adumbrated in the works of rising dramatists. Nor did he ever, willingly, go to see the performances of other great artistes. He was utterly self-centred—which may account for the fact that during his long career he never progressed one iota (apart from the inevitable progression of an enhanced technique) from the young Irving who hit the provincial cities with his Jingle and Digby Grant. From this point of view he was an unfortunate partner for Ellen Terry.

With *Faust* in view, he set out on a tour of Germany in search of 'realism'; in addition to Ellen Terry and Edy Craig, he took the Comyns Carrs (he a playwriter whose services might be useful in the final adaptation of the play), the scene-painter Hawes Craven, the stage-director H. J. Loveday, Ellen's dresser and his own functioning as lady's maid and valet, and minor personnel; all in the grand manner. Of the party, Edy got the most joy; her ambition was to study music in Germany; while Irving and his minions raked antique shops for properties, Ellen took her daughter to concerts.

Ted was at Bradfield—doing no good there; a long series of acts of insubordination culminated in a midnight tricycle ride with some friends, and Ellen to her indignation learned by telegram from the Headmaster that Ted was expelled. Eventually he was sent to Germany, to Heidelberg, from which he was sent down for some other silly escapade. Ellen resented this attempt to discipline her wayward son. She need not have troubled. Ted had only a kindly tolerance for anyone who tried to make him behave himself; he was the son of the great Ellen Terry, and dedicated to the theatre. He was truly sorry for those who did not recognize his exceptional character.

Faust afforded Ellen Terry one of her best opportunities (she described Irving's as a tuppence-coloured part). Beautifully produced, with all the artifice of the theatre, her moving performance as Marguerite left its mark in many private records, as well as in the notices of the critics. It was followed by a revival of Wills's *Olivia* —the lead of which Marion again took over, when Ellen, again, fell ill. (Fred played Thornhill in this; a beautifully dashing performance.)

Out of one of her brother-in-law William Morris's scrapbooks comes so delicious a description of Marion and Florence's appearance that one cannot forbear to quote it. Unfortunately the usually punctilious Mr Morris omitted the name of the paper from which it was cut, and the date, which was *circa* 1885. It concerns the art exhibitions which they faithfully attended as an important part of their social round. There is no record that any of the Terrys except Ellen knew good painting from bad, but it was fashionable during the season to be seen at the galleries, and doubly agreeable when the artist happened to be a personal friend.

> Three years ago the winter exhibitions displayed almost as many button-hole bouquets as there were women . . . and yet hardly a flower was to be found in the galleries a fortnight ago. Miss Marion Terry and her younger married sister were two of the exceptions, as they wore lilies of the valley and maidenhair in large, flat, spray shape on their cloaks of Paisley shawling, made with sling and dolman sleeves respectively, and trimmed with brown fur. Miss Marion Terry's bonnet was of chenille-spotted brown felt, and her dress crimson satin. Her sister wore a large black velvet hat and feather, with a greenish aigrette.

No paper I have seen gave space to Ellen's romantic draperies —she, like her sisters, had a fancy for flowers, usually roses, bunched up against the loosely tied chiffon scarves that veiled her throat —nor even to the black velvet hat with 'pom-poms' all round the brim, which brought a cry of delight from Whistler when he met her wearing it. Her positive dislike for the 'fashionable' persisted to the end of her life.

There came a spate of deaths. Charles Reade died during the run of *Twelfth Night*; then Charles Kelly, and, the following year, Edward Godwin. Three pieces carved out of Ellen Terry's life, and then another—not so deep, but part of the fabric. Fred Archer, who carried the morning milk at Harpenden, and was as famous, now, on the racecourse as she was in the theatre; Fred, who gave her the two fox terriers, Fussie, which she gave to Irving, and Drummie, who was her companion—Fred, clutching his sister in his arms, shot himself in the mouth at his home in Newmarket. In an odd way, she felt this more—or should one say, differently? —than the death of the two men who had called her 'wife'. She had outlived her love for Godwin, and the Kelly interlude had worked itself to an end. But that easy friendship with Fred the milkman had somehow persisted and its tragic dénouement shook her.

Charlie's small Minnie was engaged by Maurice Barrymore as the child in *Nadjesda*, and, terrified by the performance of the actress who played the title-role, fled screaming into the wings, vowing she would never again appear on the stage—out of which state of mind she was fortunately coaxed by her aunt Marion in time, at the age of six, to play Mignon in *Bootle's Baby*, at that reputedly unlucky theatre, the Globe. Under the management of Hollingshead and Shine, six-year-old Minnie's salary was ten pounds a week—more than her uncle Fred was getting with Mrs Kennion's Stock Company at Leicester. The Globe was not unlucky for Little Minnie Terry.

These lives seem a thousand miles away from Moray Lodge, where Minnie's almost grown-up cousin Katie was preparing for her 'coming-out'; was attending lectures on Home Nursing and Hygiene and contributing naïve little articles to the *Pink 'Un* and *The World* (undoubtedly it helped to be the daughter of Arthur Lewis); and cousin Janet, aided and abetted by aunt Flossie, was in active rebellion against Mama's starchy régime; and cousins Lucy and Mabel were good little maids in school—and all four were governed by the rules laid down for young ladies in the final decades of the nineteenth century. Proud of their connection—through aunt Ellen—with the Lyceum, they had no glimmer of the realities of life in the theatre, as known to their small cousin Minnie; through their father's and mother's friends, they knew only the theatrical aristocracy, the rich, successful element, the privileged element of which, as daughters of the great Kate Terry, they felt themselves a part. Of the four girls, all extremely intelligent and beautifully educated—they were particularly accomplished in music and languages—only the youngest, Mabel, just entering her 'teens, showed a disposition towards the stage, although Katie proved her Terry blood in her intellectual appreciation of acting and production in general, and it would seem that, given opportunity, she could have made an intelligent critic. Somewhat shy, inclined to be withdrawn, she was a voracious reader and already a fluent writer; she had a very good memory and a passion for exactitude. Her readings of the classics had given her a fine, formal vocabulary. An earnest listener, it was she above all who profited by association with the cultured society which, for affection of her father and for respect for her mother, assembled in Moray Lodge. Growing up in a little Court of the Arts, of which their father was King and their mother Consort, the young Lewises had no faintest conception of the hard road the artist has to travel. Art was served to them on gold plate!

(Kate Terry Gielgud's autobiography gives a perfect 'conversation piece' of the strict discipline that governed the débutante of the 'eighties, who, having danced until four in the morning, was expected to be down for breakfast at eight, although 'Mother felt obliged to cancel family prayers and take her breakfast in bed'! Kate was indefatigable over the chaperonage of her daughters. Although 'out', Katie had two hours in the schoolroom every morning but Saturday. It would appear that the stamina of the Victorian débutante was tougher than that of her modern prototype.)

One never, at Kate's house in West Cromwell Road, after her widowhood, met the humble old professionals, her contemporaries in the theatre, who were welcome at Ellen's at 215 King's Road, Chelsea, and, later, at Burleigh Mansions, St Martin's Lane. 'Old Kitty' (as Ellen tolerantly called her) preferred in conversation to introduce the names of the aristocracy with whom she was acquainted, and took less than little notice of reference to any actor or actress who was not 'in the top bracket'. 'Who? Never heard of him', she trumpeted, when Ellen mentioned an old actor who, having fallen on hard times, had appealed to her for help. 'Oh come, Kit; you must remember. He was with us at Bristol—and then at the Lyceum for three or four seasons.' 'What did he play?' 'Oh, I don't know, utility. A *very* nice fellow.' The bright, cold eye of Kate became glassy; Miss Kate Terry—Mrs Arthur Lewis—did not concern herself with 'utility', or with young, struggling actors who lacked important social backing.

The First World War was then over, but Kate Lewis was still living back in the 'eighties, still surfeited with her great reputation as châtelaine of Moray Lodge and her greater reputation in the theatre. (In 1917 it was fifty years since her farewell performance, and few, if any, of the rising generation had heard the name of Kate Terry. In the 'eighties, although twenty years had passed since her retirement from the stage, her glory as an actress was kept alive through a devoted and wealthy husband; and memories were not so short as they are in the present day.) As Mother to four girls she must have been formidable; one is inclined to pity them— all but Janet, who was strong enough, backed by her aunt Florence, to resist her. But the pity might be misplaced: they all adored her.

Flossie, at 13 Campden House Road (the number was later altered to 49, from when onward, according to her daughter Olive, luck deserted them), was radiantly producing a family: Olive was succeeded by Geoffrey, by John, by Hugh. It was no less 'grand' an establishment than Moray Lodge, but the lightsome spirit of its mistress so pervaded it, so filled it with delight, that the 'grandeur' never struck one. It was perhaps easier to bring up three little boys than four little girls; less prunes and prisms, more of the 'joy and jollity' of youth. It is not surprising that Janet Lewis was more drawn towards her aunt Floss's home than to her own; that Charlie's Minnie was happy there; that even the misfits, Edy and Ted, relaxed in that beneficent atmosphere. Florence appears to have been the only one who treated the young Craigs as ordinary people, and, in doing so, blew the froth off their pretensions. The Morrises' was the true 'home' of the rising generation, and Florence the 'mother' of them all: the gay, adoptive mother, full of mischief and love and understanding, which reached out beyond her own babies towards all the young fry she drew into her beneficent orbit. She appreciated—without approving—the pattern Kate was laying down for her daughters; her heart went out to Ellen—eternally involved in practical and emotional difficulties; she shared with Marion responsibility for Charlie's offspring—Minnie, Horace and the infant Beatrice. She kept in touch with her brothers, and with the squalid life of her sister-in-law, Edie-Tom (now a grass widow) and the Edie-Tom children. She was constant in attention to the old Ben Terrys in Cathcart Road, and to aunt Lizzie and uncle Tom Binsted; and all the time entertaining and being entertained, theatre-going, dressing beautifully and never for a moment neglecting her own home and family. If 'darling Floss' had a fault, it was that of burning the candle at both ends too persistently; all the vitality of a highly vitalized family seemed to collect in her small frame. Often ailing or exhausted, she acceded to the appeals of those who loved her to 'rest', in the country or by the sea; but these pauses in her hectic round were too short to mend the delicate machinery which, only ten years after her marriage, was beginning to run down. According to her diary, she was frequently 'seedy', or 'not the thing'—contemporary descriptions of what today might be called 'under the weather'. The Morrises rented a house on the river, near Moulsford, for summer holidays: Florence had a *tendresse* for the Thames. And the children loved it—with Nurse Bawtry and Alice the under-nurse, and their Terry grandparents and Uncle Tom and aunt Lizzie Binsted coming down to stay, and Tommy the white pony and Silver the grey mare.

Irving's second American tour took place in 1885. Ted—aged fourteen—accompanied his mother. An attractive boy in his own right, as the son of Ellen Terry he was the mark of every woman on the ship. He played a small part in *Eugene Aram* in Chicago, and, his taste now fully whetted for the stage, went impatiently back to college in Heidelberg—according to his ideas, a sheer waste of time.

The seeds of genius were germinating in him, but, over-flattered and very vain, he resented the discipline his mother tried, belatedly, to impose on him. Whether his art would have profited by the acceptance of that discipline may be disputed by future examiners of the career of Gordon Craig.

Wreathed in graces and talents, he had everything, in a minor degree: his mother's gift for acting, his sister's gift for music, his father's skill in the use of pencil and crayon; it took time to blend these into the creativity upon which the great reputation of Gordon Craig is based. To be a great creator and an indifferent executant was temporarily his lot. He had endless vision; as time went on he was an inspiration and a vital force to all interested in the onward movement of the theatre.

Unfortunately, he invited derision by his ignorance of the elementary mechanics of stagecraft, which he affected to despise, never having taken the trouble to master them. Had it been possible for himself and his sister to work in partnership (an arrangement temperamentally impossible for both), Gordon Craig's fame would have rested on a sure foundation and not been at the mercy of cranks and idealists who often misinterpreted his intentions, or turned them to ridicule in the eyes of serious craftsmen.

It was always the theatres which were wrong for Craig's designs, not his designs wrong for the theatres; and this may well have been true. But it was unfortunate, to put it mildly, that one of his most brilliant inspirations, which might have revolutionized the whole mechanics of setting the stage—his famous screens, whose beauty and fluidity created a sensation in the second decade of the present century—came to nothing, because he had not taken trouble to inform himself on the proper weighting of mobile scenery. It was unfortunate that when C. B. Cochran, at the zenith of his power, and one of Craig's greatest supporters and believers, offered him a theatre and *carte blanche* to demonstrate his ideas in construction and décor—a princely offer which, if it had been accepted, would have given the work of Gordon Craig a permanent home in London, came to nothing. Persuaded by his son, Craig came to London with ideas and designs for a production of *The Faerie Queene*, but his scheme, which included an orchestra of fifty performers, did not appeal to Cochran, whose notions of *carte blanche* did not run to an enlarged orchestra. Neither would give way. Disillusioned, Craig drifted back to Italy. It is unlikely that his philosophy deserted him, or degenerated into bitterness, when the news presently reached him, that Cochran had immensely augmented the orchestra for his production of *The Miracle*; resentment was not Craig's way.[1]

He had not yet learned the elements of lighting a stage (witness his

[1] I gave a false account, on hearsay, of this incident, in my biography of William Nicholson. I am indebted to Edward Carrick for the correction.

disastrous production of *The Vikings* at the Imperial, which cost his mother the better part of her hard-earned savings), or the mechanical, as distinct from the artistic, balance of a set. True, he could have engaged people to see to these details for him, but skilled theatre craftsmen were inclined to tire of working for so incalculable, so erratic a master—as servants lose heart when working for an employer who knows less than themselves, and to whom they cannot turn for direction.

He was, in the truest sense of the word, a visionary and an idealist: terms which unfortunately bracketed themselves with irresponsibility about money and human relationships. And it was he who, in the end, defeated himself.

The pure idealist cares nothing for money; Craig adored money, and spent it like water—anybody's money, excepting his own, of which indeed he had little. He could have made a fortune, for no such inventive mind has entered into the European theatre since its inception.

Could any of this have been corrected, in his youth, by forceful handling? Assuredly not. His was a formidable heredity on both sides. And the result—surely—was worth while. But all of the foregoing is ahead of our period, which is *circa* the eighteen-eighties.

Edy, deeply, conscientiously, was studying the piano under Hollander in Berlin; receiving the letters from her mother which are quoted in Ellen Terry's *Memoirs* and showing endless solicitude for her daughter. This wonderful correspondence will be published it is to be hoped, in its entirety.

All 'beauties', in the popular Press, bore a likeness to Ellen, who, according to Lady Salisbury, was '*never* immoral, only rather illegal'! For some curious reason, her portrait was never painted by the Pre-Raphaelites, who were her friends;[1] the only 'great' portrait of Ellen Terry is the Lady Macbeth, by Sargent. As a portrait of Ellen it is unconvincing; much better is the swirling study in black and white which hung over her bed in the last phase, at Burleigh Mansions, and is now in the National Portrait Gallery. All sorts of 'little' painters recorded her: Johnston Forbes-Robertson

[1] There is a crayon sketch by Burne-Jones.

(a member of the Lyceum Company), Graham Robertson, Mortimer Menpes, Solomon J. Solomon, and the Duchess of Rutland—the last a piece of pictoral journalism which is, nevertheless, an honest and respectable representation of Ellen Terry's Portia. Photographers did better by her than painters; the beautiful, if literal, studies by Window and Grove, and the few uncannily beautiful photographs by Hollyer (who recorded the Watts paintings). It is difficult to understand why Whistler—her ardent admirer—never painted Ellen Terry; it would seem she 'defeated' him. So, to see the true Ellen of the 'eighties and 'nineties, one must resort to the art of the camera—which had advanced far from the amateur efforts of Julia Cameron and Lewis Carroll in the 'seventies.

No surviving photographs give a fair record of Marion Terry. She was not photogenic, in the way her sisters were. Before the camera, her tender face—which was too irregular to be precisely beautiful—hardens; takes on angles and planes which none recognized who knew the original. I was fifteen years old when I first saw Marion Terry—not on the stage, but close at hand—and she was fifty-six; at one glance she wiped out all the Gabrielle Rays, Dare sisters and Lily Elsies whose postcards we collected in the schoolroom.[1]

III

1888 was the year of the Lyceum *Macbeth*—one of Irving's super-productions, yet unfortunate for Ellen Terry. She was young enough to play Miranda in *The Tempest* or Rosalind in *As You Like It*. As an actor, Irving was 'older than his age'. His Macbeth was bitterly attacked, yet would seem, on evidence, to have been one of his most intelligent performances. The crowd scenes were magnificent, full of original and individual business, perfect in design and in timing. Sullivan's music—revised by Irving—was exactly right. Ellen's Lady Macbeth started a controversy which was the best advertisement the play could have had. Lady Macbeth had

---

[1] A note from W. S. Gilbert, asking her to contribute to a charity performance, furnishes an illuminating vignette to Marion's personality. 'My dear Marion, you are haughty with me' (as indeed she was with everyone), 'but you are a good-hearted girl nevertheless.' It concludes, 'With my unvalued love, yours always, W. S. Gilbert.'

always been a 'banger' of a part: to be played with all the stops out
—pure villainess of melodrama. Ellen brought lights and shades
to it which no actress had previously imagined.

In her blue and green gown (now in the Museum at Smallhythe)
made by Mrs Nettleship from a design by Mrs Comyns Carr, she
was sitting for her portrait by Sargent (now at the Tate). Exhibited in
that same year at the New Gallery, it created a sensation—as did
Ellen herself at the private view. She had dyed the front of her hair
red, to tone with the squirrel-coloured plaits of Lady Macbeth, and
the dye would not come out. 'Oh Nelly, how *could* you?' wailed
Oscar Wilde, meeting her on Irving's arm in the foyer. 'Oh Oscar,
how *could* you?' she retorted, indicating the acanthus curls which
were his current affectation: and followed it up with the famous
faux pas, 'Oscar, you didn't really mean it, when you said to
Aimée,[1] "Aimée, if you were only a boy I could adore you"?' A
deathly silence fell, for gossip was already busy with the name of
Wilde, and, driving her home, Irving explained her indiscretion,
which Ellen—even then—was too innocent to take in.[2]

In that same year, a girl of most singular beauty, a protégée of
Gilbert, made her début in a charity revival of Gilbert's *Pygmalion
and Galatea* at the Lyceum. Marion Terry and Mary Anderson,
successively, had played Galatea, following Mrs Kendal, who had
created the part at the Haymarket. Mary Anderson graciously
agreed to the engagement of the unknown Julia Neilson in the
part of Cynisca, the jealous wife—an absurd part for a girl in her
teens. It was the launching of one of the most promising, and, in
the end, heartrendingly disappointing leading ladies of the
British stage.

She was of Scotch and Dutch-Jewish birth; 'tall as a tree', with
dolorous eyelids that concealed a sense of schoolboy fun, and dark

---

[1] Aimée Lowther.
[2] Ellen Terry (1921): 'When Oscar was found guilty of that unnameable sin . . .
I was revolted by his very name. . . . Then he wrote *De Profundis* . . . it purified
Oscar, and I loved him again.' She told of walking in Paris with Aimée Lowther
and 'seeing a man gazing wolfishly into a pastrycook's windows, biting his fingers.
"It's Oscar, let's go and speak to him." . . . We induced him to come and eat with
us in a quiet hotel and for a while he sparkled, just as of old. Oh, if we had only
written down the wonderful tales he told us!'

copper hair like Rapunzel's, down to her knees. Her tilted eye-brows and the natural cadences of her voice made her a gift to tragedy; the nobility of her carriage was suited to classic roles. But this sweet stupid girl, who adored the acting of Ellen Terry and strove to imitate it, persistently saw herself as a comedienne. She inherited her beauty—and her stupidity—from her mother, the Jewess Gertrude Emily Davis, whose brief married life with the Scottish jeweller, Alexander Ritchie Neilson, broke up soon after Julia was born. They had been through hard times while Mrs Neilson let lodgings in Doughty Street[1] and Julia was supposed to become a governess—the only profession open, in those days, to refined young women with some education behind them. But she had developed a voice and a gift for music, which procured her the entry to the Royal Academy of Music, where she also studied elocution. She was in demand for amateur dramatics—oddly enough, her first public appearance was in the Isle of Wight, so closely associated with the theatrical family into which she eventually married.

Gilbert wrote lyrically to a friend about her Cynisca; the critics were cool, apart from Clement Scott, who described her as 'no Cynisca', but a 'very promising Galatea of the future'—a hint which Gilbert took, and cast her (with Lewis Waller as Pygmalion) in a matinée at the Savoy.

Gilbert apparently took as much of a fancy to the lovely Julia as he had previously taken to Marion Terry. Those were the days when beauty was the first quality required of a leading lady; when such great actresses as Edith Evans and Flora Robson would not have had a look-in with any manager or producer. Julia was engaged (without salary) for morning performances of two of Gilbert's fairy comedies, and, in November of the year of her London début, surrendered her amateur status to play Ruth, at ten pounds a week, in a play he had written specially for her—*Brantinghame Hall*—which was produced at the St James's Theatre, under the management of Rutland Barrington (a member of the Savoy Company).

A young, ambitious actor-manager, Herbert Beerbohm Tree—he added Tree to his patronymic of Beerbohm for some reason

[1] Later in Montague Street.

207

unknown[1] during his amateur days, when he was a clerk in the office of a City merchant—saw Julia in *Brantinghame Hall* and offered her an engagement at the Haymarket Theatre, to which, as manager, he had transferred from the Comedy. It was not an important or particularly tempting offer: third item on the triple bill he had instituted for morning performances.

In the previous year, he had successfully presented Marion Terry in a play called *Hard Hit* by the up-and-coming young playwright, Henry Arthur Jones. According to the *Daily Telegraph*, it was Marion's first appearance after 'a long and anxious illness'— of which no record appears to survive. According to an anonymous Press cutting, she 'exercised her limp and clinging method to excellent purpose in the character of the heroine'. 'Limp and clinging', to one who saw her in her prime, would seem the last adjectives to apply to the art of Marion Terry. The *Telegraph* and the *News* speak of her 'power and variety', her 'energy and force'; the *Pink 'Un* says she 'took her audience by storm in several of her stronger scenes' and the *Observer* notes 'her increased physical strength'.

However that may be, with the notable attraction of Marion Terry, Tree made enough out of his first season at the Haymarket to justify an experiment which modern managers might do worse than follow. At his morning performances an unknown young actor or actress might be given a chance: the audience being guaranteed by the already distinguished name of Tree.

He had sent his new recruit out on tour to gain experience, and she came back to open in the autumn season of 1889 in the small but flashy part of Julie de Noirville in Robert Buchanan's adaptation of *Roger la Honte*, called in its English version *A Man's Shadow*. In the bill, as Suzanne Laroque, was Minnie Terry, not yet in her teens, but a more experienced actress than her beautiful aunt-to-be, Julia Neilson.

That same year Julia played in a piece of Gilbertian claptrap, worse—if anything—than *Brantinghame Hall*. In the triple bill for the matinée, Tree put on Gilbert's one-act called *Comedy and Tragedy*. He came to Julia and told her, 'I've engaged Fred Terry to play

[1] His half-brother Max said it was because Beerbohm was too difficult a name for the gallery to shout.

Julia Neilson-Terry and baby Phyllis

Phyllis Neilson-Terry

Dennis Neilson-Terry

Dennis Neilson-Terry
and Mary Glynne

lovers to you, because he's tall.' At the rehearsals, it was obvious that the love-scenes were something more than acting.

Out at St Albans, a Mrs Gibson, a close friend of Ellen's, lived at Ashwell House. The big Georgian house with grounds seems to have been a holiday resort for all the Terrys; Florence went there to recuperate after Olive's birth, Marion stayed there, and Ellen, with Irving and the young Craigs. Irving, by then, was 'a member of the family'. He and Ellen holidayed together, and everyone appears to have shut his or her eyes to the obvious. In April of 1889 they had received the royal command to Sandringham—from the Prince and Princess of Wales, 'before Her Majesty the Queen'. The chosen pieces were *The Bells* and the Trial Scene from *The Merchant of Venice*; in his usual princely fashion, Irving not only had special sets built to fit the constricted space, but converted the ballroom at Sandringham into a miniature replica of the Lyceum, proscenium, act-drop and all.

In the autumn of that year Ellen was again presented to disadvantage in a French Revolution drama, in which she had little to do but look heartrendingly beautiful as the mother of a young man condemned to the guillotine; as the young man was played by her son Gordon Craig, aged seventeen, she was content once more to play a 'second-fiddle part'. Sent down from Heidelberg, Ted (as he continued to be called by his friends and family), had a good stage presence, good looks and some talent; he had found, it appeared, his *métier*. His mother's rejoicing in his success was clouded by the defeat of Edy's promising career as a pianist. The dark, serious girl had come home from Berlin; not even to her mother could she talk of her bitter disappointment. Rheumatism, the arch-enemy of the instrumentalist, had already established itself in her young joints; she could no longer spend the hours in practice that her professors required of her.

It would not appear that Edith Craig, now in her twentieth year, had any deep desire to go on the stage; all her heart was in music. Steadfast of purpose, she was not the kind lightly to switch to another thing when the profession to which she had dedicated herself deserted her, through no fault of her own. One thing she could not abide was inoccupation; it was the easy and natural thing to join the Lyceum Company as a Walking Lady (from which eventually she graduated to small parts).

She had become handsome; very tall—for those days, when a 'womanly' height was supposed to be about five feet four; Edy overtopped 'womanliness' by a good four inches—and an excellent carriage; she wore stage costumes beautifully, with a true sense of period, as became her father's daughter. She had an infallible sense for the creation of costume—of which, on occasion, Irving was pleased to avail himself; he had a warm regard for Edy. And her voice was her Terry grandmother's: that deep, peculiarly resonant voice that lent value to the least of her utterances. It may seem curious that with all these qualities Edith Craig never made a name for herself as an actress; for this there could be two reasons. The first, that she, the ardent feminist, had not sufficient of the feminine in her to rouse the 'keen interest in the manly breast' described by Charles Reade. Emotionally and artistically, she was more interested in, and interesting to, her own sex than to the male. The second, that her markedly powerful—many called it aggressive—personality did not endear her to people with influence in her own profession. She suffered from the defect of 'always knowing best'. It is possible she did know best, but she had not the wit, tact, insincerity or plain common sense to disguise her knowledge, and in this was not helped by the well-meaning sycophants who gathered around her—as they gathered round her mother. And she had not Ellen's sense of humour and proportion to guide her! Edy to Edy was a very important and always-right person. And— rather amusingly—she, who encouraged a little court of her own, despised her mother's entourage of adorers, and resented the time Ellen 'wasted' on 'valueless' people. One of Ellen's great qualities was that, to her, no honest human being was 'valueless'. This was the thin end of the wedge: the beginning of the disaffection— 'estrangement' is too strong a word—which was eventually to separate Ellen Terry and her daughter; a separation which lasted for years, and was deliberately fostered by the one mainly responsible for it. Many of Ellen's friends fastened the blame on Edy; but it cannot have been easy for a young woman of powerful character to live in the shadow of so dazzling a creature as Ellen Terry, and to see the carelessness with which her brother made and discarded his innumerable conquests. To have all the Terry virtues—and, added to them, some peculiarly her own—and *not* to have charm must have been embittering for a sensitive (few credited her with that) female creature. So she sought, and found, her own compensations.

The decade closed, for Terrys, in the shadow of Sarah's rapidly failing health. The house in Cathcart Road had become a house of anxiety. Marion, characteristically setting her own wishes aside—she had long hoped for an establishment of her own—nightly came back from the theatre to her mother's bedroom, wondering whether the loving heart had failed.

Sarah stubbornly refused the companion-nurse they wanted for her, so the burden of her feebleness fell on the 'children' themselves. She was frequently taken to Moray Lodge and Campden House Road, where she faded and rallied, and was adored by her grandchildren, and kept up the pretence that there was nothing at all the matter with her. She kept it up for two more years, when a stroke put an end to her gallant pretensions.

She was thought to be dying. All her children and the Lewis grandchildren gathered around. Suddenly she became very restless, and was evidently trying to speak. Little Lucy Lewis said, 'Darling, you want them to go? *"The Show must go on."* '

Then 'as they quietly moved off, she sank back on her pillows, peaceful and satisfied.'[1]

Sarah rallied and the sun shone on her before the end of the year. George Alexander, an erstwhile member of the Lyceum Company, found backing to go into management of the Avenue Theatre—later the Playhouse—and engaged Fred Terry for the name-part in *Doctor Bill*, in which he opened in 1890. Sarah was not at his first night, but his notices, which confirmed his great success, were read to her. 'Darling Tops'—Fred Terry, with ten years of experience behind him, had at last got a London lead. He could pay off some of his gambling debts (and joyously run up some more). He could seriously contemplate marriage with the beautiful girl with whom he had been in love ever since their first meeting in Gilbert's *Comedy and Tragedy* at the Haymarket Theatre.

[1] Letter from Lucy Terry Lewis to the author.

CHAPTER THREE

Turn of the Tide

The Russian influenza epidemic which swept the country in the winter of 1890-91 caught the two old people in Cathcart Road and filled the hearts of their children with foreboding. Sarah begged them 'not to come near', for both Ellen and Fred were rehearsing and Marion playing at the St James's. Ellen drove round most mornings from her home in Barkston Gardens, but was wise enough not to go in; with her offerings of 'a little turtle soup' for her dear old Dad she left scribbled notes, asking her sisters to send or bring her news of the invalids.

The theatre was prospering as it had not done since the time of Garrick; mid-Victorian *morbidezza* had lifted and a sparkling Society galloped in the pleasure hunt led by the Prince and Princess of Wales and the Marlborough House *côterie*; there was a rush to imitate the 'goings-on' of the vulgarly called 'Smart Set' and (in the opinion of the older generation) a corresponding relaxation of morals and manners, especially among young married people: actually there was a great recrudescence of wit and elegance, and intellectuality was coming into fashion among the aristocracy. A formidable little old figure, withdrawn at Osborne or Balmoral for so long, had been galvanized by her Jubilee into activities no less gratifying than they were disconcerting to her entourage; her loyal subjects gave emphatic proof of the hold she retained upon their hearts—made stronger, if anything, by the fact that her influence on their lives was much diminished. The Grandmother of Europe was in immense form. The Grandmother of the Terrys, two years younger than Victoria, was (as her daughter Ellen wrote, only ten years later, in a book she eventually gave to me) 'wearin' awa to the Land o' the Leal'. Like all the theatrical profession, a devotee of the Throne, Sarah's twilight was warmed by the marks of Royal favour which had been bestowed on her children. The Lewis pew at St Mary

Abbots adjoined that of Princess Louise and her husband the Marquis of Lorne, who were graciously pleased to exchange greetings after matins (one may be sure, bearing her Wesleyan youth in mind, that Sarah staunchly called it 'Morning Service'), and Arthur and Kate, with young Katie, received a card for a garden party at Kensington Palace, where the Heir to the Throne stepped out of his way to speak to Kate Terry, and the blushing Katie curtsied to her future Sovereign. And the Princess of Wales's known admiration for Ellen was ripening towards the personal friendship of which the latter received many proofs up to the time of Queen Alexandra's death.

How far from St Helena. . .? How far from a tavern on Spice Island and a builder's yard to the gates of a palace?

The Dancing Girl, at the Haymarket, was 'the talk of the town'. It was supposed to be *risqué*; its heroine was a Quaker girl, innocently domiciled on an island (unspecified) off Cornwall, who became the 'favourite mistress' of a Duke. Into this play Henry Arthur Jones, a writer of little education but acute theatre sense, packed all he had got: of vice and virtue three bags full, seduction, bankruptcy and attempted suicide—the last averted by the introduction, practically at the fall of the curtain, of a character previously unheard of, who, at some equally unheard of moment in the past, had been rescued by the intended suicide from death in a carriage accident. The Duke did not down his 'cup of poison'.

The Dancing Girl would have been a riot in the twentieth-century revival of old melodramas which followed the production of an unforgettable piece called *Young England*—written in all seriousness by its author, which turned overnight into a raging farce, ran 278 nights, and netted the author a small fortune. Somehow *The Dancing Girl* got overlooked.

But in 1891, a fashionable (and, by implication, sophisticated) audience took it dead seriously. Tree's performance as the Duke brought down the house; James Fernandez, the Dancing Girl's father, in his denunciation of his errant daughter, scored an immense personal success—and the principal attraction was Drusilla Ives, the 'Dancing Girl' herself, played by Miss Julia Neilson.

Julia's spectacular beauty was her principal asset, but there was a joy, an ardour about her acting which captivated not only her audiences but also those who worked with her. She was not yet so headstrong as not to accept direction—according to old theatre-goers, Julia Neilson could have been moulded into an excellent actress under a powerful director who did not suffer from the handicap of being her husband.

That ripe, rich, very bad portrait by Collier which hung in their drawingroom, and which at her daughter's suggestion she gave to the Royal College of Music holds, for all its 'Christmas supplement' character, more than a little essence of the lovely creature who conquered the town and the susceptible heart of young Fred Terry.

Fred, playing juvenile to her lead, with one sensational scene which so terrified the author by its 'immorality' on the first night that he implored them to cut it out (which they had the sense not to do), was deeply in love with her, and she with him. But the course of true love was not running smooth.

Julia's mother, Gertrude Emily Neilson, was all against the match. She had an exaggerated idea of her daughter's talent, and was not in the least beglamoured by the name of Terry. Fred Terry, in her opinion, was an erratic young man, with no financial security. Utterly unrealistic in her approach to The Profession, she had calculated that, under Tree's management, Julia might make enough within a few years to retire from the stage and, with her self-made *dot*, to attract a wealthy husband of sober and conventional antecedants, preferably a member of the Peerage. It may be taken for granted that Fred, by his violence of opinion, his obstinacy and choleric resistance to opposition, did not sweeten the putative relationship.

The Dancing Girl ran for more than three hundred performances in town, and then went on the road. In the last week of the tour, Fred and Julia rushed up from Brighton to the Registrar's Office in Marylebone Road, and returned husband and wife: the beginning of a famous partnership. Originally a partnership of love, it became in 1900 also a business partnership, which for a quarter of a century commanded the devotion of town and country. The relationship of Fred and his mother-in-law followed to the end the classic pattern of mutual detestation.

On 1 March 1892, five months after her youngest son's marriage,

Sarah Terry died. Ellen Terry wrote to a friend two days afterwards:

> Yes, my pretty Dear has left us & I pray we may never battle to live as she did, up to almost the last moment.

Her children and some of the grandchildren came to 'look their last on all things lovely', for, the battle over, kind death restored to the tired face the serene beauty of youth. Ellen's letter continues:

> My poor little Floss was so broken up—but she & Marion too—are magnificent in hard times—they are not only sunshine women. Little Floss for 7 hours without moving on her knees, & with her little white wax fingers moistening the poor lips—& speaking cheerfully to her of the children.
> What one can go through with, without bursting!

It was Ellen who removed the wedding ring from the hand which had so often lent its warmth to their little chilled limbs in lodgings and dressingrooms, and its coolness to their feverish brows, and who cut a tress of silver hair from the quiet head. Among Fred Terry's papers was found an envelope addressed in Ellen's writing to 'Father: open with care'. It enclosed a sheet of writing paper headed 22 Barkston Gardens, Earl's Court, S.W., on which was written:

> Father to Mother.
> Mother to Father—1st March 1892. 7.30 in the evening.
>   Mother's Wedding Ring.

The ring came to Phyllis Neilson-Terry after her father's death, and was eventually given by her to her husband, Heron Carvic. The silver lock of hair is still in Phyllis's possession, last witness to the beloved 'Miss Yerret', the grandmother she never knew (Phyllis was born in the year of Sarah Terry's death).

Ellen, Marion and Fred were all acting on the night their mother died; they all went dutifully to their theatres, as a last tribute to that gallant spirit. Sarah was buried hard by, in Brompton Cemetery, where, four years later, Ben was to join her.

'What was to be done about Father?' was a problem for them all. An old gentleman in failing health (not that he would have admitted it) was a responsibility which—it was tacitly agreed among them

215

—should not fall entirely upon Marion, with her career to consider, her frequent provincial tours and her own not too solid health. Neither Ellen nor Fred (Julia was expecting her first baby) had suitable accommodation to offer; no help was to be expected from the Georges, Charlie (for all his love) or Edie-Tom; they had their own problems of existence. The sumptuous doors of Moray Lodge and Campden Hill Road, although open wide, offered no attractions to Bohemian Ben, still dapper, still addicted to the company of 'the boys' and happiest when he was strolling round the theatre purlieus, reviving sweet memories of days gone by over a tankard of ale in his favourite hostelries and eager as ever to glean the 'news' whispered around stage doors or rumoured on 'The Rialto', as the pavements round and about the Strand and Charing Cross Road were known to The Profession. He had, by then, serenely accepted his 'retirement'.

It appears from one of Ellen's notes to him that Ben had settled the question of his future in his usual independent fashion.

My dear old Father,
. . . you have elected to live by yourself now, and would soon make a mess of it if you go and get ill.

He remained at 57 Cathcart Road; there was a housekeeper of sorts, and his daughters were constantly in and out, to assure themselves of his well-being.

It was a bad twelve months for Terrys. In the August of 1891 Florence had written into her diary:

Sweet Babe [Hugh] very ill at seven o'clock in the evening.

In times of trouble Terrys drew closely together. Lucy was sent by Kate to look after her aunt Flossie; it should have been Janet, her aunt's 'familiar', but Janet appears to have been out of touch—probably away from home.

Sleeping in her aunt's bedroom, Lucy was roused by Floss springing out of bed to fling open the window. The frightened girl ran to her aunt's side, and Florence, between waking and sleeping, murmured in the voice of a somnambulist, 'Little Hughie's soul is flying to God.'

In her diary that twentieth day of August 1891 she entered, 'God called my little baby boy to him. Amen.'

It was, according to her brother Ben, writing from Mandalay with his usual solicitude for family fortunes and misfortunes, of which he knew so pathetically little,[1] 'dear old Floss's first great misfortune'.

> Thank God in her last letter to me she seems to be more resigned and quieted. . . . I am but a very poor hand at writing a sympathetic letter. . . . Does sympathy soothe the wounds or does it give another stab to the wounded one? I don't know . . . but I think I would prefer bearing my grief in silence and alone—

—as he had to bear it, when the news of his mother's death reached him within seven months.

Tom's letters from Tasmania, on receiving the news of Sarah's death, are outpourings of misery—whether at the loss of his mother or of the monthly five pounds she was allowing him is not made quite as clear as the writer undoubtedly intended.

To recover from the shock of the baby's death, Florence, with her daughter Olive, was sent by her husband to the Metropole at Brighton. It may have been Florence's suggestion that Sarah should accompany them. The fragile old lady, convalescing from influenza, was collected from Cathcart Road, and on her return to town Florence wrote into her diary 'Mother seems very ill'. (It was not long before Sarah had the stroke which paralysed her and silenced her beautiful voice for ever. Yet she managed, through somebody— probably Edie-Tom, who, for good reasons, had maintained close contact with her mother-in-law—to send the January and February remittances to Tom, who allowed, in his belated acknowledgement twenty-seven days after his mother's death, that he had heard from his wife that she—Sarah—was 'so ill'.)

Earlier in the year of baby Hugh's death, Florence was driving her niece Minnie (aged nine) to rehearsals of *Charles I* at the Lyceum. Little dark Minnie—her father Charles in miniature—was as intelligent as a squirrel; she was cast as the Princess Elizabeth, and

[1] 'It was well worth waiting for a few years, to get your kind and loving letter dated 7th Sept for the which ever so many thanks, dear Dad. . . . It was worth waiting ten years—your last to me was dated 1880—to get your last dear letter.' Young Ben to Ben.

must have looked it to perfection. Wills, the author of the play, the big, peasant-aristocrat Irishman, with his long beard and long pipe, his wild eye and his addiction to chewing raw onions, died that same year. It was he who adapted *The Vicar of Wakefield* into the play *Olivia*, in whose title-role Minnie's aunt Ellen triumphed under Hare's management at the Court Theatre in 1878, and in the Lyceum revival in 1885.

Ellen Terry found the part of Henrietta Maria, to Irving's Charles I, 'unrewarding'—although Isabella Bateman, in the original production, made a notable success of it. No records of Minnie's Princess Elizabeth survive; it was little more than a walk-on.

In some rebellious mood, Ellen bought a trivial old play of Charles Reade's, called *Nance Oldfield*, which Irving, to humour her, put on in front of a revival of *The Corsican Brothers*. This was no act of altruism on his part; there was nothing for Ellen in the *Brothers*, and it would have been bad business to leave Ellen Terry out of the bill.

There was a part for Ted, which undoubtedly influenced her in the purchase of this piece of theatrical claptrap—which she kept in her repertory for years, and left it on record that she 'never had an Alexander Oldsworthy so good as my son'—although she subsequently played it to Laurence Irving, Martin Harvey, and Harcourt Williams. This may be the place to note that, to Terrys, all Terrys were *hors concours*.

According to a note of Christopher St John's, Ellen Terry said, some time in 1928, 'My Ted . . . acts far better than he writes'. Few of their contemporaries seem to have agreed with her. Gordon Craig is a superb writer, in his own genre. Had he not been the son of Ellen Terry, it is doubtful he would, for all his charm and theatre sense, have achieved any but a minor position as an actor. He spent eight years (on and off) at the Lyceum, and some months with Ben Greet. Shaw and Granville Barker praised his work and offered him parts. Irving had no great opinion of his talent. It is fair to add that Irving had no great opinion of the talent of his son Laurence, who, but for his premature and tragic death in the sinking of the *Empress of Ireland*, was set to be the leader of the twentieth-century theatre. But to compare the son of Ellen Terry, as an actor, with Laurence Irving or Martin Harvey is unfair. (Gordon Craig was later, with no justice, to be contemptuous about Benson; neither of them was a 'great' actor; they were both visionaries. Benson was, probably, innocently ignorant about the existence of Craig. They might well have met over their mutual devotion—from totally different angles—to the art of the Theatre. Craig's view was broader and more forward-looking than Benson's; Benson's more classical, and therefore narrower. In comparison with Craig, reared in the theatre, Benson was, admittedly, an amateur: but their idealism should surely have drawn these two rare young men together.)

In *Henry VIII* both Henry Irving and Ellen Terry had parts worthy of their mettle. It was one of the most magnificent of the Lyceum productions; Irving's Wolsey was a great performance and Ellen as Queen Katherine, loaded with silver brocade and gold lace antimacassars from Whiteley's, dissolved her audience in tears and received rapturous letters from poets and painters.

Yet she was unhappy and restless. In her middle forties she was being forced into parts she could have played in her sixties. Irving was her senior by ten years only, yet, so far as his outlook on the work was concerned, could have been her father. She was burning to attack the moderns: the fashionable Mr Wilde; an incalculable Irishman called Shaw (with whom she entered into correspondence the following year, when he presented a play called *Widowers' Houses* at the Royalty Theatre, under J. T. Grein's management); a young Scot called Barrie, who, in the same year, hit the town with his *Walker, London*. Although Toole, who played the lead in *Walker*, was a personal friend of Irving, it was impossible to interest the latter in these up-and-coming playwrights. Or in Ibsen, who brought to many playgoers their first intimations of 'live' theatre.

It could be that Irving was shrewder than his critics accounted him. Neither Barrie nor Shaw (when eventually she gave them a trial) contributed one iota to the glory that was Ellen Terry. Neither had in himself anything scaled to her artistic dimensions. The illimitable vanity of Shaw, the infantilism of Barrie, both pretending to know what her son was later to describe as Ellen Terry's 'secret self'—never produced anything meet for her as an actress. Shaw, the iconoclast, only by his correspondence increased her dissatisfaction with her current situation, and was incapable of offering any alternative. A destroyer of false gods, he had nothing to offer in place of that which he destroyed. Ellen herself made no success of Ibsen, when eventually she tackled him under her son's direction.[1]

She chafed against the restrictions imposed on her at the Lyceum. In her middle forties, still young and beautiful (as few women of her age were in the eighteen-nineties, when it was usual, after passing the forty mark, to sink back into elderliness), she had never been given the opportunity of playing Rosalind or Imogen. In between Shakespearian productions she was forced into old-fashioned dramas, which gave her 'lovely' parts, but advanced her no inch in her profession. She, the ambitious, the far-seeing, the artist on many planes as well as her own, had the misfortune to be linked with an old-fashioned commercial manager, whose gifts as an actor, far from extending themselves, hardened in their narrow mould as time went on.

Incapable of jealousy, or of its milder sister, envy, she could not but be aware of Marion, with George Alexander at the St James's, acting in Wilde comedy.

Some of her admirers deplored Marion Terry's acceptance of the part of Mrs Erlynne in *Lady Windermere's Fan*. Marion, the embodiment of purity on the stage! To begin with, how could she ever look it, with her cool brow, her quiet eyes and the ineradicable gentlewomanliness of her bearing? Marion was relentless in condemnation of members of her own profession who 'looked like actresses' off the stage. 'One should not be noticeable' was one of her spoken tenets—to which she was wont innocently to give the lie when asked for her name by assistants at the West End stores she patronized. Her full-throated 'I am Miss Marion Terry' was guaranteed to switch heads in her direction from the farthest reaches of whichever floor she happened to be on, and, perfect actress as she was, she never managed wholly to conceal her satisfaction that this should be so.

[1] On several occasions she expressed her regret that she had never had an opportunity of playing *Ghosts*. As Mrs Alving she would have been admirably cast, and could have made her son into a good Oswald.

She not only realized the part of Mrs Erlynne in her every in-flection and movement, she looked it—with her dark copper hair touched up with henna (the Bad Woman's colour) and brushed with bronze powder; with her elegant figure laced so tightly into her glittering gowns that it looked as if one could break her off at the waist between finger and thumb, and her heavy eyelids painted a greenish-grey, to accentuate their Mona Lisa droop. The timbre of her voice altered, became slow and sultry. Her performance, today, would be called 'sexy', a description from which she would have shuddered away. The critics were unanimous in their acclamation of the 'new' Marion Terry. A scandalous minority whispered that, at last, they were seeing the 'real' Marion Terry. These were incapable of recognizing the 'great' Marion Terry, whose imagination and technique were equal—as any actor's must be—to spanning the gulf between private character and the character to be interpreted in accordance with the playwright's intention. Audiences in the eighteen-nineties were still naïve; when, four years later, scandal blew up about the blameless name of Marion Terry, plenty of people who should have known better looked back on her per-formance of Mrs Erlynne, and said, 'I told you so.'

That unfortunate twelve months included the letting of Moray Lodge, 'with option to purchase'. It was Arthur Lewis's decision, and to its implications Kate deliberately closed her eyes. She had four daughters to launch on Society, and when her husband informed her he had found a large country house at Englefield Green, to which during three months of the summer they could remove household and stables, her mind worked quickly. There could be no enter-tainment on the Moray Lodge scale at Englefield Green, so Lucy had better accept the Hallés' invitation to Campiglio, and Katie might be sent off with Janet on a few weeks' visit to the Medleys in Devonshire. Kate, no country-lover, resigned herself to local hospitalities, and hoped for the best.

It must have been baffling to Kate that her daughters, well educated, pretty, popular and presented against an exceptional background, had not so far attracted the attention which defines itself within an engagement ring. Katie had been 'out' six years, and had not yet had a proposal. Janet, Lucy, and even the schoolgirl Mabel were already crowding her on the social scene.

When Katie came back from her Devon holiday with a *beau*, Kate was instantly on the alert—although it seemed unfortunate that her admirer, a Mr Frank Gielgud, was a widower (fortunately without 'encumbrances'). He had impeccable connections: father in the War Office and Special Correspondent to continental newspapers. Mr Gielgud was Lithuanian on his father's side (what were Lithuanians?) and his mother Polish: a pity about all this foreign blood. But on the maternal side there was an actress of some distinction, which suggested a community of tastes.

Katie Lewis met her Tall, Dark Stranger in the year of her début (Jubilee Year), and, during the interim between that and their second meeting, six years later, his young American wife had died.

They had interests in common—the theatre, music and books— but these soon gave way to more intimate topics. Serious Katie attracted him by her unlikeness to the majority of her flighty contemporaries. They went for long, deliciously melancholy walks, in the course of which Mr Gielgud poured out his 'flood of memories'. Katie must have been a very long-suffering girl. It cannot have been inspiring, hour after hour, to listen to a spate of reminiscence about a woman she had never known, but kindly did her best to imagine.

Mr Gielgud was made welcome at Moray Lodge, and in that warm and pleasant atmosphere—to which he contributed his gifts as a musician—gradually shed his melancholy. He had, actually, a very good earthy sense of humour, which was only temporarily mislaid. By profession he was a stockbroker, which lent him the solid background which appealed to Katie's parents.

Her reception of his proposal, at a charity ball, must have been chilling: 'Only if my father approves.'

Katie Lewis had what was presently to be called 'a father fixation'. This comes out strongly in her autobiography. She was deeply sincere, and so was her suitor, Frank Gielgud; neither of them affected to be 'in love'. She had reached the age when, for all her outward assurance, she was anxious about her future. She was essentially a 'home'-girl (her mother's 'amenable daughter'), and in Frank Gielgud, with his previous experience of marriage, found compatability rather than romance.

He, who had loved his lost Evelyn with passion, craved mainly companionship, and recognized it in Katie Lewis. Her youthful conventionality and calm offered peace; her perceptivity in the arts added the 'something more' to their cool relationship.

Kate drew a breath of relief; one at least of her girls was *rangée*.

The tenant did not take up the option to buy; Moray Lodge was still theirs in October, for Kate's Silver Wedding. There was an immense *soirée*, which went on until four in the morning: a gathering of the clans—Terrys, Lewises, Morrises—and, as the night wore on, of theatre people. The Lewis girls wore silver bodices off their elegant, wine-bottle shoulders and wide tulle skirts. There were dancing and music; Fred came from the Haymarket and Marion from the St James's to perform a one-act play. Kate's and Arthur's health was drunk, time and again, in champagne, and somebody— was it Arthur?—remembered to propose Ben, who, with his silver sheaf of beard covering his white tie, was the most venerable there. Titles and Orders and great names in abundance. It was the last blaze of the famous hospitalities of Moray Lodge.

William Morris bought Bennets, at Harpenden, as a summer house for Florence and the children. 'Dear Harpy', Floss called it. She had Ellen's true love of the country; the puffy oaks—like green, captive balloons—and broad Hertfordshire commons laid balm to her spirit. Lover of London gaiety though she was, it was bliss to escape to Harpy, to gather the children round her, and have Dad and Polly, Fred and Julia, Nell (when she could spare the time), Janet and small Minnie down on holiday. She was not well; she had not been really well since the birth of Hugh. 'My legs *have* gone back to their normal condition, but I am weak still and of course find I am able to do little or nothing.' 'I have such a horrid toothache!' —such phrases recur in letters to her 'dearest Dad'.

And now, to compensate her for the loss of 'Sweet Babe', another baby was on the way.

Quiet, shy Geoffrey and gay Jack (a 'true Terry') loved Harpy, as their cousins, Ted and Edy, had loved it going on for twenty years ago. Nervous, lawless, highly strung Olive who, after two days at Kindergarten, made her Mother promise never to send her to school again, tormented the governesses and was amenable only to her adored mama. She and her brothers detested invitations to Moray Lodge, where they were tolerated only to fag after tennis balls, and found it hard to realize that four prim young ladies in long skirts, puffed sleeves and boaters were cousins, of their own generation.

Ted now petrified his mother by announcing his intention of marrying May Gibson, a young art student, a couple of years older than himself. (He had just had his twentieth birthday.) Ellen Terry philosophically noted in her diary that it might turn out well, 'if the young couple will not be too hasty'. Vain hope indeed!

No young woman he fancies in matrimony is ever good enough for the mother of an only son. May was the daughter of her old friend Mrs Gibson at St Albans: often her hostess—and Irving's; often hostess to all the Terry family. May was not at all the non-entity she was considered by her mother-in-law to be. Small, with dark intelligent eyes, she concealed beneath a somewhat colourless exterior (which misled Ellen) a strong and already determined character, and plenty of courage—all of which, as time went on, she was to need. Some forty years later, she was as hard as nails and a sharp business-woman. Ellen was right in one respect: that she was the wrong wife for Teddy. But who was the right wife for a youth who was, at twenty, virtually an adolescent?

Talented and practical, May arranged the details of their elope-ment—to which Ted lent himself the more joyously in that it was totally unnecessary. The parents, although not enthusiastic, were not positively antagonistic to the marriage. But it was all very ro-mantic and Forest of Arden-ish! It was clever of May, to make an elopement of it.

The most important and enlivening incident of that darkened year was the birth to Fred and Julia of their daughter Phyllis.

It was no leaf but an oak that fell in October of 1892; 'What a year, what a year,' murmured Ellen, when they brought her the news of the death of Tennyson. Irving's business manager, Bram Stoker, had been at Farringford only eleven days before to obtain the poet's consent to the cuts Irving wished to make in the play (*Becket*) which he planned to produce in the following year. Feeble as he was, the aged Laureate not only went painstakingly through the revised

Fred Terry

Julia Neilson

Ellen Terry

script, detecting at least one instance where the blue pencil, slipping up, had made nonsense of the text,[1] but agreed, though with hesitation due to his weariness, to Irving's suggestion, diffidently put forward by Stoker, that another speech was needed in the Northampton castle scene to strengthen Becket's position with the King and make it clear that the people of England were behind him.

Within a few days, to the astonishment and delight of Irving, Tennyson produced sixteen lines of resounding blank verse (almost certainly the last he ever wrote), which were remarkable not only for their force and dramatic fitness but also for their unity with the original work, which, not written for the stage, had been published in 1884. Irving had always seen Becket as a great part for himself, and had been tinkering with it over the years.

The year closed in darkness for Ellen. *King Lear* was produced in November, and, in spite of a tremendous reception by the first-nighters, was to prove a failure. The beautiful Ford Madox Brown production could not cover the Lear's lack of vitality and pace; he played it too old, too slow. (When W. J. Holloway, one of the most valued of the Lyceum Company, took over during Irving's attack of the grippe, the play ran twenty minutes shorter—to the relief of all, including the audience.) Ellen's Cordelia was swamped by such a performance: she could make no headway against Irving's deadly and unvarying tempo.

And now Irving's mind was full of nothing but *Becket*—in which she had a wretched part as Fair Rosamund—and he was murmuring about *King Arthur*, an even worse prospect for her. She could only hope that another American tour would interrupt these projects.

Was it all over, that radiance which, when it began in 1878, seemed as though it would last for ever? (*It was*, although her loyalty

---

[1] ' "Who is God, the Virgin?"
' "Who is *what*?" I asked. . . .
' "God, the Virgin. . . . Here it is."
'. . . To my astonishment I read:
' "I do commend my soul to God, the Virgin." '
Bram Stoker's Life of Henry Irving.

Irving's pencil had cut out the succeeding lines:

> St Denis of France and St Alphége of England
> And all the tutelary saints of Canterbury.'

Fortunately the error amused Tennyson very much.

to the Lyceum was to last ten more long years.) All those years of happy artistic and domestic intimacy, the holidays they spent together, the visits to Moray Lodge and to Divach, where Henry fitted in so beautifully that he seemed part of the family; when they entertained together at The Grange, Brook Green—the house he bought because neither his apartment in Grafton Street nor her house in Barkston Gardens was suitable for the hospitality they wished to offer their friends. He, who had no family life of his own, had appeared to enjoy the close-knit Terry circle—Edy and Ted, who took him comfortably for granted, the big-eyed Lewis girls, 'dripping devotion', the husbands, Arthur Lewis and William Morris, who made him respectfully welcome in their homes. All this, to begin with, had supplied a warm obbligato to their private life. What Ellen did not grasp was that Irving had no taste for domesticity; she had encountered, for the first time, one whose egoism was infinitely greater than her own, and who was pitiless in the pursuit of his own interests and desires. Her passion for her art was no less than his but, at this period, she was a lamb in the grip of a vulture.

Speaking of those days, she said, round about 1921, 'He began to get tired of me and to pay attention to other women. I wasn't jealous, but I said, "I love and adore you, and while you wanted it everything that was mine was yours. But when you ceased to want it—*No*." '[1]

[1] E.T. to the author, *circa* 1922.

'Henry is so nice to me lately that I'm convinced he has a new "flame".'—Ellen to Bernard Shaw, 18 January 1898.

CHAPTER FOUR

Chiaroscuro

For Fred and Julia, established with Tree at the Haymarket, those early 'nineties were halcyon years. It seemed that nothing could go wrong. On their return from their 'honeymoon' tour (they went straight out on the road with *The Dancing Girl* again, and reopened with a London revival: a piece of shrewd organization on the part of Tree) they had a tremendous reception from the first-night audience. They rushed into lodgings, and eventually found a tiny flat not far from the theatre, into which Julia flung a few sticks of furniture. (The only properly furnished room was the bedroom; that and their dressingrooms in the theatre mattered more to the lovers than apartments in which to receive their guests.)

Tree put on *Hamlet*, in which there was nothing for Julia, but Fred played Laertes to the satisfaction of his sisters—which meant more to him than the approval of the critics. In that antic production, his was one of the few sober and classical performances. Among other innovations which Tree brought to his *Hamlet* was a chorus of angels at the end; into his own performance he introduced as many tricks as a wagonload of monkeys.

In the fall of the year Julia had her first child, Phyllis, and was ready to take up the lead in Stuart Ogilvie's adaptation of Kingsley's *Hypatia*—an immensely showy production with sets and costumes by Alma Tadema, an esteemed archaeological painter of the period. 'Tad' had a vivid realization of Greek, Greco-Roman and Greco-Egyptian art, and the right technique to translate it literally into the idiom of the theatre. A special part (Issachar the Jew) was written in for Tree, who, rightly, did not see himself as Hypatia's lover, Philammon, and the 'beauteous youth' was played by Fred: another success for the young couple.

Hypatia did not have a long run; Tree was anxious to produce a new play by the fashionable playwright Oscar Wilde, whose *Lady*

227

Windermere's Fan was packing them in at the St James's. The script of *A Woman of No Importance* offered him an excellent part as Lord Illingworth, and good parts for those valuable young members of his Company, Fred Terry and Julia Neilson. Julia of course could not play Hester Worsley as Wilde intended—as an American girl; but some trifling changes in the dialogue would bring the part well within her scope. Fred's excellent and much matured acting, his youthful and romantic good looks naturally cast him as Hester Worsley's lover.

Unfortunately, Fred was not inclined to lend his youthful and romantic good looks to the part of Gerald Arbuthnot. He did not care for the part, nor for the lines he was called upon to speak. 'But I am so ignorant of the world, Lord Illingworth!' stuck in his gullet. The whole atmosphere of the part and of the play was antipathetic to his nature. He detested the *faisandé* wit of the society Wilde put on the stage. He had an already old-fashioned vocabulary of condemnation for it: 'unhealthy', 'unnatural'. Never in his life had he heard any fellow of his own age talk the way this Gerald Arbuthnot was supposed to talk to his father; 'I suppose society is wonderfully delightful!' One might conceivably get over that sort of line in a period piece, but in modern comedy . . .!

The word homosexual, in 1893, was not part of the common vocabulary; Fred and his friends had a different, less courteous description for Oscar Wilde. His gorge rose—against the part, against the play and against the author. But it is not easy, for a young rising actor to quarrel with his management, or with a leading playwright. Wilde came to lunch with the young Fred Terrys and was astute enough to strike exactly the right note. He praised Dickens—one of the gods of Fred's idolatry—of whom he, Wilde, had not read a word. A fellow who cared about Dickens could not be altogether—what they said he was! Fred agreed to play Gerald Arbuthnot, and, in due course, faced an unpleasant first night. The audience booed the author, and was not quieted until Tree came on to inform them that Wilde had left the theatre. *A Woman of No Importance*[1] brought no marked kudos to the Haymarket in spite of the distinguished cast which, as well as Mr and Mrs Tree and Mr

[1] A current witticism of the period was: 'Which is Wilde's own favourite play?' 'Obviously— *A Woman's of No Importance!*'

and Mrs Fred Terry, included Holman Clark, the indefatigable Rose Leclercq and Mrs Bernard Beere.

Julia Neilson played once again in a Wilde comedy, in 1895, to support Lewis Waller (who had played Orestes to her Hypatia) in his first venture into management. It was *An Ideal Husband*; Waller played the so-called lead—Sir Robert Chiltern—and was all but obliterated by the performance of Charles Hawtrey as Viscount Goring. Julia was given the impossible part of Lady Chiltern, and Florence West (Waller's wife) played Mrs Cheveley—Wilde's blue-print for a 'villainess'. It was Mrs Erlynne over again—an excellent part, but it needed Marion Terry to play it.

Fred was on tour in *The Home Secretary*; it was the first time since their marriage that they had been separated.

Lewis Waller was unlucky; after a few weeks, the storm burst, and *An Ideal Husband* was withdrawn. 'Public feeling ran so high against Wilde that our audience vanished', said Julia Neilson in her autobiography.

Her second child, Dennis, was nine months old when she and Fred decided to accept John Hare's offer of a four-months' tour in the United States. Julia had to choose between maternal love and a career, and the latter won; small Phyllis and the baby had to be left at home with their grandmother Morris to keep an eye on them, while their parents went off on another stage of their theatrical venturing.

Fred was in perfect agreement with Julia that the children should know nothing of the seamier side of the players' life. They had never known it themselves. Thanks to his sister Marion, Fred as a boy had enjoyed every advantage of education; thanks to his sisters Kate and Florence every social advantage. He had never experienced the toughening process that helped (for good or ill) to mould the characters of his parents and his elder brothers and sisters; never known what it was to go anxious or hungry, to be shabbily dressed and at a disadvantage in the company of his betters. Hard up he might be (and, thanks to his extravagance and his gambling, frequently was); but there is a difference between being hard up with nothing behind one, and hard-up against the background of an indulgent and generous family. Julia, also, had never had to struggle; and they were both determined to build up financial and social security for the children, as well as for themselves.

It may here be said that Fred, 'The Golden Terry', in all his gay, squandering life never failed in the tenderest sympathy to those less fortunate than himself. It is easy, if one is 'in the money', to be generous; it takes imagination and true warmth of heart to find the finest and most delicate ways in which to help the poor and the proud.

In May of the year (1895) that Fred and Julia Terry went to the States, the Lyceum Company returned. Their tour had been successful from all points of view, and her enormous personal *réclame* had done something to console Ellen for the wretched parts she had been called upon to play since the production of *King Lear*: Rosamund (in *Becket*), the Lady Soupire (in *Journeys End in Lovers' Meeting*) and Guinevere in *King Arthur*. She had had one small but delightful adventure, when Irving allowed his son Laurence (then a member of the Company) to put on his own play *Godefroi and Yolande* (based on Swinburne's poem *The Leper*) in Chicago. The play was young, was utterly different from the hidebound Lyceum productions; as eager about young Laurence Irving's work as she was about her own Ted's, she joyfully played Yolande. (Irving thought the piece 'morbid' and 'unpleasant' and declined to present it at the Lyceum.) And—things were looking up!—the next Lyceum production was to be *Cymbeline*.

There would be a lot to tell 'dear old Dad' when she got home.

When the ship docked at Liverpool she was met with the news that her father was dead. He had caught one of his spring colds, which turned to pneumonia, against which the 'Terry heart' could not hold out.

The numerous obituaries of Ben Terry are remarkable rather for their inaccuracies and omissions than for the light they throw upon their subject. Ben had 'become an actor in his teens'; had married 'a clever and beautiful actress, Miss Ballard'; had 'retired into private life' when the Kean management at the Princess's Theatre came to an end. A writer in *The Theatre* observed that, 'though of no ordinary talents', Mr Ben Terry would be remembered chiefly as the father of one of the most remarkable families known to the English stage. True enough, this last.

It does not seem to matter that Ben Terry was nothing much as an actor; his descendants may well remember him as one who, by his indomitable attachment to the theatre and his never-failing courage, blazed the trail for their own achievements. His were the personal qualities which, transmitted to his children, grandchildren and great-grandchildren, contributed to their successes. He was a 'Bruant-Alexandre' of the theatre; an impassioned 'Old Actorr' who gave all that was in him to his art.

Ben Terry is part of the glory that was Kate, Ellen, Marion and Fred; of the lesser lights of Phyllis, Dennis and Mabel; of the art of John Gielgud, of Gordon Craig and his son Edward Carrick; of Olive's son, Anthony Hawtrey, and of the many Terrys (on the right or wrong side of the blanket) who have contributed their gifts to the theatre, or its subsidiary arts of the cinema and television.

They can all look back, a century and a half, to a Portsmouth tavern and a stage-struck boy whose genes are in their blood; whose virtues are their virtues and vices their vices—for never have the characteristics of a family been more accurately reproduced down the centuries than they are in the descendants of Ben Terry and Sarah Ballard.

In 1895 Irving was knighted (the first Knight of the Stage) and Ellen set herself to the study of Imogen—something 'worth while' at last! Mr Bernard Shaw, who considered himself a better playwright than Shakespeare ('Shakespear' [*sic*] 'like an ass'—'What a DAMNED fool Shakespeare was!'), very kindly undertook to assist her in her study by writing out for her 'The Intelligent Actress's Guide to *Cymbeline*'. Ellen was amused and fascinated by the pretensions of the *arriviste* young Irishman, who offered her not only youth, of which she was starved, but a fresh approach to her own art. Bored with the Lyceum *mystique*, having been weaned on Shakespeare and having in her little finger more intuitive knowledge of Shakespeare's meanings than Shaw was ever to acquire in his lifetime, she found Shaw's letters stimulating; he had a way of putting his finger on essentials. With a remarkable lack of modesty he told her exactly how the play should be produced and acted—which so delighted her that she overlooked his jibes at Irving and the rest of the cast.

He was just what she was needing: a young, insolent admirer with brains and a facility for expressing himself which equalled her own. They exchanged bogus 'love'-letters—and it may even be that Bernard Shaw did contribute something to Ellen Terry's Imogen: the loveliest flower in the fading garland of her queenship at the Lyceum. Never again, under Irving's management, was she to have a part worthy of her mettle. Sans-Gêne, Catherine of Russia, Sylvia Wynford in a miserable piece called *The Medicine Man*, an even worse part in *Robespierre* and, finally, Volumnia, were parts she undertook only at the promptings of loyalty. Shaw assuredly had nothing to give her when she played Lady Cicely Waynflete in his dull little comedy *Captain Brassbound's Conversion* in 1906.

The long Terry-Shaw correspondence—invaluable to historians—began, and lasted for twenty years. It was life to her, during those 'dying days' of her relationship with Irving and with the Lyceum itself. Life, to get a letter from Shaw at the Winchelsea cottage where Henry and she kept up the pretence of their old attachment. 'Indifference is personified in H.I.', she wrote in her little account book, where, for six years (1894-1900), she noted, with passionless clarity and scrupulous justice, the *real* Irving. 'I wonder how his other friends and lovers feel to him. I have contempt and affection and admiration. What a mixture!'

That vivid woman, not yet fifty, physically and mentally young for her years, was yoked with a skeleton, of love and of art.

At the end, the name of George Bernard Shaw was recorded second only to Charles Reade's in the roster of Ellen Terry's friends. They never met for years after the correspondence started—which must have been a deliberate contrivance on both sides. Shaw—undersexed—would never have had the courage to propose marriage to Ellen Terry; Ellen—disinclined for marriage—would not have taken seriously any advances from Shaw, whom she rightly regarded as a delightful *blagueur*. The vanity of Shaw could not have brooked the laughter his proposal would have evoked. At the top of his voice he had proclaimed himself 'in love' with Ellen Terry and Mrs Patrick Campbell; and, with characteristic prudence and pusillanimity, married (in 1898, while still writing inflammatory letters to Ellen) a rich young woman, Miss Charlotte Payne-Townshend—from when on there is a definite alteration in the temperature of

Ellen Terry's replies. He becomes 'Dear G.B.S.', or 'Dear Bernard', or nothing at all; no more letters were signed 'Your lover, Ellen'. An absurd, dangerous signature, meaning as little as Shaw's romantic rhodomontades; knowing them both, it is more than unlikely that he so much as kissed her fingers.

There were changes at Moray Lodge. The riding horses and the bays, with the landau and mail phaeton, were sold. The head coachman was dismissed and a groom promoted. Remained the brougham, the stanhope and a couple of carriage horses, plenty of indoor servants and a surface prosperity which would pass, in these days, for luxury. But there were economies of which the mistress of the house was aware: fewer dinner parties and receptions and extravagant gowns for the girls. Neither Kate nor her daughters knew anything 'for certain'; but there was clearly worry about 'the business', and they must go carefully for a while.

In the beginning of her diary for the same year Florence Morris wrote: 'May I have as happy year in this as in 1895.' She had never fully recovered her health from the birth of her last baby. She was frequently ill with 'bad throat and fever'. Of such malaises she took small account; the 'sweet children' were her life; in the fall of 1895 she was expecting another.

She went on holiday that summer with sister Polly, to Grange-over-Sands in North Lancashire; to Polly's great friend, Agnes Mary Wakefield, whose little house was implanted in the woods sloping down to Morecambe Bay. Mary Wakefield was full of her project to start a festival of music in that musical North Country,[1] where every child seemed to be born with a nightingale in its throat. Music every day, and most of the night, echoed out into the larch forest. It was all remote from Campden House Road and the hectic social round. 'Darling Floss' came back, exhausted but radiant, to 'dear Harpy' and the children. She took little part in the London season that followed.

On a chill March morning of 1896 there was a family luncheon at Moray Lodge: Kate and the girls (including young Mrs Frank

---

[1] Mary Wakefield made the first festival of its kind in the country: the Westmorland Musical Festival.

Gielgud, the self-possessed matron of a house in Earl's Court Square, and mother of a two-year-old son, Lewis) and twelve-year-old Olive Morris, Florence's daughter, with her Terry features, dark, abundant hair, and eyes which were neither amber nor green nor brown, but changed with her changing moods. Olive was there because her mother was ill, and Nurse Bawtry, at Campden House Road, had her hands full with the boys, Geoffrey, Jack and baby Bay. She would rather have been almost anywhere than with her aunt Kate and her cousins Katie, Janet, Lucy and Mabel; their formal kindliness—well meant though it was—chilled her. Aunt Kate's fat little firm face gave nothing away, and Janet avoided her small cousin's eyes.

When the March wind swept down a poplar on the winter lawn, Olive laid down her knife and fork; it was the signal for which, subconsciously, she was waiting. The meal ended in silence, and cousin Katie rose and asked Olive to come upstairs. In one of the large, cold, grand bedrooms, the child was told her mother was dead. She could have replied that she knew it already.

Florence Morris died on 15 March 1896, at the age of forty-one. In her niece Kate Terry Gielgud's autobiography the cause of her death is described as 'an emergency operation for appendicitis'; in her great-nephew John Gielgud's *Early Stages* as 'consumption'. There was no tuberculosis in the Terry family. 'Darling Floss' died in premature childbirth, of peritonitis, a common fatality in those days of primitive medical science.

In the last of her little red leather diaries, embossed with her initials in gold, she left the hieroglyphs which reminded her of the dates when she was supposed to send money to her brother Tom. 'I post to Tom P.O. for £8, August and September', she noted in the previous year. It would appear that, after her mother's death, she took on the commitments to 'the wandering boy'.

For Polly—Marion—it was a shocking blow. Floss was her second self: an attraction of opposites. Superficially there was little in common between impulsive Florence and the elder sister who, behind a veil of impenetrable reserve, weighed every word and action. From their childhood, Florence was the outlet for Marion's sensitive and secretive nature: the one above all to be loved and trusted.

In view of that love it was natural for Marion to offer her brother-in-law, Willie Morris, her help in caring for her sister's motherless children.

Olive Morris had always loved her aunt Marion. Unhappily, her grief for her mother took the searing form of hatred for anyone who tried to take Florence's place. When Marion moved into Campden House Road, to look after Olive and the boys, the love changed to antagonism, and the situation became so intolerable that Olive was sent to boarding school, which was the thing above all that she dreaded and that her mother had promised should never happen to her.

Miss Russell, who kept Waterside, Westgate—a very elegant boarding school 'for the daughters of gentlemen'—must have been a remarkable woman. She had Austrian blood; she was brilliant, understanding and kind. She realized the state of mind of a twelve-year-old girl desperate for the loss of her mother, resentful of what she regarded as her 'betrayal'—and so gained her confidence that Olive eventually opened her heart to her. One of the girls was allowed to keep a dog; why, asked Olive, could she not keep her baby brother, Bay?

Miss Russell—she was indeed an exceptional headmistress!—wrote to Olive's father. Bay Morris—not yet three years old—was accepted as a 'pupil' at Waterside, where he and his sister Olive spent between three and four happy years.

Meanwhile arrived at Waterside, Olive's younger cousin Phyllis, the lovely spoilt daughter of Fred and Julia Terry. The cousins shared a bedroom.

The year after Florence's death, when Marion Terry was at the Criterion with Charles Wyndham, a paragraph appeared in an evening newspaper called the *St James's Budget*:

> That clever and delightful actress, Miss Marion Terry—seen on the boards all too seldom of late—will soon desert her profession altogether, for it is now an open secret that as soon as their term of mourning shall have passed, Miss Terry is to be married to her brother-in-law, Mr Morris.

'Be thou as chaste as ice.' Willie had taken her about a little, as a reward for her kindness to the children, and from those innocent visits to galleries, theatres and the houses of their mutual friends had sprung this horrid harvest.

The notice was offensive on four counts. It threw doubt on the sincerity of Marion's grief for her beloved sister. It implied an 'understanding' between her and William Morris so soon after Florence's death as to suggest to scurrilous-minded readers an attachment, if no more, during the latter's lifetime. To advertise her imminent retirement would mean no more offers of work, at home or abroad (she was just then hoping to get an American tour which, however, did not materialize until 1908). And finally, the rumour that Mr Morris, partner in the legal firm of Ashurst, Morris, Crisp & Company, was proposing to marry his deceased wife's sister might, by its absurdity, raise chuckles in legal circles, but would be taken in dead earnest by laymen and laywomen with a smattering of law, who would snatch up their pens to inform the peccant couple that such a marriage was illegal and any children born of the union would be illegitimate.

Marion must have dreaded opening her post for many mornings after the appearance of this dire announcement.

Rather oddly, Mr Morris does not appear himself to have taken steps to refute a statement which reflected as unfortunately on himself as a lawyer as on his loyalty to the memory of his wife; but he may have been the author of the denial and apology which in due course appeared in the *St James's Budget*. Meanwhile, he advised Marion to go to Sir George Lewis, the great Jewish lawyer who on more than one occasion safeguarded Terry interests.

On 7 April the case came before Lord Justice Grantham—Miss Marion Terry *v.* Mr Edward Steinkopf (proprietor of the newspaper), to recover damages for alleged libel. Marion appeared in court and gave evidence in her usual composed and well-bred fashion, although inwardly sickened by the vulgar publicity of the whole affair, and the jury, without leaving the box, found verdict for the plaintiff. She was awarded £500 damages, which might be considered not excessive for the seriousness of the libel; but £500 in 1897, was worth almost three times as much as today, and she and her counsel appear to have been satisfied.

Among those who were assiduous in their offers to console the wealthy widower was Mrs Neilson, Julia Terry's mother. She was (to judge from her portrait by Eves) as beautiful as her daughter; she had the softness, warmth and *ruserie* of her Jewish blood, and it may have been she who influenced Willie Morris in his purchase of a house called The Wilderness, at Baldock, as a holiday home for the children. (Geoffrey and Jack, by then, were both at prep. school, and entered for Harrow.) She was there, *en châtelaine*, to welcome them to the big Georgian house—and, before the end of the holidays, when they had returned to London, Olive in a red dressing-gown (which she felt added to her importance) marched down to her father's study to lay down an ultimatum. Either Mrs Neilson went, or she.

It was aunt Marion over again, but worse. Olive, this time backed up by her brothers, Geoffrey and Jack, would not tolerate the usurpation of their mother's place by an outsider. It would appear that Emily Neilson was not so tactful as she might have been; she accepted gifts of Florence's jewellery and clothing, and wore them in front of the children. For this, Mr Morris was more to blame than she; 'Gertie'—as the children called her—was sweet, stupid and insensitive. She meant no harm and would have hated to hurt anybody's feelings.

William Morris was not to be dictated to by a teenage daughter. Mrs Neilson went, and Olive and her brothers believed they had triumphed until they were informed of their father's marriage to uncle Fred's mother-in-law. That Fred's brother-in-law married his mother-in-law was a standing joke in the family, but made it difficult for the younger generation to sort out relationships.

William Morris and Gertrude Emily Neilson (born Davis) were married in 1898 at St Mary Abbots; Fred and Julia came up from tour for the wedding. The bride was lovely, in silver grey; apart from Fred, her son-in-law, no Terrys were there. How could they be? 'Darling Floss' was still green in earth. Her daughter, Olive, returned from Lausanne, had gone out as her aunt Ellen's companion on the last (as it proved) of the Irving-Terry tours. Her reaction to what she regarded as the betrayal of her beloved mother took the form of a rude telegram to her stepmother and earned her a reproof from Ellen. Rudeness has no place in the Terry tradition.

CHAPTER FIVE

Dark Days

In 1898 the Stock Exchange was shaken by rumours of disaffection in South Africa. War had not broken out, but was felt to be imminent. Among many firms caught in the inevitable commercial slump was Lewis & Allenby. It had been faltering for years, and this was the end. Arthur Lewis walked into his wife's boudoir and quietly said, 'It's all over. I'm finished. Bankrupt.'

The daughter of Ben Terry and Sarah Ballard took the news with majestic calm. She who had known poverty intimately was not dismayed; nor were her daughters, Janet, Lucy and Mabel. The Terry blood came out strongly at that last of all Christmas dinners at Moray Lodge; they paid fine disregard to the tolling of the bell that broke into the Christmas carillon. For the last time, Kate and the girls looked down that long expanse of damask, crystal and silver around which, for more than a quarter of a century, the distinguished guests of Arthur Lewis had gathered. They raised their glasses dauntlessly to the incalculable future.

For Kate, it was just a swing-back to her youth; for the girls, who had known nothing but broad lawns shaded by chestnut trees, flower beds and fountains, spacious apartments, servants and stables and grooms, it was something quite other: lifting their proud young heads, they took their tone from their mother, like members of an orchestra obeying the conductor's beat.

Indomitably, as in the past, when she had moved the Terry family from one set of theatrical lodgings to another, Kate set out in search of a place where they could afford to live, and eventually discovered a sober terrace house in unfashionable West Cromwell Road. It was actually a prolongation of the Cromwell Road, then a resort of painters and writers, so not 'lower class'. William Morris bought it and settled it upon his sister-in-law for her lifetime, and there she lived until her death in 1924, at the age of eighty.

There was no garden, no large reception rooms, no space in which

238

to conduct the fine social life to which, since her marriage, she was accustomed; an ugly square drawingroom, overstuffed with the furniture and *bibelots* she had transported from Moray Lodge. Instinctively she chose the worst. Looking at that drawingroom, in the nineteen-twenties, one might have been forgiven for questioning the authenticity of the glories of Moray Lodge; the bad oil-paintings, the horrid convolutions of mahogany and walnut, prostituted to the craft of the Victorian cabinet-maker; these may have been swallowed up in the gravely handsome spaces of Moray Lodge. A Canaletto or Zuccarelli was the same to Kate as a greasy daub by a contemporary painter: something to fill up space on the wallpaper. Her artistic perception was all turned towards music and the theatre. It is rare to come across this divorce between the arts.

To the tune of 'Soldiers of the Queen', the Lewis girls re-organized their lives. Janet found a post as secretary to the Gramophone Company (later the Gramophone and Typewriter Company Limited: the gramophone of those days being an enormous wooden or metal horn and the record a vulcanite cylinder slipped on to a steel column. The title of the piece was recorded on the cylinder and was followed by the portentous announcement 'Edison—Bell—Record!') which she held for two years and abandoned only to keep house for wealthy friends in Ennismore Gardens.

Lucy, who had always professed an interest in teaching, became a governess in a private school, which uninspiring labour she shortly abandoned for the Foreign Office, where she was employed as stenographer and précis writer—a post of considerable responsibility for an unexperienced girl.

Mabel, on the attic floor of the ugly terrace house in West Cromwell Road, established a sewing-room, and employed her skilful needle in the creation of lingerie for sale to her friends and acquaintances. She was a most beautiful sempstress, and made all her own clothes and some of her sisters'. She also painted miniatures on ivory, and on at least one occasion exhibited at Burlington House. But her heart was in the theatre.

She had already availed herself of the family friendship with the actor-manager John Hare to get small parts in Hare productions. She had a faint Terry likeness—mainly of voice and carriage—which grew more pronounced with the passing of time. Eventually she became a good and reliable though uninspired actress, sure of parts in the West End.

In 1898 John Hare put on a cheapjack comedy, *The Master,* at the Globe. Thrown together with cynical under-estimation of popular taste, it contained every known cliché of dialogue, business and situation, and there was not a part in it (including Hare's own) worth playing. He himself began to have doubts of its success, until the idea occurred to him of offering Kate Terry an enormous salary[1] to appear in the insignificant role of Mrs Faber. 'Return of Kate Terry' on the bills was bound to attract the public, especially old admirers who had never set eyes on her, except in a theatre box or driving down Regent Street, for close on thirty years. The younger generation, which knew her only through the rhapsodical descriptions of parents and grandparents, would surely come out of curiosity, if nothing better.

Kate Terry accepted the offer, for good reasons: the move to West Cromwell Road was pending, they urgently needed the money, and she felt her support would be of value to Mabel, who had been 'resting' for nearly twelve months. She was also doing a good turn to her old friend Hare. Yet it would seem to have been an unfortunate policy on the latter's part, to bring Kate Terry back to the stage in so trivial a piece and a part. She had a few lines to speak and little to do but smile, look charming and manipulate a property 'baby'. Her entrance was greeted with 'thunderous' applause, but even the Kate Terry legend could not save the play from its well-merited failure. Amid an orgy of sentimentality from the critics (who, on Kate's account, forbore to damn *The Master* as thoroughly as it deserved) Mabel, as Kate's daughter, received a few modestly complimentary notices—and, when the play came off, went on tour in T. W. Robertson's *Ours.*

Why, one might wonder, having 'broken the ice', did not Kate Terry receive other offers? She did, but turned them down. Ellen Terry said that Kate was 'very expensive' and that it was the managements who turned *her* down on hearing the terms she proposed. E.T. undertook to 'talk sense to old Kitty'—apparently to no avail. But there may have been ulterior motives for Kate's

[1] The exact sum is not known; but it was well above that earned by a current leading lady, and doubtless gave Kate 'ideas'.

reluctance. Acceptable as would have been the money, did she feel
unequal to repeating the effort which had come to so disappointing
an end? She may well have doubted her own power, not to act,
but to memorize a long part—for the Terry curse of failure of
memory had, in spite of the long years during which she had not
been obliged to exercise it, caught up with her. 'The sweet voice of
days gone by' (*vide* Edgar Pemberton) was not again to be heard on
the stage.[1] However, Mabel was now an established member of
John Hare's Company, and, when the move to West Cromwell Road
took place, was playing Muriel Eden in *The Gay Lord Quex* to Irene
Vanbrugh's Sophy Fullgarney.

Lewis & Allenby had been made into a Company, with Arthur
Lewis as Chairman. He still had his office in Conduit Street to
which, when weather permitted, he walked the long stretch by
Cromwell Road, Knightsbridge, Kensington Gore, Piccadilly and
Bond Street. No more the phaeton, with liveried groom sitting
up behind; no more, at the end of the day, the glow of handsome
rooms crowded with artists and actors who looked to him as their
friend and their patron. There was no space in West Cromwell
Road for more than two or three dinner guests. To this small
compass was George du Maurier's 'princely fellow' reduced (Du
Maurier was now living in prosperity on the proceeds of his novels,
the discovery of his talents as a writer consoling him for his fading
eyesight)—perhaps by his own lack of foresight and providence.

It was a pale life for one who had lived so richly and fully; there
can be no bitterer thing for one accustomed to dispense largesse
than no longer to be able to do so. But in Arthur Lewis there was
no bitterness; that handsome and gentle face (unfortunately,
according to the fashion of the time, bearded) with wide-set eyes
is the face of one whose values transcend the material. His regrets
were not for himself, but for his wife and the litter of daughters
he had fathered; he must have longed for a son, to whom to pass
on the responsibilities he was soon to abandon.

He had his compensations: the Club which was his contribution
to the Arts he desired above all to serve, and the small room with a

[1] She helped out the family finances by giving 'coaching' to young *ladies* who
wished to go on the stage.

north light he rented in Kensington, where—an artist *manqué*—
he kept up his weekend dabbling, persuading friends to sit for him.

He had not much longer to endure this truncated existence. He
died suddenly in the night of 24 November 1901. His beloved
daughter Katie gathered holly and periwinkle from Moray Lodge to
deck his bier. His wife Kate, strong, unimaginative, insensitive,
sank her grief in plans for the future; she must keep up the home
for Janet, Lucy and Mabel, so she took as lodger an American lady,
the mother of one of Mabel's friends. Katie, the most conventional,
in a sense the most limited of his children, was the one to feel most
deeply the death of Arthur Lewis. He had been the centre of her
life, dearer to her even than her husband and her children—until
the birth of little Arthur John, in 1904; the child to whom she
transferred all her idolatry, with whom she shared every interest
from nursery to stage, and of whom she would never brook a breath
of criticism. She supported him with her love and confidence to the
end. Her boudoir was papered with photographs of John Gielgud.

With the abandonment of Moray Lodge the pattern of family
life disintegrated. There was no longer a centre where, from time
to time, they could all collect. 57 Cathcart Road was a shell inhabited by strangers, and at Campden House Road and Baldock,
Emily Morris reigned in the place of 'darling Floss'; she was
beautiful, kind and generous, but to the children she remained an
outsider; she did not 'belong'. Her daughter Julia and her son-in-
law Fred Terry, at Elm Park Gardens, were absorbed by their
professional and domestic life. Marion, at last, had found independence, the flat at Buckingham Palace Mansions she filled with
her collections of china, her books, piano and music (she not only
played but composed: on one occasion a waltz called *Olive* which
was published by Boosey); and her few intimate friends, who were
not 'of the theatre'. Katie in her little house in Earl's Court Square
had her hands full with her social life and the children.

Ellen, at Barkston Gardens and, intermittently, Tower Cottage,
Winchelsea, was isolated in a private unhappiness, of which loyalty
prevented her speaking even to her closest friends. After *The Medicine Man* played itself to its dreary end, Irving was seriously ill—
for the first time in his life. They were on tour with *Sans-Gêne*,

doing excellent business, when he caught a chill which, on top of the chronic pharyngitis from which he had suffered for many years, turned to pneumonia and pleurisy. For the sake of the Company the tour had to go on, and, with Irving out of the bill, resulted in a heavy loss. In the earlier part of the year he had suffered an even more crushing financial disaster, the burning of the whole Lyceum storage at Southwark. On the premises which, owing to an uncharacteristic attack of economy on Irving's part, were insured for little more than half their value, were the scenes and properties for forty-four productions. This shocking blow, added to the sum of his other losses and debts on the administration of the Lyceum, undoubtedly weakened his physical resistance, and it was not until the first week in December that he could be moved from Glasgow to London; a ten weeks' drain on his already depleted capital.

Convalescing at Bournemouth, he wrote briefly to Ellen that he would like to see her. She, if not he, was sharply aware of the 'nothingness' between them when he informed her that he was planning a provincial tour for the spring, with a small Company *which did not include herself*, and 'for the present' she could do as she pleased. For a few moments she could not believe the evidence of her hearing; could even that monstrous egoism, that total indifference to any interests except his own, eliminate twenty years of faithful partnership which included, not seldom, personal immolation, as an artist, to Henry Irving? It could. It presently dawned on her, by way of Irving's halting phrases (he had the grace to be a little sheepish), that he regarded her, 'for the present', not as an asset but a liability.

Her independence triumphed. Of course she could look after herself—could fix a tour of her own: which, to the delight of her agent, she proceeded to do—*Othello* and *The Lady of Lyons*, with Frank Cooper as her leading man; two easy parts for Ellen, she having studied and played them before.

Meanwhile, Irving had had other views. There was a proposal of the formation of a syndicate to take over the insolvent affairs of the Lyceum Theatre, but the members of the syndicate refused to sign unless Ellen Terry were 'part of the Show' (her own words). Irving had not the courtesy himself to put this proposition to Ellen, but sent Comyns Carr as his emissary. Loyal as ever, she replied through the same intermediary that she would conform to the proposed terms, although this meant curtailment of her own plans and the acceptance of a mediocre part in Sardou's *Robespierre*.

It is difficult to see why Ellen Terry accepted this contract; she was not impractical, and it was to her disadvantage as an actress. There was no reason for her to put herself out for Irving, who had treated her badly from all professional and personal points of view.[1] By preserving her independence, she would have had opportunities of adventuring she would certainly be denied at the Lyceum. One is inclined to suspect sheer feminine weakness; although, as we have noticed, not impractical, she was not a business woman, and may well have misdoubted her capacity for managing a Company of her own.

She did a couple of months' successful business 'on the road' with Frank Cooper, a valuable member of the Lyceum Company, and came back to rehearse *Robespierre*—a one-man show for Irving, an overwhelming production which took in two hundred and fifty supers, and for her meant spending the greater part of the evening in her dressingroom, answering letters from her admirers, most of whom resented the summary disposal of Ellen Terry by her manager. The show closed at midsummer, with a deficit of £4,000, and, in conformity with her contract, Ellen went out with Irving on the provincial tour which was partly to recoup their losses on the London production.

During the tedious weeks she read *Captain Brassbound's Conversion*, sent to her by her ardent correspondent Shaw—whose ardour was temporarily and only slightly reduced by his marriage in the summer to Miss Charlotte Payne-Townshend; dreamed of playing it, and got as far as giving it a copyright reading in Liverpool. Her enthusiasm for this piece of early Shavian twaddle can only be accounted for by her dissatisfaction with her current situation. Lady Cicely Waynflete (supposedly created from Ellen's own letters to Shaw) was presumably a more attractive part than Clarisse, in *Robespierre*—but its threadbare qualities were revealed when the play was produced in 1906. The character was nothing and meant nothing; even the genius of Ellen Terry could not lend life to it.

The century, for Ellen, was coming to a mournful end, with

[1] She denies this in her *Memoirs*, but facts speak more loudly than E.T.'s generous disclaimers.

nothing in view but a nine months' tour of the United States, and a relationship which had once meant everything to both of them, and was now so meaningless that they transacted necessary business through Irving's manager, Bram Stoker.

For Fred and Julia life was as radiant as it could only be for two gifted and successful young people, strongly established in their profession. Fred at the Haymarket, and later the Garrick, was an admired *jeune premier*; Julia, as Constance in *King John*, was tearing down her magnificent hair nightly in Tree's fine new theatre, Her Majesty's—a gesture she loved all her life to demonstrate. It was her first tragic Shakespearian part and she revelled in it; in latter years she often declared that Constance was her favourite part. She was to follow it up in the new year with a shocking Oberon, which Tree's direction allowed her to play like a principal boy, and a Rosalind with Alexander, which was not much better. Always her beauty procured for her these great classic parts, and always her accomplishment just failed to keep pace with the opportunities that came her way. 'That beautiful, sacred white *cow*'—as Tree described her, in an access of fury at Julia's angelic impassivity. The outstanding quality which ten years' experience had developed in her was a radiant confidence; the torments and agonies experienced by Fred in every new part he played were unknown to Julia. On first nights he died a thousand deaths; she took them in her serene stride. Sure of her words, her business, her positions on the stage—what had she more to do than send the moonlight of her smile out into the house, which thrilled to the lovely and eccentric cadences of her voice? She seldom considered a part deeply or discussed its shades of meaning: but this may have been because she was a very inarticulate young woman (the inarticulacy increased as time went on). Sometimes she had startling patches of intuition— Mary Queen of Scots.

They had long been ambitious to set up in management on their own account, and, with the dawning of the new century as an omen, they felt the time had come. It would not have seemed the happiest moment for such a venture; negotiations with the Boers had failed, the ports were crowded with troopships, 70,000 soldiers (the largest number so far contributed by England to any war) were sent to

South Africa and, with Mafeking, Kimberley and Ladysmith in state of siege, and constant reports of British defeat and disaster, there was 'a red sky' on the horizon of the dawning century.

But the immortal words spoken by the half-blind, eighty-year-old Queen, 'We are not interested in the possibilities of defeat; they do not exist', sent their oriflamme through the country. It was with no lack of confidence that, at midnight of the old year, the guests at Lewis Waller's New Year's Eve party, lifted their glasses to the new century—destined to be so richly rewarding for Fred Terry and Julia Neilson.

Marion too, sedately 'bringing in the New Year' with sister Kate and the girls, had no need to fear that red dawn; after rather a dull season with an undistinguished play called *When a Man's in Love*, she was contracted to play Rosalind and Beatrice as a guest artist with Frank Benson at Stratford-on-Avon, this engagement to be followed by a long tour with Thalberg, the repertory including Lady Teazle and Mrs Erlynne. Mabel, too, had prospects: a tour, and—perhaps!—a part, later on, in a Shaw play in town. (The part, Gloria Clandon, in *You Never Can Tell*, materialized in the month of May.)

In New York that same New Year's Eve, the nearest and dearest to Ellen Terry was Irving's younger boy, Laurence, of whom she said, 'I always felt he should have been *my* son.' The deep understanding and affection that existed between the young man (he was in his twenty-ninth year) and the experienced actress were increased by her admiration of the seriousness of his purpose, both as actor and writer, and he turned to her for the sympathy which was missing from his relationship with his father. As a member of the Lyceum Company, Laurence was consistently slighted and had the constant mortification of seeing other young actors promoted over his head to parts to which, by equipment and experience, he might have been considered entitled. It has already been said that Irving 'did not think much of' Laurence's work; the opinion of one member of the Company, the late Alfred Kendrick, a contemporary of Laurence's, was that he thought, on the contrary, too much of it for his own ease. In his own plays, *Godefroi and Yolande* and *Peter*

246

the Great, although his acting in some parts was rough and unfinished, Laurence showed great power and promise. Trained for the diplomatic service, he had intellectual qualities which came out strongly in his approach to his art. Essentially modern and simple, his style accorded ill with that of his father, which, as Irving aged, became progressively more stagey and artificial. The rest of the Company taking their cue from their manager, it can well be assumed that no stage was large enough to contain both Irving and Laurence; and that Irving perceived the anomalies of the position is at least as likely as that he was actuated by jealousy of his son Laurence.[1]

The pair of them more or less 'in Coventry' so far as the Great Man was concerned, Ellen Terry and Laurence Irving were drawn together by community of tastes and ambitions; he shared her enthusiasm for Shaw and the 'new' theatre; while preserving a scrupulous loyalty to Irving, she helped him over his patches of discouragement, let him read to her, criticized the new play he was writing, and sympathized with his latest and most thankless task. It was he who had translated Sardou's *Robespierre*; he was now commissioned to translate the same author's *Dante*. When he read bits of this fustian to her, they both knew that, for her, it was the end.

The First Lady of the English Theatre, when the new century dawned, was in exile, trailing round America in the caravanserai of a moribund tradition of acting. Knowing her, it may be taken for granted that she made the best of it; her inextinguishable spirit, her luminosity and laughter kept her and her companions alive, and entranced her audiences. Financially, the tour was an immense success ('I felt I'd earned my keep,' said Ellen).

But as the shores of England approached, at the end of that long nine months, the future was indeed incalculable for Ellen Terry. She had to play out her contract with the Lyceum Syndicate. After that—*le déluge*.

[1] The other son, Harry (H.B.) was more to his taste, giving promise of being the sound, commercial actor into which he developed.

Fin de Siècle

Of the younger generation, the Craigs were, if not the dominant, the most vivid contributors to the build-up of Terry tradition.

Their cousin Minnie—now married to a promising young actor, Edmund Gwenn—sparkled erratically in the theatrical firmament, but was too temperamental to make the position for herself she might, with application, have achieved; she was constantly on tour, often in the United States. The children of Floss and of Fred were still in the schoolroom. Olive Morris, a rebellious and lovely child of sixteen, was sent back to school in Lausanne, the elder Morris boys were at their prep, and the youngest, Olive's adored Bay, had gone from Westgate to a 'baby-school', with his cousins Lewis Gielgud and Dennis Terry; Phyllis, Fred's girl, was idling her time away at Westgate with Miss Russell. So wide a gap of years separated these younger ones from their Lewis cousins and Craig cousins that it was hard for them to grasp the relationship; to the little ones, Minnie Terry, Mabel Terry Lewis[1] and Edith Craig seemed rather of their aunt Marion's generation than of their own.

Edith Craig, at thirty, was a serious, striking young woman who commanded devotion from those who recognized her qualities. Having transferred her allegiance (*faute de mieux*) from music to the theatre, she had spared no pains to perfect herself in the *métier* to which she was now dedicated. She proved in small parts at the Lyceum that she had the makings of an actress; a devoted admirer of Irving, as an actor, her intelligence rejected the Lyceum school in so far as productions and plays were concerned, and she found in J. T. Grein's Independent Theatre an intellectual outlet.

[1] Mabel and, after the death of Arthur Lewis, Kate both added Terry to their surnames, and were copied by Janet and Lucy. Katie Gielgud, not to be left out of the picture, became Kate Terry Gielgud. To distinguish themselves from the numerous Terrys currently on the stage, Phyllis and Dennis added their mother's name to their patronymic and were known as Neilson-Terry.

Grein, a Dutchman (later he was naturalized), founded his Independent Theatre in 1891, with the object of presenting plays of 'literary and artistic rather than commercial' value. Launching his venture with a private performance of *Ghosts* at the Royalty, he proved himself a rebel against the old artificial standards of playwriting and production, and, as a critic, was in a position to defend himself against the attacks his revolutionary ideas provoked. Under his aegis Edy had the opportunities she had wished for, of acting intelligent parts in intelligent plays—but she was cheated of success by her own personality, at once too aggressive and too shy (the one being the concomitant of the other). Capable of speaking a line exquisitely, of playing a little scene to perfection, she had not got 'what it takes' to carry an important part. She had the overwhelming personality of the 'true Terrys' without their power to charm, except within the circle of her intimates.

Undefeated, she applied herself to those aspects of the theatre in which she was eventually to excel: the mechanics of the stage and the creation of costume. When Irving, hard-up after the disaster at the store, commissioned her to dress *Robespierre*, she did it with economy and common sense, backed by the impeccable sense of historical period that derived from her father. No detail escaped Edy's attention, and she knew exactly how, out of a few yards of sateen, of flannelette, of flimsies from a coster's barrow, to create an effect of richness or its opposite, the robe of Clarisse de Mauluçon or a citizen's overcoat. *Robespierre*, according to the records, was one of Irving's most spectacular productions; it was certainly, so far as the wardrobe was concerned, one of his cheapest.

Encouraged by this success, she set up her atelier as a theatrical costumier, which might have been successful had she had the ability to commercialize her talents or made up her mind to devote the whole of her time to it. 'If only she would concentrate', wrote her brother of Edy, 'all would go forward with her.' She was receiving a weekly allowance of seven pounds ten shillings from her mother,[1] and even on that generous sum and her own earnings was not making ends meet. Little of the money was spent on herself; there were

[1] It was originally twenty pounds, but Ellen's finances were not as sound as they had been, and Ellen was probably aware of demands on Edy's purse which she herself was not inclined to carry.

plenty of parasites to batten on the generosity of Ellen Terry's daughter. Presently there was a more persistent one—but that was largely Ellen's fault.

It was Ellen who interfered with Edy's love-affair, and diverted the normal pattern of her daughter's life into the channel it followed from 1899 onwards. In the fifth American tour, 1890, Edy met and fell in love with a young American actor of whom, for some reason, her mother did not approve. There were bitter scenes, and after the final one Edy retired to her bedroom in tears. Ellen, in some *crise de nerfs*, ordered the distracted girl down to dinner; she had a party, and Edy was needed to balance the table. She sullenly dried her swollen eyes and descended at her mother's bidding. That incident affected their relationship; there was on neither side a diminution of love, but an indistinct antagonism—later to be exploited by those who stood to gain from disaffection between Ellen Terry and her daughter—grew up between them.

Once again, some fourteen years later, this warm-hearted and tender-hearted woman was to fall in heterosexual love, and to face her mother's angry opposition. 'He was not good enough for Edy!' and 'He was disfigured!' were the grounds of Ellen's objection to the young musician, a friend and collaborator of Gordon Craig's to whom Edy's shy heart had gone out. Those who supported Ellen Terry's view and called Martin Shaw 'mediocre' as a musician overlooked the fact that the last quality to attract either Edy or her brother was mediocrity; each was quick and contemptuous in the dismissal of the second-rate, in character as in achievement. As for the birth-mark which evoked Ellen's shuddering distaste—it was just the kind of thing to draw Edy's tenderness more surely towards her admirer; the compassion that ran beneath her surface brusquerie always inclined her towards anyone 'at disadvantage'.

She was strong enough, by that time, to stand up to her mother's disapprobation, but she was not proof against the threatened suicide of the friend with whom for several years she had been living.

She had formed an attachment to a young writer, called Christabel Marshall, the legitimate daughter of Emma Marshall, a Victorian novelist. The legitimacy is emphasized because it was her fancy sometimes to represent herself as the offspring of a romantic episode.

This could have been to put herself in line with Edy, for whom she had developed a *Schwärmerei*. She would have no place in this record but for the fact that it was she who brilliantly ghosted Ellen Terry's *Story of My Life*, and collaborated with Edy on the notes which later amplified it into the *Memoirs*.

'Chris', as she chose to be called, had started as a devotee of Ellen's but, at her first meeting with Edy, transferred her devotion. Ellen Terry liked her very much; she was always prepared to like any friend of Edy's, and respected talent. 'Chris' had personality, an excellent education, a genuine gift for writing and a rich appreciation of the arts; she may be said to have consolidated her position with Edy's mother when she supported the latter's objection to Edy's lover by an hysterical demonstration of which she left a full account in an anonymous, semi-autobiographical novel called *Hungerheart*, which was accepted by Methuen and published in 1915. If it had not foundered in the war tempest it might well have made the kind of sensation made by *Marie Claire*, and, in these days, of *Bonjour Tristesse*. As a first novel, it is superior to either. Its main interest lies in the admirable portraits it paints of Ellen Terry ('Louise Canning') and Edith Craig ('Sally').

It was owing to this lifelong (as it was to prove) attachment that Edy did not accompany her mother on that last Lyceum Company tour to the States; she and Christabel Marshall[1] had set up house in Smith Square, on Edy's—which is to say, mainly Ellen's—money. (The address—7 Smith Square—was unfortunate for Chris, who had an impediment of speech which altered her Ss to a kind of nasal H. The story of a cab-driver who, unable to make out Chris's 'Heven, Hmith Hquare', drove off with 'Oh, go to hell!' is not apocryphal.

Edy's life expanded, from the time of this breakaway from her mother, yet she was never free of a sense of guilt. In a clear-eyed fashion, she was a devoted daughter. That this devotion took the form of furies and scenes agonizing to spectators (they became more painful and even brutal as time went on) in no way denies its validity. She had no illusions. Ellen, to her daughter's way of thinking, was someone to be cared for and protected from the results of her own

[1] After her conversion to the Roman Church, C.M. took the name of Christopher St John.

indiscretions. Ellen, violent and headstrong as her daughter,[1] resisted protection, yet, in another mood, depended on Edy for every smallest practical detail of her life. She must deeply have missed Edy on that last American tour with Irving.

Gordon Craig—it is time to dispense with 'Ted'—was busily laying the foundations for the great reputation which, later, was to be his. Disillusioned with the theatre in its existing form (he had stopped acting in 1897), he was already obsessed with his vision of the Theatre as it might, and should, be. For him and his collaborator, Martin Shaw, the new century dawned auspiciously, with their production of *Dido and Aeneas* at Hampstead, under the auspices of the Purcell Operatic Society. It was Gordon Craig's first opportunity of putting into practice all the poetry, the sense of line and colour he had cultivated through his association with the poets and artists of the era. W. B. Yeats and H. W. Nevinson (the latter after the revival at the Coronet Theatre in 1901) wrote lyrically of the achievement of the young *metteur-en-scène*, who had brought something new, imaginative and unrealistic into the dusty world of the theatre.

Since his stage début in 1885 (the year before the death of his father, Edward Godwin), he had served his apprenticeship at the Lyceum, and, during Lyceum vacations, in the provinces. He enjoyed some privilege as the son of Ellen Terry; he got parts which would not have come in his way had he been an unknown youth, struggling for a position in the theatre. He had married, and, soon after his marriage, struck a black patch of unemployment, which he filled up with intelligent reading and with the practice of—to him —a new art.

He and his wife May, on return from tour, were given domicile by the young painter, William Nicholson, at Denham. James Pryde, Nicholson's brother-in-law, was also staying there, and,

---

[1] 'Don't let them call me "sweet"!' she implored me, when we discussed the writing of this book; she had suffered from the lucubrations of those who, rating her character from the parts she played, heaped her name with honeyed adjectives. Having known her well, I agree that 'sweet' was the last word to apply to Ellen Terry. Charm, grace and tact add up to a much more formidable combination when blended with the hot Terry temper and the cold obduracy which, on occasions, accompanied it.

between them, Nicholson and Pryde were evolving the famous Beggarstaff posters. Nicholson was working on the woodcut, his personal extension of the work of Bewick and the elder Crawhall, and fired Ted with his enthusiasm. It was stimulating society for the young actor who had in himself much more than the art of acting; with characteristic industry he applied himself to the woodblock and the chisel, and although his woodcuts were for some years imitations of Nicholson and Pryde, his own originality and inventiveness asserted itself, as he progressed from small book labels, letterheads and decorative motifs towards larger and more serious compositions.

He had an astounding number of talents—even for a Terry—and cultivated each one with assiduity. His just intolerance of amateurism preserved him from the lot that too often overtakes the many-gifted. A saying (in later days) of Ellen Terry's: 'I would never be contented to do anything unless I could do it supremely well', applies also to her son, of whom it might be said that the record of his life was the slow search of and progress towards technical perfection in those arts out of which, eventually, he created his vision—a vision as yet faint as a cloud along the eastern horizon, yet positive, and increasing in positivity from year to year. He practised sketching in chalk, pencil and pen, he taught himself the use of the tools of etching and lithography, not with a view to excelling in these media, but of serving 'The Gleam'. His painting was acceptable to artists, his writing to writers; in both he proved himself a person to be taken seriously (a tribute denied to him for long years by his contemporaries in and out of the English theatre). He read voraciously—English, French, German, Italian.[1] He had begun to publish his artistic miscellany called *The Page*, which was favourably noticed in Belgium and Italy, and received commendation in London from a small group of artists.

Thus far, at the start of the new century, had the 'spoiled' son of Ellen Terry progressed, by dint of his own effort and ardour. He was, to some extent, a phenomenon—and the English (of those years) did not take kindly to phenomena, which reminded them too uncomfortably of their own mediocrity. They preferred

[1] He had but a garbled notion of foreign languages, and spoke none fluently: yet he could read in them.

not to notice that which they were incapable of understanding.

So, in the year 1900, we find E.G.C. professing to be hard-up—which, as his mother's son, he certainly should not have been, had he had commonsense in the handling of money, or any sense of responsibility to his wife and the four children of their marriage, Rosemary and Robin, Philip and Peter. It was part of his pose to sweep domestic commitments aside, and he was always a great poseur. He had an already old-fashioned conception of the privileges of the artist, the Murger conception—which he was never to outgrow.

He was big, handsome and healthy, apart from short sight, a weakness he shared with his uncle Fred; both of them, in their dashing youth, were obliged to wear spectacles, which they both detested; it must have been cramping, to play the gay deceiver in the thin, realistic, gold frames of the period. What fun they could have had—both of them—in the 'romantic' black rims of the third decade of the century! Uncle Fred, after all, was only seven years older than Ted, and they had more in common than biographers recognize. They cursed or laughed at each other. Fred both disliked and admired the nephew whom he was quite incapable of understanding.

Ted lived, in a day, a more vivid life than his young relatives lived in a year, for he was totally emancipated, morally and spiritually, from the conventions of the age. He was utterly charming, utterly without principle—in the common interpretation of the word; he admitted no moral obligations apart from those he owed to his work. There was about him a certain loftiness, not recognizable by those he called, with a twinkle in his eye, adopting their own pronunciation, 'hoy polloy'.

Those who, later, belittled his devotion to his mother, and hers to him, overlooked the fact that Gordon Craig was the true projection of Ellen Terry's soul. Had she been a man, she would have been a Gordon Craig; hers was that same happy levity, that wildness of creative spirit, that reaching out towards far horizons. Edy was the child of her heart, Ted the child of her soul. The antagonism between sister and brother was largely due to Edy's jealous incomprehension of this delicate relationship between her mother and brother, of which she could only see the material demands he made, and his 'neglect'—which Ellen Terry herself perfectly understood, while weeping over it.[1]

His supreme gift to his mother was the laughter which Edy, that stern young judge, could not supply; Edy had little appreciation of humour, no gift at all for creating it—and if there was one gift grateful to Ellen Terry, it was the gift of laughter. It was not a gift common to Terrys, who were (and are) inclined to take themselves seriously; 'darling Floss' had it, but in Kate and Marion, and in the former's descendants, there was not a glimmer. Fred had it doubtfully, in a schoolboy's degree; Charlie undoubtedly had it—but not George, Tom or Ben. Ellen alone inherited the robustious sense of humour deriving from Ben Terry of Spice Island, the delight in the Rabelaisian jest, the sharp sense of the ridiculous which she transmitted to her son.

It was a pity he did not apply it to himself; he invited derision on many occasions by his disregard of practical considerations.

Yet it would appear that, at the beginning of the century, this extraordinary young man, who had little at that moment to show in the way of achievement, was the Terry of the Future; the one to outsoar them all in permanence; the one to leave his indelible impression on the Theatre—when the exquisite art of his mother and aunts was scattered by the wind. The names of Kate, Ellen, Marion and Fred Terry are already cold as the engravings on a memorial tablet; to the present generation they are as remote as Garrick or Siddons. But the most mediocre student in the most mediocre little so-called 'academy' of dramatic art in the whole of Europe is—or should be—aware of the name of Gordon Craig, from whom the modern *metteur-en-scène* derives, not altogether his inspiration, but his motor power.

There are two distinct people, Ted and Gordon Craig: Ted, the fool, the irresponsible, the maker of trouble for all with whom he was associated; and Gordon Craig, the serious man of the theatre, the prophet and the visionary. The two were too frequently confounded—and that was their own fault. A parallel suggests itself with 'E.T.' and 'Nelly' in E.G.C.'s record, *Ellen Terry and Her Secret Self.* He was aware of her dual personality, as he appears *not*

[1] Their correspondence, during her student years in Berlin, plentifully shows how Edy 'neglected' her mother.

to have been aware of his own. That book is the only true record of Ellen Terry, capturing the butterfly, the Ariel imprisoned within the shell of the Great Actress. Written by an idolized and spoilt son, who loved his mother with tenderness, humour and imagination, and revered her as an artist—how it was hated by Edy and her cohorts. No woman—least of all her daughter Edy—was capable truly of *knowing* Ellen Terry; two or three—Lady Alix Egerton, Aimée Lowther, Lady Maude Warrender came close to knowledge by way of the rareness of their own temperaments, their individual fineness. It was Ellen's instinct only to reveal herself to men: to her close friends, Graham Robertson, Norman Forbes, Sir Albert Seymour (Bertie the Bart), Tom Heslewood, and half a dozen more. None of these were her lovers; they loved her, and she loved them, and they talked the same language, and communicated through spirit and sense. They were bitterly resented by Edy and her 'regiment of women', who lost no opportunity (in particular after the publication of *Ellen Terry and Her Secret Self*) of discrediting Ted—Ellen's 'lover-in-chief', in the sense of having more knowledge of his mother, of whom he was indeed her second self, than any man with whom her name had been associated. It would appear that Godwin knew Ellen a little, Watts and Kelly not at all; Irving—never a glimmer. The beauty and closeness of the relationship between mother and son are fully confirmed in their unpublished correspondence.

In the first year of the new century, Gordon Craig was putting into practice all the theories his mother had dimly envisaged during her latter years at the Lyceum: those restless years, disturbed by the egregious Mr Shaw's endless correspondence, which (so she assured her son) she 'did not take seriously'—one of Ellen's rare lapses from complete sincerity. She took the letters more seriously than she admitted—even to herself. And she was right to do so. Unvaluable as Shaw was artistically, he stirred up in her a divine discontent.

Her sister Marion, her brother Fred and her niece Mabel were dedicated to the commercial theatre, from which it was her ambition to break away; she had had enough of it. Her vision was fixed on broader horizons. She was aware of something more in herself, something that belonged to the future, rather than to the past;

something that her daughter Edy, in her limited fashion, recognized, and her son Ted deeply understood. Edy's approach was severe, academic (she would have made an admirable don); Ted's was gay, forward-looking and charged with fantasy. Ellen turned instinctively towards her son.

In 1901, Ellen Terry played her last part at the Lyceum—Volumnia, to Irving's Coriolanus; bad box-office, poor houses. 'They don't want Coriolanus, they want Kitty Rubbish', was Irving's sour comment, when he heard of rival theatres 'packing them in'. He was an embittered old actor, out of pace with the times; but he was also a sick man, gallantly struggling against his disabilities.

Ellen Terry refused £12,000 to go to America in *Dante*. In this her brother Fred, who played Thornhill in the revival of *Olivia* which followed the last American tour, supported her. Devoted as he was to Irving, Fred Terry recognized how little his sister had to gain by such a contract. He himself was sunk in his first venture into management; he and Julia had got hold of a masterly piece of theatrical twaddle called *Sweet Nell of Old Drury*, which was to prove a money-spinner for thirty years.

Fred Terry, like his master, Irving, had no artistic perception whatever (art, in those days, had not yet invaded the theatre) but an unerring commercial sense—which does not imply that he did not make mistakes over the succeeding years, as when he put on *The Heel of Achilles* and a shocking piece called *Mistress Wilful*—the latter for the benefit of his wife, Julia Neilson. Fred Terry bought this originally for his daughter Phyllis; an American tour fortunately intervened, and Julia gleefully picked up a part written for a girl of eighteen, and played it with aplomb at the age of forty-five.

He was an exquisite actor in his own idiom, which was that of the Lyceum, deriving from the Keans. He was technically incapable of putting a foot wrong; he was the true son of Ben Terry, achieving all that Ben Terry aspired to and never achieved. He was dedicated to the old drama and could see little, if any, virtue in new schools of acting. Sixteen years younger than his sister Ellen, he was already set in the ancient idiom—yet he was capable of recognizing a talent superior to his own.

Playing Thornhill to Ellen's Olivia (having sworn he would never act with her again), brother and sister effected a temporary *rapprochement*. Ellen was grateful for Fred's confirmation of her own disinclination towards *Dante*, in which, indeed, her part was beneath the consideration of any actress of her stature. For all his heroworship of Irving, Fred was not blind to the latter's misuse of the gifts of his leading lady. She was very glad of 'darling Tops's' considered opinion; always it was her instinct to turn for advice to a man.

Holidaying in Geneva, before she took up her engagement with Tree, she wrote:

> Dear Fred,
> Perhaps you've settled it all, *but if you haven't* I must tell you that *Ted* is a most wonderful hand at *Fairy Scenes*—arranging—lighting—and clothing them, and being full of very original ideas might be of use to you. . . . Don't trouble to answer this, but if you care to write to Ted, his address is 8 Downshire Hill, Hampstead.

Fred had in view a play called *For Sword or Song*, his only venture into the artistic theatre. He had as little use as Irving for his sister Nell's 'whiteheaded boy', but, to please her, commissioned two sets, which were exquisite, and cost as much as the whole production, which was a failure, because neither Fred nor Julia were the right people to put on that kind of show.

The address given in Ellen Terry's letter is of interest, because it brings into the picture the family of Meo: Gaetano, the gallant Italian immigrant, whose daughter, Elena, became the mother of two of Gordon Craig's children—Nelly (known to the family as 'Little Nellie')—and Edward ('Little Teddy')who later made his own name as Edward Carrick.

The story of the Meos must be left to Gaetano's grandson, who alone is qualified to describe how the transfusion of Meo blood enriched the Terry-Godwin stock.

CHAPTER SEVEN

Ellen

In the northern woods, in the heart of the bosky growths of oak, elm and pine, it is not uncommon to come upon a single larch of such soaring height and beauty that it seems from a distance to dominate a whole hillside, not alone by its luminous colouring but also by its matchless shape. A naturally regal tree, it rises like a pale green spear from the squab growths surrounding it; it is often partnered by a sister tree, a little smaller, and the pair of them fling their green tassels, their minute ruby buds on the winds, to which they bow with inimitable resilience. Up there, in my North Country home, I have seen many trees brought down by tempest, but—it may be coincidence—never a larch; I have heard the screaming and the whining, as the tall shaft bends over, tugging on its obstinate roots, but, come the calm after storm, there is the larch, shaking out its fragile-seeming branches over the battered forest, asserting its regency to a wind-riven sky.

In the packed Terry forest, Ellen was surely the larch, head and shoulders above her own and the following generation: which they all, with perhaps the exception of jealous Marion, proudly accepted. Marion's jealousy is both touching and reasonable: she had so nearly the divine spark that illuminated Ellen, she caught the reflection of it now and again, but *it*, the thing itself, constantly eluded her. And this was a matter of temperament, not of an inferior talent.

Marion was sober, inclined to be genteel, and drew on her imagination for her (theatrical) emotions. She was, as all members of The Profession are at some moment in their careers, inevitably touched by the finger of scandal; her name was linked with that of Squire Bancroft—which petrified the pair of them. Ellen herself declared[1] that her sister was 'in love' with Bancroft, but that it

[1] On one occasion, at the top of her voice, at a first night, with Marion sitting within touch of her. Much of the Marion 'scandal' may be ascribed to Ellen's mischief.

came to anything must be for ever incredible to anyone who knew either of these cautious and conventional people. Another 'affair' which was attributed to Marion arose out of her sympathetic and wise advice to a young man who was deeply in love with a girl of her acquaintance; Marion and the young man used to sit in a London Square and talk about his troubles; very occasionally she would ask him to tea—always in the company of a third person. Her discretion irritated sister Nell, who, 'for the hell of it', sometimes invented stories about Polly.

Ellen Terry had the 'divine madness' which is an ingredient of genius. With her tongue in her cheek, she bowed gracefully to public opinion. Privately, she did exactly as she pleased, controlled only by her devotion to her children. It happened that her taste was not for promiscuous 'love'-affairs; it was not for love-affairs at all. She was in love with Edward Godwin—for a while; she was in love with Henry Irving—for a while. Her true love was for her art— which, with typical realism, she called her *work*. She could love any-one—temporarily—who contributed to that. Any departures from the dedicated path were due to the womanish dread of loneliness. That accounted for her second marriage to Charles Kelly (Wardell), and for her third marriage (1907) to James Carew (Usselman). It is interesting that these two husbands of Ellen Terry were 'much of a muchness': young, vigorous he-men, who supplied some need in her for commonplace masculinity. It is not suggested that she loved either of them; towards both she preserved an aloofness which must have been galling. Yet—they gave her something. Ellen Terry did not—as the more maudlin of her admirers chose to believe —live on honeydew.

What had she, that set her above them all? Something that Kate never had, Marion never had, and the boys never glimpsed for all their devotion to The Tradition.

Some foolish writer of one of Marion's obituaries referred to her 'intellectuality': the last quality that was ever attributable to Marion Terry. Only Ellen had ever that fine, that aristocratic approach that identified her with all the arts. Kate had no glimmer; Marion was equally blank, apart from her music; Fred thrust out his jaw—the term 'artist', to him, was almost an obscenity. Charming, humble Charles made no pretensions, and his daughters Minnie and Beatrice regarded the Theatre mainly as a means of earning a living. Kate's daughter Mabel had a smattering of painting and music, and a neat talent for the stage.

Only Ellen, from her sixteenth year, had had the privilege of close association with the arts, which coloured her work and enriched her personality and freed her from the bourgeois considerations which governed her sister and nieces. She had a natural disposition towards learning; she mopped up literature and history and archaeology like a sponge. She loved, and was at home in, the company of poets, painters, musicians and writers: and they all contributed something to her quality as an actress.

At the end of the century she had passed her own half century; her hair was greying; her once sylph-like form had thickened; there was a shadow on the 'fabulous face'. And what wonder? She had taken, with philosophy, Irving's infidelity—personal and professional. She was a public idol—and sometimes she wondered why, for she had, in the last few years, little opportunity of demonstrating her art in the Theatre. In November 1900 she wrote to Shaw—

> I feel so certain Henry just hates me! . . . We have not met for years now, except before other people, where my conduct exactly matches his, of course. All my own fault. It is *I* who am changed, not he.

It was always Ellen's 'fault', not other peoples.' Whether true or not, this did not make it easier for her.

She was the only English actress who ever teamed up, in critical opinion, with the great continental *lionnes* of the theatre, with Duse, Réjane and Bernhardt.[1] And how little she had in common with them! Bernhardt had, during her lifetime, a great reputation which has to some extent been preserved in the writings of James Agate; most of those who remember her and are able to compare her with the moderns find it a little difficult to believe in the

---

[1] Having seen Bernhardt's *Dame aux Camélias*, I saw that of Rachel Behrendt at the Odeon in 1926. It was a disaster that this beautiful and gifted young actress retired from the stage shortly afterwards; she had the simplicity that Bernhardt lacked, and that was absent from the elegant performance of Edwige Feuillère, a few years ago. Both of these actresses realized the part in a way impossible to Bernhardt, whose single aim was to exploit her own personality.

greatness of an art so overladen with the baroque. Bernhardt's acting resembled some of her preposterous gowns, so loaded with frills and furbelows, with tinsel and jewels, that no 'line' remained; she throttled herself with mousselines and tormented her hennaed hair into a frizzled mop that concealed her brow and left only a pair of eyes burnt into the white paper of her face and a vermillion square of mouth revealing unpleasant teeth. Ellen Terry admired her extravagantly, but, as we have seen, she was tuned to reverence; there was nothing in herself of that *Vénus toute entière à sa proie attachée* which was Bernhardt's approach to her audiences. Ellen was far too simple ever to have become a *lionne*.

Nor was there in her any of the agony that informed the art of the Duse: that divine, that supernatural actress, who translated all the privations and humiliations of her youth into her work; who was a tragedienne by nature—although also, when called to be, a brilliant comedienne. After all, true comedy has its roots in tragedy— as every clown or comic has proved down the ages. Ellen Terry had had enough griefs in her youth—and managed to dispose of them, as a bird flirts drops of water off its wings. Her most prejudiced admirers never claimed for her that she had the qualities of the tragic actress; her Lady Macbeth was—just perceptibly—a piece of acting. It was lovely to act, but she never wholly believed in the Sleepwalking scene; its horror did not grip her, although her impeccable technique enabled her to grapple with it. She could be sad, she could be pathetic to a degree that dissolved her audiences; but she never quite conquered the frozen peaks of tragedy. So she never—and she herself was the first to admit it—approached the stature of the Duse.

English and French comedy are hardly comparable; it would be foolish to measure the dry, brittle and brilliant comedy of Réjane against the warm and genial comedy of Ellen Terry, with its delicate nuances conveyed in the incomparable lift of an eyebrow, twitch of the mouth. If any criticism can be levelled against Ellen Terry as a comedienne, it is that her art was essentially insular; that it belonged to our climate as our rich autumns and our thin summers belong; it adumbrated the subtleties of English weather, and the incalculabilities of English character. She never tried it out against the harsh backcloth of the European theatre. Was she right in evading that challenge? In America, to polyglot audiences, made up of European orts and shreds, she had overwhelming success. Insular, superficially, she was; but there was something in Ellen Terry's acting which embraced the whole of the human race.

She had something none of her continental rivals could claim: a romantic beauty, of face, of frame, of movement—which might well have swamped her talents as an actress, had it not been wedded with the deep glory of her personal genius. That beautiful, irregular face, with wide mouth, square jaw, aquamarine eyes and frail skin, like cherry-blossom, needed little to enhance its beauty for the stage; the proportions were so right. The long arms and thighs, the low bosom and generous hips, the movements like flowing water, not only glorified, but dominated whatever costume she was required to wear; and these held good to the end of her life.

She seldom knew her lines. Already, in her early fifties, her memory played traitor to her;[1] scraps of paper were pinned up all over the stage to supplement the offices of the prompter. Yet, so acute was her sense of theatre that she seldom inconvenienced her fellow players. She would cover any gap with a piece of business, an improvised line that belonged to the part and led naturally into the line another was obliged to speak. She so identified herself with the parts she played that she was incapable of speaking any words out of tune with the character.

She would be late on her call, and at the last moment stab in a safety-pin to catch up some piece of errant drapery, while her dresser (Sally Holland) agonized in the wings. So radiant, so *sure* was she, from the moment the lights shone up into her divine face, that criticism was disarmed.

To see Ellen Terry only in her sunset, was to be sharply aware of the indescribable magnetism that reduced to papier mâché the people who played with her. One of the less unfortunate was Edith Evans, who put up some kind of artistic resistance as Mrs Ford to Ellen's Mrs Page. A victim was Doris Keane, an American actress who had created some sensation in a melodrama called *Romance*, during the First World War; she aspired to play Juliet, and the management

---

[1] Gordon Craig wrote that she had trouble only with memorizing trashy lines (as in *Robespierre*) and could always memorize Shakespeare. *Wrong*: E.G.C. never had the painful experience of prompting his mother in her last Shakespearian parts.

was so ill-advised as to engage Ellen Terry for the part of the Nurse. The result was to be foreseen: nobody saw the Romeo or the Juliet, and only the graciousness of Ellen Terry prevented a débâcle.

She had no vanity—ah, here we come to it. The affectation of the modern actress was something outside the range of her understanding. All she wanted (and ever had) to prepare herself for the stage was reasonable space, a roomy table for her make-up, good lights, a comfortable chair or two for visitors and a couch to rest on. She would have opened her beautiful half-blind eyes wide at a 'specially-decorated' dressingroom, at a Picasso or a Renoir or a William Nicholson hung on the walls; she, who knew about painters and painting, did not require that sort of 'inspiration'; nor did she find it necessary to advertise her erudition. I saw at the Lyceum, before its 'conversion', its leading lady's dressingroom; it was perfectly adequate—and no so-called 'star' today would accept it.

Nor would Ellen Terry have accepted the conditions which Sarah Siddons took for granted: the hutch, the walls streaming with damp which infected the costumes, the hand-basin with a modicum of warmish water, the chamber-pot. She had had all that before she came to the Lyceum (as, in the 'twenties, we, the small people of the theatre, had it). She required only what was strictly necessary for the proper fulfilment of her duties to her public. (On one of her last engagements she was surprised, and even embarrassed, that I, who happened to be looking after her, insisted that a drugget should be laid down in her dressingroom.)

At the turn of the century, Ellen Terry, daughter of the strolling players Ben and Sarah, granddaughter of a Portsmouth tavernkeeper and a Portsmouth builder, with some Scottish and a little Irish blood in her veins, had outstripped not only her own family, but the whole of the contemporary theatre and was established as the Queen of the Stage. Surrounded by adulation, by true affection and by the respect and admiration of her peers in all the arts— Ellen Terry was unhappy; was unfulfilled. Ambitious, not for herself, but for her work, she could see no future.

She had come back from the third American tour to play *Olivia* in London; an absurd part, she considered, for a woman of her age, and it made her self-conscious. Yet it was a tremendous success in the provinces, when they took it on tour. Shaw was still pestering her to play in *Brassbound*[1] (which Irving detested, he was right; there was nothing for an actress of the dimensions of Ellen Terry in the trivialities of Shaw), and she regretfully rejected the part of Lady Cicely Wayneflete.

The only good thing that happened to Ellen Terry that year was her purchase of the Elizabethan farmhouse at Smallhythe (now the Ellen Terry Museum) which was to be her home until (literally) the day of her death. She and Irving had found it when she was living at Winchelsea, but it was not then for sale. She later sent Edy down to look at it, and bought it on the nail. On the edge of the marsh, it was surrounded by meadows emblazoned with king-cups; the evening air stirred to the baa-ing of innumerable lambs; bats scooped up the twilight in their swift wings; the scent of hay blew across the toll gate which no longer exists.

That primitive, Tudor house was the small harvest of nearly half a century on the stage. Her open-handedness, to family and friends and greedy hangers-on, left Ellen Terry, in 1900, a comparatively poor woman. But Smallhythe Place, as it had been called for a century or more, included two cottages, Yew Tree and Priest's House, and a handsome parcel of land. An added attraction was the legend of Henry VIII's sojourns at the 'Place' to visit his love Anne Boleyn, then living at Yew Tree. There is actually a property near by known to this day as 'Bullen's'.

This, to Ellen Terry, her grandchildren and her friends was *home*, for twenty-eight years. She always cared more for simple, country-minded folk than for the grand acquaintances of her professional life.

---

[1] It was produced in December of the same year, Laurence Irving creating Brassbound and Janet Achurch Lady Cicely.

SECOND INTERVAL
Historical

The days of peace and plenty were drawing to a close—although there was little indication of that in the brief and glittering reign of Edward VII which ushered in the new century. The new King had made himself tremendously popular as Prince of Wales; his oddly imperfect knowledge of the English language and his thick German accent, far from offending, rather endeared him to his subjects: they were part of the charm of 'Teddy', as he was called by the proletariat. There were plenty of thick German accents around the town in those days, for the Prince had always cultivated the society of wealthy Jews—not, it was said, from entirely altruistic motives. It was 'an age of silk and money', according to a (not very shining) wit of the period; and not a little of the money flowed into the Theatre, whose auditoria, night after night, were crowded with a fabulous array of elegance and fashion. No cloud ventured to impose itself on the golden Edwardian horizon; not even the most prescient committed themselves to a forecast—that the twentieth century was to be torn to shreds, morally, materially and artistically, by two wars, in comparison with which former wars were virtually Ruritanian.

By the time the first war broke out, in the burning summer of 1914, the complexion of Society had suffered a sea-change; Edward VII had died, and his son George V had come to the throne. A well-intentioned, limited man with no social flair, 'The Sailor King' (as he was dubbed, most inappropriately, as he never willingly set foot outside Great Britain from his accession to his death) had no faintest understanding of any of the arts, and was sadly recognized even by the most loyal of his subjects as a wet-blanket on the gay Edwardian tradition.

The Theatre received only the most perfunctory support from George V and his Consort. Queen Mary enjoyed a good musical comedy; King George used seamanlike language when dragged

266

away from his stamp collection or his game of cards to make an obligatory appearance in the Royal Box. Once installed there, he guffawed at the simpler jokes and scowled when the laughter of the audience defeated his understanding. Queen Mary, who had three times the intelligence of her husband, interpreted, and still the King persisted it 'wasn't very funny'. As for a serious play, or a Shakespearian performance, wild horses, on very rare occasions, succeeded in dragging them to it; but their Tussaud effigies could have contributed no less than did their presence in the box.

It was 'back to Victoria'. It was certainly not encouraging for the players, who continued, in loyalty, to describe themselves as 'Their Majesties' Servants'.

Between 1914 and 1918 there was no general evacuation from London, as there was in the Second World War. When the raid warnings sounded, people descended sedately to their cellars or, if caught out in the street, to the Tube stations. The Zeppelins, with their bellies full of murder, were slow and ponderous in comparison with the aircraft of the nineteen-forties; in a student's hostel a young woman delayed until the enemy was almost overhead, threading blue ribbons into her lingerie, and explained when ordered down by an irritable warden, that it was her ambition to be described as 'a well-dressed corpse'. There was no closing of shops or cessation of public services during the hours of daylight; the first daylight raid was regarded as an act of monstrous incivility on the part of the Hun (Germans had become Huns).

The Theatre was harder hit than any other business during that war. Petrol for private vehicles was rationed and taxis became rare as the call-up went on; such bold spirits as, in pursuit of their favourite diversion, were willing to risk the black-out, were likely to find themselves pinned down in the Tube until long after the rise of the curtain, because from the warning to the All Clear, all exits were blocked by the wardens or police. So the general rule in London theatres become two evening performances and six matinées in a week.

A harder blow fell, in the imposition of Entertainment Tax: the stupidest of all taxes, if one considers the importance of keeping up public morale in time of war. This led, inevitably, to a rise in the price of seats, and—I have never met anyone who could explain, let alone justify, the second measure—to a reduction (sometimes amounting to 20 per cent) in actors' salaries. The tax was levied not only on seats booked and paid for in the usual way, but also on 'paper'—the box-office term for complimentary tickets, which were traditionally issued to members of The Profession, as well as to non-professionals it was desirable, for some reason or other, to cultivate. Considerable skill went to the successful 'papering' of a house—which, included, on first nights, the representatives of the newspapers and magazines on which the production counted for publicity.

Ellen Terry, newly returned from an American lecture tour, was persuaded to go with H. B. Irving and Sydney Valentine to the Prime Minister, as representatives of the Actors' Association, and appeal for the removal of the tax on 'paper'. Largely owing to Ellen Terry's irresistible powers of persuasion, the tax was withdrawn, which meant much, not only to managements, but also to actors who could not afford to pay for seats, but whose contacts with contemporary theatre were essential to their work.

The war ended in 1918, and, on the face of things, the Theatre was all set for a boom. A galaxy of stars attracted packed houses, not only in London but also in the provinces; seats were booked up for every performance, queues for pit and gallery snaked for blocks outside every theatre—regardless of the quality of entertainment offered on the bill. The love of the English for the drama demonstrated itself extravagantly throughout the 'twenties, and the know-alls winked, and gave it as their opinion that certain managements were 'making a packet'.

The truth was that many theatres whose House Full boards went out every night were not large enough to make a profit against an exorbitant rise in rents and costs of production, which included salaries, costumes, stage sets, lighting and advertising. Apart from 'the golden galaxy', actors profited not at all from those crowded houses; what they earned was seldom more than just enough to keep them off the breadline.

Thousands were out of work; many, both old and young, too pitifully shabby to present themselves for auditions. Hundreds existed bitterly on some form of charity—yet, when offered chances of earning a reasonable living apart from the Theatre, the majority refused. The Actor's habit of living unfits all but a few for any calling apart from his own; this has nothing to do with professional pride, as some of his supporters choose to maintain; it is quite impossible for the Actor, accustomed to late hours, to lazy mornings, to a kind of innocent social indiscipline, to adapt himself to the routine of wage-earning outside his own specialized orbit. The Theatre was the Actor's life-breath; old, middle-aged and young, they chose to sit in waiting-rooms, where they were in touch with their own kind, where there was a little warmth, idling away the hours with gossip, furtively fingering the few coppers that might buy them a little food—they chose that, rather than put their names down at an agency where they might have been offered regular money for a regular job which entailed early rising, punctuality and the efficient performance of simple tasks, well within the range of their abilities. Let it be taken into account that, down the ages, many have described themselves as 'actors' on the meagerest premises: people of little talent and less character who chose The Profession as an 'easy' way of living. Their illusions were surely dispelled during those painful 'twenties.

There was the problem of finding work for actors returning from the trenches. This was partly met by the establishment of Repertory and Resident Stock Companies[1] in the provinces, but these were unable more than to touch the fringe of the general distress with which the Benevolent Funds and the notorious generosity of actors to their own kind were unequipped to deal. The Profession was monstrously overcrowded; there were not theatres, plays or parts enough to give employment to the thousands who, calling themselves 'actors', competed with the true professional—i.e. the one who was, first, a dedicated actor, and, second, dependent on acting for his living—for such work as was going. ('A massacre of the

[1] The distinction between Repertory and Stock Companies may be roughly defined as follows: the Repertory originally consisted of members sharing on terms of equality, the Hamlet of one performance acting as Walking Gentleman in the next. The Stock Company was made up of actors engaged for definite parts, and implied a professional hierarchy. In this respect, the modern Repertory approximates more closely to Stock, as there is always a Leading Man, or Leading Lady, who plays the 'star' parts, and minor members have few opportunities of distinguishing themselves.

innocents,' declared one old actor, 'would have been very useful!')

Against this gloomy picture must be set a resurgence of talent in the Theatre.

In conformity with a new school of writing, a new school of acting had come into being, of which the principal exponents were Charles Hawtrey, Seymour Hicks and Gerald du Maurier (each, presently, to be rewarded with a knighthood, as much for his good works as his acting).

Hawtrey and Hicks were, in a sense, 'old actors'; their reputations were established long before the outbreak of the war. But they both had sufficient flexibility to adapt themselves to the new medium. Du Maurier was the brilliant *arriviste*; he had none of the elegance of Hawtrey, none of the sagacity of Hicks; he had something that 'matched with the hour'—the dry, careless throwaway of the so-called Bright Young People, whose rather dreary antics governed contemporary society.

To the contemptuous eye of the Old Actorr, it seemed as though every actor who had the advantage of a classic training was endeavouring to forget all he had learned: voice production ('elocution' had long been at a discount), the measured speaking of important lines (which were now to be 'thrown away', as one might throw a dead match) and deportment. It was fashionable to clip the speech, to mutter, to slouch, and to dispense with gesture, because gesture was not 'realistic'; nobody, off-stage, used his hands or his body to express opinions or emotion. *Speed* was of the first importance. Of this, Hicks was the most entrancing exponent; his torrential utterance and his small, flashing movement—'the quickness of the hand deceives the eye'—were inimitable.

The Old Actorr would have been shamed if 'Speak up!' had been shouted at him from the pit or the gallery; the first thing he learned was to plaster his voice on the back wall of the auditorium. In the 'twenties 'Speak up' was shouted not seldom from the cheap seats, which did not feel they were getting their money's worth. The new, 'naturalistic' school disregarded these admonitions.

Artistically, it was an unhappy period for the Theatre. Musical comedy and farce monopolized the London stage, with Barrie and Shaw on the side-lines. These were crowded by crook drama, a new form called the 'revue' (a mixture of music-hall, ballet and excerpts from Parisian *boîtes de nuit*) and, eventually, the all-conquering ragtime from the States. This was the reaction from the war; people did not want to have to *think*; their desire was to escape from their individual nightmares. They were trying to reorientate themselves—and the rubbish they saw in the theatre presumably helped.

Serious productions were driven into Sunday-night shows, or out into the provinces, where, as always, there was a more thoughtful and intelligent public than in London. The Old Vic was the only London home for Shakespeare. Benson gallantly bore his tattered banner out into the wilds. Fred Terry, Matheson Lang and Martin Harvey (now to be rated as Old Actorrs) popped briefly into town, and retreated to the provinces, to lick their financial wounds. Lewis Waller, the pre-war idol of every woman in her twenties or thirties (the K.O.W.—'Keen on Waller'—club still strove against the derision of the Bright Young People), made himself slightly ridiculous by attempting to adopt the new idiom. 'Gents' evening suiting', combined with the spotlight, did not become that hero of the cloak and dagger, of the resounding Shakespearian phrase.

The Theatre was suffering from growing pains. Unlikely as it seemed, to those who took their theatre seriously, it was actually advancing. A lanky youth, with Terry blood in him, serving his apprenticeship to the Old Vic was to profit not only from his classic training but also from the flexibility which emanated from the breakaway of intelligent artists from the old pattern of acting into something new, and far from perfect, which yet contributed to the soil in which, eventually, he was to plant the seed of his own idealism.

Up to the time of the First World War, the Actor's publicity, apart from his name on the bills and the critics' notices, consisted in the sale of little cabinet photographs, priced from twopence to sixpence, according to size, and later (from the beginning of the new century) of the picture postcard. Occasionally a 'sketch', or a few discreet paragraphs on an actor much in the public eye appeared in select magazines, with photographs and a bowdlerized 'interview'.

No actress of distinction was seen in a public restaurant before the beginning of the century. Actors ate—according to their status and means—in their clubs (the Green Room or the Garrick), or in taverns whose lay *clientèle* respected their personal privacy. This was part of the barrier of exclusiveness and mystery which the actor raised between himself and the public, and which contributed to the glamour of The Profession.[1]

Autographs were not solicited—except by the very young or the ill-bred—other than by a respectful letter, or by personal application at the stage door. The autograph, if granted, was apt to be written on a printed card, bearing some such inscription as the following:

> I send you my autograph with pleasure. Will you in return send me a trifle for one of the charities I wish to help.

The appeal was seldom ignored, even when the means of the applicant enabled him only to send a few postage stamps. The autograph rarely went unacknowledged. Good manners were then the vogue; idolatry (of which there was plenty) did not take the form of milling round the stage door, shoving dirty bits of paper into the actor's hand, obstructing his passage to his cab or car: far from it! It was commonplace for the 'fans' to form a cordon between the stage door and the cab or car, and to hold back *hoi polloi* who intruded on the passage of the actor or actress.

'Bohemianism' went out of fashion; the Actor's aim, off-stage, was to ape the affluent bourgeoisie, in dress, in manners and in morals. He aspired to the best of two worlds: for his children, the dubious advantage of public school education; for himself, social advancement, running tandem with his art. He jeered—not unkindly—at the Old Actorr, whose simple world he could no more appreciate than the Old Actorr could understand his. He was nervously aware of a new element encroaching on his own: the cinema, inspired by Hollywood—that is to say, bearing no sort of relationship to the English way of living—was already threatening the music-hall, most English of all institutions; it was presently to threaten the legitimate theatre—mainly because it was cheap, comfortable and in tune with the laxity of manners and morals that inevitably follow a war. For the expenditure of as little as sixpence, young men and women could enjoy petting parties in the

[1] Gordon Craig wrote to Ellen Terry during the First World War: 'I am going to try and bring back mystery about all that concerns the theatre; it used to be one of its greatest attractions and was so right.'

Kate Lewis

Marion and Ellen Terry

Edward Gordon Craig, Edith Craig and James Carew at
the funeral of Ellen Terry

dark; as a secondary consideration, could guffaw at Fatty Arbuckle and get a thrill out of Ramon Novarro or Theda Bara.

The dignity of the Actor was further shaken by a figure also emanating from the States: the Press agent. Persuaded by this insidious character, the Actor—most simple of souls—came to believe it might be good for business, or for his personal *réclame*, to be seen eating in public; to lend his presence, as well as his name, to certain projects which were receiving expensive publicity. The thin end of the wedge having been inserted, Big Business stepped in. Through the advertisement columns, the Actor or Actress was offered not only free but lucrative publicity, in return for his endorsement of products ranging from cosmetics to fountain pens.[1] Few apart from the top-liners had the moral strength to stand out against this easy money.

Worse was to follow: the invasion of their private lives by the spotlight of the Press. Encouraged by many, deplored by a few, the Camera's Eye penetrated the Actor's home, tore the last veils which protected him from the curiosity of the mob. Admittedly it was invited by those who rated a paragraph in a gossip column higher than their personal privacy.

So fell the Ivory Tower of the Actor; curiosity, familiarity and vulgarity crawled in over its dust. There was no more mystery, and progressively less glamour—of which mystery is a vital element.

One generally approved change entered the life of the Actor, affecting him both professionally and domestically.

For something like seventy years, disinterested and philanthropic people had been aware of the exploitation of the Child Actor by unprincipled or ignorant parents and guardians.

Kate Terry, her brothers and sisters, never suffered from that exploitation, because they were the children of cultured parents who cared as much about their moral and physical welfare as for their contributions to the family exchequer. In the old stock companies this was the rule rather than the exception; growing up under the watchful parental eye, few children appear to have been the worse

---

[1] This was not entirely a new idea. Julia Neilson had contributed the glory of her hair to advertise a product called Harlene before the First World War.

for their rough-and-tumble rearing, their late hours, casual education and bohemian associations. In patches of poverty, whoever went short it was not the children. Sharing the hazards of the player's life, they were inevitably precocious, but their innocence was jealously preserved, not only by their parents but by every adult member of the company to which they made their small contribution. Ellen Terry said she had never heard foul language or seen *louche* behaviour until she was grown up.

But there were others to whom the guardianship of a promising child actor stood for hard cash: hollow-eyed children, coerced, frightened and bullied into The Profession. Outside of the theatre they were as little human as trained animals; they had not even the delight and pride of the animal in its performance—for all but the lowest of trainers knows that the way to get the best out of an animal is not through fear. These unfortunate children cried mutely for protection, which was originally extended to them in a clumsy form of legislation which raised the age at which they could be granted a licence for performing in the theatre.

The writer recalls from as recently as forty years ago, a famous—or infamous—school which specialized in supplying 'child' artists to productions which advertised for them. These miserable little characters were trained to the limit of their undeveloped powers, deliberately underfed, given lemon juice in place of milk to retard their physical growth. Their IQ was barely up to the child of eight or ten whom they successfully counterfeited. The majority came from slum families whose interest, naturally, was only in the pay-cheque. They had, according to the legislation, to be more than fourteen years old. A particular instance which comes to the mind is that of a girl in her early twenties who was able to pass, both on and off the stage, as a ten- or twelve-year-old. A pitiful dwarf, she was seldom out of an engagement. She had not the intelligence to play an adult part, neither had she any interest in acting, except as a means of earning her living.

The case of these unhappy young people was shown up by Brenda Girvin (among others), and the government belatedly decided that something more than an age-limit was needed to protect them. So it became obligatory that Child Actors should have regular hours of schooling, and that children on tour should be accompanied by a qualified governess; that their hours in the theatre, whether rehearsing or performing, should be strictly defined, and that, without a special licence, they should not be allowed to appear on the stage after nine o'clock at night.

Thus the Child Actor today is protected against exploitation. He is also 'protected' from the true life of the Theatre, its incalculable hours, its hazards, its community spirit—which produced the great Actors of the past. The actor, whether Child or Adult, has 'never had it so good', as working conditions go. Much water has flowed under the bridges since Kate Terry at the age of three, and Ellen Terry just over four, nodded and slept at midnight rehearsals, and gaily went on to play their parts at an hour when today's little actor is supposed to be tucked up in bed. Kate and Ellen survived, in excellent health, to the age of eighty apiece.

In 1890, theatre artisans—scene-shifters, carpenters, electricians and baggagemen—were already banded for their mutual protection. Controversy raged over the case of the Actor, unemployed, or victimized by the many bogus managements that took advantage of the helplessness and poverty of Actors to dishonour their contracts, leaving companies stranded, and with no means of reprisal. So a General Theatrical Union was proposed, to embrace managements and artists, and, incidentally, to procure for the latter better working conditions. Oddly enough, it did not receive, from The Profession, the support it might reasonably have expected. That unfortunate word 'Union' stuck in the gullet. Actors had their own aristocracy, and objected to their (tacit) classification with labour. Although, in 1889, two young actors had died of fever, due to the insanitary conditions of dressingrooms, few were inclined to stand out for the modicum of cleanliness and propriety that made the difference between disease and health. Bogus managements continued to flourish, actors to dress in unheated rooms, stinking with sewage, where costumes hung up overnight were infested with bugs, and make-up was nibbled by mice and rats.[1]

None the less, the Actor resisted the label of Unionism—by

[1] This is no exaggeration; these conditions were prevailing, in the writer's experience, into the early nineteen-twenties, in a modified degree. What they must have been like before the First World War passes imagination. But, for some extraordinary reason, we never complained! And, of course, the stars' rooms were very different, although not comparable with a star's dressingroom today.

implication, Trade Unionism—which struck at his pride as an artist, and reduced him, in his own estimation, to equality with the lower ranks of the theatrical cosmogony.

By courtesy of the British Actors' Equity Association, I have been permitted to consult an unpublished work called *The Rise of British Actors' Equity*, by Joseph Macleod, which quotes what Mr Macleod describes as the Actor's budget, applying to the actor immediately before, during and following the First World War. The average actor had 35 weeks' work in the year, and out of total earnings of £75 spent £32 on food; the rest went on clothes and lodgings. There was no surplus for drink, tobacco or newspapers. Seventeen years after the formation of the Actors' Association, Ben Terry, as a Walking Gentleman and 'bit' player in his son Fred's Company, would have been entitled to the munificent sum of four pounds a week—the women were paid less.[1] Frank Benson was offering less to his people, and continued to do so even after the Actor's Union (the description this time was accepted) formed itself inside the Association, and attempted to enforce a minimum salary of two pounds a week, with extra for matinées *and rehearsals.*

This last was an important innovation; actors were apparently expected to live on air during rehearsals. No less important was the projected measure against amateurs, who paid premiums and received no salaries—who were, in effect, blacklegs on The Profession. According to the Union's ruling, all company members, regardless of their experience, were to be paid on a professional scale. And finally, all engagements were to be for the run of the piece. It had formerly been commonplace for an actress who had rehearsed and perhaps opened satisfactorily in a play to be replaced, without notice, by the *chère amie* of the backer or manager.

It seems curious that these measures, so patently designed for the betterment of the Actor's status, did not receive the whole-hearted support that might have been expected. The pusillanimity of the Actor's temperament and his stubborn individualism defeated the

[1] 'How did you expect them to keep up an appearance and a morality on three pounds a week, Chief?' Fred Terry was asked. The glassy Terry eye focussed. He liked to believe that 'the girls' were moral—as most of them were. And he liked them to have beautiful shoes and beautiful gloves—although how he imagined they acquired them . . . ?

Union's honest attempt to bring justice to bear on the relationship between actors and managements. Until the formation of the Stage Guild in 1924, little if any progress was made.

There followed a period of lobbying and intrigue, of party politics, private interests and Trade Unionism, of clashes between the Association and the Guild, which came to a head when the Association was affiliated to the T.U.C., and its members 'deserted' to the Guild in bulk. On the Grand Council of the Guild actors, managers and authors had equal representation, and the Standard Touring Contract was devised which, temporarily at any rate, satisfied and safeguarded all parties.

Some ten years later the Actors' Association and the Stage Guild finally sank their differences of opinion and amalgamated as the British Actors' Equity Association. The English Theatre, at last, was regimented—whether for good or evil time alone may show.

One unfortunate result came of that well-intentioned clause about payment for rehearsals. Owing to the unwillingness, or in some case inability, of managements to conform to the clause, plays too often were put on under-rehearsed.

The sense of dedication somehow got mislaid, together with the authority of the actor-manager who, at the fall of the curtain, might call for a rehearsal, going on into the small hours, to improve a scene which had 'flopped' at the evening show; who, in the heat of production, was free to carry on from morning, through noon and midnight, until dawn was in the sky; who was freely and loyally supported by his company, whose desire to give of their best matched his.

No willingness, no loyalty, could prevail against the Trade Unions. The painter, the writer, the creative musician are happy in that their art is solitary. The actor is pinned down by his dependence on people whose business is to turn on a light and turn it off, to lock the door of an office or dressingroom, to see that the theatre is shut up after rehearsals: all elementary tasks which the actor is perfectly capable of doing for himself, but under union rules is not allowed to do, for these switchers on of lights and lockers of doors are granted a monopoly and their working hours are strictly controlled. Managements found themselves required to pay exorbitant overtime; little wonder if—in view of the gamble involved in putting on even a small production—they kept down expenses to a bare minimum.

During the second and third decades of the present century the Theatre became, not an Art, but a Business. Little wonder if this mercenary attitude infected the artists themselves. The theatre itself, the theatre of bricks and mortar, of lath and plaster, the theatre smelling of grease and gas and size, was no longer their *home*, but an office. The few whose devotion to the *métier* would have driven them to work on to all hours were defeated by the many who, if the rehearsal was timed to finish at five, started looking at their watches at a quarter to four.

It was a far cry from Mr and Mrs Shalders at the Portsmouth Theatre; from Mr and Mrs Kean at the Princess's; from Mr and Mrs Chute at the Bristol Theatre Royal; from all the little provincial companies who cared, naturally, about the pay-cheque, because they had to put food into their own mouths and those of their children, but who expected in return to give their unlimited utmost, regardless of time or personal convenience, to their manager.

For the change in the theatrical climate Equity must shoulder part of the responsibility. The arts are not amenable to regimentation.

PART THREE

CHAPTER ONE

1900—and Onwards

The first years of the new century were 'bumper' years for Marion Terry. Having played, in the Stratford-on-Avon festival of April 1900 as guest artist, the parts of Rosalind and Portia, she departed on a strenuous provincial tour, which included, among other heavy parts, Lady Teazle and Mrs Erlynne, and came back the following year to open at the Court Theatre in a revival of *The Real Little Lord Fauntleroy*, and went on to the Vaudeville with *Quality Street*. The parts of 'Dearest' and Susan Throssel were what the more sentimental of her admirers liked to call 'Marion Terry parts'; she herself liked playing them because—a weakness she shared with her sister Ellen—she believed in giving the public what it expected of her, personally, as an actress; experiments, in her opinion, were rarely good box-office, and to the box-office Marion was as dedicated as her brother Fred and her sister-in-law Julia. Past mistress of the elegant saccharine, she had, fortunately, another string to her bow.

Oscar Wilde died in 1900, and was buried in the cemetery of Bagneux, whence, nearly ten years later, his remains were transferred to Père Lachaise; and those who, in 1893 and 1895, had booed his plays off the stage, not because they were bad plays but because English Puritanism is for ever incapable of dissociating the work of art from the morality of its creator,[1] now prepared to accept revivals of Wilde's comedies, as the scandal had died down, and the plays themselves were good entertainment. *Lady Windermere's Fan* was revived in 1904 and again in 1911; *A Woman of No Importance* was revived in 1907.

Marion Terry belonged to, and interpreted, the epoch as no modern actress has succeeded in doing. Dame Marie Tempest said[2] that one of the most impossible roles for an actress of the twentieth

[1] If he has the misfortune to be an Englishman; a 'foreigner' can get away with murder, because, of course, no 'foreigners' are moral!
[2] To the author.

century to attempt is that of a late-Victorian or Edwardian Lady. (The men, for some reason, come off better; John Gielgud, Jack Hawkins and George Howe, among others, have succeeded in capturing the 'native wood-notes wild' of Victorian comedy.) For the women, the quiet assurance instinct with good breeding appears to be unrealizable; a flashy exaggeration approximating to caricature blots out the authenticity of Wilde's feminine characters, and no playgoer of the last two generations has ever seen a Wilde 'heroine' or 'villainess' played for what she is worth. (The 'last' Lady Bracknell[1] was Aida Jenoure at the Liverpool Repertory in the 'twenties; she was then in her sixties and knew the idiom. The 'last' Mrs Erlynne, the 'last' Mrs Arbuthnot were Marion Terry.)

This is not to belittle recent attempts to interpret these parts; the actress of thirty, forty or fifty years' experience today is too close to Victoriana and Edwardiana to catch the authentic note. Contemporary manners and morals are more easily teamed up with the Elizabethan and Georgian than with those delicate, subtle and complicated conventions of late-Victorian and Edwardian society. A century from now, there may be research which will enable Wilde, Pinero and Jones to be presented at their true valuation: as admirable craftsmen of the theatre who, apart from 'fashion', contributed something permanent to the art of the dramatist, and should be given their dues in production and interpretation.

A few years ago, I took a friend who, in her very distant youth, had moved in London and Viennese Society, to a Wilde revival; one of her comments, trumpeted from the stalls, was, 'Doesn't the woman know better than to take her parasol into the drawingroom? Vulgar; nothing like us. My dear, you should have seen Marion Terry; she was one of us!'

She was strikingly good-looking, with her dark copper hair, her heavy eyelids and somewhat buxom figure; her superb carriage and convincing aristocracy (in days when aristocracy comported itself as such) made her a natural choice of managers, producers, and authors who had plays of elegance to present. Within a somewhat narrow range she was an exquisite actress; no one but a fool would have considered casting her for Mrs Higgins in the 1920 revival of

[1] Poor Lady Bracknell has been the principal sufferer from the dramatic distortion of Wilde's characters in the modern theatre.

Pygmalion at the Aldwych. Her own judgement failed her, for once, in accepting the part; but Shaw was the playwright of the moment. Marion's art called for beautiful sets, beautiful clothes and well-bred people; she had no faintest understanding of what, in her day, were called 'the lower classes', and no idea of interpreting them. In a cast that included Mrs Patrick Campbell (already too old to play Eliza), her Mrs Higgins was one of her few failures.

Up to the outbreak of the 1914-18 war, she created no fewer than eighteen parts. Usually she was a titled lady—Lady Claude Debenham in *Mollentrave on Women*, Lady Astrupp in *John Chilcote, M.P.*, Lady Mary Crewys in *Peter's Mother*. Her final performance was the Principessa della Cercola in *Our Betters* which, produced in 1923, ran for over a year.

Marion did not care for reminders of the humble beginnings of the Terry family; she had 'thought herself' into the grand manner she so admirably interpreted, on and off the stage. She never, when on tour, welcomed—as Ellen did—attentions from small, humble Terrys, proud to claim their kinship with the great Terrys. She disclaimed relationship with the little butchers, bakers or candlestick makers who sprang from the original Portsmouth root. Ellen visited them, gave a baby a christening cap (cherished today, because it was given by Ellen Terry), and sat down for tea at humble tables, as Ben and Sarah, sixty years before, sat down.

After a blazing start with *Sweet Nell of Old Drury*, the young managers Fred Terry and Julia Neilson were not doing quite as well as they had expected. Fred, that noble gambler, backed two losers in succession: *The Heel of Achilles* and *For Sword and Song*. Expenses ran to £1,000 a week, and at the end of the season the Company was more than £10,000 'in the red'. They had lost every penny they had made in *Sweet Nell*, and Julia—it would appear—lost her head; it was not like her to panic, but the one thing that ever shook her shrewdness and serenity was the fear of being 'in reduced means', as the Victorians called it. She had seen enough of that in her youth. Without taking Fred into her confidence, she went to her stepfather, William Morris, to ask his advice. The disaffection between Fred and his mother-in-law having spread to his stepfather-in-law, Mr Morris agreed to put up some capital

—on condition that Fred Terry had no part in the management of the Company. It is all but incredible that Julia Neilson accepted terms so insulting to her husband (her excuse, later, was that she had to think about the children's education).

One can picture the short-sighted blue eyes pinpointing, the formidable Terry jaw jutting, the beautiful crooked mouth thinning to a line. Fred was never to forgive Julia for what—himself passionately loyal—he saw as an act of monstrous disloyalty. He made instant reprisal; a Canadian friend, Charles Hosner, came to his help, and furnished him with the means of retaining his share in the management. From this unhappy incident dated all the trouble which was presently to arise in the relationship between him and Julia: trouble sedulously covered up for publicity reasons, but active for many years.

For Sword and Song had been a very expensive production (Fred's nephew Gordon Craig and Percy Anderson had contributed to the *décor*), and after that, Fred, wagging his wise young head, decided that 'art' was not for him or for Julia.

One of the qualities of greatness is to recognize one's own limitations. Another is to steer steadfastly by your guiding star, and not be led astray by some *fata Morgana* of the tides.

Contrary to the opinion of those who have belittled him, Fred Terry was a very great actor. It is a pity that these misinformed critics never saw Fred conduct a rehearsal: direct a block-headed girl in the delicacies of a love-scene, or a nervous and rather stupid man in the pathos of madness. He had no vocabulary whatever (apart from great richness in profanity), and such terms as 'method' or 'motivation' would have been regarded by Fred as obscenities, not to be uttered before 'the ladies'. But he could 'show how' in such a fashion that one was not tempted to *copy* him, but one's imagination was kindled.

He was already a slightly 'old-fashioned' young actor, in the sense of deriving from Kean and Irving, and of having a bent towards the romantic school. The attitudes, the speech and the costume of historical (or pseudo-historical) drama both attracted and became him; he brought conviction and sincerity to them, and the spectacular handsomeness he shared with Julia contributed to the vein they now decided to make their own.

Fred was only once more to appear in a play worthy of his immense talent. In *Much Ado About Nothing* he played a Benedick so perfect that the part might have been written for him—a performance only rivalled by the Benedick of his nephew, John Gielgud. Julia tried to imitate her sister-in-law Ellen's Beatrice with unfortunate results; she was acted into the shadows by one of her understudies. But her beauty, her grace and her radiance blinded the majority to her shortcomings as an actress.

They were perfectly clear about what they wanted. Both Fred and Julia loved luxury: Julia loved beautiful, fashionable clothes and they both liked rich, expensive food (Fred's taste was, actually, simpler than Julia's; he was a connoisseur of good, plain, English cooking—meat, vegetables, sauces all 'of the best'), and were extremely hospitable; Julia, as was natural, liked to show off the resources of her *cuisine*. They wanted a handsome house with servants, an exceptional cellar, governesses for the children—and Phyllis to be 'finished' in Paris and Dennis to go to Public School.

If Fred sold his birthright for a mess of pottage, as certain critics accused him of doing, the bright Terry eye was wide open. Actually, Fred did nothing of the sort; it was not in him or in Julia to be pioneers of the 'new' theatre. In *Sweet Nell* they had discovered their *genre*; a few more 'Sweet Nells' and they could indulge to their hearts' content in Fred's gambling on cards and horses, Julia's mania for beautiful, preposterous hats. They would not have to worry unduly about their rather disquieting health; Fred's clear, bright eyes, his clear, fresh colour and vigorous carriage gave no indication of the obscure heart condition (shared by his brother Ben and his sister Ellen) from which he had suffered since babyhood. The sedentary life of the theatre was crowding flesh on to his big bones, and he had already preliminary twinges of the gout which made martyrdom of his later years on and off the stage. And Julia had had several miscarriages, and had begun to be nervous about herself. 'Be dimmed'[1] to Art, as such; the thing was to find plays of a calibre to appeal to the big-hearted, mutton-headed public which had taken them both to its bosom in the respective roles of Charles II and Nell Gwyn.

[1] The Terry bowdlerization of an oath which Fred never hesitated to employ in its original version in his private life.

In 1903 they discovered their supreme piece of romantic tushery, *The Scarlet Pimpernel*, which remained the sure card in their theatrical pack up to their retirement. They had recouped a little of their losses with a trivial comedy called *Sunday*. They tried out *The Scarlet Pimpernel* in Nottingham, and after eighteen months of revision and rehearsal, brought it to the New Theatre. The critics were rude and the public indifferent; it took courage to nurse the new play for four weeks against a stagnant box-office. But Fred's genius for making bricks without straw, his unerring instinct for good 'theatre', his inventiveness and his power, with his own jolly laugh, of invoking laughter, blazed it into success. As *Sweet Nell* had been Julia's play, the *Pimpernel* was Fred's. They played it—intermittently with other productions—over twenty years. They had other successes, but it was the *Pimpernel* which paid for the big house on Primrose Hill, the servants, the governess, the Rolls, the chauffeur, the children's education, the upkeep of a big permanent Company touring in the grand manner (it was known as The First Company on the Road), Fred's variegated diversions, Julia's collections of antique furniture and the lavishness of their private and public expenditure.

It appears not to be generally known that the novel of *The Scarlet Pimpernel*, a best-seller of its period, owed much to the dialogue and business imposed by Fred Terry on the Baroness Orczy's clumsy little play; without acknowledgement to their originator, she incorporated them into her novel—and eventually brought (and lost) a copyright action against the Terrys.

It is easy for those who never saw Fred Terry in *The Pimpernel*, who only know it from revivals or in its screen version, to overlook the basic excellence of Fred's version of the old play; the first scene in particular, the whole of which was invented and scripted by Fred, was a masterly introduction to the play, and the scene which followed it, of which Fred invented all the comedy business and situations, a model of romantic drama with all the elements of tension, suspense, surprise, and comedy, backed with a creeping atmosphere of unease, deepening towards the fall of the curtain.

One of the good things in the Company was that the new or young members were not only allowed but encouraged to stand in the wings; in some of the smaller provincial theatres this led us into trouble with the Stage Manager, but we became skilful in dodging him, in suspending ourselves from ladders or flattening ourselves up in the flies. And not only the small-fry but also the principals often crowded the wings to see the Chief's first act, from which we learned far more of our business as actors than we gained from half a dozen rehearsals.[1] Fred Terry could teach from example, rarely from precept.

In 1904, Kate's youngest daughter, Mabel Terry-Lewis, married a Captain Ralph Batley, of the Dorset Yeomanry, and retired (temporarily) from the stage. Mabel's talents, like those of her contemporaries, Lilian Braithwaite and Sybil Thorndike, were slow in ripening—and never rivalled theirs. But when she returned, in 1920, she did not lack for 'engagements' (as, imitating her aunt Marion, who disdained the professional vulgarism of 'job', she called them), it was not until she was well into her forties that she was generally recognized as a valuable actress in her limited *genre*.

Like Marion, she was usually a 'Duchess', a 'Countess' or the wife of a titled individual: to all such impersonations she brought a dry, convincing stylishness, deriving—such was the impression she gave—from her private life. She was not, in the pure sense of the word, an 'actress', for all she did was to carry *herself* on to the stage. She was quite incapable of realizing any character or any class apart from that with which she was acquainted, but, within a narrow range, she was impeccable. Her recreations and hobbies, as listed in *Who's Who in the Theatre*, are illuminating: 'Miniature-painting and shooting, farming and dog-breeding.' In and out of the wings, she was the perfect exposition of The County: the patroness of the point-to-point, the Lady of the Manor, the opener of bazaars, the President of local committees. She was the unlikeliest of all sports of the Terry breed.

In the year of Mabel's marriage, her sister Katie gave birth to another son, Arthur John. The Gielguds had moved from Earl's

---

[1] He had little idea how good he really was; he used to send the 'boys and girls' off to Aldwych farces, to learn 'timing'. With all honour to Tom Walls, Ralph Lynn and Robertson Hare, Fred Terry's split-second 'timing' more than matched theirs. He may have meant 'pace'; as an actor he was often bogged down in later years by an inferior Company.

Court Square to Gledhow Gardens, off the Old Brompton Road:
a bigger, more important house, which the increase in the family
demanded. The eldest boy, Lewis, ten years old, and the second,
Val, were at prep. school near Shackleford—both already showing
a bent for acting. The Great Gielgud of the future lay in his cradle,
a very delicate baby, constantly sicking up his food, running tem-
peratures and agonizing his mother who, having brought up a
couple of healthy children, was disproportionately worried by
Arthur John's nonconformity to the family tradition of heartiness.

They were all, in that first decade of the new century, well
established: even Charlie, who, as business manager, was in constant
demand for touring Companies. Everybody loved Charles Terry, and
liked to have him around; he got on with all the small-fry of the
theatre, was respected and liked by the big-fry; he understood the
moods and tenses of the players, and—incapable of organizing his
own finances—was never a farthing out in his theatre accounts.

Ben, by now in Cawnpore, was not doing so well, and had separated from his wife, to whom he was allowing half of his small
income. He wrote to his brother Fred:

> I don't often write to you but I hope you & yours are all well and
> comfy. . . . As for me old man I'm getting fairly old but hearty still
> except that I've no teeth and indigestion is playing the dickens with me
> . . . they promise me a full set of teeth to last my life time and guaran-
> teed to chew up one of India's hardest beefsteaks provided I pay them
> Rs 200. Now Fred old chap to get rid of my indigestion will you help
> me? My pay is very small or I would not trouble you. . . . I think
> I'm like the dear old Dad can't stick too much preaching.[1] Anyhow
> old man if you can't don't let that stop you from Droping [*sic*] me
> a line. . . .
> When do you intend going to America? Don't think of coming to
> this Godforsaken place Fred it wouldn't pay the passage money—
> India is a wipe out now and its mostly for the Indians with a bit more
> since Lord Curzon came out. He played to the gallery first and now he
> wants to play to the Stalls but they are not taking any . . .
> How many little ones have you?
> Send Photo if handy also one of Mrs Fred.

Fred's response to this appeal is not to be doubted.

---

[1] A reference to his wife.

Phyllis Neilson-Terry

Olive Morris

Mabel Terry-Lewis

Val Gielgud

John Gielgud

An actress in her fifty-fourth year cannot, whatever be her equipment, play a virgin in her teens. When Henry Irving revived *Faust* at the Lyceum there was no possible part for Ellen Terry. She agreed to play two matinées a week, and took herself off to Stratford-on-Avon, to play Queen Katharine in F. R. Benson's revival of *Henry VIII* for Shakespeare's birthday.

A few weeks afterwards, Tree came down to Tower Cottage, to propose she should play Mrs Page to Mrs Kendal's Mrs Ford in his projected revival of *The Merry Wives of Windsor*. When she telegraphed Irving for his reactions to this proposition, he graciously assented to her appearance in the rival theatre, provided she fulfilled her contract at the Lyceum.

It was almost the last *leading* Shakespearian part she ever—in its entirety—played. She and Madge Kendal (then Robertson) had detested each other way back at the Bristol Theatre Royal, and it was Mrs Kendal who spread it abroad, when Ellen Terry had her poisoned arm during the run of *Twelfth Night*, that she (Ellen) was having 'riotous supper parties, dancing the can-can and drinking champagne behind drawn blinds'—all risible to anyone with the least knowledge of Ellen's simple habits.

The production of *Merry Wives* at His Majesty's Theatre in 1902 made history; it would have made history of a different kind if the back-stage encounters of the leading ladies had been recorded. Mrs Kendal was a brilliant comedienne, but a malicious, jealous and selfrighteous woman. Her venom was fully matched by Ellen Terry's barbed mischief, and the bickering of Mr Tree's 'Ancient Lights', as Cyril Maude wittily called them, afforded even more comedy than that of the text to privileged listeners behind the scenes.

During the first week of the run there was a fire in Ellen Terry's dressingroom, and her beautiful dress of hunting pink was destroyed. The origin of the fire was never discovered and led to much theatrical chit-chat, but within twenty-four hours, using common red flannel and upholsterers' braid, Edy Craig produced from her Henrietta Street atelier a gown even more effective than the original. To say that the quality of clothes is in their wearing is platitudinous. One was always conscious, under Mrs Kendal's robes, as under Mrs Kean's, of the busked corset, the Victorian pantalettes and petticoats and a dreadful garment called 'combinations', which belonged to her private wardrobe; to dispense with any of them both ladies would have considered indelicate, if not immoral. So however fine the material or the cutting, their costumes always lacked authenticity.

In whatever she wore for the stage, Ellen Terry gave the impression of being authentic 'to the skin'—which is not to say she carried her passion for archaeological perfection so far as the cotton shift, the padded and pocketed divided petticoat worn over nothing at all. Every actress who has played 'costume' parts knows the necessity of protecting herself against the filth those ample gowns sweep up. But Ellen Terry never confined her lithe, expressive body in a corset; when necessary for the period, her bodices were boned to give her more bust and waist than were hers by nature. She knew that an actress's physical equipment did not stop short at face, hands and feet, but included spine and ribs and thighs. On or off the stage, she was never convincing in modern clothes.

The family was entranced by her overwhelming success at His Majesty's. Marion and Fred alone had some perception of what their great sister had uncomplainingly endured at the Lyceum. In her mute, discreet fashion, Marion would not have admitted it; Fred, strangulated by hero-worship for Irving, might have rumbled inwardly, but would have gone to the stake before putting into words his private opinion that Nell had had 'a raw deal'. A simple soul, Fred must have suffered between two loyalties—the great Terry solidarity and his personal devotion to the Guv'nor.

Both Fred and Julia were aghast at the project at which Ellen had hinted: her intention, when the run of *Merry Wives* came to an end, of taking the Imperial Theatre,[1] and giving her son his head as director.

Ellen had no commercial sense whatever (although capable *on behalf of someone elese*, of striking a hard bargain). Ted—the young Freds had had their experience of him: that ugly overdraft, after *For Sword and Song*, owed not a little to his irresponsibility, his grandiose notions and his practical inexperience in carrying them out. Ted, within a month, was capable (according to Fred) of

[1] The Imperial, built by a contemporary actress, Mrs Langtry, brought her no luck, and certainly none to Ellen Terry.

bankrupting his mother. Edy was sharp and knowledgeable, and would exploit the venture as a means of finding jobs for all her women friends—who would work up a very pretty, backstage hell-broth. And the fact that Charlie had been approached by Ellen to act as her business manager was not reassuring: dear old Charlie—about as capable of handling a wasps' nest as of controlling such a set-up! He was eventually to declare that he would never again act for his sister; good business man of the theatre though he was, he admitted himself helpless against that combination of Ellen and Edy and Ted—all three of them grinding their separate axes.

The Imperial season opened with Ibsen's *The Vikings*. No one in his right mind would have cast Ellen Terry as Hiordis. Gordon Craig depended on his mother's name to attract a public unlikely, otherwise, to interest itself in Ibsen. She can never have visualized herself as the big, raw-boned Scandinavian Hiordis is intended to be, but, in the same spirit as that in which she sacrificed herself to Godwin, to Watts and to Irving, she sacrificed herself to the son in whose work she steadfastly believed. She was not alone in her belief; Gordon Craig had gained artistic *réclame* with his productions of Purcell's *Dido and Aeneas*, Handel and Gay's *Acis and Galatea*, and Housman's *Bethlehem*; he had published woodcuts, etchings, engravings and (between 1898 and 1901) his magazine, *The Page*, now a collector's piece.

The Vikings was a bold and adventurous exploit on the part of Craig, a gallant one on the part of Ellen Terry, who, by lending herself to this unfortunate production, hoisted the banner not only of maternal devotion but also of faith in the advancing Theatre. Anxious to please and encourage her, various intellectuals and artists wrote flattering letters; but *The Vikings* ran for twenty-four performances.

Gordon Craig claimed that one of his biggest sets only cost a hundred pounds—which could be true. He overlooked the expense of virtually disembowelling the theatre before his scenes could be mounted, and the elaborate lighting system which he insisted on installing—with the result that the curtain rose almost on pitch darkness: no recommendation to playgoers who, even from the stalls, were obliged to strain their eyes to detect a few actors straggling blindly about the stage. The *effect* of darkness and the *actuality* of darkness were matters between which Craig had not yet learned to distinguish (and the playgoer reasonably expects that the price of his seat should include the ability not only to hear but also to see).

Stricken, perhaps, with eleventh-hour doubts, he ushered his Hiordis on in a blaze of limelight, totally destroying the atmosphere he had been at pains to create (which, according to Bernard Shaw, was in any case untrue to Ibsen's picture. Shaw, pontificating on a matter of which he had superficial knowledge, had evidently not read the play, or paid no attention to Ibsen's stage directions. Craig's realization of the 'stormy, snow-grey winter day' was true to the text; but he need not have made a black-out of it.)

Much Ado About Nothing was rushed on after the withdrawal of *The Vikings*; but even the legendary glory of Ellen Terry's Beatrice could not draw a sufficient public to rescue a venture already bogged-down in production costs. Her tenancy of the Imperial Theatre lasted a poor two months, and sent her out on the road, in the hope of salvaging *les pauvres restes* of her by no means lavish resources. Among the parts she played on that tour was that of a Dutch fisherwoman, in a translation of Heijermans' *The Good Hope*. She was about as fitted to Kniertje as she was to Hiordis. She undertook Hiordis in support of her son Gordon Craig; her daughter Edy persuaded her into Kniertje because the translation happened to be done by Edy's friend Christabel Marshall, now calling herself Christopher St John.

How weak it makes Ellen Terry sound; yet weakness was not in her nature. Adrift from the sure anchorage of the Lyceum, she was prepared to listen to anyone who encouraged her to strike out into those uncharted seas of the 'new' theatre. It is touching, how ill-advised, at this moment in her life, she was; how simple she was in accepting the direction of those mainly intent, through her, of furthering their own interests.

She had none of the security of her sister Marion and her brother Fred, both firmly lodged in niches they had made their own, beyond which they had no intention of straying. In her middle fifties, Ellen was the divine adventuress—with, unhappily, no one to give her disinterested advice. Laurence Irving could have helped, but he, a young married man with his (too brief) future to consider, was sunk in his own career. He was one of the few to appreciate her effort to interpret Kniertje. One cannot believe that he would have encouraged her in her next venture—although Mr Barrie was an established playwright, with *Walker, London*, *The Professor's Love-Story*, *Quality Street* and *The Admirable Crichton* to his credit, as well as *Peter Pan*, already a children's classic.

He wrote a regrettable piece of whimsy, called *Alice-Sit-by-the-Fire* (of which the title alone might have been enough to warn off a less simple person), for Ellen Terry; on his small acquaintance with her, he packed a lot of her personal idiosyncrasies into the text —and the part fitted her about as well as an off-the-peg garment fits a woman of generous proportions who ordinarily employs an expensive *couturier*. Kate at West Cromwell Road, Marion at Buckingham Gate, Fred at Elm Park Gardens and Katie in Gledlhow Gardens wagged regretful heads; that kind of twaddle was not for Ellen Terry...

But worse was to come; inevitably she yielded to the flattering importunities of Bernard Shaw and committed herself to the part of Lady Cicely Waynflete in *Captain Brassbound's Conversion*.

CHAPTER TWO

A Light Goes Out

On a gleaming October morning, with fallen leaves laying a pall of gold over the autumn grass, a short, upright man walked into a Lakeland kitchen; he had soil on his hands and tears running down his honest North Country face. The breakfast porridge was being prepared, and a child of eleven was holding the bowls into which it was to be dished. He said in a strangled voice, 'Henry Irving is dead'—and the bowls crashed on the brick floor and the porridge was burnt.

The little girl had never seen Irving or Ellen Terry; he had seen them once, on a provincial tour, at the height of their glory. But the name of Irving was a legend in that remote northern cottage.

To thousands who had never set eyes on him, the death of Irving was the death of a sovereign. That much painted and much photographed head, as familiar to them as their own, was an emblem of kingship and, with Irving's death, kingship departed from the Theatre. He was the first actor to be knighted, the last to be buried in the Abbey. Men wore black ties and women bits of *crêpe* for Henry Irving.

He died in Room 20 of the Grand Hotel at Bradford, and the final words of his part in *Becket*, 'Into Thy Hands, O Lord', were seized upon by journalists and by the public as 'Irving's last words', which would have pleased him. Actually, he made a speech to the audience, spoke to the local manager, to Bram Stoker and to a boy who asked for his autograph at the stage door. His last coherent words were to his valet Walter Collinson whom, as was not his custom, he asked to accompany him back in the cab to the hotel, and who was present when he collapsed and died on the night of Friday, 13 October 1905.

It has been said that he was a greater actor off the stage than on, and this could be true; he was poignantly aware of his personal grandeur and guarded it jealously. Not even his closest associates—they cannot be called friends, for Irving had no genuine gift for friendship, which implies intimacy and mutual confidence—were ever allowed to see him in a moment of weakness; if they chanced on such a moment, reverence closed their eyes and their mouths. This, surely, is kingship.

How much he was, or was not, of an actor can never now be resolved; he was unquestionably a spell-binder, for even his bitterest critics continued (if with a somewhat virulent pertinacity) to follow his career. His eccentricities of speech and deportment made him God's gift to the mimic; it was almost pitifully easy to give an imitation of Irving. All actors are egoists; it is an essential part of their equipment. But Irving was the Ego itself.

The greatness of his reputation rests upon his influence on the Theatre. He made it not merely respectable, but venerable.

He carried the dignity of the parts he interpreted into his private life. He commanded respect from the Throne downwards, and an almost superstitious devotion from his immediate entourage.

It is generally known that, in spite of the fact that during his twenty-seven years of management he made over two million pounds sterling, Henry Irving died a poor man. The greater part of his earnings was ploughed back into the business, either in the form of production accounts or in what were called 'Expenses on the House', which included Irving's vast and lavish hospitality. The capacity of the Lyceum when he took it over was only £228; it cost him £12,000 in 1881 to increase it by another hundred. In 1898 he had suffered the crushing loss by fire of the greater part of his stock-in-trade, and when, a few years later, he was forced to conform to the new regulations for public safety in places of entertainment, he knew he was beaten. By modern standards, the old Lyceum could be described as a death-trap. The money to carry out reconstruction was not there; he had for some years been borrowing from friends eager to help in the saving of what everyone but Irving himself recognized as a sinking ship, and his bank overdraft had got out of hand.

He did the only thing he could; sold out to the syndicate which, under the name of the Lyceum Theatre Company, offered him a contract on excellent terms for themselves, and very poor ones for Irving.

There were none apart from his family—the wife he detested, his son H.B. (Harry—married to Dorothea Baird), his son Laurence (married to Mabel Hackney), and his grandson Laurence, son of H. B. Irving—at whom the death of Henry Irving struck more sharply than at the Terrys. He was part of their cosmos, had entered into their personal lives and was an object of veneration to the young, who had known him only distantly. Not only Ellen, but Marion, Florence, George, Charles, Fred, Minnie and the Craigs had had close contacts with Irving's Lyceum. The Lewises and Morrises through family relationship with Ellen had also a personal tie.

Ellen Terry was acting in Birmingham when, at six in the morning, reporters came to her for 'expressions of sympathy'. By some oversight, she had not received one of the innumerable telegrams despatched by Bram Stoker within a few moments of Irving's death. Her sensible maid refused to have her disturbed before eight o'clock.

'Oh, mistress dear' (all Ellen's maids were trained to address her as 'mistress'), 'there is dreadful news. Sir Henry——'

'Hush,' said Ellen. 'I know. Leave me quite alone.'

She had already had her warning; when he was taken ill at Wolverhampton in February of the same year, she had gone down and seen the doctor, who gave his opinion on Irving's condition. He ought never again to play *The Bells*, because of the emotional strain the part of Mathias imposed on him. Ellen Terry was later to say, 'Henry died after *Becket*, but he died of *The Bells*.'

The news reached Marion, rehearsing with Charles Wyndham at the New Theatre for *Captain Drew on Leave*, and Fred, on tour with his *Scarlet Pimpernel*. Fred, as emotional as his sister Marion was the reverse, was described by a member of the Company as having given his only bad performance as the Pimpernel that night; not only did he constantly dry up, but inspiration seemed to be withdrawn from him. To Fred, it was the death of a hero, as well as the loss of a leader.

After the failure at the Imperial Theatre, Gordon Craig had withdrawn himself to Germany, had published his important work on *The Art of the Theatre*, and '*Craigische Vorstellung*' was incorporated into the vocabulary of German theatrical art. At thirty-three 'Ted' had made himself a name respected throughout the continent of Europe—but not (it goes without saying) in the country of his birth.

All he knew of the practical, as distinct from the visionary, art of the Theatre he had learned at the Lyceum. Irving did not care for him and frequently mocked him. And Irving's mockery could be very cruel. Yet the youthful reverence never wavered; Gordon Craig had venerated Irving as a man, and, as an actor, had striven to emulate him.

Gordon Craig should have been at the funeral in the Abbey. He was born to figure on all occasions of pomp and circumstance; he had exactly the right manner, the right bearing. He had, moreover, some of the qualities which Ellen Terry listed as Irving's own: impersonality, gentleness, craftiness, incapacity for caring for anything outside the scope of his Art. He should have been there to support his mother, who was deeply moved when she saw the pall of laurel leaves which covered the catafalque; she was not told then that this superb tribute was contributed by the last of Irving's ladies, Mrs Aria.[1] Had she known, her great heart would have felt nothing but gratitude.

In their boarding schools, respectively at Lausanne and Westgate, Olive (Florence's daughter) and Phyllis (Fred's daughter) received the news with awe; they had both seen Irving, although they were too young to have known him. Olive had been on tour with her aunt Ellen and Irving. Phyllis had been presented to him in the wings after *Coriolanus*, and instantly accepted him as god and hero. The tears streamed down her face as she walked in the school crocodile along the Westgate front. The Gielgud boys, Lewis and Val (John was still in his cradle) caught the prevalent awe from their grandmother and parents. The Lewises and Gielguds went into modified mourning for a week or two, to indicate their personal attachment to the dead. Katie, Janet, Lucy and Mabel remembered the golden

[1] Mrs Eliza Aria, indefatigable first-nighter and devotee of the theatre, died, as she herself would have wished, in her box at a first night in 1934.

days when Irving was the honoured guest at Divach and at Moray Lodge.

Minnie Terry had played with Irving in *Charles I* and in *The Holly Tree,* the curtain-raiser before *China.*

In that same year occurred various happenings which had immediate bearing on Terry history.

When Gordon Craig went to Germany his marriage to May Gibson had been for some years at an end. By May he had four children: Rosemary (of whom a charming portrait by William Nicholson survives, and who was briefly on the stage), Robin, who was for a short time in films, then took himself to Paris, where he drove a taxi, Philip and Peter. Peter was drowned in saving a young woman from the sea at Bognor. May was a brave, determined and gifted young woman who, when left to fend for herself, made a career of her own as a theatrical costumier and dressmaker, with a shop in Baker Street.[1] She called herself Mary Grey. She was, admittedly, the wrong wife for Ellen Terry's son, in that she was practical, hard-headed and had little understanding of the workings of the artist's mind. She was bitterly disappointed in her marriage, which had brought her none of the kudos she envisaged in marrying into the illustrious family of Terry. From the beginning, her mother-in-law (who had always disapproved of the match) was 'agin' her, and her awareness of Ellen Terry's sweet antagonism did not bring out the best in her.

'Big Ted'—as he now became to the family—was not in England

[1] She designed and made an exquisite set of costumes for Fred Terry's production of *The Marlboroughs*—regardless of cost. Fred was furious when the account came in, and the only dresses retained were Julia's and a single Walking Lady's—my own. I had one brief appearance of less than three minutes: for this May had designed an elaborate Marlburian gown, perfect in every archaeological detail, of a copper-green velvet, loaded with incrustations of bronze. The lace of my head-dress was real. The weight of the gown was so excessive that I reeled over in a long dress-rehearsal. I have no idea why this dress was kept and others rejected. The dress-rehearsal was a glorious spectacle; it was something of a shock, on the first night, to meet the other Ladies of the Company in costumes, effective and elegant, but not as worn at the rehearsal. Julia Neilson (and I) alone wore the originals: Julia's the most fabulous she had worn in any of the plays. Edy Craig would have conjured the same magnificence out of sateen and cotton and stiffened muslin. May was able to indulge her obstination for expensive materials when, later, she went to Hollywood. She had no more commissions from the Fred Terry-Julia Neilson Company.

when his son 'Little Teddy' was born; he had become infatuated with the art of an American dancer, Isadora Duncan, and artistic infatuation progressed, automatically, into love. Or what passed for love. His true love was his Art, which he put ahead of all human considerations.

There was a god-like quality about Craig: pitiless, indifferent, cool. He made some rather inept drawings of the Duncan[1] but it is doubtful that he was deeply moved by the fact that she was pregnant with his child. He was always mildly taken aback by the inexorable processes of nature; he may even subconsciously have felt that there ought to be an exception in the case of The Son of Ellen Terry, absolving him from the tiresome consequences of a brief, but rather often fatal, attraction. To his intense surprise, Isadora Duncan gave birth to a little girl, Deirdre, declared to be his daughter, doomed to be drowned, with Isadora's son Patrick, in the Seine.

Three years after the birth of 'Little Teddy', Elena and the children were summoned to Florence where 'Big Ted', by then, was domiciled. Presently they moved on to Paris, where they were living when their little half-sister was drowned. Where, then, was the father? Not at hand to lend support to the distracted Isadora. At that moment he had not a thought in his head but Eleanora Duse, and the production she had commissioned from him.

A boy from Indiana came to town: a young man of German-Jewish extraction who, ten years previously, having seen Henry Irving and Ellen Terry in Chicago, where his family was then living, had conceived a passion for the Theatre.

The family name—Usselman—was unfortunate for an actor, so he changed it for Carew—pronounced as it is written. As James Carew, he got himself on the English stage, worked hard—and not wholly successfully—to get rid of his American accent, and, in 1905, made his London début as Sam Coast in *Her Own Way*, with Maxine Elliot's Company.

He scored a big success; he was broad, handsome, tough and immensely masculine. Women fell for him. He had taken pains to make himself into an actor—not first-class, but attractive and dependable enough to catch the eye of (among others) Bernard

---

[1] To be seen at the Museum at Smallhythe.

Shaw. Jim Carew was a simple and likeable person, kind, generous and unpretentious. He was ambitious, as all young men should be, and much gratified to be cast for a part in Shaw's *Man and Superman* at the Court Theatre. He had no idea what was coming to him when he was offered the part of the American naval officer in *Captain Brassbound's Conversion*, in the following season. If he had known, it is all but certain he would have plunged at it. His London successes had changed the character of 'the boy from Indiana'; he was not quite so simple, and he had a rush of success to the head.

Olive, expelled from her boarding school in Lausanne, came home to Baldock, and expelled herself. Rightly or wrongly, she felt she was a bone of contention between her father and her stepmother— her aunt Julia's mother. The boys, Geoffrey and Jack, were at Harrow; her beloved Bay still at his prep.

She was eighteen years old, tall, slender and very like her aunt Ellen, except for colouring. Olive's eyes were brown, grey or hazel, according to her mood, but never that perilous mermaid-like aquamarine, and her hair was dark. During her school holidays she had been out on tour with her aunt Marion, for whom the dear love of her childhood had revived. It was not difficult when she turned, as seemed inevitable for any 'true Terry', towards the stage, with her beauty and her Terry background, to get what Marion called 'an engagement'.

To play the lead in *Doctor Wake's Patient* on tour (it was a popular drama) was a fantastic start for an inexperienced girl. As Lady Gerania, Olive was paid five pounds a week and got good notices; she came back to town, into Bourchier's production of *The Walls of Jericho* at the Garrick, and when Bourchier revived *Macbeth* played the Crowned Child and understudied Violet Vanbrugh. It was a desperate understudy for a tender-faced girl not yet out of her teens. Violet Vanbrugh was (physically) a 'natural' Lady Macbeth: her height, her narrow bones, her sharp short nose and long upper lip contributed to her characterization of the most controversial of all Shakespeare's female characters. From the moment of her entrance she 'looked the part', which is a great help with audiences, and if she did not extract from it the utmost of its majesty and its dark implications, she succeeded with the public and most of the critics. Olive, as behoved the daughter of Florence Terry, tackled her understudy bravely, but—perhaps fortunately—was not required to go on.

She was sharing a flat with another young actress in Gordon Mansions, Battersea. One night, in the lift, she met a man old enough to be her father: Charles Hawtrey, who, as an elegant comedian, has never been equalled on the English stage. His flat was opposite Olive's. He had seen her that afternoon at the Coronet Theatre in Brieux's *Les Hannetons*. The lovely girl, not yet twenty-one, and the middle-aged *bon viveur*, whose reputation with 'the ladies' was hardly less than his reputation in the theatre, eyed each other. Hawtrey's name, by then, was a household word; Olive Morris had not yet had time to impress herself on the public, but in every gesture and movement, in the inflections of her voice, she was 'true Terry'. They fell in love at a glance.

Fred's Phyllis, returned from Paris with a smattering of French and a vital urge towards the theatre, was packed off to the Royal Academy of Music, to study under her mother's old professor of singing, Randegger.

She had never wanted to be a singer. Having been warned that if she forced her exceptionally high soprano her voice would break, she had already done her best to bring this about. By forcing and bad production (Phyllis was a show-off student), Randegger completed her efforts. She had a brilliant upper register and nothing whatever in the middle by the time she left the R.A.M.

The Freds did not want their children to go on the stage. They wanted—— It would appear they were not quite sure of what they wanted. They idolized their young—Phyl, as tall as a tree, with a remote and empty beauty; she had her father's pure blond colouring and the fabulous eyelids of her mother, the voice of a nightingale, the deportment of a camel (she wore her shoulders under her ears and, like her mother, was slightly knock-kneed), and the vanity which came partly of being a Terry and partly from the spoiling she received from her childhood, from her parents, from those who wished to curry favour with them and from others who were carried away by the charm of Fred's 'Golden Girl'. Nobody appears to have recognized the exaggerated humility which underlay Phyllis's insolent façade; she was certainly not aware of it herself; she was far too busy 'putting on an act' which, to her, seemed obligatory, as a Terry.

Among her contemporaries at the R.A.M. was Clara Butterworth (later to star in *Lilac Time*). One day they had an argument, and, for once, the flaming Terry temper got the better of Phyllis's normal placidity. She hit out at Clara, and Clara retaliated in like fashion. Taken aback, Phyllis drew herself up to her full five feet eight and a half, and observed icily, 'You don't seem to realize who I am. I am the daughter of Miss Julia Neilson and Mr Fred Terry.' To which came the withering retort, 'And I am the daughter of Mr and Mrs John Butterworth.'

Phyllis, like her cousin Olive, was 'True Terry', lavish and laughter-loving. Her physical and mental indolence were not Terry at all, but more probably derived from the Dutch-Jewish strain in her mother's blood; and, at the age of sixteen, to have arrived at going on for six feet was enough to make anyone lazy. In modern times, 68 inches is by no means out of the way for a woman; it is, in fact, almost standard height for model-girls. But in Phyllis's youth it was exceptional, and in some odd way Phyl always managed to look taller than she was; uncurling from a sofa, even in the lofty rooms of her parents' house, there was something that reminded one of a lovely young golden cobra, whose head would presently brush against the mouldings of the ceiling—an optical illusion which provided one of the handicaps she had presently, as an actress, to overcome; it was not easy to find a leading actor who could match that soaring height.

In the matter of indolence she was the antithesis of her brother Dennis who, at Charterhouse, was already a brilliant scholar and, by his fond parents, dedicated to the Bar. Extremely good-looking, fluent and opinionated, Dennis's brains irritated his father who, living on heart and instinct, abhorred argument and was incapable of conducting it without losing his temper. He was proud of Dennis, but lovely, lazy Phil was his beloved one; she could twist him round her little finger.

Enamoured of the stage, Phyllis coaxed herself out of the R.A.M. into her parents' Company, in another of their costume dramas, *Henry of Navarre* (almost as permanent a success as *Sweet Nell* and the *Pimpernel*). Two years later, her brother Dennis dispelled his parents' ambitions by making his début in *The Popinjay*.

The children of Fred and Julia had a featherbed introduction to the stage, and every sort of theatrical and social advantage. But they were honest enough not to wish to make capital out of the Name. Phyllis re-christened herself Phillida Terson —which lasted only until her aunt Marion overheard some Mrs Know-All in the stalls of His Majesty's Theatre announcing that Phillida Terson was the daughter of Tree. One can visualize the Terry hackles rising. Phyl became Phyllis Neilson-Terry virtually overnight. Meanwhile, Dennis had become Derrick Dennis, and, as such, had taken off into Benson's Company; but as everybody in the Theatre, and not a few of the public, knew they were young Terrys, the laudable intent of Miss Terson and Mr Dennis was defeated.

In an effort to keep the generations more or less parallel we have skipped some years; neither Phyllis nor Dennis was on the stage in 1906, which must go on record as Ellen Terry's Year.

It was the year of her stage Jubilee; fifty years since a child of eight, playing Mamillius, stumbled across the stage of the Princess's Theatre, pulling a Grecian go-cart, in the wake of Charles Kean. In those fifty years, fantastic changes had taken place in the theatre; changes no less fantastic in Ellen Terry's own life. In 1904 a relatively unimportant, material change had come—when she left the red-brick Victorianism of Barkston Gardens for a small house in the King's Road, Chelsea. Number 215 was a Carolean house, set back behind a wooden paling and a little flagged courtyard and a few down-leading steps; there was a plane tree or two—but I cannot remember whether these were actually in the court, or whether they overhung from next door. Indoors there was some panelling, in not very good condition, and in conformity with her altered domestic conditions Ellen proceeded to build out at the back a modern studio. The stairs were tumbledown; you could look out between the treads into the little garden behind. A more suitable domicile for Ellen Terry than the suburbanism of Earl's Court, a pretty shady house, it had character and quality; its single dis-advantage was its situation on the King's Road, already beginning to be a route for heavy traffic, which eventually obliged its mistress to install double windows on the first floor which, originally her drawingroom, later became her bedroom.

There she could have been—and at intervals was—very happy, but for the intrusion of an element which, temporarily, changed the whole pattern of her life.

CHAPTER THREE

Indian Summer

At every hour of the day the place was seething with women. Some of them she liked, and tolerated others. It seems curious that there was no one to protect Ellen Terry from these female cohorts, most of whom owed their acceptance to Edy who, heading her band of feminists, waving her banner of Women's Franchise, sponsored their introduction to Ellen Terry—who could not have cared less whether or not women had a vote, although she pretended, to please Edy. Then there were the elderly 'fans', the pseudo-artists, the amateurs with pen or brush or pencil, who wrote poems to her and made drawings of her, were passionately addicted to her, and made scenes of jealousy over and around Ellen Terry. She appears not to have had the moral strength to scrape them off, and there was constant friction between these and the satellites of Edy. Actually Ellen rather enjoyed scenes and often encouraged them for her own entertainment.

The result was that the men in whose company Ellen Terry had formerly taken pleasure were scared by this female bodyguard from battling into her presence. There was something a little ludicrous in attempting to conduct a conversation under the inimical glare of some person who openly considered that she had a prior call on the interest of Ellen Terry.

Edy herself attempted (not unsuccessfully) to police her mother's masculine society. A few accredited males—who had tactfully paid their tribute to Edy—were admitted to The Presence; for the most part they were gentle, romantic beings, whose devotion was never likely to overstep the line drawn by Edy herself. Shaw was an exception—but he was prudently tied up to his Charlotte, was *le grand blagueur*, and might some time conceivably write a part fit for Ellen Terry to act.[1] Burne-Jones and Ben Webster, both comfortably married, were on Edy's 'safety' list, and so were Sir Albert

[1] He never did.

w   305

Seymour and the young Harcourt Williams, the latter because of his known attachment to Jean Mackinlay, whom he was presently to marry. 'Dear little Barrie' was a fireside pet. Tom Heslewood, a dear favourite of Ellen's, married her (then) companion, and became 'one of the family'. She loved Graham Robertson. There were others—tolerated by Edy for their 'insignificance'; it is positive that no human being was insignificant to Ellen Terry.

Edy's curious, jealous watchfulness—perversion of love—over her mother undoubtedly cramped the latter's sunset years. Edy had no understanding whatever of that final upsurge, the Indian summer of a still beautiful and eternally vital woman, that prompted Ellen Terry's third marriage.

Edy had been her companion, her business and stage manager, almost her all-in-all after the severance with the Lyceum; Ellen leaned on her, trusted her and endlessly sang her praises. She endured Edy's over-earnest women friends, with their political affiliations and their obscure antagonism to the opposite sex. Edy could be tender, could be sweet—and could be the very devil. So, if it came to that, could Ellen.

It would require a separate book to do justice to that complicated and often painful mother-daughter relationship, which, since the death of Edith Craig, has been perverted into a sentimental legend risible to the few surviving witnesses to the true situation. They fought incessantly—Edy nearly always winning, because she had youth, a loud voice and a violent self-opinionation on her side. But at any moment she would have died for her mother, whom—constantly—she wounded, as she, undoubtedly, was wounded by Ellen. She knew Ellen loved Ted more than she loved Edy. And that was primarily because Edy had the misfortune not to be a man. But they never sang in tune.

A Liberal daily newspaper, *The Tribune*, now had the inspiration of celebrating Ellen Terry's Jubilee by a shilling fund, which raised £3,000. Her Jubilee Commemoration performance at Drury Lane raised £6,000: a noble benefit for a veteran actress. Properly invested, these sums could have secured Ellen Terry a competence for the rest of her life. Yet, within fifteen years, she was again in money trouble.

Astonishment is professed by the late Christopher St John, in her notes to the American edition of the *Memoirs*, that 'not a single woman was invited to join the General or Executive Committee' constituted to organize the performance at Drury Lane, and that the Executive arranged a programme as nearly as possible all-male. The Executive was shrewd; its object was to star Ellen, and it did not want Edy—known far and wide as a trouble-maker—on the Committee. It was impossible to invite other women and yet to exclude Ellen Terry's daughter.

The trouble-maker, on this occasion, was Ellen herself. In the immense and elaborate preparations for the Drury Lane matinée she took only a perfunctory interest. It was hard on those who were 'setting the nostril wide' to do her honour; the distinguished players and painters who had pledged their contributions to a historic occasion. No less than twenty-two Terrys were lined up to take part in the masque which concluded the programme. Coquelin, Réjane and Duse were coming from the Continent to lend their glory to the scene.

But Ellen Terry was preoccupied. In rehearsals for *Captain Brassbound's Conversion* she had met the 'boy from Indiana', the young James Carew, with his Red Indian profile, his vitality and something about him which offered escape from the atmosphere which was stifling her. She was fifty-eight and he in his thirties. It made no difference. James was what she needed.

He was young, fresh, handsome, and, to Ellen Terry 'smothered in women', like a breath of fresh air. Presently he was noticed as her escort, not only in but out of the theatre. Everywhere she went, 'Jim' was sure to be. He was to be met at the King's Road and at the Farm. It was puzzling, for he was a rather commonplace and at moments brash young man: what Edy and her satellites called 'unsuitable', although they gave him a patronizing friendliness because of the evident pleasure Ellen took in his company. But James Carew, amenable as he was to start with, was not cast for the role scornfully assigned to him by Ellen's entourage, who could not forgive her—at her age!—for attracting the younger generation.

'Well, Bertie; so you're another of Ellen Terry's tame cats!'

'No, Lady Alexander; only her very devoted friend', was Sir Albert Seymour's dignified reply to the accusation. 'Bertie the

Bart', as Ellen christened him, was indeed a devoted friend, not only to her, but to her nearest and dearest. The plain little man, with a vocal impediment and a sense of humour that could beguile Ellen out of her darkest moods, remained their friend to his death —and beyond.

Nobody—except perhaps 'Bertie the Bart' and Ellen's other dear and close friend, Lady Alix Egerton—seems to have recognized in James 'the danger'.

How could she? What has Ellen Terry got in common with James Carew? He's ordinary! He's got no sort of fineness! He's altogether *unsuitable!*

Few of the innumerable people who cried Havoc upon Ellen Terry's third marriage seem to have recognized it as a supreme tribute to her ageless beauty and charm. That an ageing actress, heavy and grey-haired, could attract a man young enough to be her son, seemed to some ludicrous, to others indecent. Malicious people said James married her in order to further his own interests; this was not true. James loved Ellen, and never ceased to love her to the day of his death.

As for 'How could she?'—had those people who deplored her new adventure, forgotten, or never known about, her marriage to Charles Kelly? There was more than a little in common between Kelly and Carew. They were both actors, and both what was contemporarily known as 'he-men'. Handsome, masculine, intellectually commonplace, but good, sound and healthy.

> Through what wild centuries
> Roves back the rose?

There are at least two good reasons for Ellen Terry's attraction to James Carew: that, beneath all that 'honeydew' aspect propagated by her admirers, ran a healthy, earthy nature, and that she looked to a husband to hold back the relentless tide of women which was gradually swamping her existence. She did not then realize the price she was going to pay for this indulgence of a natural instinct: the struggle to live up to the demands and expectations of a man in his thirties when she was approaching her sixtieth year.

She went on an American tour with James as her leading man,

and they were married in Pittsburgh. How they managed to keep the marriage a secret is a mystery; even Edy did not know until the returning voyage. Knowing her 'secret self' as none other did, Gordon Craig wrote to his mother: 'I hope you are really very much in love. If not . . . poor James.' Many of his letters to E.T. contain friendly and understanding references to his stepfather.

James had the worst of the bargain. Very naturally, his conquest of the Leading Lady of the English Stage went to his head, and he assumed airs of importance which became him neither as Ellen Terry's husband nor as an actor. He had exactly Kelly's weaknesses: violence, impatience, jealousy—and Ellen was no longer of an age to combat or cope with these. To be made to feel that you 'don't belong'—the attitude of Edy's coterie—is not calculated to bring the best out of anybody. Exacerbated, not by Ellen Terry herself, but by her *milieu*, James became more and more intolerable. As an actor he was ambitious and vain; as a husband uncertain—which enraged him.

He was later to tell his step-grandson, Edward Carrick, that he had never wanted to marry, but Ellen Terry insisted; she said she was too much in the public eye, and could not afford any more scandal.

The marriage lasted little more than two years. Ellen Terry wrote a letter, of which one sentence stood out: 'You simply must not treat any woman the way you have treated me.' Knowing James Carew as a quick-tempered but gentle and generous person, I could not refrain from asking to what particular atrocity this referred. 'He kicked my dog!' answered Ellen, in accents of doom. Some years later, I asked James himself for his version of this incident. James, by then, was much mellowed, an altogether happier and more established person, and devoted, as he never ceased to be, to Ellen Terry. He smiled reminiscently. 'Yes, of course I did. She and those bloody women got me into such a state that I lost my temper and took it out on the poor brute!'

It was always an imperceptible breeze that swung the weather-cock of Ellen's decisions. 'He kicked my dog!' That remained when all of James's other misdemeanours had faded from her memory. Godwin's puerile anger when he found her trying to harness the pony soon before Teddy's birth touched off something which altered the complexion of her attachment to her first lover.

She had fortunately, at this disturbing time, another interest on which to focus. There was no work for her; Shaw had not produced anything to her dimensions, and the plays she was offered were beneath her consideration. Such parts as she had played with James Carew added nothing to her reputation; there was no question of immolating herself (as she would gladly have done) in the career of a rising actor, for James, apparently, had ceased to rise.

The long empty days went by on a deadly rhythm, until the arrival of Elena Meo, with the two flaxen-haired children, Little Teddy and Little Nelly, from Paris. Little Nelly had a deep, dark voice, and already wanted to go on the stage. Little Teddy was an enchanting child, sweet and imaginative, the image of his father at the same age, but utterly lacking in 'Big Ted's' conceit. The mother and children became the centre of Ellen Terry's life. They lived with their father in John Street, Adelphi, but spent more time in King's Road with their grandmother and step-grandfather. They liked James, and he was fond of them. 215 King's Road rang to children's voices and the old stairs creaked under their small feet.

For five years Gordon Craig had lived and worked on the Continent: Berlin, Vienna, Florence, St Petersburg. With writings, etchings, woodcuts, theatre designs and scenic models he had built up a reputation not confined to Europe, but known wherever two or three were gathered together in the name of the Arts.

By many he was regarded as 'mad'; by the intelligent minority as the only sane man in the contemporary theatre. One of the few to recognize him as such in England was C. B. Cochran. He had produced *Rosmersholm* for Eleanora Duse, and written about it. He had brought out the first number of *The Mask* and secured the Arena Goldoni as a permanent workship and school, which settled him in Italy. The volume, variety and quality of his work, for a man in his middle thirties, were remarkable. As always, he was the visionary and, on the technical side, was weak: but he was what the confused and wholly commercial theatre of the period required to lift it out of the abyss into which it had fallen. He had a pure and disinterested approach to the theatre, and although he has been accused of the irresponsible squandering of other people's money, only microscopic sums, far less than he was entitled to by his labours, found their way into his own pocket. He managed to live 'like a lord' because he happened to be gifted with the lordly manner, but this 'lordly' living, when it comes to be examined, was really very simple. He had the art and the grace to conjure fineness out of simplicity—and the artist's perception of what was and was not valuable. There is a legend that a few hundred lire contributed by a well-wisher to the Goldoni school was spent on the purchase of a coach and horses, in which he and the students travelled magnificently around. Why not? The sum involved was too trivial to be of practical use to the school, but provided a touch of the 'divine madness' that seems absent from the modern world.

So Gordon Craig arrived in London—the last city to appreciate him—with his Elena, his Nelly and his Teddy; his broad-brimmed hats, his capes, his long hair and his romantic flourish—a creature of charm and of joy to his mother, foundering in her third matrimonial failure. He brought her light and laughter—of which she was in need. He was bursting with vitality; put on a show of etchings, found a publisher for them, dashed to Russia, came back and laughed off Tree's proposal of a revival of *Macbeth*[1] at His Majesty's. The association of Craig with a producer who had introduced a chorus of angels into the last Act of *Hamlet* and visualized Oberon as a principal boy part, was indeed enough to make the angels themselves laugh. He arranged to produce *Hamlet* in Moscow and, at 6 John Street, set up a model stage for screens, added to his woodcuts and wrote on theatre problems, morning, noon and night.

Everything but the theatre he found impossible to take seriously: domestic and human relationships, anything that involved 'unpleasantness'—these he brushed off, as one brushes off a mosquito. That Ellen was unhappy about James, that Elena worried about money meant nothing to him. His deathless charm was at anyone's disposal; his occasional bursts of ill-temper were reserved for those who could not, or would not, see through his eyes. He had all the qualities, lovable and maddening, of authentic genius. 'My son who

[1] Craig actually drew a magnificent series of sets for *Macbeth*, of which Tree never made use.

is my sun.' They had everything in common, those two. Edy, feeling herself pushed into the background, suffered; after all, it was she who had carried, unsupported, the burden of her mother's affairs. She was presently to take on some of her brother's. According to her lights, she was a good daughter and a good sister; the pair of them would have done badly without Edy who, in her uncompromising fashion, accepted responsibilities neither Ellen nor Gordon Craig was capable of shouldering.

In 1906, another little Terry was born, the grandchild of 'darling Floss': Anthony, the son of Olive Morris and Charles Hawtrey. They had not married, on account of some obligation on Hawtrey's part to a lady he had given an undertaking to marry, if and when she became a widow. The lovely Olive had endured the *Sturm und Drang* of Hawtrey's incalculable life for two years: the writs, the bailiffs, the complications that crowded the charming Edwardian buck, the great actor and *flâneur* that Hawtrey was. A formidable heritage for a baby—that combination of Terry charm and Hawtrey charm.

Kate Gielgud wrote that it was 'a pity', and it looked for a while as if history was going to repeat itself. Edy and Teddy Craig had not been acceptable at Moray Lodge; Anthony Morris (he took the name of Hawtrey by deed poll) was, by implication, not acceptable at Gledhow Gardens. But the social picture had altered. Olive was not 'cast out' by her father and stepmother, her dear aunt Marion, her uncle Fred and her aunt Julia. And the list of godparents was impressive: Lady Mabel Egerton, Lena Rathbone and Henry Ainley. Even West Cromwell Road and Gledhow Gardens were obliged to admit this put a different complexion on the situation.

There was no future, from Olive's point of view, in her life with Hawtrey, and soon after Anthony's birth she got an engagement for New York. The contract was with Charles Frohman. The acoustics of the theatre in which she made her New York début were impossible, and the play, inevitably, 'flopped'. She had the baby and his nurse with her, and no money except her salary. With typical Terry courage, she bought the rights in a farce—and this also was a failure. The florists' windows infected her with nostalgia; she longed for the English spring, the primroses and cowslips of the English countryside. And for her brothers—the shy and quiet Geoffrey (now farming in the Argentine), Jack with his beautiful singing voice, a 'true Terry', and the dear Bay, loving and kindly. A friend came to her rescue with a cheque for a hundred pounds which paid their passage back—herself, Tony and the nurse—and in 1911 Olive married one of her many suitors, Charles Chaplin, by whom she had, in the following year, 'a nice little black baby, dark and curly, with a delicate heart'—Michael Chaplin, who was eventually to join his half-brother Anthony in the latter's venture at the Embassy Theatre.

Both the little boys went to school at Westgate—Reece's; then Tony went on to Bradfield. Michael's health was a constant anxiety to his mother. The local doctor said he had a mastoid; Harley Street said no mastoid at all, but so bad a heart condition that he might die at any moment.

Willie Morris's love for his lovely, wild daughter—the image of her aunt Ellen—came out strongly. It was he who, when the doctors suggested a sea-voyage for Michael, sent them to South Africa on a Union Castle liner, and sent them again, after Michael had influenza. He gave Olive an allowance, and built her a house near Windlesham in Surrey. She was able to take the boys to the South of France in winter, where Michael got stronger, and Tony endlessly played boule.

After her marriage, Olive gave up acting. All of her devotion went towards her two little boys and, presently, towards her grand-children. She cared for The Family, and was loved as her mother, 'darling Floss', was loved, by all of them. Terry sentimentality was diluted, on Olive's side, by the coolness of Morrises. Besides sensibility, she had sense.

In Gledhow Gardens (number 7; it was actually on the corner of the Old Brompton Road) a little boy and his baby sister played with a toy theatre. Arthur John and Eleanor naturally knew nothing of upheavals in other branches of The Family. In their rarefied life, controlled by a German governess, a staff of servants, elder brothers at public schools, and parental conventions, they never met two little contemporaries called Nelly and Teddy, or a baby called Anthony, in whose veins ran the same bloodstream as their own.

Theirs was a very similar upbringing to that of the Lewis girls at Moray Lodge: the secure background, the slight sense of superiority to children less well placed than themselves.

But in the veins of Arthur John, aged five or six, ran the blood not only of Terrys (his mother's family) but also that of a Polish great-grandmother, Madame Aszperger, an actress sufficiently important to be celebrated by a marble bust in the foyer of the Opera House at Lvov.

John Gielgud, in *Early Stages*, has left so enchanting an account of his childhood, and the aspirations of himself and his brother Val towards acting and production, that to attempt to add anything, or even to quote from it, would be superfluous. John Gielgud is one of the articulate Terrys—like his mother, his great-aunt Ellen and his second cousin, Gordon Craig. He has left a perfect pastiche of a nervous and neurotic little boy, brought up in privileged conditions: the sort of little boy who could hardly have survived the conditions from which his grandmother Kate, his great-aunt Marion and his great-aunt Ellen derived their strength, but within whose frail body was the germ of that same greatness which they blazoned to the theatrical world.

Everything was 'on velvet' for Arthur John: a stable background, the prestige of his Terry connections, the Aszperger legend. Naturally he was a conceited little boy; yet he was not—as might have been expected—'spoiled' by it; he was too serious.

CHAPTER FOUR

The First World War

In 1914, the calm tempo of a prosperous country was interrupted by war. Fred's boy, Dennis, and Katie's eldest son, Lewis, both enlisted on the outbreak—Dennis, at eighteen years of age, already a seeded actor, with a three years' contract with Granville Barker and an outstanding Romeo to his credit; Lewis was at Oxford reading for Greats. The younger Gielgud boys, Val at Rugby and John at his prep., were mercifully too young to be swept into the war machine; but their aunts were active. Janet effectively controlled two hundred women clerks in one of the Ministries and Lucy was a secretary in a department of National Savings. Their mother Katie was a canteen worker and sorted clothes for the refugees, Polish and Belgian, who were pouring into London.

Olive's brothers, Geoffrey, Jack and the beloved Bay, Charlie's son Horace and Tom's son Ben (?), all joined up, and contributed to the web of anxiety which drew the older generation closely together. They all came through safely—except Bay, who was one of a party of untrained youths ordered to dig themselves in under gunfire at Suvla Bay. Bay Morris was wounded, and taken aboard a hospital ship which was torpedoed. He was not among the survivors.

Fred and Julia 'carried on'. They had a twelve-months' lease of the Strand Theatre and were playing the Second Act of *The Scarlet Pimpernel* when a Zeppelin dropped a bomb which missed the theatre by inches. Fred, in his fine striped silks, with his impeccable wig and imperturbable smile, walked down into the audience. The air was full of dust, his business manager who had taken the stairs from dress circle to stalls in a leap (he was not an athletic person) was pulling himself together, there was chaos at the stage door, the call-boy from the Gaiety Theatre had been blown by the blast into the Strand with a piece of shrapnel lodged under his heart, there was death outside. Then the second bomb fell, blowing a hole in the

315

street large enough to swallow a bus. Fred walked calmly to the orchestra pit, leaned over and directed the conductor to strike up 'God Save the King'. The house, coughing and choking with dust, rose, to save, not only the King, but Fred Terry.

The date was 13 October 1915.

Among their many contributions to the war effort, Fred and Julia donated a car and driver, to pick up the wounded from trenches and help to clear the field hospitals; a little bundle of pencilled letters witnesses to the gratitude of the survivors of Mons and Ypres. Fred contributed generously to 'Form Fours', a civilian organization to assist the families of men on active service. No record has been kept of the largesse scattered by 'The Golden Terry', on any who, whether in wartime or in peace, were in need or sorrow. The scattering was done secretly, confidentially, and to publicize it was bitterly to offend Fred Terry.

Like his niece, Katie Gielgud, he went through the personal torment of having a son in the front line.

The relationship between Fred Terry and his handsome, gifted son was curious and touching. Proud of Dennis's devotion to the Theatre, of his successes and of the high esteem in which 'the boy' was held by an intelligent minority of the critics,[1] he was puzzled and exacerbated by his intellectual qualities: by a sense of humour for which a later generation coined the term 'off-beat'. Fred, a great lover of laughter, knitted his brows and thrust out his formidable jaw at many of Dennis's 'jokes'; he simply could not understand

---

[1] One of the intelligent critics, Sydney Carroll, wrote of Dennis Neilson-Terry's performance in *Fear*:

'I have never seen a performance by a young actor that so greatly impressed me by its nervous force, its sincerity, its emotional power and its gradual building up to the necessary climax. . . . Most of the notices I have read in the papers have failed utterly to do justice to Dennis's interpretation of what was, if the writers had only had the discernment and the wit to see it, an almost impossible task. The reception was unbelievably enthusiastic and had the principal actor been a foreigner or a young man who had not previously aroused prejudice and unreasonable antipathies, he would have been hailed by those outrageous incompetents of the pen as a Heavensent genius.' (In a private letter, 29 November 1927.)

The 'unreasonable antipathies' to which Sydney Carroll refers in the afore-quoted letter may well have been aroused by Dennis's violence of opinions and his uninhibited expression of them—which Fred himself, a man of no moderation, might well have appreciated if they had not too often clashed with opinions invariably based on emotions, and seldom, if ever, on reason.

them, and a forced smile frequently concealed the suspicion that Dennis was 'getting at' him and his friends—the last thing on earth the invariably affectionate but quick-tempered Dennis intended. It was sad for them both that Fred hated and mistrusted intellectualism, and took it, in effect, as a personal affront. Julia did not know what it was about, and accepted it with bland sweetness. But she suffered during the flaming rows which often took place across the long table at Primrose Hill Road, when father and son joined issue on the painful subject of politics, and Dennis's forensic brilliance invariably defeated, without convincing his father.

'My dear Dad,' wrote Dennis, after one of these unhappy controversies,

> I'm very sorry to have argued with you last Sunday. I tried not to, but failed & I'm quick-tempered at times which doesn't help things. . . . My opinions on certain subjects I must ask you to let me keep till such time as they are definitely proved wrong, but I do feel that in the manner of expressing these opinions I have been over headstrong. I hope you will accept my apology for a rudeness of manner towards you, the outcome of a sincere conviction at that time that I was helping & not hindering. All love to you, which I hope you will wish for.
>
> Dennis

Whatever acrimonies may have lingered between father and son were blotted out during the war. Of the volume of Dennis's correspondence with his parents from the time of his departure to France, one letter (too private to reproduce here) is marked in Fred Terry's writing, 'The most beautiful letter I have ever had in my life.' It is a remarkable correspondence and, bearing in mind the restrictions of the last war, it seems remarkable that some of the letters got through; but, as a commissioned officer, Dennis was probably his own censor. The majority were letters of devotion, gratitude and repentance for past 'sins'.

During those war years, both Phyllis and Dennis married. Phyllis, lovely, beguiling, headstrong as her brother, had gained *réclame* in Shakespeare, in a revival of *Trilby* (the part created by H. B. Irving's wife, Dorothea Baird), and in some trivial but successful plays. She was immense box-office; her name, her beauty and 'the Terry charm' wafted her to the heights. She could be very good indeed, and unbelievably bad—as the mood took her. She was almost invariably careless and, like her mother, allergic to direction.

Beautiful and stubborn, she now elected to bestow her favour on a commonplace actor, Cecil King. All the Terry tradition was there, at her disposal; she chose, for a caprice, to play ducks and drakes with it. 'He made me laugh' was her incredibly frivolous excuse for her descent from the Terry throne, which petrified her family and friends.

King was married to an actress, Maud Godden, so there had to be a divorce. Her father, when he heard of it, lost his head completely and swore to horsewhip King outside His Majesty's Theatre, at which King was currently stage-managing. To the son of Ben and Sarah Terry, the grandson of Peter Ballard, lay preacher of the Wesleyan meeting, divorce was anathema; Fred held by conventional morality (with notable exceptions in his own favour).

So the divorce took place. King's wife, who afterwards became a good friend to Phyllis, regretted it for the latter's sake. They— Phyllis and King—might never have married but for the disastrous tour to the United States which, in conformity with puritanical American law, obliged them to legalize their relationship. She, by then, was already disillusioned; he was wide awake to the advantages of marrying a rich, successful, famous young woman with the all-conquering name of Terry.

The marriage did Phyllis no good, professionally, artistically, intellectually or emotionally, and ended in a separation which King refused to confirm by divorce. There was stormy weather ahead for Phyllis, and long years of alienation from the father she adored, and who adored her. She continued to have her successes, but it was generally agreed by those interested in the career of Fred Terry's daughter that her marriage to the commonplace, jealous and possessive King was a misfortune. In Phyllis, as in her father, generosity amounted to a vice; of that generosity King availed himself to an indecent degree. And something in Phyl dried up; that drying up was not good for her as an actress.

The year after Phyllis's marriage, Dennis, invalided out of the army, married a young actress whom he had known from their mutual childhood, and to whom, in George Alexander's production of *The Aristocrat*, he played the stage lover (Fred and Julia over again). He wrote to his father,

My Darling Dad,
  Bless you for your gift and your adorable letter, every word of which I understand and appreciate & shall work hard to live up to. It will be strange being away from you, at least I should say living away from you, because in spirit we shall never be apart & of course we shall see each other often. I say it will be strange because it's a mighty big step to take even with great consideration and deep love & I've always loved my home with you & Mother. You do think I'm wise don't you to get married quietly, don't you loathe ceremonies of any kind with tons of people looking on critics & reporters & God knows what, that's what I want to avoid!!!

Mary Glynne, as she called herself, was the daughter of a North Country doctor called Aitkin, had Welsh blood in her and was related on the maternal side to the Scottish shipping firm of Renwick. She was a pretty, gently-bred, conventional girl and a promising young actress; she idolized her dashing young husband—and would have adored a slap-up wedding, crowded with Terrys and theatrical notabilities, but gave it up for Dennis's sake. They were quietly married at the parish church of Highgate. They presently had two children—'the gentle Hazel' (her grandfather Fred's name for her) and little red-headed Monica. Monica had nothing to do with the theatre, so passes from this record, which is a pity, because Monica had an enormous personality of her own.

In 1914, before the outbreak of the war, Laurence Irving and his wife Mabel Hackney, died in the collision of their liner, the *Empress of Ireland*, with a Norwegian collier in the St Lawrence River. Never was there a more needless tragedy. Lifeboats were manned to take them off, but Mrs Irving lost her head and clutched her husband, impeding his effort to lead her to the boat. That delay of seconds cost both of them their lives. To the gentle and sensitive Frank Benson, of all people, who happened then to be touring Canada, fell the task of identifying their bodies on the dockside at Quebec.

So perished a great Hamlet—'curious, sinister, faulty, rare': so Agate described it. Every playgoer has his 'only' Hamlet; Laurence

Irving's was mine (I saw it four times)—which is not to disparage more recent Hamlets.

Having seen both of them at their best, I see nothing amiss in a comparison between the Art of Laurence Irving and that of Dennis Neilson-Terry.

Laurence had not had three years cut out of his acting life by war; he died at the age of forty-three and Dennis at thirty-seven. Each had the potentiality of leadership. They had much in common: heredity (in Dennis's case longer and stronger than in Laurence's), and a modernistic and psychological approach to the drama. Neither believed in the falsities and contrivances of the commercial playwright, although each was obliged to make use of his craftsmanship in order to make ends meet. There was a certain coldness, a 'sinister' (*vide* Agate) quality in Laurence's work; in Dennis's a kind of quivering warmth—'a nervous tension superhuman in its result . . . gifts of voice and person that redeemed even his cheapest impersonations. If he had given', wrote Sydney Carroll after Dennis's death, 'the time and trouble he spent to make successes out of mediocre plays to more ambitious efforts, his abilities would have received wider and greater recognition.' In comparison with Laurence Irving he might be described as a lightweight; yet his Takeramo, in the revival of Laurence's last success, *Typhoon*, although perhaps lacking in the 'sinister' quality the part demanded, was not only brilliant, but deep.

In Grandfather Ben's day, Dennis would have been hailed as a a 'great' young actor. But times had changed; the advancing theatre required more than Dennis—although he had it all there, in his quick and sensitive brain—was prepared to give it. Three years before his death, he wrote in a letter to his parents:

> Those I envy are the real artists in life, those that can make music in their minds or mould or paint with their hands, oh the absolute incompleteness of an actor's life. I hope I never have a son to lead such a useless existence unless you are a success & success is chance and luck in this profession just as much as hard work and talent; we have nothing to fall back upon, it's a grand woman's profession but not a man's.

How far that cry of the heart got through to Fred and Julia Terry is incalculable. It could have angered Dennis's father, and baffled his mother. What was 'the boy' talking about—'absolute incompleteness' and 'useless existence'?

Later on in the same letter Dennis wrote:

You were right I wish I had been a lawyer, but I should have failed worse at that probably too emotional.

In some mood of profound discouragement, he wrote this to the two people most incapable of understanding him—for all their parental love.

Dennis Neilson-Terry should have played Shakespeare, Ibsen and Tchekov; should have lent his great talents to the oncoming British dramatists. He had all the qualifications—and he knew it; hence that cry of the artist *manqué* in 1929. He played for safety, played claptrap, for the sake of an extravagant young wife, who thought nothing of spending a hundred guineas on one evening gown, and of two idolized children, whose least whim was to be gratified in the most expensive fashion. As for Mary's pretty frocks, Dennis got as much pleasure out of them as their wearer; he liked elegant women, and little, blonde Mary chose and wore her gowns admirably. Dennis himself sometimes made suggestions—of which couturiers were sharp to take advantage.

'Ten guineas for a bloody ribbon!' exploded his father, when an unpaid bill of Dennis's boiled to the surface of the chaos left after his death. For some reason that unlucky bit of ribbon stuck in Fred's gullet, and he went to the length of ringing up the shop about it. Oh yes, the bill was quite correct; Mr Neilson-Terry had chosen the ribbon as a finishing touch to one of Miss Glynne's gowns. Barely containing himself, Fred smashed the receiver back and smouldered off to write another cheque. Julia's beautiful, heavy-lidded eyes followed him reflectively through the slammed door. 'Poor darling.' (Fred, or Dennis, or both?) 'He wouldn't have given it a thought if it had been a bookie's account for a couple of hundred.' Julia was in the fortunate position of not being obliged to submit her own bills to anyone's scrutiny except that of their business manager, Garrett, who was too well aware of the side on which his bread was buttered to query any of 'The Missus's' spending.

In 1915 Ellen Terry returned from lecturing in Australia and the

United States. She had suffered the shock of Laurence Irving's death; she was sixty-seven years old—not 'so' old, as age is counted today; the impression she made was not of age, but of excessive fragility—and this, as it turned out, was a false impression. She was now as slim as a reed, and as resilient. She was very nearly blind— and that was largely her own fault. Her sight had been fading for a long time, and when she reached New York on her way back from Australia, she took the sudden decision to be operated for cataract. It was no fault of the surgeon's that the sight of her left eye was damaged irreparably; impatient of the darkness imposed on her after the operation, Ellen snatched off the bandages, and paid for this folly for the remainder of her life. The gay swiftness of her move- ment was replaced by a gentle groping, but she had recaptured the beauty of her middle age, of the Imogen period—she was, in effect, a white-haired Imogen, having cast off the unbecoming trappings which, for a while, to keep pace with her young husband, she had unwisely affected—the modish hats and the tailor-mades in which, unfortunately, she allowed herself to be photographed. All that was rejected; the Ellen Terry who came back in 1915 was draped in Godwin's Tyrian silks and wore lace on her lovely head.

Indifferent to war hazards, she came back to war charities.[1] Did I say 'groping'? The 'groping' was confined to the stairs at 215 King's Road. In a letter describing her performance in one of the charity matinées, in which she played the Queen in a version of Andersen's *Princess and the Pea* (with Little Nelly and Little Teddy in the cast), I see I wrote (and still remember) of her entrance that it was like '*Ha ha, la belle jaune giroflée!*'

During the war years, Gordon Craig was in Naples, Pompeii, and Florence, visiting ancient theatres, writing puppet plays, end- lessly active, earnest and valiant in all the projects he undertook.

---

[1] Having promised Edy not to return on an English boat, she rejected Charles Frohman's offer of luxurious accommodation on the *Lusitania*, and sailed on the *New York*. The *Lusitania* was torpedoed before the *New York* reached Liverpool.

A letter from a fellow-passenger on the *New York* describes how, when they got off the coast of Ireland, where the waters were infested by German submarines, it was customary to put on a show, to keep up morale. Ellen Terry, half blind and exhausted by the trip, flung herself eagerly into the production, and when a gloomy chairman attempted to start a prayer, to save them from disaster, struck up 'It's A Long Way to Tipperary' in which all the passengers and ship's company joined.

On the outbreak of the war he suffered a tragic setback in his work, which he took with characteristic fortitude: he had been constructing, for more than a year, a great wooden model for a projected performance of Bach's St Matthew Passion. With shocking suddenness his resources dried up; the friends and patrons who had supported his School, the Arena Goldoni, were prevented by restrictions on international currency and personal problems of wartime existence from continuing their contributions. In that very year, 1914, he had published, from Florence, his work *A Living Theatre*. Complementing his earlier works, *The Actor and the Über-Marionette*, *The Artists of the Theatre of the Future* and *Towards a New Theatre*, this gave a description of the activities at the Arena, and was of most exciting interest to people intelligently interested in the Drama. This 'little candle, burning in the night' was put out by people more interested in murder and destruction than in life and creation.

Undaunted, Craig broke up his wooden model for a production which would never now see the light of day, and directed all his ardour into reading and writing. He was forty-two at the outbreak of the war, and, apart from a public dinner convened for him by a group of actors, writers and miscellaneous artists in 1911, had had little recognition from the land of his birth. Incapable of resentment or bitterness, he went on quietly working for a world which might, in due course, recover its sanity; producing his journal, *The Mask*, sporadically; ideas, ideas, ideas all the time—and the slow, painstaking improvement of his triple arts, writing, woodcutting and drawing. His letters to his mother during this period are heartbreaking and gallant, and written as from soul to soul. 'Poor Ted Dear Ted—Great Ted' she inscribed on one of the envelopes.

When Craig returned to Italy, Elena, left in John Street with the children, continued to devote herself to his interests and ideals. Money had to be raised for the School, and to this end she made of herself a prophet and mendicant, preaching the gospel of Craig and, as her son says, 'praying hard in between'. Her faith and her powers of persuasion were rewarded; the late Lord Howard de Walden and three or four other public-spirited people agreed to subscribe to the vision, and Elena was able to return in triumph to Italy, with promises of financial support for the School. "Poor mother . . .' writes her son: 'she was never mentioned in despatches, but father inscribed a book to her . . . "To Elena who brought me my school in her hands." '

The children never suffered the disadvantages of English schooling; Teddy had a month's tutorship with Francis Palgrave (a friend of his grandmother Ellen) and made aquaintance of the Greek classics. Nellie, with her deep, dark voice, was more than ever determined to be an actress (it seems likely she could have been a good one).

There were lots of laughter and something very near to poverty, for the money subscribed to the School was held in sacred trust for that and no other purpose. Elena went out and bought the cheapest possible food in the markets; there were always a minestrone and pastas—it was all very close to Ben and Sarah, to Ellen and Godwin—and very remote from the "grand" London Terrys.

When the cold Roman winter came, and they all froze in the vast Roman studio, they started looking for "a warm place to work in," and found it at Rapallo—the Villa Rassio, next to Max Beerbohm's Villa Chiaro—just by luck.

Edith Craig was working like a beaver—when she got the chance; but her chances were few. She had founded a Sunday play-producing society, Pioneer Players, dedicated to the Advanced theatre; there was obviously no money in that, although her productions were widely praised. Among others, she put on one of the Japanese No dramas: a small masterpiece, achieved on a shoe-string exchequer.

She was an autocratic and bullying director, and an impeccable technician, so she got on better with the artisans than with the artists of the theatre. She had no glimmer of her mother's tact and delicacy, none of the charm of her brother Gordon Craig; so no West End manager wanted her through his stage door. It was no fault of hers that a play she was directing never reached production. The producer, Anthony Ellis, was so incensed by the interference of her friend Christopher St John (Christabel Marshall) that he packed it up. Edy was notorious as a nuisance—and it was not always her fault, but her aggressive personality and 'always rightness' set many against her who could have been valuable to her advancement. Few apart from her personal friends detected beneath Edy's unprepossessing manner, and even less attractive manners, the warm heart and basic kindliness to which her few intimates could bear witness. She was a great director *manqué*, but she had not sufficient genius to over-ride the antagonism which her singularly unpleasing personality aroused.

Where her brother could raise hell, infuriate everybody and leave not a wrack of ill-feeling behind, the wounds Edy inflicted in her single-minded devotion to the work went deep, rankled and became permanent. She was surrounded, inevitably, by a group of female sycophants, of whom the chief was her house-mate, Christopher St John; these, unhappily, encouraged Edy in her arrogance and tactlessness, built her up into a tin goddess, and applauded her resistance to even the mildest form of criticism. It was unfair to Edy, who, under all her brusquerie and bad manners, was a warm and tender-hearted creature, and not vain at all.

> The evil that men do lives after them,
> The good is oft interred with their bones

might well be said of Edith Craig; there are, unfortunately, too many who remember 'Edy's hatefulness', too few to subscribe whole-heartedly to the tributes assembled after her death. But that she had a kind of twisted genius neither enemies nor friends can deny; that she was a magnificent friend, loyal and loving, and a devoted aunt to her nephews and nieces—to this there are many to bear witness. She was keenly aware of the dislike she inspired, which naturally brought out the worst in her; it increased the acrimony between herself and her mother, and the brother who had only to lift his finger to command the affection for which Edy longed.

She and her friend Christopher St John were at this time living in a Bedford Street flat; the household had been enlarged to include a painter, Clare Atwood, to whom it was intimated that if 'Chris' objected, she would have to go. A quiet, wise, shrewd little woman, she fitted herself in with tact and grace; she accepted her sobriquet of 'Tony', in conformity with a contemporary affectation which conferred masculine names on women (Radclyffe Hall, a mutual friend, was known as John) and dressed them up in trousers, before trousers were admitted as women's wear. 'Chris' and 'Tony' described themselves as 'the Matka's Boys', the Matka being Edy.

'Chris' was also known as 'Master Baby' and 'Tony' as 'The Brat'. How far Edy, in her innermost self, subscribed to this fantasy is not to be resolved; Christabel Marshall came into her life in an unhappy hour, and established an influence it is difficult to associate with so powerful a character as Edith Craig. She had the strength to resist 'Chris's' attempts, as a Catholic convert, to proselytize her. There was an integral honesty in Edy; she did not see how Catholicism fitted into their pattern of living.

It is not difficult to imagine how the *ménage à trois* was antipathetic to Ellen Terry. She made, nevertheless, a notable present to her daughter: the Priest's House, part of the Smallhythe Place demesne —and, in due course, suffered all the *Stürm und Drang* this brought across her quiet threshold: the constant interference in her private affairs, the flaming rows, usually emanating from 'Chris', whom, oddly, she liked, because 'Chris' was intelligent, clever and, despite her vocal impediment, could read aloud from the classics. She dismissed an aspect of her daughter's life which she could not understand, and heroically endured the trouble in which—indirectly —it involved her. She was absolutely incapable of imagining treachery.

Shaw, writing to Christopher St John after Edy's death, had the naïveté to propose that 'Chris' should write the history of the *ménage à trois*. Naïveté, or mischief? Pretending to some degree of intimacy, he must well have known that such a history was unwriteable. 'Chris', very correctly, rejected the suggestion.

There was little, if any, *rapport* between Smallhythe, Primrose Hill, Rapallo and Gledhow Gardens. Katie Gielgud had spent thirteen agonizing weeks in the Casino at Le Touquet, now converted into No. 1 Hospital, B.E.F., watching over her eldest son Lewis, gravely wounded in the battle of Loos. 'Old Kate' had had a stroke, but, by the time Katie came back, was hearty as ever— more hearty than her exhausted daughter.

Young John (now at Westminster) could not take air-raid warnings and sleepless nights, so got permission to sleep at home; a sensitive and neurotic boy, he could not stand up to the war which his (much older) Terry and Morris relatives were taking 'in their front teeth'. He was (temporarily) dedicated to Art, and messing about

with chalk, charcoal and poster paints; he had joined the Westminster Art Class, and showed a little talent. He gained a scholarship for Oxford—and threw it away. His heart was in the theatre.
At the end of the war he got himself into Constance Benson's School
of Drama. Lady Benson was a bad actress but a good teacher. In
John Gielgud she had exceptional material. When he came to her
he could neither speak nor move; Constance tackled his speech
(he had, actually, a beautiful voice) and Ruby Ginner (not yet the
leader of the Revived Greek Dance) tried to do something with his
movement, which, as he had no kind of athleticism, was deplorable.
Yet, as an actor, he had all the potentialities; both Constance and
Ruby recognized this.

Young John Gielgud did not know—he had barely heard of—
his cousin Anthony Hawtrey: the brilliant boy, destined to become
a distinguished producer, under whom John might have served
with advantage; or his cousin Teddy Craig, later, as Edward
Carrick, to become an outstanding figure in the film world.

His mother, Katie Gielgud, had accepted, with a gulp, and only
after they became 'famous', her cousinship with Edith and Gordon
Craig. Anthony and Teddy were both born 'on the wrong side of
the blanket', and had therefore no claim to the hospitalities of
Gledhow Gardens. The loss was Arthur John's. Whether or not
they were individually compatible, that sensible and sensitive boy
might have profited by the companionship of his cousins, whose
approach to the theatre was tougher and more realistic than his
own.

The Freds up at Primrose Hill were god and goddess to John
Gielgud, but in no sense part of his life. Great-uncle and great-
aunt; distant and glorious. Bestowers of gifts and favours. Ellen,
of course, was ELLEN: one could boast of being her great-nephew—
but one had never casually opened that little wooden gate, walked
down the steps under the plane trees to the front door and sat down
at the long diningroom table for tea, with Elena and Little Teddy
and Little Nelly—Teddy laying his fair head down on a big fruit
cake, and shooting an imaginary arrow at Nelly—and, when tea
was over, gone through into the studio, with William Morris's
fishes biting their tails in lustre all round the fireplace, and

great-aunt Ellen tracing the pattern with her thick, sensitive finger. John should have had all that: and Ellen's romantic, nostalgic monologues, and her laughter with the children and whoever else happened to be there. He had none of it; only his great-aunt's Christmas Day visits to his parent's house, when Ellen was vague (and irresistible), and had not the assurance she felt within her own walls.

John was at Lady Benson's academy; lunching with his brother Lewis at Magdalen, punting by Chinese lantern light down the Cherwell, taking part (thanks to his brother) in Oxford amateur dramatics. He had not the faintest contacts with the Theatre (as known by his young relatives) towards which he had nevertheless romantic yearnings.

Apart from casual meetings which, since they are not recorded, are only conjecturable, he had no acquaintance with his great-uncle Charles—'dear old Charlie', beloved by Ellen and Fred: apart from his job, the most delightfully irresponsible of creatures. Out of sheer light-heartedness, Charles caused 'a peck of trouble' to his family: in particular to open-handed, easy-going Fred. But who could say No to Charlie?

'Lend me a fiver, old boy; I've got the bailiffs after me.'

Fred, having backed a succession of losers, was also, at the moment, sailing a little close to the wind, but he sent round to the box-office and extracted a fiver for Charlie, which he handed over rather solemnly.

'For God's sake, old boy, let me have it back as soon as you can; I'm in a devil of a mess myself.'

'God bless you, old boy,' returned Charlie, with equal fervour. 'I certainly will.'

When a member of the Company came round to Fred's dressing-room and proposed their lunching together, Fred wagged his head gravely.

'Sorry, old boy; it won't run to it today.'

'Nonsense; I'm asking *you*. I've just had a bit of a windfall. Come on: let's have a bloody good bottle and a steak at the Coal Hole.'

So out they went—and the first person on whom they set eyes in the famous and by no means inexpensive restaurant of the Coal Hole was Charlie—entertaining a couple of ladies on his

borrowed fiver. Without a flicker of embarrassment, he invited his
brother to have a drink.

This was one of the stories Fred Terry delighted to tell and Ellen
(having had it from Fred) recounted with glee.

Short, fine-drawn and dapper, Charles Terry was in all but stature
the 'spitten image' of his father Ben; he had the same pink face, high
cheekbones, fine thin nose and delightful voice and manner. He had
a neat little grey moustache. He was dearly loved by all the young,
who were later to say that they owed some of the best advice they
were given in their lives to Charles Terry. When this was repeated
to Fred, he said, after a long pause, 'Wouldn't it have been fine if
the old boy had taken some of his own advice?'—which was
undoubtedly true.

Charles regulated his life on a set of naïve precepts, such as the
one he wrote into the autograph book of a Post Office clerk:[1]

> God gave us life not just to buy and sell
> And all that matters is to live it well.

According to his lights, he lived his life well. He, his brother
Fred and his sister Ellen were birds of a feather. There was not much
rapport between them and 'Old Kate' (as she was affectionately
known to her brothers and sisters), or Old Kate's descendants, the
hot-house products of a social and educational system to which
neither Ellen, nor Charlie, nor Fred subscribed. Those three were
in sympathy with their brothers, poor, lost Ben, 'the illustrious
old G' and the reprobate Tom, none of whom was mentionable in
West Cromwell Road, in Gledhow Gardens or Buckingham
Palace Mansions (where Marion had established herself), except in
hushed family sessions, out of hearing of the younger generation.

But no Terry brooked adverse criticism of a Terry. Ellen broke
this unwritten law when she described one of her young relatives
as 'an emetic' on the stage—which enraged Fred, subscriber-in-
chief to the tradition.

At the end of the war Dennis's first child—'the gentle Hazel'—
was born. Not so 'gentle' as her grandfather Fred thought, but

[1] Charles Terry wrote a beautiful hand, which on the testimony of an old note-
book, he was at great pains to perfect during his schooldays. His letters are models,
not only of orthography, but of old-world courtesy.

Fred had the Victorian idiosyncrasy of inventing characters for those he loved. Gentleness and patience were qualities associated with the women he loved and glorified—his mother and his wife; he instinctively bestowed these qualities on his nearest and dearest without considering how aptly the descriptions applied. He made ideals of mother, wife, daughter and granddaughter, ideals to which, like a homing pigeon with crippled wing, he returned from his wilder flights for comfort and reassurance. None of the women who imagined they 'counted' in Fred Terry's life stood up for a moment against those four dearest, for all the times Julia and his beloved Phyl infuriated him. Hazel was too young to infuriate; she was only to be loved.

Hazel was presently sent to a private school, close to their Hampstead home. She had the freedom of her father Dennis's library of politics, crime and theatre—a liberal education for a child not yet in her teens. She accompanied her father everywhere —often as his *garde-chienne*, for even the most persistent ladies were unlikely to press their attentions upon Dennis with a big-eyed, intelligent child in attendance. Those big, beautiful eyes—deeper in colour than her great-aunt Ellen's and her aunt Phyllis's—took in much; 'the gentle Hazel' was a very sophisticated little girl. Her doting grandfather would have exploded if he had realized the depth of intelligence those great blue eyes, the crooked mouth, the obstinate jaw directed across the glittering panoply of luncheon at 4 Primrose Hill Road.

CHAPTER FIVE

'Wearin' Awa' to the Land o' the Leal'

The war was over, and it was the fall of the leaf. The sturdiest of
the 'leaves', Old Kate, fully recovered from her stroke, was tramping
around the house in West Cromwell Road, blowing a police whistle
to summon her stone-deaf servant, acting the matriarch to her
unmarried daughters—and was inclined to condescend to the
physical frailties of her younger brothers and sisters. She was turning up in full regalia at first nights, where she competed for public
recognition with Ellen and Marion. Few of the post-war generation
were aware of the name of Kate Terry; this she never grasped, fortunately for her peace of mind. But there was always a degree of
rivalry between the sisters on public occasions.

Advancing in her seventies, Old Kate, hard and round as a Rib-
stone pippin, bade fair to see her contemporaries out—which,
actually, she did not. She beat Ellen by four years and Marion by
six to the tomb; Fred outlived her by nine years. This would not
have suited Kate; she would have liked to make the star exit—The
Last of the Terrys. The three surviving daughters of Ben and
Sarah died in the order in which they were born—which was
seemly.

In 1923 Kate went with her daughter Lucy on a short visit to
the States, in time to see her daughter Mabel (whose husband had
died, and who had returned to the stage) make her début on Broad-
way. Approaching her eightieth year, the indomitable old lady
perhaps could not stand up to the pace of the New World; when she
returned to West Cromwell Road, to her Victorian relics, her police
whistle and the narrow routine of her domestic life, she was visibly
reduced in strength and energy.

In 1924 she had another stroke, and died, as many old people die, of senile pneumonia, 'leaving no wrack behind'. The great Kate Terry was unknown to a post-war generation, a mere handful of family and friends attended the funeral. Fred cut a rehearsal to go to his sister's burial service, and a young member of the Company who went, inconspicuously, to pay his tribute of respect to the eldest of the four great Terrys, sadly reported, 'A shocking house, worse than an August matinée at Wimbledon; let's only hope the old lady didn't *see!*'

Dauntless to the last, during the war Ellen Terry had acted and lectured and made her début on the screen. The year after the war she played her last full-length Shakespearian part, the Nurse to Doris Keane's Juliet.

In 1915, Miss Keane had created a furore in a melodrama called *Romance*, with the 'matinée idol', Owen Nares, as her leading man; her Juliet was completely obliterated by the Nurse. ("I'm keeping all the rude bits in,' Ellen wrote to me gleefully. 'They shan't prune my Shakespeare for me!' To a postcard asking if Mr Shaw had supplied her with 'An Intelligent Actress's Guide' to acting the Nurse, she replied on a postcard 'Not likely!' with a spattering of exclamation marks.)

Miss Keane's supporters ascribed her own failure to the 'famous Terry charm'. It might more justly be described as the 'infamous' Terry charm, since it blinded so many (including professional critics) to the strenuous labour, the impeccable knowledge of the Art of the Theatre on which that so-called charm was built. (Olive's son Anthony Hawtrey was particularly virulent in his condemnation of the catchword which provided an easy get-out for people too idle or too ignorant to examine the elements which accounted for the eminence of Terrys in the Theatre.) Had Ellen Terry chosen to exert all of her 'charm', as well as her experience, that production of *Romeo and Juliet* could have been a fiasco; it very nearly was, and it was Ellen who wrested (partial) victory from the jaws of defeat by her sense of balance. She deliberately damped down her own performance so as not to over-shadow the Juliet; but it was for Ellen Terry that the audience called midway through the play—the kind of call, John Trewin reminds me, that vanished soon after the war, or in the early twenties. Archibald Haddon wrote in his *Green Room Gossip*:

There was a great and memorable scene when the curtain fell on the episode of the Nurse's teasing of Juliet over Romeo's message. The enchanted audience called the actress again and again and, very rightly, would not be content until Miss Terry answered the call alone.

At the end there was a furore for Ellen Terry and for the Mercutio (Leon Quartermaine), in which, by Ellen's inimitable grace, the Juliet was included.

So frail, by that time, was Ellen, so wracked by ills of the flesh, that many wondered why, for all the inspiration which informed her last performance, she continued to accept engagements. Surely she could not be short of money?

As it happened, she was. She was cluttered with dependants and obsessed with the necessity of providing for Edy, Ted and Ted's children after her death. Neither of her children had helped her to save money—conspicuously not her daughter. She kept a 'secret' pass book and cheque book ('Edy must never know about these'), from which she dispensed largesse to whoever came to her in want or woe. She had the least money-sense of anyone I have ever known. One night, when I stayed until the small hours at Burleigh Mansions and discovered I had hardly enough in my purse to take a taxi back to where I was staying in Kensington, I asked Ellen Terry to lend me half a crown to cover the tip. Ellen was shocked by the meagreness of the request. 'But you must have five pounds—or ten pounds! What use is half a crown?' Fortunately, there was not as much as five or ten pounds in the flat; she thrust a handful of silver into my handbag—of which exactly a shilling was used, and the remainder taken back to her in the morning. I found her still distressed that I had to ask for so little as half a crown; she kept on insisting that I must be 'hard up', and eventually, to put an end to this fantasy, I felt obliged to show her my pass book—a vulgar, but, it seemed to me, necessary thing to do. She was then worrying about trifles, and it was important to remove this trivial worry from her overladen mind. She was almost childishly impressed, and there were no more arguments when I paid for a taxi, a meal in a restaurant, or some small luxury she was—at that time—denying herself.

Into such confusion did her generosity and charity lead her that, in 1920, the home she loved, 215 King's Road, Chelsea, had to be given up. The grandchildren and their mother had gone back to join Gordon Craig in Italy. There was a sale. While her tangled affairs were sorted out, Ellen Terry was moved by her daughter into an old-fashioned block of flats in St Martin's Lane.[1]

The one redeeming feature of this deplorable arrangement was that Burleigh Mansions housed, on an upper floor, Ellen's ever devoted husband James Carew who, during her tenancy, found many ways of proving his devotion. Ellen herself had wanted 'a little flat near the theatres', when it was explained to her that she could not afford to keep up the Chelsea house. But, when established there, she panicked.

There was neither space, light nor air; her friends were horrified by the approach—'like a goods lift on a railway station!'—to the couple of hutches which were Ellen Terry's reception and bedrooms; there was a closet for a servant, a narrow kitchen and 'the usual offices'. She had a few of her lares and penates about her: her portraits by Watts, Burne-Jones and Sargent, the remains of Whistler's blue and white china, some scores of books and bits of furniture whose beauty was lost because they had virtually to be piled one on top of another to get them within the strait confines of the flat.

She learnt in time how to avoid hurting herself against chairs, tables or cabinets; moving slowly, half-blind, she learned the exact position of each piece, and it was the duty of anyone waiting on her to make sure that nothing was displaced by so much as an inch. Never since childhood in Stanhope Street, or before Lyceum days, in theatrical lodgings, had she moved in such limited quarters.

There were compensations: being close to the theatres—she could walk with ease to five of them, and also to her favourite restaurant, the Gourmet in Lisle Street; and, on starry nights, to be helped up a dangerous little staircase to the leads, from which

---

[1] Among the things sold was a set of Gordon Craig's wood-blocks. Knowing that the last thing Ellen Terry would have desired would be to part with any of her son's work, I ventured, having gone to the view on the day before the sale, to write to Edith Craig, suggesting that these blocks, piled in a cupboard, might have been overlooked. I was told to 'mind my own business'. The only reason for bringing this matter up is the false claim, in the Notes to the *Memoirs*, that nothing personal to Gordon Craig was sold. Ellen Terry was not responsible for the sale.

she could look down upon 'the iron lilies of the Strand' and on the lighted globe of the Coliseum just across the way: she called this 'walking on the ramparts'.

It was not, this time, Edy, but Gordon Craig and Ellen Terry's friends who said that the situation was 'unsuitable'. For Edy, within a stone's throw, in Bedford Street, it was a very convenient arrangement: she could keep her eye on her mother, and on her mother's 'unsuitable' friends, and to some extent control the household.

The psychological effect of this arrangement on Ellen Terry was very marked. Accustomed to trained service, to respect and to some degree of (very elastic) formality in the conduct of her domestic affairs, she found it all but impossible to adjust to post-war conditions: to 'companion-maids' who, although well intentioned and reliable, had not the approach to which she was accustomed. She became an impossible employer; servants came and went with such frequency that the name of Ellen Terry was black-listed on the books of the most famous of the West End agencies.

She panicked. The conditions of her life, so far removed from those to which, over nearly half a century, she had become accustomed, gave her illusions of poverty. It was difficult to persuade her to spend a few pounds on the barest necessities of living.

Shortly after taking up domicile in St Martin's Lane, Ellen signed a contract for a week's engagement at the Gaiety Theatre, Manchester, whose transformation into a cinema was inappropriately to be celebrated by the appearance of Ellen Terry in 'Excerps' (*sic*) from her 'Repertoire'. She was offered one hundred pounds for twice-daily performances. Although hotel expenses for herself 'and attendant' were included in the contract, there was a general outcry among her friends, who knew how unequal Ellen was, physically, to carrying out such an engagement. Her stubborn rejoinder was, 'Edy needs a hundred pounds.'

Never was a hundred pounds harder earned than in that steaming week of July 1921, when it was the author's painful duty to force Ellen Terry twice a day on to a tiny rostrum, and prompt her halting delivery of Shakespeare to audiences little capable of appreciating what that combination of Shakespeare and Ellen Terry amounted to. The programme in which she appeared was of an unbelievable vulgarity—'The Orchestra with a Soul', Gaumont 'Round the Town', a Vitagraph Comedy, a Pathé Gazette. Ellen Terry's contributions to this symposium were the Mercy speech, the Sleep speech from *Henry IV* and a Christina Rossetti poem, *The Round Tower at Jhansi*. She was persuaded out of 'When daisies pied', and I flatly refused to play Mrs Ford to her Mrs Page in an 'Excerp' (*sic*) from *Merry Wives*.

The management was better than its word; it not only paid for Ellen Terry's personal maid, but (when I unexpectedly arrived from the North, having heard that Edy, who was supposed to have accompanied her mother, had been obliged to change her plans) for my room ('and all expenses') next door to Ellen's suite. When, at the end of the week, I went to the office to collect Ellen Terry's salary—one hundred and five pounds, of which Ellen's instructions were to enter fifty pounds to her 'secret' account—I was offered, to my astonishment and embarrassment, a cheque and a cigarette-case, warmly inscribed by the manager (little Ludwig Blattner, inventor of the Blattnerphone, whose heart of gold ceased to beat too soon; he got into financial trouble and committed suicide). 'We'd never have got Miss Terry on to the stage unless you'd been here.' True enough; but I started by refusing the cheque and ended by accepting it; it came in very usefully for tips in the theatre and the hotel. The remainder went into the kitty.

Edy got her cheque for a hundred pounds. Ellen Terry got two weeks in bed after that Manchester engagement which—nothing to a woman in full possession of her health and strength—taking into account all the conditions, was a nightmare on which one prefers not to dwell.

In 1922 Gordon Craig came to London to open his International Exhibition of Theatre Art and Craft at the Victoria and Albert Museum. Just entering his fifties, to the young, Craig was a venerable and picturesque figure; with his long, white hair, his broad-brimmed hats, his vast 'disguise'-cloak, he appeared very, very old: older than his uncle Fred (eight years his senior), old enough to be the grandfather of his Terry, Lewis and Morris cousins. It was an optical illusion; the eternal jester, Ellen's 'Ted', was younger than any of them.

Ellen Terry, blind and beautiful, was radiant on the opening day; she wore one of her robes of silvery Tyrian silk—and borrowed a hat of mine to which she had taken a fancy, broad and overlaid with flat ostrich plumes on a foundation of black lace. At any moment the presence of her son was enough to kindle her into the beauty of which she had, in his absence, become a little careless. She was triumphant in the honour which was paid to her son—at last. Not only the English art world, but that of France, Italy and Germany was there, to acclaim Gordon Craig as the prophet of theatrical Art. That was Ellen Terry's legacy, and Edward Godwin's legacy, through their son, to the modern theatre. No wonder she was proud.

The Exhibition was a great success. It went on to Manchester, Glasgow and Bradford, and was visited by more than 350,000 people. Those costume designs, masks and puppets, those miniature illuminated models not only demonstrated the great advance in theatre art for which Craig was responsible, but fascinated people who had nothing to do with the theatre at all. For the first time the general public had a chance of seeing the contribution of an English artist to the theatrical scene. They saw, were fascinated without understanding, and, inevitably, forgot. Whatever is original, unrealistic and imaginative in theatre art today derives in some measure from this Exhibition which, originally staged in Amsterdam, was brought to London through the interest of the late Lord Howard de Walden, as President of the British Drama League.

Marion Terry was suffering from the first intimations of the arthritis which eventually bowed her magnificent, straight back, and tormented her for the short remainder of her life.

Having played her unfortunate Mrs Higgins in the London revival of Shaw's *Pygmalion*, it was three years before she accepted another engagement—her last—in a Maugham comedy, *Our Betters*, as support to Margaret Bannerman, an actress whose great gifts and beauty were too briefly exploited on the stage. Marion's charm and elegance were unimpaired; she was bent, her memory was treacherous, yet she more than held her own against a cast which included

Margaret Bannerman and Constance Collier. The play ran for over a year, but Marion had to give up before the end. Arthritis had her in its grip, and she was never again seen on the stage.

Sad, small and twisted, supported by the arm of brother Fred, her last Press photographs were taken at her sister Ellen's funeral; but the heavy-lidded beauty was still there.

A small collection of Marion's diaries was snapped up in a sale after the death of her sister-in-law, Julia Neilson; Fred Terry had cherished these relics of his dear sister Polly. They must have been a sad disappointment to the purchaser, for they contained no indication of Marion's thoughts, interests or occupations apart from 'Luncheon Lady X', 'Bridge Mrs Y', 'Tea Lady Z' (the names often indicated only by initials). Not a word of plays, concerts, exhibitions she must have attended; above all, no opinions of people, places or events. Was she, unlike her sister Ellen, incapable of expressing herself?—or was that a part of the almost morbid discretion which developed in her youth, and might be attributed to her childish sensitivity to the scandal in which light-hearted Nelly involved the family?

It would be easy, on data, to describe Marion Terry as a shallow, fashionable, Victorian-Edwardian actress—yet nothing could be farther from the truth. The secretiveness of her childhood deepened after the death of her beloved sister Floss. Very critical and contemptuous of standards that did not match her own, she had a horror of what she called 'vulgarity', and resisted with all that was in her the encroachment of publicity on the player's private life. Outside of the theatre, the affection of her family, her own small home, her music and a small, picked circle of friends were all she desired; on the latter she imposed her own discretion. From the few survivors, nothing is to be gained of Marion's 'secret self'. They may have known nothing of the secret self; if they did, their lips are sealed in loyalty to the dead.

She destroyed every letter she received; kept none but 'business' communications. When writing to friends, she guarded her pen, except for an occasional outburst to her beloved brother Fred.

It is not easy to visualize Fred Terry, that big blond hero, on and off the stage always the Scarlet Pimpernel, as the weakling of the family. The last of Sarah's children, he had a complicated heart condition and bad eyesight, which obliged him always to wear glasses. As time went on, he was increasingly tormented by gout and other ailments less mentionable in polite society, to which his addiction to high living contributed. He bore with heroism the penalties of his too, too solid flesh, but was dependent on doctors and on his annual visits to a German clinic. His understudy and Julia's worked overtime, never knowing when, at an hour's notice, they might have to go on. Provincial managers booked Fred Terry-Julia Neilson, crossed their fingers and hoped for the best; instead of Fred Terry, audiences might be obliged to accept Frank Royde (nearly as popular as Terry in his native North) or one of Julia's understudies.

Julia, having torn herself to shreds by over-acting her Gwyns, Marguerite Blakeneys and Valois, was now offered the best part she had ever had a chance of playing under her husband's direction. *The Borderer* was another piece of hack writing, of contrived situations and unlikely dialogue, but it held a superb part for Julia as Mary Stuart, and a wretched one for Fred as Bothwell. Fred—capable of making bricks without straw—in effect offered the play to Julia. She swooped upon it, and proved herself for what she was: a great tragic actress, who had persistently perverted her art into slapstick. No more over-acting; it was the artist arriving, through spiritual travail, at the inner meaning of the part. She swept like a swallow over the cheapness of the lines, the rubbishy situations. Both Duse and Bernhardt triumphed in fustian; so did Ellen Terry. Julia Neilson, in *The Borderer*, did exactly the same.

Naturally, the public detested it. They always expected to guffaw at Terry plays. They were called upon to weep—not the facile, sentimental tears they willingly shed on the Garden Scene in *The Scarlet Pimpernel*, but painful tears of pity and horror. There was not a laugh from start to finish of *The Borderer*, except the artificial tinkling of the Queen's Marys. The shadow of the block lay on the scene from Julia's first superb entrance to the tune of bagpipes, through the absurd marriage scene and the blood-freezing murder of Rizzio. The audience sat, puzzled, defeated and uneasy, for the atmosphere which Julia projected across the floats was not at all that which they had come to expect of her.

The production was full of faults—most of them due to Julia, for Fred's performance was impeccable. Ellen Terry's criticism was just: 'all those tinsel veils you all wear, and Julia's white stuff all over her head; one can't see what she's *doing!*' Ellen was right; Julia had insisted on putting the Walking Ladies into copper veils, wonderful colour, but too brilliant against the sombre scene; she put me into a seven-foot train which, when I rushed across the stage, on one dire night, lashed itself round the legs of the Chief, and it was a mere act of God that Bothwell was not brought grovelling to the floor.

London, unfortunately, missed Julia Neilson's Mary Stuart, which had earned her (and, incidentally, the play) the finest notices she had received since she went into management, not only from provincial but from London critics, when the Company came within reach of town. The long, arduous part drew so strenuously upon her physical and emotional energy that she eventually played it only twice a week; she had so identified herself with it that, eventually, she could not support it. She was supposed to open with it at the Strand Theatre, but after a few rehearsals she broke down, and the part was taken over at very short notice by her daughter Phyllis, who may fairly be said not to have had a chance of showing what she could do with it.[1] She had not time to think herself into the part with which, then, her mother was obsessed. On stage and off, Julia was, temporarily, Mary Stuart; it was trying for Fred, and difficult for her 'Marys'. The play had a brief run in town.

Fred and Julia went on acting round the provinces; it was a triumph of mind over matter. More often than not in acute pain, Fred went on Pimpernel-ing it, or Navarre-ing it, or Henry VIII-ing it, with beads of agony rolling down his handsome genial face. A tremor of the boards was enough to set hell-fire raging in those gross, gouty legs. Nobody in front ever glimpsed the martyrdom he endured—not for money. He should, for the good of his health, have given up at least ten years before he did. A dedicated actor, he remained with his 'boys and girls' (one of the 'boys', James

[1] Phyllis Neilson-Terry had only four rehearsals for this lengthy and arduous part.

Carter Edwards, was old enough to be Fred's father and when, in his cantankerous fashion he chose, could act Fred off the stage).

It was the First Company on the Road: the last of the great Stock Companies inheriting the traditions of Kean, Garrick and the 'circuit players' to which Ben and Sarah Terry devoted their young lives. We travelled in the Grand Manner; on our long journeys we were entertained *en prince* by 'The Chief' and 'The Missis'. The best of theatrical lodgings were taken for granted as 'Terry's'. We were fêted wherever we went. As 'Terry's' we were given preference. There was an uproarious party at the end of every tour, with wine flowing like water, and Fred and Julia shedding their light on the most insignificant members of the Company.

When Fred and Julia retired to the big square house on Primrose Hill, the bell tolled for Terry's Lambs (as we were inappropriately called); it was the breaking-up of a family, each member of which was an object of consideration and solicitude on the part of the leaders. Most went out, with modest confidence, to find themselves new jobs; five, six, seven or more years with Fred Terry seemed good enough reference at least to procure them auditions. But the wind had changed. Terry's Lambs were considered too stylized by post-war management and post-war playwrights (among the latter a young man called Noel Coward—he had not then adopted the diaresis—had had a blazing success with a comedy called *The Vortex*, which, incidentally, raised to stardom an ex-Terry actress. Lilian Braithwaite had served her apprenticeship to the Terrys in 1900 and was the original Lady Olivia Vernon in *Sweet Nell of Old Drury*.)

It was the Ben Terry story over again; as those old stock actors were not acceptable to the increasingly sophisticated theatre of late Victorian and Edwardian ages, so most of Fred Terry's people, who knew 'the job' down to the flick of an eye-lash, were coldly regarded when they went for interviews or auditions. It was reasonable; costume drama does not make for flexibility, and, of *les beaux restes* of the Fred Terry-Julia Neilson Company, few but the two principal understudies, Frank Royde and Violet Farebrother, were heard of again. A notable exception was an eager and ambitious young actor named Donald Wolfit, who had stayed with 'the old

341

firm' only long enough to profit by its excellences, not long enough to get bogged down in its apparently inescapable idiom.[1]

For many of the Company the outlook was bleak: especially for those who had families to support. No longer could one aspire to digging oneself cosily into an old, permanent Company, from which only ambition or misdemeanour or death dislodged one. Such security was undoubtedly bad for the artist—and bad for Fred Terry's reputation as a manager. There was too much dead wood in the Company, too many (and obviously not the best) who hung on for personal, not artistic, reasons. It was contemptuously said by his critics that, as Terry would not pay good salaries, he could not expect to attract good actors. That was not true; knowing that his reign was coming to an end, he was too kindhearted to lop off the rubbish he had accumulated down the years. As a good man of business, he was too shrewd to pay more than it was worth.

Two aged and ailing stars, supported by a mediocre Company, could not stand up to the sharp competition of the 'new' Theatre, already sufficiently shaken by the invasion of revue and jazz. Fred and Julia took their graceful farewell of their devoted public in 1929. He retired to his club, the Green Room, of which he was President, and she to her beautiful home, to her curtains and carpets, to antique furniture and china (for which she had a mania) and to the sweet idleness of long days whose uneventfulness was only broken by the visits of young relatives and friends, luncheon and dinner parties, occasional visits to theatres and the lively conversations of Davises, Foxes, Morrisses, Kerins and Jacobsons— her own people.

The leaves now fell rapidly: Ellen in 1928, Marion in 1930, Fred three years later.

Ellen Terry had been failing visibly from the time of the Manchester engagement. She was weary, vague, her memory increasingly erratic.

In 1923 or '24 (my diaries of the period were lost in the second

[1] The list of the pre-Wolfit actors who ascribed their later success to their schooling with Fred Terry is too long to enumerate. The actresses seem to have been less capable of profiting from that great direction. Royde, when he joined Fred Terry, had a reputation of his own, gained with Tree, Compton and Matheson Lang.

war) I was staying at the Farm. I was summoned to Tony's studio in the loft at the back of the Farm, and told 'they' had decided that Ellen, 'for her own good', must be put into a 'home'.

That very morning I had been sitting on Ellen's bed; we had been talking about D'Annunzio's *Il Fuoco* (which she had given to me) and about the Duse—of all contemporary actresses the one with whom Ellen was most in tune; about those last great appearances at the New Oxford in 1923, when Ellen herself presented me to the great Italian. She had been recalling moments and movements in *La Donna del Mare* and in *Spettri*—in which last (*Ghosts*) she herself would have liked to play Mrs Alving. This was the woman 'they' were proposing, for 'their' own convenience, to commit to a 'home'.

It is not conceivable that the idea originated with her daughter. Edy worried about her mother—and had good reason to do so. The worry could have been resolved if Edy had moved the few yards from the Priest's House to the Farm, to sleep within hearing of Ellen, of the nightly restlessness that drove her uncertain feet down the steep, dangerous stairs to the uneven flooring of houseplace, passage and parlour. Down there, the portrait of Sarah Terry called her 'old child'—Ellen's name for herself—on many moonless nights. It was admittedly a perilous exploit for a feeble and nearly blind woman. It angered her to be followed. But it would not have angered her if Edy had been there, to share her little nightly pilgrimage through the past.

But this the possessive fury of 'Master Baby' would not brook. Tormented by the reports of housekeepers and casual visitors to the Farm, Edy weakly gave in to the suggestion that her mother should, 'for her good', be removed from her dear Farm, and put into a 'home'—a suggestion mercifully thwarted by (among others) Ellen's brother Fred. The news spread, and created an uproar among Ellen Terry's friends and family; Gordon Craig got wind of it in Italy, and wrote incredulously. None knew better than he that though his mother's memory might fade—never her brain.

The unseemly project was dropped. After a series of unfortunate experiments in 'companion-housekeepers', the solution was found in the indomitable Yorkshirewoman Hilda Barnes, who, despite every sort of obstruction from the Priest's House, staunchly and devotedly cared for Ellen Terry to the end. 'Barney', with her voice of a corncrake, her uncompromising exterior and her heart tenderer than a Persian kitten's fur, survived all the malice, commanded not only the respect but also the affection, of Ellen Terry's old friends. Ellen's last call was not for 'Edy', as in the Notes to the *Memoirs*, but for 'Barney'. It was like a child crying out for its nanny. Barney was all that, and more, to Ellen during those last dim years: servant, protector, friend—the trusted one.

Ellen Terry died where she would have wished to die, at the Farm, Smallhythe, now known as the Ellen Terry Museum. She would have disliked the grisly description; the word 'museum' is not to be associated with Ellen, or even with her relics which, at dusk of a summer's evening, when the sun slants through the low windows, seem to stir and to give off that faint and lovely perfume which clung to her through life: that fragrance as delicate as small flowers which was in her thick, silver hair, in her fine, healthy flesh, unblemished to the end, and in all the garments she wore. A dress of Ellen's, given to me by her as a memento of one of our expeditions, although faded and its rich batik pattern blurred, still holds that scent of rice-powder which, with her lipstick and the charcoal she rubbed on her eyebrows, was her only cosmetic. After the door is closed and the footsteps of sightseers cease to echo overhead, that sweet, subtle scent still pervades her bedroom.

In 1925 Ellen Terry had accepted the title of Dame Grand Cross of the Most Excellent Order of the British Empire. The dear friend of Queen Alexandra, it was left to Alexandra's son to 'knight' her, as she expressed it. Most people felt that she should have been given the title earlier: that, as Irving was the first Knight, she should have been the first Dame of the Stage.

Wirepulling, however, had procured for another actress that notable honour. 'Who's Genevieve Ward?' not unnaturally inquired *hoi polloi*, to whom the name of Ellen Terry was a household word.

Miss Ward was an American actress who under the name of Madame Guerrabella, had started her career as an opera singer, lost her singing voice as the result of an attack of diphtheria in Cuba, stormed successively the New York, Paris and London stages and made a success in 1879 in a play called *Forget-me-Not*, which she eventually played all over the world. An accomplished but old-fashioned actress, who was often compared with the Italian Ristori, she played with Irving at the Lyceum, occasionally with Benson and, for the last time, at the Old Vic, as Queen Margaret when she was accorded rapturous notices by the critics. Her 'dame'-ing in 1921, was deeply resented by those who considered that the honour should have gone to an English actress. She made her curtsy four years before Ellen Terry's, and died in the following year, at the age of eighty-four.

The bitterness created by the precedence given to Genevieve Ward over Ellen Terry in the matter of the title was immensely increased by the official opposition to Ellen's burial in the Abbey. A petition signed by the eminent in her own profession, and by many famous and distinguished people in the arts and sciences, was withdrawn when it was privately intimated that the petition would not be granted. Ellen Terry was not to be laid beside her partner and lover ('ay, there's the rub') in the Poets' Corner. And it was more than twelve months before the faculty was obtained for placing her ashes in a niche in the actors' church, St Paul's, Covent Garden.

On a shining July morning, the funeral took place at Smallhythe church, and the cortège set out for Golders Green, past the closed shops, the drawn blinds of Tenterden, to the ringing of church bells. Not the tolling; tolling would have been out of character with the singularly joyous procession, the coloured flowers and streamers of ribbon that loaded Ellen's chariot. 'No funeral gloom, my dears, when I am gone'—in her own last exhortation—was scrupulously observed. *La belle jaune giroflée* went back to dust on the same tripping measure which had borne her across innumerable stages into the hearts of her innumerable lovers.

Not only the Kentish countryside, but all England, mourned for Ellen Terry as, twenty years earlier, it had mourned for Henry Irving. Creature of love and light, she carried love with her to the tomb.

> Here let thy clemency, Persephone, hold firm,
> Do thou, Pluto, bring no greater harshness.
> So many thousand beauties have gone down to Avernus
> Ye might let one remain above with us![1]

Someone should have chanted that over Ellen Terry's bier.

[1] Ezra Pound.

Marion Terry died in 1930, two years after her sister Ellen; died as she had lived, with a certain aloofness, remote from a world with which she had not closely associated herself. She had many admirers but few friends in The Profession.

From the time she withdrew from *Our Betters*, she, crippled with arthritis, had been chasing relief in continental resorts, among them Nervi and Monte Carlo. She was devotedly writing to her 'darling little brother', with whom she shared, not only love, but the sympathy engendered by mutual physical torments. Fred, at the Dengler Institute, was striving to slough off the too, too solid flesh that affected his heart; Marion, after her treatments at Acqui and Nervi, was able to walk a little, but wrote, 'I'm getting so *fat*, I'll be able to be *your* understudy for Henry VIII without *your* padding!'

She came back to England in time to see the last of the Fred Terry-Julia Neilson productions, *Katherine Parr*, where she 'felt like a peacock with its tail spread out absolutely bursting with pride!' —a typical example of Terry prejudice in favour of Terrys, for the play was a poor one and both Fred and Julia were too tired and ill to make the most of the few opportunities it afforded. Marion may have been present on one of their good days; more likely, Fred was fired by his sister's presence to cast aside the ills of the flesh, and to give one of his inspired performances, of which, by then, there were alas too few.

A letter written by Marion to Fred from the Bayswater flat to which she had retreated from the expensive purlieus of Buckingham Palace Mansions is mainly concerned with the rising generation:

I have been to three of John Gielgud's performances of Shakespeare's plays at the 'Old Vic' and I can't say how really thrilled I have been with the work he does, Macbeth—Oberon—Hamlet—the last without cuts!! I was in the *uncomfortable* stalls for Hamlet, for just *five* hours, and didn't *want* to move (tho' I'd have liked to do so but couldn't, the place was crammed), I wanted to go tomorrow, the last of his performances, but there is no seat to be had, and I hear today it's going to the West End in a fortnight, so I'll see it then—it's *very young*, very thoughtful (without dragging it with long pauses and mouthing) graceful without effort and every word distinct and of course he looks charming—I told him I was proud of my nephew, he replied he 'was proud of knowing he had some of the Terry blood in him, and hoped to go on doing better'. I hope you will be able to see it.

This was the last of his sister's letters preserved by Fred Terry; if there were more, they must only have been scraps, for the disease which had bent her proud spine and disabled her movements now attacked her arms and hands. She died three months later, supported to the end by Fred's love and care for the sister who, in his childhood and youth, had looked after him. ('Again a duck of a chicken! and a chicken of a duck—for it is beautifully young and tender', wrote Marion—as good a trencherman as the rest of her family—'and I feel with, or rather after, each mouthful, I want to say "Thank you, Freddie dear, it's *so* good".')

The Press did not devote much space to the death of Marion Terry; the quickening tempo of contemporary life obliterated memories which, a decade earlier, would have been lively.

There was a short service at St Paul's, Covent Garden, and she was buried at St Albans, close to her beloved sister Florence. She had lived to the age of seventy-seven.

The Younger Generation

In the late 'twenties, Gordon Craig was producing—among a thousand other things—his designs for *Hamlet*, for *Macbeth* and for Ibsen's *The Pretenders*. He was living in Rapallo (not then the tourist resort it has since become), and there was some job connected with his work which had to be done in London, so he sent his son, 'Little Teddy', to look after the business for him.

Eager, adventurous, full of ideas, a small, fair young man arrived in London in 1927: his father on a miniature scale.[1] Edward Craig (he did not yet call himself Carrick) was just twenty-two: he bore with him the rich harvest of years of close association with one of the most cultivated minds in Europe: an acquaintance with the arts and their various techniques which anyone in close contact with Gordon Craig could not, unless he were an idiot, fail to imbibe.

Once arrived, he made up his mind to stay. His capital consisted of good looks, immense charm, wit, courage and vitality—which he had inherited from his Meo as well as his Terry grandparents. He had a very clear idea of what he wanted to do. The cinema, anathema to his father, was the Art of the Future to young Craig. He saw clearly, as his father did (and does) not, how the cinema lent itself to the fulfilment of Gordon Craig's visions, and, exactly as Gordon Craig had attacked the vulgarized theatre of his own period, so his son dreamed of making use of the vast resources of the New Art to produce truth and beauty instead of the bad taste and frippery in which, under the Hollywood influence, it threatened to be swamped.

A young man arriving out of the blue from Italy, even if he bear the illustrious name of Craig (which, so far as the film world was concerned, might have been Brown, Jones or Robinson), does not easily find opportunities for proving his quality. 'Teddy', as he was affectionately known to his family, was very soon penniless. He found,

[1] 'My boy Teddy is a rare boy'—E.G.C. to E.T.

however, a friend whose name must for ever be dear to all struggling writers, painters and sculptors: Leoni, of the Quo Vadis restaurant in Dean Street (in those days it was one little room). Leoni fed us all, cheered us all, and when we self-consciously offered the shilling or two which was all we could afford for a meal that ran to half a guinea on the menu, brushed our silver aside—'You will pay me back some day, when you are rich and famous.' (That the bread he scattered so lavishly on the waters came back to him buttered is proved by the modern Peppino Leoni's; none of his early clientele can go there today without dedicating a thought of love and gratitude to the kind and generous little man who saved some of us, literally, from starvation).

But being able to take prospective clients to Leoni's and grandly sign a bill which would never be called in was not enough for a proud, ambitious and industrious young man who was just managing to keep himself afloat by designing book jackets, selling an occasional wood-engraving and doing occasional Art criticism for papers in Italy, Holland and the States.

His first break into the film world came through his ever kind and generous step-grandfather, James Carew.[1] A year after his arrival in England, he got, through James, the job of Art Director to the Welsh Pearson Elder film company at the Stoll Studios, Cricklewood. The name of W.P.E. is forgotten today; George Pearson was the 'father of British Films'. Edward Carrick[2] (he took the name then, to distinguish himself from his father, who would not have taken kindly to the association of the name of Craig with 'the bastard art') was the youngest Art Director in England, and George Pearson wrote of him in his autobiography:

> In Carrick we had an Art Director with that vivid imagination so vital to his work. Since then, the years have revealed his genius. To my mind,

[1] James Carew died a few years after Ellen Terry and his last request, that his ashes should be scattered on the garden at Smallhythe, was reluctantly granted by Edy. But there was no one there to receive the ashes when they were brought down by James's friend, Malcolm Keen. A muddled gardener could not understand what it was all about: were the contents of the casket to be dumped on the bonfire? Mercifully, Olive Chaplin arrived on the scene, and James Carew's ashes were gently bestowed at the bottom of the garden, beside the pool, where Olive continues to lay flowers on the resting place of Ellen's last and most devoted husband.

[2] 'Carrick' is the Irish equivalent of the Scottish 'Craig'.

he is the supreme master of his Art; his published books on film technique have become classics, treasured wherever films are made. All who have worked with him have benefited by his influence, for he has the unique gift of inspiring others by his own vision.

With the security of his new job behind him, 'Teddy' proceeded to get married. His wife's name was Helen Ruskin Godfrey; the children of that marriage, John Edward and Helen Paula, struck out in their early teens, not towards the theatre, but towards painting, and, in Helen's case, towards photography.

Edward Carrick went from strength to strength. He did sets for *Volpone*, and for the Old Vic production of *Macbeth* in 1932 (which he also produced and designed the costumes and props). His most ambitious venture was the establishment of a school where the Film should be studied as an Art, as a medium of expression—to which the war put a stop; Carrick was requisitioned by M.O.I. to organize and staff the Crown Film Unit. Such valuable films as *London Can Take It* and *Target for Tonight* (among many more) with which he was associated were a direct contribution to the war effort and made a great impression on both sides of the Atlantic.

For a young man barely into his thirties already to have established himself as Art Director, Art Critic, Book Illustrator and Theatrical Historian, to have his work exhibited in America, Australia, and Canada, and purchased by the Victoria and Albert Museum, the British Museum (print room), the Museum of Modern Art (N.Y.C.), Yale University and the Kupferstich Museum, Berlin, might prompt from the envious or ignorant 'Very nice to be the son of Gordon Craig'. Yes, it was very nice to be the son of Gordon Craig: to have that fire in the brain and the blood and the relentless determination to achieve; to have the creative passion so highly developed that indolence was virtually a sin; to have a completely selfless dedication to 'the job', whatever that might be, and no interest in self-advancement, except in so far as increased authority might profit the job itself. These virtues are common to the *true* artist. The protean gifts with which the Craigs, both father and son, were endowed could well have been their ruin; they welded them into success.

In his autobiography John Gielgud, writing of his apprenticeship to the Old Vic, does not mention that his cousin Anthony Hawtrey was there at the same time. Gielgud says that he himself was not auditioned—'perhaps some kind person had recommended him', which seems likely enough, for the Terry grapevine was liable to buzz in favour of younger members of the family. For some reason it did not buzz for Olive's Tony, who went through his audition with nothing but his talent and his outstanding good looks to recommend him.

Sir John Gielgud would be the first to admit that a large element of good luck sped his advancement in the theatre. For once, the capricious gods had justice on their side; with or without privilege, Gielgud would have scaled the Everest of his profession. The conquest might have been a little delayed, but he had it all within him, and no living actor is comparable with Gielgud at his best. As a triumph of mind over matter, it is questionable whether the whole history of the English theatre affords a parallel.

His cousin Anthony Hawtrey had an advantage John had not: the spectacular good looks of the Terrys. Sometimes he looked exactly like his great-uncle Fred, more often like his second cousin Dennis. He had the debonair carriage of his father and his great-uncle. Instinctively speaking and moving well, he had none of the tussles with a rebellious physique which John Gielgud candidly describes in *Early Stages*. As an actor, he turned out very well and got some excellent notices from the critics, but his heart inclined towards production, and it was as a producer that eventually (after the Second World War) he impressed his name on theatrical records with a series of plays which, originally put on at the Embassy Theatre, scored successes in the West End.

He had the great gift of light-hearted humour, a shrewd commercial sense, no highbrow pretensions whatever, notable originality and much artistic perception. People liked working for him—and what better can be said of a producer? After he established himself at the Embassy, he took his half-brother Michael Chaplin in as his business manager. Michael was not 'a man of the theatre'; he had passed his law examinations, was in his grandfather Morris's office, and had done well in the Inns of Court Regiment, but like many young men who had finished their war service, he was not anxious to go back to his pre-war routine, and was glad to fill in with brother Anthony until a new career offered.

351

Two young men, meanwhile, were emancipating themselves from the pleasant but restrictive surroundings of the parental home, 7 Gledhow Gardens.

To look at, there was nothing about Val and John Gielgud that reminded one, even remotely, of Terrys. Physically, they both took after their Polish-Lithuanian ancestry; Val in particular (especially after he grew a beard, in order to distinguish himself from his brother John) was a direct throwback to the Zamek[1] of Gielgudyszky, on the Niemen River. He survived Rugby, and in the First World War trained to be an infantry subaltern. As a child he had had a romantic passion for the art of warfare, but his illusions were slain in camp at Bushey. He chose between two years with the Army of Occupation in the Rhineland and a History scholarship at Oxford—in favour of the latter.

He had already ruined his eyesight with excessive reading and wore glasses which, at school, earned him the sobriquet of Beetle; actually, he was a very distinguished-looking youth, with an uncertain bent towards the Theatre. Unlike his brother John, he had no powerful sense of direction. He could write, he could act; he subedited, unsuccessfully, under the incomparable Reeves Shaw, of Newnes. He understudied his brother John on various occasions, filled in as ASM for Fagan at the Royalty and played a couple of seasons at the Oxford Playhouse. He wrote novels and short stories and managed to get some experience in films.

Coldly considered, it looks as though Val Gielgud was well on the way to becoming a rolling stone, for he had made no conspicuous success in any direction, until, in 1928, his star rose with his appointment to Assistant Editorship of the *Radio Times*. Suddenly, all those adventures in the art of earning a living clicked into place; the experience he had gained in various fields stood him in good stead. He gravitated from editorship into the drama department, and with breathtaking abruptness was promoted to Director of the Corporation's Productions.

By the time the BBC moved from its homely quarters on Savoy Hill to the big, pretentious building in Portland Place (losing, in transit, its easy-going, semi-amateur character), the young Director of Productions was a personality and a power whose

[1] Fort.

influence reached far beyond the walls of Broadcasting House. In the teeth of opposition from leaders of the theatrical profession, who saw in the new medium nothing more than a threat to the box office, Val Gielgud not only presented great plays, but persuaded great artists of the legitimate stage to interpret them. By the mid-nineteen-thirties, the name of Val Gielgud was at least as well known as that of his brother John.

The fact that John Gielgud's earnestness, his passion and his serious devotion to the Theatre were contained in a slight and insignificant body may have been good for his advancement in The Profession. His physical shortcomings, of which he was aware, obliged him to work harder than the young actor who is lent confidence by a ready-made equipment of beauty, grace and all the delightful if superficial qualities that captivate the common public. William Terriss, described by Ellen Terry as resembling 'a butcher boy flashing past, whistling, on the high seat of his cart, or of Phaeton driving the chariot of the sun', was inconsiderable as an actor, but 'got away with murder' on account of his personal charm. Even in the present day, when audiences (and directors) are more enlightened, it is generally accepted that the chances of the young stage aspirant are assisted by a presence and good looks.

Arthur John Gielgud had neither; he had rather a frail physique (largely owing to his aversion to physical exercise) and irregular features. For some years after his professional début, although he worked unremittingly at building up a 'presence', he suffered unless, on the stage, he could disguise his unimpressive features with 'hirsute appendages', or (as in *The Constant Nymph*, when he took over from Noel Coward) in glasses and a pipe—which lent him the confidence he lacked when, bare-faced, he was obliged to confront an audience. This want of confidence he was apt to mask, both on and off the stage, with an air of insufferable conceit, which naturally disposed many against him.

Of course he was conceited. He was too shy, and had been brought up in too exclusive a society to be a good mixer. His air of withdrawal, which was invariably interpreted as superiority, was actually the measure of his insecurity when he was required to mingle with people of a different *milieu* from his own.

Of his Terry blood he was inordinately proud, but had the praise-worthy ambition to make good under his own patronymic; he was simple enough (to begin with) not to realize that his honest desire to be accepted or rejected on his own merits was defeated by the fact that, from the moment he took to the stage, he had a shoal of Terrys, Terry-Gielguds, Terry-Lewises and Neilson-Terrys rooting for him!

His grandmother Kate, his parents and aunts 'knew everybody'; he grew up, not in the limited world of the Theatre, but against a broad and impressive background of Important People. His parents were deeply and intellectually interested in the arts—his father in music, his mother in the theatre and literature. Mr and Mrs Gielgud moved in a wide, social circle of cultured friends whose means kept pace with their tastes. There always appeared to be plenty of money; at all events, there was a very positive security—of all elements the most valuable to a sensitive child. Those who profess to sneer at 'money' have little appreciation of the security that 'money' lends, when one is young.

Arthur John was indubitably an artist, from the time he played with his first toy theatre—which to him was not a toy at all, but an intrinsic part of his childish life, and the foundation of his eventual career. From his nursery to his kindergarten, to his prep. and public schools (which, as a 'petted' boy, he naturally detested), he spent a very exclusive youth. Of contacts with the theatre he had few, apart from meetings with his great Terry relations, either at Gledhow Gardens or West Cromwell Road, Primrose Hill, dressingrooms and stage doors; the theatre, to the boy, was a spectacle viewed from boxes, stalls or dress circle. There is no record during his boyhood of his buying himself a ticket out of his own pocket-money for pit or gallery: of his standing in a queue for pit or gallery, or subjecting himself to any sort of discomfort for the sake of the Art.

Little wonder that when he went out on his first tour, with his cousin Phyllis's Company, he was shaken: found it difficult to adapt to the rough-and-tumble of a shared dressingroom, of 'digs' and the 'pub'.

He had his private world of books into which to withdraw; he knew a little about music and painting. But it was long before he found people, in his new profession, with whom to share these esoteric tastes. Besides being an actor, John was an intellectual, and

354

intellectualism, in the commercial theatre, was not yet in vogue.

It is now, unhappily, most damnably in vogue; actresses who do not know the difference between Degas and Cézanne, between Epstein and Henry Moore, are invited to open exhibitions; actors to write—or to lend their names to—brochures on subjects of which they have no knowledge whatever. An embarrassing, even a ludicrous state of affairs, to which it is impossible to imagine the Old Actorr lending himself (Ellen Terry's name was once used in this fashion to 'boost' a book on the Diaghilev ballet, announced on the jacket as 'By Ellen Terry', it was actually written and illustrated by a young acquaintance of Edy's. When asked to sign it, she said, 'I certainly won't; what do I know about the Russian ballet? I never wrote a word of it!').

Visualizing himself, in a humble way, as 'a Terry', John Gielgud was not, at the time, paying much attention to his paternal ancestry: to the Polish Gielguds and to his great-grandmother, the shadowy Madame Aszperger, who cannot have been at all shadowy in her time, immortalized as she is in marble in a Polish opera house. According to Kate Terry Gielgud's autobiography, Val Gielgud's *Years of the Locust* and John Gielgud's *Early Stages*, so little is known of those early Gielguds that it is natural they were blotted out by Terrys, all alive-o, dominant and vigorous. But John Gielgud's grandparents were Polish on both sides, and it would seem to be the Polish blood which lends its peculiar coloration to this actor's work.

The limitation of Terrys has lain, always, in their insularity. They were as English, each one of them, as the cliffs of Dover. The returning exile might well make for a theatre where Terrys were acting, to breathe the authentic air of his homeland. None of the Great Four, Kate, Ellen, Marion and Fred, had the temerity to pit their gifts aganst a European audience. It was not a matter of speaking a foreign language; Fred spoke admirable French (if not 'French' French); his sisters had the perfect ear, and could memorize lines in any language, like parrots.

Foreign actors came over here and, speaking their own language, gained immense *réclame*: Coquelin, Guitry *aîné*, Bernhardt, Duse, Réjane had not a syllable of English between them; the Dutch actor, Bouwmeester, playing Shylock in Dutch with an English-speaking cast, created a furore in the 'twenties. The English, most allergic of all races to foreign languages, took these players to their hearts; they did not understand a word of what they *said* but the purport of their acting was not to be mistaken. French, Italian, Dutch— there was a universality about their art which required no pedestrian knowledge of verbal idioms to translate it to the mind and the heart.

That universality would appear to be in the art of John Gielgud, and derives without question from the Polish side of his family. In no European country could Gielgud conceivably appear and not receive the homage due to an actor of more than common distinction.

Admittedly, the poets and playwrights of his age have offered him finer material than ever was offered to his forebears, yet there must be the 'something more' before the actor, however gifted, can fully avail himself of such opportunities. That 'something more' was John Gielgud's.

Had Ben Terry and Madame Aszperger looked down upon a man in his middle fifties, in whose veins stirred corpuscles of their own blood; who, with no props and no costume—who wearing contrari-wise a thin suit of deplorable cut—conjured magic from the air with his voice and his hands,[1] might they not have exchanged glances that said, 'So long may greatness be deferred'?

II

Of the children of Ben and Sarah Terry, Charles, George and Fred alone survived. Time was when it was hardly possible to pick up a London playbill without encountering the name of Terry; now Mabel Terry-Lewis and her first cousins Phyllis and Dennis Neilson-Terry were left to carry on. But, disguised as Craig, Hawtrey or Gielgud, Terry blood survived.

Edith Craig, the *doyenne* of her generation (this is to discount Kate Terry Gielgud, only because the latter's connection with the theatre was not immediate, but through her children), was nobly toiling in the non-commercial Theatre, producing plays in churches and pageants in private parks, stage-directing in the suburbs and the provinces; endlessly industrious, wholly disinterested, so far as her personal advancement was concerned. She was in her sixties when her mother, Ellen Terry, died in 1928; she was a gallant

---

[1] John Gielgud in *Ages of Man*, Queen's Theatre 1959.

figure, commanding respect from those who appreciated her contribution to the contemporary theatre.

After Ellen Terry's death, she instituted at Smallhythe the Barn Theatre, in commemoration of her mother, and produced several shows a year up to the outbreak of the Second World War. Between the two wars Edy had become an object of veneration to her own profession, best equipped to estimate her value as a woman of the Theatre; old battles were forgotten—whatever might have been her private failings, her integrity in connection with the Stage was unassailable—and actors and actresses of distinction rallied round and supported her venture at the Barn, not only with encouragement but with their services. To begin with, these offerings were to The Immortal Memory, gradually they included Edy herself.

Ellen Terry had left the Farm to her daughter, and Edy's first object was to establish it as a Memorial.[1] The Barn Theatre and the Barn Players' Society, organized somewhat on the lines of her Pioneer Players, were part of her project. Around this revolved the supporters of Edith Craig and the last fifteen years of her life must have been the happiest, for during those all the finest in her character rose in a great wave to the surface. Apart from the affection of her inner circle, she enjoyed the affection and adulation of many who became her friends only during these last years. She was able to dispense her rich scholarship, her passionate enthusiasms and the innate warmth of her personality over a wider field. Autocratic and dictatorial she remained to the end, demanding to be waited upon and listened to regardless of the convenience of others; but, somehow, these peccadilloes came to be accepted just as 'Edy's way'. The whitening of her hair softened her hard, handsome face and brought out the beauty of her dark eyes which, although capable of a terrifying concentration, had actually never been hard at all. Not called upon, in those days, to be ruthless, she forgot about ruthlessness.

A curious transformation came over Edy from 1928 onwards; more and more she grew in physical resemblance to her mother; consciously or otherwise (she had talent as an actress) she adopted Ellen's mannerisms and gestures—even to groping for a door, and

[1] In 1939 it was taken over, together with the Priest's House and adjoining Cottages, by the National Trust. The Barn is part of the Farm itself.

357

pretending blindness: Edy, who had the eyes of a hawk! She bore with fortitude the burden of constant pain from rheumatism and arthritis, and perhaps the impersonation helped (she did not trouble to put it on in her domestic circle).

Her cousin Mabel Terry-Lewis, three years Edy's junior, was poles apart in sympathy from the world of the older and younger Craigs, although she never went down, as a member of the Family, to take part in a performance at the Barn.

Following on her return to the stage in 1920, she pursued her neat, accomplished, busy way. Never out of an engagement, she created not fewer than thirty parts between her return and the outbreak of the Second World War; she played in revivals—including a revival of *The Importance of Being Earnest* at the Lyric, Hammersmith, in 1930. One may hazard the opinion that Mabel Terry-Lewis's Lady Bracknell was very good; at least she would not burlesque or overplay it—Mabel was incapable of overplaying anything. She brought her cool judgement and her innate good taste to all her parts; she had much of her aunt Marion's quality, without Marion's tenderness.

Her reputation built up steadily to the time of her retirement —forced on her by the Terry scourge of failure of memory; it was not possible, in swift modern comedy, to indulge in Ellen Terry's light-hearted flitting from chair to table, from table to screen, on which bits of her part were written out.

Mabel was less of a public favourite than she was a favourite of managements who knew that, in Mabel Terry-Lewis, they had an artist of impeccable accomplishment and loyalty, who was incapable of letting a scene down. Somewhat strangely, her greatest personal successes were made in New York.

A list of her parts draws a smile to the lips of the reader; a mixture of *Burke's Peerage*, *Debrett* and the *Almanach de Gotha*, they include Lady Sarah Aldine, Lady Frinton, Lady Heriot, Lady Mabel Cardale, Lady Elliott, Lady Emily Temple, Gräfin von Raben, Princess of San Luca, Lady Damaris Mocque-Stallyon, Lady Bracknell, Lady Melbourne, Lady Morley, Lady Loxfield, the Countess of Brocklehurst, the Duchess of Sutherland and the Duchess of Berwick! What impression did these names, or the plays in which they were billed, make on the contemporary theatre? They convey nothing to the modern playgoer.

Ambitious actors and actresses were already groaning at what had begun to be known as type-casting; Mabel Terry-Lewis was one of its principal victims. Whether or not she groaned is unrecorded. Whether or not she was capable of extending herself beyond the narrow boundaries of her particular idiom is unresolved. Very rarely, as in *Frolic Wind* (Lady Damaris Mocque-Stallyon), *The Importance of Being Earnest* (Lady Bracknell) and *A Hundred Years Old* (Doña Filomena), she got a break. She went on polishing the small but perfect jewel of her art, and, in private life, became more and more like the characters she acted on the stage. As time went on, she gave the impression of being more interested in her farm and kennels and in county life than in the creation of another peeress or another woman of Society; she was notably more real in these than when she was called upon to play a middle-class housewife. Off-stage, like Marion, she liked nice, well-bred, well-off people, did not invite publicity, and was inclined to avoid theatrical occasions.

And so to her young cousin: the incalculable Phyllis Neilson-Terry—her mother's daughter in that she was capable of acting like an angel and—apparently without perceiving the difference—like a clown.

Phyllis had 'inherited the earth'—on the face of things: fantastic beauty, a cross between her mother Julia's and her aunt Ellen's; the Terry legend—of which, to the general public, she was the living witness; a background of authority, to which her cool and somewhat aloof personality lent weight; immense charm—when she chose to exercise it; inherited talent—on which she relied over much.

She had never, like her father and her aunts, had to 'sing for her supper'. Wherever she went, a red carpet labelled 'Terry' was (figuratively speaking) laid down for her; if it was not there, she demanded it, if not directly, by her attitude to the people who, in her estimation, should have had the carpet down, ready and waiting, for her young, royal feet to tread.

Few recognized, behind the assured façade of this big, beautiful, young woman, behind her empty laughter, an innate loneliness and disappointment. Unlike her brother Dennis, she was not intellectually gifted, but she had inherited her father Fred's qualities of utter truth, utter honour and utter loyalty. She had married a man incapable of appreciating these qualities, as he was incapable of helping her to develop the potentialities in her art; and came back from a long American tour to face formidable competition in her first venture as actress-manageress in London. Marie Tempest, Irene Vanbrugh and (of Phyllis's own generation) Gladys Cooper were ruling the theatrical waves; Mrs Patrick Campbell was still—intermittently—on the scene; and not less than half a dozen accomplished actresses were established figures in the London picture— among them Marie Löhr, Lillah McCarthy, Mary Clare, Sybil Thorndike, and a couple of rising stars, Gwen Ffrangcon-Davies and Edith Evans.

Phyllis Neilson-Terry opened at the Apollo in a play called *The Wheel*, by J. B. Fagan: a drama in which, two or three times a week, she displayed all the quality of her mother's Mary Stuart, hypnotized her audiences—and, in interim performances, left them wondering what they had come to see: 'a reed, shaken with the wind'?

Except briefly, with her father and with Tree, she had never had the advantage of a hard, dominant direction. As a Terry, she thought she had all the answers, and the critics backed her up in her opinion. She was, furthermore, struggling with her private problem of a marriage she recognized, too late, as the worst mistake she had made in all her headstrong young life.

On her cousin Kate Gielgud's recommendation she engaged a young relative, a youth still studying in Lady Benson's academy, for the provincial tour of *The Wheel*, which had had a great success in London. Blood, to Phyllis, was a great deal thicker than water. The young second cousin, whose work she had never seen, should have his chance and four pounds a week, to speak a few lines and understudy. Fortunate young man—with the silver spoon lodged firmly between his teeth! A score of gifted youths would have crawled for his opportunity, would have given all they had for the chance of an audition—but John Gielgud was *invited*, in a letter from his cousin Phyllis, to join the touring Company. It was one of the few instances when privilege justified itself; the gangling student, whose unprepossessing appearance and manner cloaked a passionate addiction to the drama, was to become the leader of the English-speaking theatre.

It was Phyllis Neilson-Terry's fortune (or misfortune?) to be endowed with a dual talent. Her nightingale voice had been 'discovered' in *Trilby*, so parts for Phyllis were expected to include 'a song'. This led to some outrages of which the critics were not slow to take advantage; James Agate and Herbert Farjeon cried Havoc upon her Singing Olivia in *Twelfth Night* at the New Theatre in 1932, which, despite Agate, she repeated in Regent's Park the following year. 'This is an unwarrantable and damaging mutilation of Shakespeare's pattern, which I must believe to have been thrust upon Mr Atkins', wrote Agate—implying that the initiative was Phyllis's; that it was she who had snatched the Clown's song and absurdly incorporated it into the part of Olivia. Agate was wrong: it was none of Phyllis's doing. Whosoever the responsibility, it was an unforgivable lapse in taste and artistry, and unfortunate for Phyllis's reputation with people who took their Shakespeare seriously. It made Farjeon 'pray for a sudden thunderstorm', and inspired him to launch an over-virulent attack on her Oberon three years later.

As for the general public—people said: 'Which is she supposed to be, an actress or a singer?' Sometimes she sang better than she acted, sometimes acted better than she sang.

One play, at the start of the third decade of the century, had offered Phyllis the opportunity of which, unhappily, too few came her way. Ashley Dukes translated Bruckner's *Elizabeth of England* (originally presented at the Deutsches Theater, Berlin)[1] and dedicated it to Phyllis; Meyer produced it at the Cambridge Theatre, with every possible advantage—a grand cast, including such names as Leslie Perrins, Frank Vosper and Matheson Lang; costumes and décor by Charles Ricketts, music by Constant Lambert, direction by Heinz Hilpert of the Deutsches Theater. An exquisite production, in 1931 it created a sensation by its originality and beauty—the dual sets, a Chamber in the Escorial and the Privy Council Chamber in Whitehall Palace, being presented on different levels, with synchronized dialogue: nothing like this had previously been seen in the English Theatre.

[1] Phyllis herself went over to Berlin, saw it, and bought it.

It was not Phyllis Neilson-Terry's first Elizabeth; she had played the Tudor Queen in *Drake* at His Majesty's Theatre under Tree's management, a piece of dramatic claptrap in which she had scored a success of youth and beauty. Bruckner's Elizabeth was another proposition; a mixture of romance and dry realism, of old and new theatre, it called for a different approach from the 'blue-print' she had learned as a schoolgirl in her father's Company, and continued to follow with Tree.

The interpretation of the wizened, sour-faced Elizabeth I, with her bad teeth, high, furrowed brow and carroty wig by Fred Terry's big, golden girl was, on the face of it, ridiculous, even though the public of those days was not as purist as modern audiences; yet, in this one part, Phyl managed in some odd fashion to live her beauty down. In at least one scene—that in which she is surprised by her lover Essex with her toilet not yet made—she threw everything away; jaded, bent, pallid, crawling among the furniture, she managed to convey the impression of an old and ugly woman. Acting throughout with great majesty and authority, there was an immense sincerity in her rendering of the character, leagues removed from her stereotyped performance in *Drake*.

To most of her contemporaries, Phyllis's Elizabeth of England must stand for her highest achievement in the serious theatre. The word 'serious' is to exclude the shallow comedies such as *The Wheel* and *A Roof and Four Walls* in which she made great popular successes. It mercifully did not occur to anyone to present her as the Singing Elizabeth.

In 1931, Dennis Neilson-Terry booked a long South African tour, with his wife Mary Glynne as his leading lady.

It was their second visit: in 1926, when they took out four plays, *The Scarlet Pimpernel*, *The Cat and the Canary*, *The Man with a Load of Mischief*, and *Carnival*, they had had success beyond their wildest dreams. They were still passionately in love with each other; Mary's small talent had ripened and expanded sufficiently to make her a fitting partner for her brilliant young husband. They took the children out with them, and a Nanny (who proceeded to fall in love and get married within a few weeks of their arrival, and was replaced by a German governess); they stayed in the best hotels, excusing the extravagance on the score of prestige, and Mary in her pretty frocks enchanted everybody. Dennis's letters home recorded a princely progress: bumper houses in every town, fêtes and glorifications and presentations to himself and Mary. The box office flourished and, in spite of extravagance, they arrived home well in pocket. I never saw Dennis's Pimpernel, but have it on good authority that it was the only one comparable with his father's; the name of Terry and the title of the play lit beacon fires in all the townships they visited.

But between the 1926 and 1932 tours the relationship between Dennis and Mary had altered. She cared for him too much, and was basically too unbusiness-like to accept with equanimity a situation on which her mother-in-law Julia had lowered her eyelids.

Some of Julia's intimates were shocked by the apparent complacency with which she accepted Fred's matrimonial aberrations; actually, she was not complacent at all. Devoted to her errant husband, she suffered acutely. But neither she nor Fred would have dreamed of breaking up their marriage, which would also have meant the dissolution of their artistic partnership. Fortified by the knowledge that Fred's excursions were but *passades*, and that his true love was hers, she endured with patience and dignity the many pangs he caused her. She sweetly and loftily accepted the companionship of his mistresses, which circumstances not infrequently imposed upon her; so far as history relates, she only once made public reprisal—on an occasion spoken of within the Company with bated breath.[1]

Mary Glynne was too young and inexperienced to deal with a temperament like Dennis's; like all the males of his family, he was highly sexed, and an easy mark for attractive or designing women. With her simple background, Mary could not understand that Dennis's flights of fancy made no difference to his love for her.

[1] A birthday party, given by Fred for his lady of the moment, one of Julia's understudies. Fred at one end of the table, and Miss X at the other, were leading the revelry, when the double doors at the end of the room were flung open and a servant announced, 'Mrs Fred Terry!' Julia, supposed to be ill in London, entered dripping velvet and pearls; kissed Fred with 'Hello, darling,' and said to one of the waiters, 'Move Miss X's place.' The tax on the *savoir-faire* of the Company must have been considerable. According to accounts, she was absolutely charming to Miss X.

Tension had mounted between them. Having made some success in London, she did not want to go out on that second South African tour, and the children (Hazel now fourteen) were too old, in her opinion, to be dragged round at their parents' heels, in a climate to which they were unaccustomed, living in hotels, having more excitement than was good for them. She had no one to turn to for advice, least of all her parents-in-law. Julia, who had sedulously sacrificed motherhood to the demands of wifehood and 'the business', could never have understood Mary's hesitation. Fred had no more than a tolerant regard for his daughter-in-law and, had he been consulted, would have taken it for granted that Mary should accompany her husband, whatever their private differences. He was never to forgive her for the decision to which she was forced.

The split came at Durban—when Mary could no longer endure Dennis's too-marked attentions to another member of the Company. Those attentions—had she been wise enough to accept it—were of no more importance than the many other flirtations he had conducted 'back home'. But a sub-equatorial climate plays havoc with the judgement of inhabitants of the Northern hemisphere. Mary, with the children, made for home—leaving Dennis, with his ephemeral inamorata, to complete the tour. It was a pity; they were doing wonderful business, and her name carried no less weight than his.

A cable reached the big house on Primrose Hill, reporting Dennis seriously ill in Bulawayo. He was in hospital with pneumonia— then regarded more seriously than it is today (owing to the advance of medical science). But the doctors and nurses had to cope with an obstinate, highly strung and exhausted man, carrying a load of mischief: who, at the end of his Salisbury engagement, should never have taken that long journey into the Rhodesian hinterland.

Phyllis was playing in the black-and-white production of *Twelfth Night* at the New Theatre; an ebony and ivory Olivia, she was sitting for her medallion portrait by a young amateur artist.

'Good madonna, why mournest thou?'
'Good fool, for my brother's death.'
'I think his soul is in hell, madonna.'
'I know his soul is in heaven, fool.'

There was a strong psychic *rapport* between the children of Julia Neilson and their mother. In her flat in Welbeck Street, Phyllis was disturbed by the sound of running water. Dennis had been swimming in a stream at the foot of the Matapo Hills the day before he was taken ill. On the night of his death, in her dressingroom at the New, all the flowers lay down and died.

The sister of the ward in which Dennis lay wrote to Julia after his death:

> Two days before the end he told me that you had all come to his room that night, dressed in the most gorgeous cloths [*sic*] and had been talking to him, and all seemed so happy, especially his Mother.

To Fred Terry, it was not just the loss of a dear son; it was the sudden, overwhelming realization that there could never now be a coming-together, a resolution of all past misunderstandings, a loving forgetfulness of quarrels and bitterness. Julia and Phyllis sublimated their grief in ministering to Fred's spiritual agony; 'They're like a couple of angels, looking after me', he groaned.

With Terry resilience, he recovered; he was outwardly the debonair clubman, the genial host, but those who knew him well were aware of the shadow behind the sunshine. His wife and daughter kept continual watch over him, and pretended not to, for that would have infuriated him. He was often ill, often confined to his bed, opposite to which now hung a crucifix—'to remind me of what a little I have to bear, in comparison with *that*'. A singular gentleness and patience came over him. In one of the long night watches he wrote a letter to Julia: the one enduring of his many loves. And next day, most probably, he went off to the Green Room, to laugh and drink and gamble with 'the boys', to back a possible winner—and to return, racked with pain, dependent on the support of one of the taxi-drivers who all knew Fred Terry.

Phyllis, on tour, was weekending with her friends the Howard de Waldens at Chirk. Among the guests there was a young white Russian, with whom she, usually the inarticulate, felt *en rapport*. It sounded crazy, but 'Something terrible is going to happen to somebody here this weekend', she told him.

On Monday night, in the theatre, a message came through, to ring Primrose Hill at the end of the performance.

Julia's steadfast voice asked if she 'had finished her work'. When Phyllis answered yes, she was told her father was dead.

They had dined alone, Fred and Julia, on that Monday night. Their places laid at opposite ends of that long, beautiful table, shining with silver and coloured glass, they had gone in, and Julia had seated herself in her throne-like chair. Julia's appalling portrait as Nell Gwyn, Fred's as the Pimpernel and his mother-in-law's, as silkenly and satinly herself, looked down on them, with a romanticized Phyllis and Dennis on the sidelines. Fred as himself, inappropriately severe, hung opposite the fireplace. It was the family portrait gallery.

Fred went to the sideboard and picked up the carvers. Behind him stood Timson, the old, frail, bad-tempered butler. By some accident the knife slid from Fred's hand and missed by a fraction Julia's King Charles spaniel. Fred made some explosive comment—and dropped. The arms of Timson just managed to break the fall of that grand, heavy body.

A happy, sudden, thoughtless death; just the death Fred would have wished for himself. The Golden Terry was gone. It was the end of an epoch, the end of the Glorious Terrys.

Why 'Glorious', one might ask? What of those who remained to carry on the tradition?

The next generation grew up with a silver spoon in its mouth, with the name of Terry as a passport to the Theatre. This, at once its fortune and its misfortune, may account equally for its successes and its failures. The part-Terry, John Gielgud, has demonstrated that talent may develop from a background of comparative luxury and privilege, such as True Terrys, Glorious Terrys, never knew.

The year after Fred's death, Julia astonished her family, her friends and her public by accepting an engagement with Seymour Hicks, to appear in a farce at Daly's Theatre.

With Fred, she had been in retirement for six years; within her private circle there was a legend of Julia's semi-invalidism. She seldom came downstairs before luncheon, she rested in the afternoon; her activities were limited to a slow promenade on Primrose

Hill, or round 'the village', which meant the shops down Regent's Park Road; to an occasional shopping expedition to one of the West End stores, or her favourite antique shop, or a matinée. All of these were carefully planned, so that there were not more than one, or at the most two, engagements each day. She preferred entertaining at home to visiting; did not care to accept invitations which meant travelling.

The habit which had grown on her, through the tours, of conserving her energies for the work, developed, in retirement, into a peaceful indolence, pandered to by her court of paid and unpaid retainers—which included her daughter: with the result that Julia, at sixty-five, was a remarkably well-preserved old lady. There was no reason why she should not accept the part of Madame Bobinot in Hicks's farce called *Vintage Wine*.

The temptation, once again to rollick about in a piece of amusing nonsense was irresistible. No more Mary Stuarts for Julia! Despite the weight which aversion to physical exercise and addiction to the flesh-pots had crowded on to her, she was still romantically beautiful: her rich hair, sparsely seamed with silver, fell to her thighs, or was bunched up on the crown of her head in a confusion of coils, with little corkscrew curls partly concealing her exquisitely small ears. From the magnolia whiteness of her face a pair of great blue eyes looked out—the eyes of a tragedienne: the tragedienne she had betrayed with her trivial Nells and Wilfuls. The expression of her face was one of habitual sweetness, belying the formidable will that lay behind. Gazelle-like ankles and long narrow feet appeared too fragile to support the heavy weight they carried.

She draped herself in silks, satins, velvets, furs and oddments of fine wool; on the hottest summer day she swathed herself in mousseline scarves or bits of Shetland, her favourite scent of Roman Hyacinth or Lily of the Valley surrounded her with an air of hothouses. She would wear six or seven diamond brooches, sown at random about the massive *étalage* of her bosom—not for display, but carelessly caught up and pinned on, for pleasure in something pretty and shining—and not less than half a dozen strings of pearls. Julia was the last of her generation to look romantic. Her dressing derived not at all from contemporary fashion, but from the opulent gowns she had worn on the stage. So when Julia 'made an entrance', whether into a theatre box or a private drawingroom, the house was inclined to rise. Here was something legendary, something which belonged to a world not yet disrupted by war, not infected by the 'Bright' youth of the period; something that kindled the imagination, by virtue of its total unreality, its dissociation from contemporary living. For that unreality, that dissociation, Phyllis was, presently, to pay the price.

Julia Neilson and Seymour Hicks fought their way, somehow, through *Vintage Wine*; one might say, *on ne vaut pas la peine*. It was a drivelling play; Seymour's swift, lightning-sharp method was at odds with Julia's ponderous comedy, deriving from her Sweet Nell. She looked divine, and never quite caught up with him; they were duettists, at odds with each other's tempo. With her last obeisance to the audience, the last of the traditional stars, the exponents of the old romantic Theatre, withdrew.

The mystique of 4 Primrose Hill Road became not unlike that of 38 West Cromwell Road:

> A Chinese Queen on a lacquered throne
> With a dragon the size of the side of a house
> All empty and silent and sitting alone
> In an empty house . . .[1]

It was Phyllis's self-appointed responsibility to look after that empty house.

She was on tour with a play called *Mary Tudor* when a young man joined the Company. She knew him vaguely as an unimportant member of the cast; he came to rehearsals in dark glasses—an irritating habit to those who were obliged to play scenes with him. The dark glasses enhanced the chalkiness of a pierrot-like face. He was extremely thin and fragile-looking. Because he was unsure of himself, he affected airs of superiority which far from endeared him to his fellow actors. He had a slicing sense of humour which always seemed to be aimed (it was pure defence mechanism) at making somebody uncomfortable. He demonstrated a palpable contempt of every member of the Company, including its leading lady—to whom, nevertheless, in their rare encounters, he was

---

[1] Ford Madox Hueffer—later Ford Madox Ford.

Gaetano Meo

Edward Carrick

Elena Meo

Anthony Hawtrey

Nicholas Hawtrey

ditheringly polite. Behind that façade of self-satisfaction lay a humility so exaggerated that, on an occasion when Phyllis smiled at him, he could not believe that the smile was intended for him; poker-faced, he wondered who was standing behind him, what fortunate being, towards whom that unexpected radiance was directed.

The grapevine of the theatre had informed Phyllis that this far from prepossessing young man had had his meagre salary stolen in the last town the Company had visited; her True-Terry reaction was to send a message, inviting the 'child', as she regarded him, to supper. Incredulous, and more than a little panic-stricken, he waited in a dark dressingroom near to the leading lady's; perhaps she would forget her invitation. He hoped she would—and, on the next breath, hoped she wouldn't. How should he know that Phyllis Neilson-Terry was as little capable as her father of forgetting *that* sort of invitation?

In the course of supper, his nerve went completely. He proceeded explosively to vent his opinion of Phyllis's performance in the evening show: a performance in the opinion of young Heron Carvic grossly unworthy (*a*) of Phyllis, (*b*) of a Terry. He had seen her Elizabeth of England, and was infuriated by her betrayal of the talents she had demonstrated in that.

It was a piece of combined courage and impudence: courage, because it might well have lost him his precarious job, and impudence, because what he knew about acting, apart from the rough and tumble of French touring companies, could have been put in a thimble and covered with a gooseberry leaf. He had, however, the courage of his convictions, and was prepared to stand by them. And what Terry does not respect courage? What Terry is not nauseated by its reverse—especially if it takes the form of sycophancy?

Nobody had ever talked to Phyllis like that—assuredly no actor twenty years younger than she, a young man of no importance, a very minor member of the Company in which she was leading lady. When she got over the shock, it occurred to her that this rude young man might be worth knowing.

Heron Carvic was twenty-three and looked much older. The son of a Wimpole Street neurologist, he had bolted from Eton to earn a living for himself in France. His improbable-sounding stage-name derived from his grandmother; he adopted it to spare the sensibilities of his outraged family. He was devoted to his mother, but the antipathy between him and his father was so acute that no roof and four walls could contain the pair of them. A very delicate youth, his experiences in France (which included marriage and the death of his young French wife) completed the wreckage of his health, and he came back to England at the end of five years to see if he could make a living in the chancy world of the Theatre.

He was something completely new and fascinating in Phyllis's life; to begin with, he 'amused' her (she had already been fatally drawn to one who 'amused' her, which might have rung a warning bell. Fortunately for both of them, no echoes from that dreary interlude disturbed their felicity, although King was still hanging on, bringing moral blackmail to bear on Phyllis to prevent her from claiming her liberty), but she soon discovered that the attraction went beyond 'amusement'. Here was somebody who brought no kind of sycophancy into their relationship; whose unconcealed attachment was peppered with irony, sarcasm and ruthlessness, and whose driving mental energy was often betrayed by physical ailments of the most painful and harassing nature.

Phyllis's days of mental and physical sloth were at an end. Heron Carvic had nothing in particular to contribute to her art, but he forced her to use her excellent Terry intelligence and was passionate about the minutest details which had bearing on her work. He was the kind of tonic a woman in her forties, bluffing against a creeping discouragement in her life and her art, requires.

It need hardly be said that the attitude of most of her friends to Phyllis's young lover, in the early stages of the attachment, was very similar to that of her aunt Ellen Terry's friends, when Ellen became 'infatuated' with James Carew. There was the same wide age-gap, the same apparent incompatibility of background. What the self-appointed critics overlooked was that Phyllis's was no infatuation, but a slow and steadfast appreciation of one who brought her that which, unconsciously, she had sought from her youth, someone who could give her not only laughter but a blistering criticism (often misplaced, but to Phyllis any criticism was better than none) and encourage her to stretch her lazy mind.

The one person wholly incapable of recognizing what Heron Carvic had brought into Phyllis's life was her mother. Julia's word for the situation was 'undignified'. It took bitter years, patience on Phyllis's part, tolerance on Heron's and, eventually, a war, to bring about reconciliation with one who, had she lived long enough, would have been legally Heron's mother-in-law.

Meanwhile, none of her friends knew actually how much Heron was doing for Phyllis. They had set up house in a small flat in Gloucester Place, at a wartime rent, but did no entertaining—which seemed odd, for a Terry. It could hardly be a matter of convention, for True Terrys don't deal in convention.

Everyone knew Phyllis Neilson-Terry by sight, if only as a romantic figure stepping out of car or taxi, hunching her imperious way across a yard or two of pavement into the most expensive of the West End stores, saluted by commissionaires and given precedence by shopwalkers and assistants. To meet Phyllis loping in the Marylebone purlieus, with perhaps a couple of baskets and a paper carrier in her hands, took many by surprise, but was accepted as an eccentricity of the affluent and great. They would have been more suprised if they had followed her home to a ramshackle kitchen and an old, leaking gas stove, on which she cooked the economical midday meal. Sometimes it was eggs and bacon; sometimes an egg and a slice of bacon; sometimes it was a choice between an egg and bacon.

The mystery of Fred Terry's Will must remain for ever unresolved. How did a man who had lived so full, rich and successful a life come to 'cut up' for so little money?

Part of the answer to this may be found in the 6th paragraph of the Will:

I DECLARE that all monies at any time or times advanced or paid by me to or on account of any legatees under this my Will were intended by me as gifts or have been forgiven by me and that nothing is now due to me from any of the said legatees in respect of any such advances or payments and no claim shall or can be made against such respective legatees if they or any of them shall be dead against his or her estate in respect thereof.

Apart from specific legatees, the sums of money lent or given away by Fred Terry to friends or acquaintances putting up a hard-luck story, would, if they had been recorded, add up to a respectable fortune.

Among other modest bequests, he left to his Dear Wife Julia Emilie Terry £2,000; to his business manager and to a lady friend £100 apiece. 'Dear Old Charlie' died too soon to come into his legacy of £250. The grandchildren had their provision. Old servants were remembered to the tune of between £100 and £25. Specific gifts were left to friends.

To his dearly beloved Phyllis—the darling of his heart up to the very end—nothing.

It was stunning—not only to Phyllis, but to her friends who regarded it as a public affront. Not a jewel, not a piece of furniture, not a solitary relic of the days she had loved. More than the money (which indeed she needed), she would have loved a desk or a chair; something of her father's, left to her by her father.

There is simply no explanation of this. Who that ever knew Fred Terry could imagine him capable of any act of unkindness, of discourtesy to the most casual of his acquaintances, let alone his daughter?

Some part of the financial straits in which Phyllis now found herself may have been due to her reasonable expectation of a small share in her father's estate.

Heron Carvic was determined to get Phyllis out of the financial confusion into which her extravagance and generosity had led her; to pay off the bank overdraft which had soared because she had not the very smallest conception of the cost of living. 'Economizing', to Phyllis, meant a cold meal, and a cold meal was a terrine of *foie gras* or a pound of caviare. Up to the time of their setting up house together, she had taken for granted an expensive flat in Welbeck Street, an Italian maid and every possible luxury in living. She had been brought up to all this by her mother, who set a disproportionate value on all the material aspect of success. She laughed off the climbing overdraft—until Heron introduced her to the facts of life.

Like a lamb she accepted her initiation. Phyllis, who had never lifted a finger in all her golden life, washed, scrubbed floors, cooked, ironed and nursed the sick and delicate man who had brought reality into her hot-house existence.

There was lots of laughter. They agreed it was important to keep up façade. Phyllis must always be beautifully dressed—or give the impression of being beautifully dressed. So a burst of diamonds covered up a stain or a hole in an ancient gown. One of Julia's outworn winter coats, flung at Phyllis to be given to Julia's old dresser, Polly Convey, who now waited on her daughter (they had managed, at last, to find money for a daily woman), was snatched by Heron—'You haven't got a winter coat!'—and, elaborated with *soutache*, was Phyllis's best coat for a couple of winters. She wore it like a Lanvin creation. Heron rightly refused to allow Phyllis to sell her jewels, their only capital.

They made a little—a very little—money now and again: one, two or three pounds. In a moment of desperation, they took themselves to luncheon at the Berkeley, to ask the head waiter if he would take Heron on as a waiter. This was regarded as an immense *blague*! Miss Neilson-Terry had spent big money at the Berkeley in the past. Nothing came of it—and they had spent money they could ill afford. Neither had a shade of snobism; they laughed a little wrily over those wasted pounds.

The problem of their poverty could to some degree have been solved, if, during the war years, Heron had been able to take on any kind of war work. But he was not even classified 'C4'. After his medical, when he asked the Chairman of the Board in which class he belonged, he was told, 'Just to please you, an honorary Z.' He eventually discovered that no Government undertaking would accept him, for fear of his becoming immediately pensionable.

Phyllis's work was not advancing one quarter of an inch, but she was learning what she had never glimpsed over the long, opulent years: the art of living. It's all very well—it's almost to be taken for granted—to be poor when you are young; when poverty abruptly descends on one in one's middle years it is not so easy to laugh. Phyl learned to laugh—not bitterly, but sweetly and deeply.

A very odd thing took place during those years of stress and strain; Phyllis developed an astonishing physical likeness to her grandmother, Sarah Ballard Terry. The likeness was more than physical; it went deep. The one-time empty beauty was no longer empty; it was expressive of her inner happiness and security.

Nothing could prevent her being over-generous, and often too open-handed; but the overdraft was paid off. Heron took on any job which would bring in a little money; he had protean abilities, and directed them towards building security for them both. For this he got little credit from Julia, who had not the smallest clue to the struggle through which her daughter was living. Wan and weary, Phyllis climbed Primrose Hill to the 'empty house' three or four times a week. Why, wondered Julia, didn't she take a taxi?

Heron wrote and produced a play which they toured; it was a shocker, and did nothing to enhance Phyllis's reputation, but it made a little money, and every little helps. It proved exactly what Heron intended it to prove: that Phyllis could wear modern fashions, and look elegant and convincing in them. There was a ridiculous *canard* that Phyllis could only wear costume and play costume parts. Heron's bad little bit of drama gave the lie to that; it was seen by a few managers, and the harvest came later—when Phyl got an important part in a Rattigan play.

CHAPTER SEVEN

Terry Twilight

In August 1940 a beautiful old lady was inflicting distress and exasperation upon her family and friends by her stubborn refusal to move out of London, or at least out of the air-raid orbit. Almost immediately under the guns on Primrose Hill, she occupied herself in turning the big square house on the corner of the Hill and Ainger Road[1] into a cardboard fortress; windows were strapped with tape, buckets of water and bags of sand lurked in every darkened corner; each time the raid warnings sounded every blind was drawn, every window opened, light turned off at the main and the front door not only bolted but chained. With immense skill and application, Julia turned 4 Primrose Hill Road into what amounted to a death trap for its occupants—the youngest of whom was sixty, the eldest over eighty—and sat down, a Queen on her 'lacquered throne' (usually the study sofa), to defy the hosts of Midian in pitch darkness.

'But don't you see, darling, if you stop a few firebombs all these draughts will suck the flames through the house in seconds?' 'But Timson or May will fall over these buckets in the dark!' 'But Nan[2] will come down the stairs arse over tip and break her neck in the hall!' 'But if any one of us comes to see if you're all right we won't be able to get in or make anybody hear!'

On such expostulations she turned her beautiful, mute gaze; as well argue with the Venus de Milo. The fact that people, anxious for her safety, came up and hammered on the door, at peril of their lives from falling shrapnel, meant nothing to Julia, as also meant nothing the protests that she was adding to the responsibilities and difficulties of ARP and AFS services. In her opinion, if no one else's, it was Her Finest Hour. With her lifelong gift for brushing

[1] Demolished in 1960.
[2] Miss Jenny Furnival, sometime governess to the children, who remained to her death at the age of 86 a member of the household.

aside any opinion at variance with her own, she dismissed the fact that she was not helping the war effort, but impeding it. Racial caution came out strongly; despite Lord Woolton's appeals against hoarding, her provision cupboards were stocked as for a siege.

It is not too much to say that Julia enjoyed the war, which provided her with a series of thrills and mainly self-invented occupations, in which, once more, she held the centre of the stage. Fools —mainly casual acquaintances—came to tell her 'how brave' she was, and she accepted these fatuous tributes as radiantly as she had formerly accepted the applause of her audiences. Probably the only intelligent people who did not look upon her conduct as folly were her servants who, sure of a solid roof over their heads and not dependent on rations, supported Mrs Terry's refusal to leave her home. Inspired by the mistress's example, there was no hysteria belowstairs when walls cracked and windows fell in under the volleys of the guns.

The first daylight raid took place on an afternoon in May. Down came the blinds, clank went the chains on the front door, and Julia made her stately descent to the basement, dodging sandbags and buckets of water more by luck than good management. I slipped out into the garden, where Timson was already, proudly wearing his tin hat of the First World War, grinning like an old elf. The German planes were coming over like a swarm of bees—and not an English plane in sight or a gun to check their formidable advance.

'There—that was a gun, wasn't it, Timson?'

'No, miss, them's bombs,' said Timson, still grinning grimly. ' 'Ere they come—right over us.'

'I think I should come in if I were you, darling', called Julia calmly. She was standing in the middle of the kitchen, with Hazel's French bulldog in her arms, soothing him: as little disturbed as though she were calling us in from a shower. Cook (who refused to draw the blinds in the basement) was perkily sorting apples; if it came to nerve, she wasn't going to be beaten by Mrs Terry!

Then noise like a solid block took shape and rocked the floor on which we were standing. Flung against the wall, Julia tried to hold the little dog and put her hands over her ears at the same time. 'That's the guns', said Timson in a satisfied voice, as if he were personally responsible for them. Three more blasts brought down a shower of plaster and a big crash of glass overhead. 'Oo,' said Cook, in a high, superior voice, 'look at Mrs Timson, she's passed out!' Timson's wife had been given shelter, together with her husband, at Number 4.

I was in the house on the occasion of many more raids and never saw Julia blench or even give an exclamation of fear. When tempted to cry out, 'Why aren't you away, all of you, in the safety of the country, instead of here, where you can do no good?' respect closed my lips, respect for a woman in her seventies, whose folly was surely redeemed by her impeccable courage. It was not that Julia was never frightened, or that her unsteady heart never quickened its beat, but that the strength of her will and her sense of personal dignity enabled her to control unseemly manifestations.[1] By the time the raids were over, her friends had forgotten they had ever thought of her as 'foolish', and only admired her possibly wrong-headed but magnificent intrepidity.

She had the part-time companionship of her granddaughter, Hazel. Hazel had walked on as a Page in the George Robey production of *Henry IV, Part One*, played Beauty in Sydney Carroll's *Everyman* (a seemly choice, for Hazel, at seventeen, had grown into the image of her aunt Ellen), married a young actor, Geoffrey Keen, and presently had a daughter, Gemma. The marriage was not a success; when the war broke out in 1939 the baby Gemma was sent for safety into the country, and Hazel went to live with her grandmother Julia under the thunder of the anti-aircraft guns. She had beautiful manners—and so had Julia. That was the extent of their compatibility. Julia was mildly baffled by a granddaughter who went out at luncheon time, leaving her bedroom in chaos, and came in at the small hours, with shrapnel pattering around. Conversation was difficult—on Julia's part; on Hazel's not at all; she was the true daughter of Dennis. It was just a little trying that she and her grandmother spoke different languages. Hazel had done two years with the Oxford Repertory and a season in New York. She was now 'in films', and Julia had not the film vocabulary.

[1] From friends in the Defence services I have had many instances of this fantastic courage in the old. It does not seem unreasonable that teenagers were, on the whole, least capable of facing the horrors of the raids; it was only among them that I ever personally encountered uncontrollable hysteria.

In the third year of the war—1942—a stroke of luck came Hazel's way. Peggy Ashcroft was engaged to play Ophelia to John Gielgud's Hamlet; caught in one of the blitzes, Miss Ashcroft was disabled by flying glass within a week of the opening. Hazel, in her early twenties, with relatively small experience, had the unnerving experience of partnering at short notice an established and distinguished Shakespearian actor. Haunted by tradition—the tradition of her great-aunt Ellen's flower-like Ophelia—she acquitted herself so well that she was engaged for the Indian tour which followed the short British run. Like all Terrys, Hazel had immense 'presence' on the stage; the tender young face of her childhood, however, had hardened; it was plain that her future lay in character parts, or in the intellectual drama—she herself inclined towards Tchekov and Ibsen, for which she was 'a natural', as indeed would have been her father, Dennis, had he lived to fulfil his ambitions. That Shakespearian engagement served, however, one good purpose: it cemented the affectionate attachment between the cousins, Gielgud and Hazel Terry, which was to be of value in dark days ahead.

Julia's greatest anxiety was, naturally, for Phyllis. When Phyllis was out in the provinces, where, like the majority of The Profession, she spent most of her time, they were often unable to communicate. During and after raids the telephone lines were closed to civilian subscribers. Telegrams were as unsure, owing to the Post Office's habit of closing from the Warning to the All Clear. A telegram sent to a friend in London whose telephone had been blasted out of existence took five days in delivery.

As the raids increased in violence, one after another the theatres closed down: a serious blow at the morale of Londoners, a still more serious one to the rank and file of The Profession. To cope with the problems of the latter, Basil Dean had already formed the Entertainments National Service Association (known as ENSA), with headquarters at Drury Lane Theatre, which served a double purpose: that of providing employment for thousands of out-of-work actors and musicians, and entertainment for the camps at home and abroad. Among its other good works, ENSA rigorously excluded amateurs, which got rid of plenty of young people who were trying to dodge the call-up by getting themselves on the roster. (The BBC and the film studios were also popular bolt-holes for those intent on combining safety, pleasure and a regular salary with a modicum of patriotism.)[1]

Meanwhile, the touring companies poured out to the provincial cities and towns, some of which were running repertories of their own, and vacancies, as they occurred owing to the joining up of members, were easily filled—although the standard of peacetime was difficult to maintain.

Companies went out with a minimum of scenery and costume (the one-set play became *de rigueur* for touring, because of lack of labour and shortage of transport), material for both being of the cheapest. Train journeys seemed endless, and, in winter, were bitterly cold. Dressingrooms and offices were frequently unheated, and audiences shivered in the front of the house.

The worst discomfort suffered by the actor was the change in his domestic conditions. Between the wars, his 'digs', as theatrical lodgings were professionally called, were his home. Landladies (known as 'Mas') took pride, with a few hideous exceptions, in providing as much comfort as possible for 'the poor wandering creatures', as a landlady described us, and in calling after us on our departure on Sunday morning, 'See you next year, love', knew they would not be disappointed. Having found 'a good address', one went back like a swallow, confident that on returning at midnight after the show (those were the days when theatres opened and closed at a civilized hour), there would be a good fire blazing on the hearth and a hot, tasty supper—and no complaints if you happened to bring back a friend to share it. With a heaped coal-scuttle to keep you company, you could sit up to any hour, play the piano—behave, in fact, as freely as in your own home. Going to bed, your room was like ice (unless you happened for economy's sake to be enjoying a 'combined chat'—Th. for bed-sittingroom), but the by

[1] It is not to imply that all who went to, or retained, jobs at the BBC and in films were shirkers; some were genuinely indispensable, some unfitted physically for active service, and a few more sincerely conscientious objectors. Many sacrificed their present and their future to the call to arms. But it was a matter of common knowledge that if one was professionally qualified, a bit of astute wire-pulling might preserve one from the unpleasantness of service in the Armed Forces.

now tepid bottle in your bed had nicely warmed it, and you pulled up your blankets and eiderdown and slept until you were called to bacon and eggs and another roaring fire.

This blissful state of affairs did not obtain in all digs, and bad theatrical lodgings were indescribably squalid; but comfort had little to do with price, and some of the most sought-after lodgings were in little working-class cottages—where the fact that there was no bath and the 'convenience' was out of doors counted for nothing beside the big fires, the good cooking and the Ma's readiness, without asking, to wash the ladies' smalls, sew on ribbons or buttons and mend the men's socks. Ma doctored us when we were ill, listened to our woes and rejoiced in our successes.

On the board inside the stage door were usually pinned up land-ladies' cards, for the benefit of those careless or unfortunate enough to arrive without booking. These cards were always hand-written, and one of them became a classic in the Terry Company: 'Comf. Bed Sit, piano with lavatory inside where Mr Cariello spent seven years.'

All this good cheer vanished in the Second World War. The landladies had too many troubles of their own to concern them-selves with the comforts of the 'poor wandering creatures'. Coal, gas, electric power and food were all rationed. A faint trickle of smoke stood for the once blazing fire, and the coal scuttle no longer stood by the hearth; no more hot suppers—sometimes no supper but a mug of cocoa or bogus coffee. The meal was cooked at the landlady's convenience, which was in the afternoon. Baths were rationed (often to one a week) and bits of laundry had to be done surreptitiously.

These conditions prevailed, of course, throughout the country; the civilian, who was holding down the hard end of the war, who was taking the bombing night after night, was given no concessions of food or fuel. It is not to claim undue privilege to say that touring actors were among the principal sufferers, the arduous and nerve-wracking nature of their profession making them particularly de-pendent on warmth and nourishment. The wartime duty of the actor was to keep up morale, but he was given no help. Civilian rations were grossly inadequate for people in all walks of life; into the garbage bins of the Armed Forces went joints which would have fed a family for a week.

Acting is hungry work; after the theatre restaurants were closed and depleted hotel staffs rebelled at serving suppers in private rooms. The energy briefly generated by a meal at one o'clock was burnt up by the evening performance, and many a player went ravenous to bed, to be cheated of sleep by the pangs of hunger, and the lack of a hot bath to relieve his tension. He did not complain; he was making his contribution to the war effort.

Phyllis Neilson-Terry stayed in England, to be in touch with her mother; sang at Ensa concerts and lectured for the Ministries about fuel and washing machines. She rushed back from the provinces to look after Julia and Heron Carvic.

The war ended. Heron had regular work in the theatre and with the BBC, and they had a house in Beaumont Street, with endless staircases, for which he wove the carpets. There was seemingly nothing he could not do: building, plumbing, architecture, designing Phyllis's gowns, her hats, her jewellery. The horrid overdraft had been paid off, and now he was set upon consolidating their mutual life.

And the empty house on Primrose Hill?

Those vast, over-crowded rooms held out no attractions to the post-war domestic. The butler and cook departed. Chars came and went. According to Phyllis, there were never less than three servants —of a sort. They had a genius for being invisible; for not opening doors, not answering bells, not—except at their own convenience— serving a meal.

Julia sat in the study, apparently indifferent. There was the usual gabble among ill-informed acquaintances—indirectly aimed at Phyllis: how dreadful it was, Julia Neilson being left all alone in that great empty house! Various friends and acquaintances came in as 'companions', and got short shrift. Nobody appeared to recognize how Julia's character had altered during her widowhood, from the (superficially) amenable wife to the dominant old lady she latterly became.

The dominant old lady was spending money like water—as she had always done: in trouble with her bank manager, her lawyer and her accountants, but always managing to square it by the sale of some of the valuable antiques she had accumulated down the years. Some of the antiques were supposed to go to Phyllis—and vanished overnight. Advisers tried to coax her out of that big house, which ate money, into a smaller domicile, to which her means would have been adequate; Julia was not having it.

But all those rooms with their soaring ceilings, their elaborate 'drapes' and period furniture were too much for one old lady, endlessly beautiful, crawling about the ground floor, supported by her stick, with no one within call, refusing all permanent companionship.

She was persuaded at last to let the top floor as a flat. To the relief of all, she took to her bed—not for reasons of health; apart from her winterly bronchitis and her rheumatism, Julia was as sound as a bell. But her bedroom was her refuge from troublesome callers, lawyer, accountant, bank manager—who were doing their utmost to put Julia's affairs in order, with very little co-operation on her part. She could nip downstairs, as blithe as a bird, to hear an interesting programme on the radio, or to receive some favoured friend, but the mere breath of 'business' reduced her to her beautiful four-poster, left her gasping among her pillows. 'Mrs Terry isn't seeing anybody—she isn't very well—this afternoon.' A blue eye would wink at the personal friend who happened to be up in the bedroom. Mrs Terry would love to hear social gossip, theatre gossip —but she would not talk *money*.

Phyllis got an excellent part in a Rattigan play—*Separate Tables*. For her it was a new adventure in acting: a beautiful, smooth, hard-as-nails part—the antithesis of the parts she had been offered before the war. When the London run was over, the production was booked for New York.

Money was needed at 4 Primrose Hill Road. The house in Beaumont Street, where Phyllis and Heron were then living, was marked for demolition, and Phyllis wanted to be able to buy a permanent home in the country.

Julia was perfectly amenable to the idea of being left in Heron's charge; she was now as attached to him as she had formerly been averse, and had become completely dependent on him for the practical regulation of her life. She was as well as she was likely to be. She had always sacrificed personal considerations to 'the work', and took it for granted her daughter should do the same.

But she was very old, and she had a touching fear of death. Religion, for Julia, was always more a matter of superstition than of dedication to a Faith; falling between two stools, the Jewish *fond* of her mother and her Gentile upbringing, it did not help her, towards the end. She always turned on the religious programmes on the radio, and recited the Lord's Prayer in rhythm with the Patience cards she played down. She never went to church.

A message reached Heron Carvic, that Mrs Terry had had a fall. He rushed up from Beaumont Street, to help lift the great weight of Julia from the floor on to her four-poster. She had lain on the parquet floor all night—out of stubbornness. She could well have reached the bell or the telephone. With wilful courage, she crawled about the floor, dragging rugs about her; hoping perhaps, eventually, to get herself on to her bed.

Her one terror was to be moved out of her house, her home, her shell, her refuge from the troublesome actualities of a world with which she had ceased to have *rapport* or sympathy.

She was persuaded, with great difficulty, into an ambulance; there had to be an X-ray, to determine the extent of the damage. She gave in, only on condition that, when the examination was over, she was brought straight home. In great pain, she exhibited magnificent fortitude.

For the last time, Julia Neilson descended her broad staircase, down which she had swept in her velvets and jewels—on a stretcher. Fear suddenly overcame her; clutching at the banister, she nearly brought about disaster, for herself and her bearers. Heron's intervention prevented a fatal accident.

The X-ray confirmed the worst; her pelvis was shattered.

For a few more days, in a hospital bed, she swung between darkness and light. Letters, flowers, messages poured in; in her lucid moments, Julia would none of them. She had said Goodbye to all that. She died, as she lived, in beauty, at the age of eighty-eight.

The glamour of a generation faded out with her. Few remain to witness to the glory of her middle age (which far eclipsed that of her youth), to the devotions she evoked, to the romantic graciousness of her personality.

Born out of her time, in the age of Siddons she might have gone down in history as a great actress. She was a tapestry figure—and a *tragédienne manquée*.

Hazel, the lovely child 'born to trouble as the sparks fly upward', got her life into great confusion during and after the war years. Hard hit by her father's death, she was not only strikingly like her great-aunt Ellen, but had much of Ellen's nature at the same period of the latter's life. 'Unthinking, idle, wild and gay', she could not, with her heredity, help being an actress; but she had not nearly enough work of importance to satisfy the restless intellect inherited from her father, Dennis Neilson-Terry.

The disorganization of the Theatre and of her private life combined to break Hazel, as they broke many other 'golden lads and girls', with futures ahead of them, of which they lost sight in the attempt to shake off the horror of the war years.

Ellen Terry once said in reproof of a criticism too hastily passed on a girl she did not even know: 'People only behave badly when they are unhappy.' A truism, but she disliked harsh judgements, and doubtless had her own youth in mind.

A few people, among them her aunt Phyllis Neilson-Terry and her cousin John Gielgud, understood Hazel and stood by her; Gielgud took her out on a tour with his Company in the States. But that was not much help, nor was it a help that her mother, Mary Glynne, died in 1954, and that her sister Monica (who served in the WRNS through the Plymouth blitz) married happily and went out to live in the Dominions.

The true help came from the young actor, David Evans, Hazel's second husband who, from the time of their meeting, dedicated himself to the unhappy girl he married: the girl with Ellen's wild eyes, passionate nature and basically strong character: the inheritress of all the 'glory that was Terry', with which, for a while, like her great-aunt, she elected to play ducks and drakes.

It is to be hoped that Hazel Terry will one day write the story which is hers alone to tell: a story of magnificent courage and persistence which contributed to the near-miracle which, in 1960, brought her back to the stage in a part worthy of her mettle. The play, unfortunately, was drivelling and pretentious, but with an

Hazel Terry

Gemma Hyde

Edward Gordon Craig C.H.

all-star cast (including her cousin John) it briefly achieved the West End, and Hazel, in a tough character part, gave a performance which would have gratified her father and her grandfather. She looked beautiful, and was one of the few members of the cast who appeared to be perfectly clear about what she was doing!

She is the last bearer of the illustrious name of Terry in the English Theatre.

Edith Craig died in 1947, two years after the war. Those years revolved, for Edy, round the annual performances at the Barn Theatre which managed to keep going throughout the war. Helpers rallied around on foot, by bicycle and on horseback, in farm carts or ancient pony traps—for there was no petrol to be had, except by the 'privileged'.

Queening it over them all, Edy was in her element; none argued with her, or questioned her decrees. In anything to do with the theatre, Edy was 'always right', and at this last, working on her own ground with familiar materials, without the tiresome presence of people who considered they knew as much, or more, than she did, nobody disputed it. Because they accepted without question all her directions, she had always had more success with amateurs than with professionals, working magic with raw material unspoilt by previous handling. The professionals came down to Smallhythe at the last moment, and she left them to do very much as they pleased, within the compass of her production. Such suggestions as she made they accepted respectfully; Edy had become a *culte*.

She would be a great subject for a biography, if anyone had the temerity to attempt it; in this age of candour, biography is valueless unless it tells the whole story. A symposium of tributes, edited by her friend Eleanor Adlard, bears witness to the *culte*, and is contributed to by (among others) Dame Sybil Thorndike, the late Dame May Whitty and her daughter Margaret Webster, the late Harcourt Williams, the late Sheila Kaye-Smith, the late Christopher St John and the third member of the *ménage à trois*, Clare Atwood. Personal friends, among them V. Sackville-West, Irene Cooper Willis and Violet Pym, added their tributes. Gordon Craig wrote about his sister in a short article called *Edy Playing* (the piano), and claimed genius for her.

The most permanent of Edy's works (for, unlike her brother, she contributed nothing original to the arts) was the establishment of the Ellen Terry Museum: the natural outcome of her industry, her historical scholarship, her endless patience and perseverance in the classification of material and facts. All her life she had kept up the Victorian ritual of the scrapbook, and had jealously preserved all her mother's possessions, which, of latter years, Ellen Terry had been inclined too freely to give away: going so far, on occasions, as to beard the innocent recipient of such gifts with, 'You must give that back at once! Mother had no business to give it to you.'

After the death of Edy, the Farm became a little oppressive, a kind of theatrical Lourdes, jealously policed by Christopher St John and Clare Atwood, self-appointed temple virgins, whose unauthorized interference reduced curators to despair. Tony had a mild, but formidable persistence, and Chris's rudeness was a by-word. Owing to these two, the Museum might well have closed down for want of a curator. It was rescued by Olive.

Olive, daughter of 'darling Floss', dearest niece of her aunt Ellen, was living in Smallhythe. She was there when Ellen died; she was endlessly kind to her cousin Edy—of whom, as a matter of fact, she was very fond; Edy had been very kind to her, during the turbulent years. When she offered, temporarily, to take over the curatorship of the Museum, all concerned drew a breath of relief. When Olive Chaplin took over, and reorganized the Farm structurally and artistically, when eventually she took upon herself the Herculean task of rearranging and cataloguing the library, she brought life and gaiety back to the still rooms; recognizing that reverence was not incompatible with light-heartedness, she delivered Ellen Terry from the cere-cloths in which its former custodians were driven, by the interference of the ancient vestals, permanently to enshroud her.

To be welcomed to the Farm by Olive Chaplin gave one a slight shock. Bearing no distinct resemblance to her aunt in her youth, she grew, over the years, into the living image of her: more like her than Edy ever was. The shape of the two faces is almost identical, the colour of the eyes different, yet alike in expression, eyes and face and mouth all shaped by a fine sensitivity. She has the long, lithe limbs and the bowed shoulders of Ellen Terry in her latter years;

her penetrating glance sums up the visitor—whether friend, seeker or merely curious sightseer; and to each she extends the Terry courtesy—warm or cool, according to the impression made at the first encounter. Draped in one of her aunt's Tyrian robes, one would say it is Ellen, moving through the mottled sunlight. It might be said that Ellen with her smile full of amusement moves in her niece's shadow, prompting her with nudge or a wink when Olive's memory gives out under the barrage of questions she is called upon to answer. 'Go on: make something up!' prompts Ellen, to whom the whole thing is an immense joke. Only dull people, superficially acquainted with the real Ellen Terry, could imagine her lending herself to the 'Lourdes' mystique.

There are no cords to prevent sightseers from approaching Ellen's dressing-table, on which, unguarded, stand the simple implements of her toilette, or to fence off her bed, her tables, chairs and sofas; no locks on her bookcases; even her old handbag lies there, with a diary and some letters stuffed inside it, as she left it. She might just have gone out into the garden. . . .

This is the way she would have wished it to be, the way Olive has preserved it. It is good to know that their trust has seldom been abused. There are a few objects which Olive would show only to initiates. With her skilful needle she repaired robes, with her sensitive hands she dusted, polished and rearranged. This year (1961) Olive retires, and the Farm may become like Anne Hathaway's cottage, out of which trippers have tramped the last vestiges of life; so it behoves all who can to see it while it is still living.

When the Museum was first established, it was almost inaccessible, except to people with cars of their own, or money to hire them. Cheap transport has disposed of that disadvantage. Buses come out from Rye, but pause much too briefly to satisfy any but those who are content with no more than a fleeting glimpse of the interior of the Farm. In Ellen Terry's lifetime charabancs used to come out and pause long enough for the conductor to bawl, ' 'Ere you see Miss Hellen Terry's 'ouse', and Ellen, holding out her hand to be pulled up out of her chair in the garden, would mutter, 'And 'ere you see Miss Hellen Terry beating it like 'ell for 'er 'ouse'—before curious faces were poked over the hedge. It is easy enough to reach Smallhythe by motor bicycle, moped or (if you have enough enthusiasm) by push-bike from London nowadays: a fact of which students seem insufficiently aware. The Farm enshrines two hundred years of Theatre history, and the accredited visitor might even gain access to the library, although that, very wisely, is fenced off from the long passage which leads, by way of the wardrobe, to Ellen Terry's bedroom.

It was during those post-war years that Anthony Hawtrey, Olive's eldest son, made his name as a producer. The West End successes, *No Room at the Inn*, *Red Roses for Me*, *Worm's Eye View* and *The Boy Friend* all had their original presentation at the little theatre up at Swiss Cottage. He had married an actress, Marjory Clarke, and by her had a son, Nicholas, who was presently to head for the stage, and a daughter, Annabel, who showed an early talent for painting. The death of Anthony Hawtrey, of a coronary thrombosis, at the early age of forty-six, deprived the stage of a producer of originality and vision, whose tradition, by which it is inconceivable he would not have allowed himself to be governed, would have preserved him from many of the eccentricities and affectations which bring confusion upon both playwright and actor today. There was no ' 'ark at ME!' about Tony; born gay, like his father, there was one subject upon which he was wholly serious, and in which his excellent brain never failed to distinguish the wheat from the chaff. A potentially great young commander, he would have been in the van of any movement that concerned the advancement of the theatre, but he would have been able precisely to detect the line over which acting or playwriting toppled into a meaningless exhibitionism.

And so, John Gielgud: the gangling youth from Lady Benson's academy who, within the space of little more than a decade had moved slowly, and it seemed inevitably, into his rightful place at the head of the English theatre.

If asked on what I base my estimation of John Gielgud as our greatest living actor, I would sum it up in six words: 'He nothing common did or mean' in any part I have ever seen him play.

Terrys are no less eager to claim John Gielgud than he is to claim them. Physically, he bears no faintest resemblance to any member of his Terry grandmother's family. It is now generally accepted that physical traits do not, by themselves, indicate character, but John Gielgud is markedly lacking in Terry characteristics, particularly on the male side. He is not that for which a famous Victorian coined the word 'clubable'. Hospitable within his own circle, and an excellent host, he is not to be described as bonhomous. A poor mixer, he may be seen in a social gathering of people with whom he is but slightly acquainted, sitting apart, as exquisitely ill at ease as a débutante at her first ball.

He has none of the jocund pugnacity of his Terry uncles, their gift for being 'at home' in every kind of society, and his humours, both good and evil, take a different pattern from theirs. He is not a trencherman on the grand Terry scale, and he is abstemious of alcohol. He has not followed the family tradition in marrying and producing a family.

All these negatives, however, add up to one positive: that the much-diluted stream of Terry blood which circulates in a slight frame is active in Gielgud's art.

It is a pity that more is not known of the foreign spring which contributes its powerful quota to the British (Lewis and Terry) bloodstream. Frank Gielgud, born in England, had British nationality, but both his parents were Poles, his father (Adam Gielgud) having acquired Lithuanian nationality by the accident of being born off-shore in the Gulf of Riga when his parents were in flight from the Polish Insurrection of 1830. The great grandparents (of John Gielgud) were Polish on both sides, Mrs Adam Gielgud's mother being the Madame Aszperger to whom reference has been made. So John Gielgud inherits almost equal parts of English and Polish blood, the latter coming out strongly in his appearance and that of his brother Val, and to a notable degree colouring his acting. For obvious reasons it was clearly detectable in the Russian plays and in *Richard of Bordeaux*; it appeared in *Noah*. I venture to think that none of those parts could have been played in that particular way by an all-British actor. Its beat is audible in his verse-speaking.

It is impossible, without descending to verbal banalities, to define the 'foreign' element in Gielgud's acting; at one moment it is there, in a split second it is gone, yet leaves some kind of glow. It reveals itself in an inflection, a movement or a sudden turn of the head;

it mutters like the distant echoes of an inaudible storm, or brushes the scene with an all but imperceptible current of air. But I can recall none of the many occasions on which I have watched John Gielgud act without being made aware of its presence.

And so the saga draws to an end—with just one more voice to conclude it.

CHAPTER EIGHT

Three Candles and a Cake
of Soap

In a fold of the Alpes Maritimes, almost as withdrawn as a Yeti, sits an Old, Wise Man. But soft! why should wisdom be regarded as the supreme attribute of age? I should like to think that Gordon Craig, in his eighty-ninth year, is as superbly capable of playing the fool as in his roaring youth. He would tell you that Shakespeare's Fools are stuffed with wisdom, and that it takes a Fool to make a Wise Man, as surely as it takes a Wise Man to be a Fool.

If Gordon Craig's folly, in these days, is a little subdued, it may be (indirectly to change the metaphor) that, apart from the passage of time, 'all his lovely companions', of both sexes, 'are faded and gone'. One can imagine him softly and ironically humming the tune—he had always a taste for musical tags, but they were usually of the music-hall. Better not inquire how long it is since E.G.C. was inside a London music-hall, or take too seriously the faint note of melancholy which sounds in his recent notes from his Provençal fastness. It is winter; 'winter is the v. devil', he writes. Come spring, the wood-notes wild will rise again. One cannot be expected to carol, surrounded by those peaks of snow and ice, those lethal ice-green torrents, by now frozen into stillness.

On Christmas Day and on New Year's Eve 1960, thanks to modern science, the voice of the last of the True Terrys was brought through space to reverberate under our holly and ivy: the voice of the eternal visionary, the indefatigable rebel, its endless tolerance peppered by a Damn or two—just as it were, to preserve the character. No note of bitterness or resentment intruded upon that easy voice; if, ignored by the country of his birth, he felt either in the past, it has left no wrack behind.

Actor, Draftsman, Craftsman, Creator; Rebel, Visionary, Wise

391

Man, Fool. Let us salute the Fool, whose folly has resulted in so rich a harvest for the Theatre.

I have at various times employed the epithet 'True Terry', and the time has come to define it. It most certainly has nothing to do with being born in or out of wedlock; there is, as a matter of fact, as much or more True Terry across the bar sinister as in the legitimate line.

Taking as our starting-point Ben Terry and his wife Sarah Ballard, the True Terry may first of all be described as one who sets the Theatre ahead of all other considerations, brushing aside, if necessary, the tenderest human relationships with a ruthlessness bordering (to the uninitiated) on brutality. For this reason the True Terry marries into The Profession, for it is next to impossible for anyone not bred to the *métier* to appreciate its egoism. It is possible to effect a bridge if the chosen partner is in close sympathy with the Stage and its affiliated arts, but it is a bridge to which T.Ts. are chary of trusting themselves.

The True Terry is essentially simple in his tastes; contrariwise —he is nothing if not contrary—he enjoys social grandeur and is more than something of a snob; great names and titles are as sweet music in his ears. But his snobism is never extended to members of his own Profession, or touches his true friendships. Allergic to fawning and flattery—plenty of which meet him in his day of success —he is quick to perceive their falsity and accepts them with a wink until they grow too offensive, when the flatterer is apt to find himself out of favour.

Proud, he is capable of hauteur; convinced of his importance as a Terry, he is apt to take umbrage if it is not recognized (this applies mainly to the distaff side).

Physically courageous, and of unbounded fortitude, he is morally an odd amalgam of pugnacity and pusillanimity; detests squabbles unless he starts them himself—which he is not slow in doing— and will usually avoid taking sides. He bursts into blind rages, often over trifles, and is invariably astonished, and even hurt, when people take these seriously; he himself has forgotten what they were about within a hour. Incapable of resentment, he cannot imagine it. Malice is beneath his dignity.

He is both shrewd and incredibly stupid; he is inclined to judge human nature by rule of thumb, has little patience with cases to which the rule cannot be applied and, except where his affections are involved, will not trouble to seek motivations. Apart from his peculiar genius, he is a very average Englishman, prepared to lay down his life for King and Country, taking for granted all honourable standards of conduct—even when he fails to live up to them: when he covers his lapses with bluff and suffers almost childlike qualms of conscience. To Church and State he pays polite lip-service.

He is lavish, generous out of all reason and excessively courteous. By nature an amorist, he derives much of his vitality out of a normal sex life—not confined to a single individual (although there is usually one person to whom he is faithful in his fashion), but diffuse, changeable and totally unpredictable. He is fanatically loyal to his family—which is to say, to anyone who can claim a drop of Terry blood.

Like a loose piece of knitting, this pattern is adaptable to all True Terrys. On the female side, it has to be pinched in here or let out there; the Terry ladies have not, by and large, been amorists, and have shown on many occasions remarkable moral courage.

The pattern, with a few modifications—a dropped stitch here or a few rows added there—fits Gordon Craig; to it he has added embellishments largely deriving from his father, Edward Godwin, to whose memory he professes, in *Index to the Story of My Days*, a devotion which is less filial—since Godwin parted from his family when 'Ted', as E.G.C. was then called, was barely four years old —than deferential: the respect of one artist for another. To read the *Index* is to recognize that Craig is, rightly, as proud of being the son of Godwin as he is of being the son of Ellen Terry.

No young man ever came into the world with a richer endowment of the arts: from his mother, the Theatre and Acting, from his father, Archaeology, Architecture, Drawing, Music, Literature and —more important than any—the disposition, the endlessly inquiring and creative mind from which evolved what in earlier chapters I have called the Vision, exploited by Max Reinhardt, supported by the Count Kessler and, needless to say, ignored by Craig's own countrymen. The belated recognition in this country of the fact that scenery is not merely a background for moving bodies, but an important element—Craig would say the most important element—in the dramatic climate which the actor is endeavouring to create, must be traced back to the *Craigische Vorstellung*, and to the eminence of its inspirer on the Continent. Intimations of the Art of Craig began to percolate this island's fogs, were made the base for timorous experiments and rejected by commercial manage-ments—whose memories, sluggish regarding his early success, were lively on the subject of the fiasco at the Imperial Theatre, when E.G.C. was only beginning to feel his way.

Anything brave and revolutionary in the mounting of a play within the last forty years may fairly be traced back to Craig, who would detest and disclaim association with many—perhaps the majority—of them. He is nevertheless responsible for the break-away from the literalism of Irving, the Barnum and Bailey-like showmanship of Tree, to the imaginative freedom of which the modern scene designer and director is at liberty, according to his lights, to avail himself.

Not long before the war, Mussolini proposed to Craig that the latter should produce *Quo Vadis?* in the Colosseum: a great 'honour', which left Craig unmoved. 'Pa said that he was not a Ringmaster but a Theatre Producer, or some sitch words . . . gathered up his train and swep out of Rome!' wrote his son Edward Carrick.

E.G.C. could have had a very comfortable time in his beloved Italy during the dictatorship, if he had chosen to pay tribute to a bogus Caesar. He loathed politics, did not profess to understand them and refused to prostitute his Art in their service. War lay clearly ahead, and he hated its wastefulness and violence. So he returned to France, where—in his simplicity—he imagined a little integrity, a little civilization might survive. Why not to England? Who would seek sanctuary in a country which had so thoroughly demonstrated its indifference to his existence—and to what counted with Craig more than the arbitrary act of living, the work to which he had dedicated his life? All he sought was some place where he might get on with the work. Paris seemed a good centre, handy for materials and communications. E.G.C. had been so long out of

France, knew so little of the dry-rot that had set in at the country's heart, that it never entered his mind that France would not fight to a victorious end.

The war broke out in 1939; on 14 May of the following year the French betrayed their Allies, and a fortnight later the Belgians. The Germans poured into Paris, and Gordon Craig, bearer of an English passport, was among the first batch of 'enemy' internees.

Enemy? He was educated at Heidelberg; his first recognition as a Theatre Designer came from Berlin and Weimar. In Germany— not the Germany of a housepainter called Schicklgruber, who called himself Hitler, but of the Hohenzollerns—he had a name and a reputation, before his native land accorded him either. Up to the outbreak of war, he had been in constant communication with friends in various parts of the country. It was difficult to regard Germans as 'the enemy', even when he, his young companion Daphne and their infant, 2.2., were taken to the prison camp at Besançon.

With typical German thoroughness, the van of the invading regiments was followed by representatives of the Arts; with so rich a city as Paris to be looted, the Führer and his officers and aides-de-camp wanted to be sure of not missing anything, and of getting the best.

Two young men—Heim and Conrad—were at the head of the Arts administration. One of their first and most respectable actions was to procure the liberation of Gordon Craig, his companion and little daughter, from the prison camp. They made no conditions, proposed no *quid pro quo* in the way of German propaganda. Had they done so, E.G.C. would certainly have refused; whatever were his sentiments about Germany—the old, arrogant but essentially noble Germany, which bore no relationship to Shicklgruber's spiritual slum—he would not, as True Terry, have consented to anything which implied disloyalty to England. Being, however, completely penniless, he was grateful to Heim and Conrad when they made him an offer for his Collection of books, prints, pictures, programmes and theatrical records, for which, on his acceptance, they paid him an immediate advance.[1]

---

[1] The high esteem in which Gordon Craig was held by German artists received further confirmation when, at the end of the war, the entire Collection was returned to him, with the seals unbroken.

This was all Craig had, temporarily, to live on; but it enabled him to rent a big, bleak studio on the rue Ampère. No help was forthcoming from England. ('My fault,' writes he cheerily, 'for I hadn't the special gift of ASKING and GETTING!') There was very little to eat, for under the Occupation food prices rocketed and the black market was triumphant; rationing was a farce. The common necessities for cleanliness were at a premium. With the onset of winter, the cold was terrible; light and power were cut, to keep the Germans' quarters ablaze. As clothes wore out, there was no means of replacing them.

But work piled up on long tables in the studio on the rue Ampère: woodcuts, designs, drawings—although materials for these were running short and each stub of pencil, scrap of paper and drop of ink had to be hoarded.

Shortly after the end of the war, I went to Paris for my paper, the now defunct *Sunday Graphic*. The assignment from my Editor was to bring back a cross-section of French society since the Liberation, but I had a private assignment of my own.

Paris was pitilessly blanketed in fog and ice, through and over which young women in fancy dress dauntlessly flitted round the Place Vendôme and under the dark arcades of the rue de Rivoli; it happened to be the day of St Catherine when I set out to find Gordon Craig in the wilds of the XVIIth *arrondissement*. All Paris was freezing and starving; I had been warned that the most grateful gifts I could take to my friends would be soap and candles. Unhappily, the baggage allowance on our ex-Army Dakota was so small that I had only been able to pack a couple of boxes of candles and a few cakes of soap (still in short supply at home). On the flight I had been mentally apportioning these among my many friends, and figured out to my dismay that it would run to a candle and a third apiece and soap only for 'specials'!

Taxis were to be had only by V.I.Ps. I thrust three candles and the largest piece of soap into the pockets of my coat and plunged into the Métro; having no sense of direction, when I came up at Wagram I turned north instead of south, and dusk was closing in before I found the grey canyon of Ampère. No lights in any windows; at least my candles might be welcome.

When the door on which I knocked (for of course there was a power-cut at the time of my call) opened, I recognized the bright, small eyes and inquiring nose of E.G.C.: swaddled in coats, capes, shawl and mufflers of diverse patterns, his hands mittened, a rug clutched round his knees, there was no more of him to be seen. When the excitement of meeting was over, he pulled me into the studio, professing fear I might find it cold. After the arctic cold of the streets, it seemed to me warm, but a muggy, airless warmth; to preserve that little modicum of warmth one would not have dared, even for a moment, to open a window. Looking around, while E.G.C. divested himself, out of politeness or pride, of part of his woollen cocoon—it all seemed very familiar; still more so with the entrance of the devoted young woman and the charming child, Terry in every line and limb. She was christened 2.2. because she happened to be born on the twenty-second of the month. I felt that Toutou was a hard name for a serious girl to carry—if she happened to turn out that way—but reflected that she would probably re-christen herself.

The light, to my surprise, was good enough to need (as yet) no candles, for the big studio window faced westerly, on a livid sky. Impatient before all to show me the Work, E.G.C. drew me over to the table. Suddenly I found my eyes misted over; terrified they should overflow on to some precious bit of paper, I made a performance of wiping them and blowing my nose—it was coming out of the cold, I excused myself. I need not have troubled; E.G.C. eagerly handing me print after print, was aware only of the Work. Beautiful, complicated designs, cut with the knife or drawn with the pen: today I cannot remember which, probably both. I only remember that they were among the best black-and-whites of Gordon Craig's that I had seen. To make such a comment would have been foolish and, on my part, presumptuous, since I was hardly qualified to give an opinion on the medium. That which impressed me most deeply was his complete taking for granted that, while the whole world was engaged in destruction, he had been quietly getting on with his work of creation, under conditions which might well have daunted the artist of half his age—then seventy-five.

L'homme qui n'a rien fait! as he was slightingly described by one jealous, no doubt, of his achievements. Hardly less fatuous is a description in *The Times*, 23 October 1957, of 'vintage' Craig as 'hushed, exquisite, a little austere'. No less appropriate trio of adjectives could have been found, at any moment of his artistic career, for the work of Gordon Craig. Well—jealousy and ignorance alike give rise to strange misunderstandings. If *The Times* contributor, in his groping, had found the word *fastidious*, there would have been something in it. In 'vintage'—by which presumably is meant 'early'—Craig, there is plenty of fastidiousness, which increases through the years of his progress; there is also a robustious dash of bawdy and more than an echo of sardonic mirth, E.G.C. probably preparing himself to laugh at the writers of high-sounding twaddle about his work!

He has left it on record that he was 'excessively attracted sexually by women'—which proves itself down the years through a mixture of history, legend and apocrypha. Risking the accusation of naïveté, I would say that Craig's principal form of excess is work. When, during the war, food failed (he admits to being greedy) and women —apart from the faithful Daphne—failed, he lived on work, he ate, drank, slept and fornicated with it. There, in the rue Ampère was the proof of it; his mittened hands too frozen to handle a tool, his face a shrunken mask of yellow wax printed with his small, devilish smile—he was undefeated.

Back in the comfortable flat I had been lent, a servant came to bring me a bowl of hot soup and to take my coat and boots. I said I would keep the coat until I had thawed out, and sat down beside the stove to think about the scene I had just left. It felt shameful to be sitting in a warm room, with a hot meal ahead of me and enough light comfortably to read by. . . . Light!

I plunged my hands into my pockets and brought out, with horror, the candles and the soap. I felt inclined to rush straight back to the rue Ampère, and remembered that in half an hour I had an appointment with an important person on whom I was depending for facts and figures to take back to my Editor. By the time I was through, the household at the rue Ampère would probably have gone to bed, and I was due before dawn at Le Bourget. I tried miserably to figure out how I could get my wretched offering to Daphne: what a fuss for three candles and a bit of soap. I reminded myself they were not without light, for before I left Daphne had lit some kind of lamp.

It was close on midnight before I was free to reconsider the problem, and the importance of my mission had dwindled in my eyes. I could send nothing to the rue Ampère to compare with what I had been given; the light of that studio would not dwindle out for want of three little sticks of tallow!

The war was over, but there were no artistic opportunities and money was shorter than ever; life in Paris was very expensive.

Sick of it all, Gordon Craig made for the sweet South, and crushed himself and as many of his possessions as he had been able to transport into one small room of a *pension de famille* in Vence. He was grievously crowded for space, but, for once, he did not find this much of a trial. He had a comfortable bed and a table on which to spread out the things he wished to look at or to read; he had a big pair of scissors and there were walls and oddments of woodwork on which he could pin up things of which he particularly wished to be reminded. From Peter Brook's description in 1957, the 'reminders' must have crusted the walls inches deep, before they overflowed into cupboards and drawers. His engraver's tools were within reach, but, even had he had the space, he had no inclination, for the present, to use them. He was quite contented to browse over the multitudinous letters, cuttings and catalogues for which there had latterly seemed to be no time: oddments covering three-quarters of a century, relics of a century or more.

He was naturally very tired; having borne the brunt of the war years, his mind and body both needed rest. Curling himself into the past, he managed nevertheless to be alert to the present—the latter to an astonishing degree, considering his isolation from post-war artistic and intellectual circles, upon whose doings he kept a bright eye, occasionally breaking into profane condemnation. The chief butt of his antagonism continued to be the cinema (of which he knew almost nothing), despite the fact that it had provided 'Little Teddy' with a brilliant career.

In 1957 the Miracle happened.

The Bibliothèque Nationale (he spells it 'Bibliotec Nationel': all those years of living on the Continent never taught E.G.C. to speak or write any language other than his own. He can 'make himself understood' in a variety of tongues, but in this respect the laziness of the young 'Ted', his refusal to attempt to master any subject save those directly connected with his own interests and therefore, in his opinion, necessary, has persisted)—the Bibliothèque Nationale made him an offer of thirteen million francs, equal in sterling to about £13,000 as the exchange then went, for his Collection—the same which had been restored to him at the end of the war, through the kind offices of his friends Heim and Conrad. With Terry shrewdness—the commercial *fond* has survived through the generations, and it is unusual to find a Terry making a bad bargain for himself—he parted with only a quota of the Collection, reserving, according to his own reckoning, £19,000 worth, as values are today.

This windfall liberated E.G.C. from one room in a pension and enabled him to rent a house—*le mas André*—within sight of the Maritime Alps. It is pleasant to think of him in that scented country, where in spring every breeze comes laden with violets, and in summer with thyme and rosemary and the antique earth is fertilized by Visigoth, Lombard and Saracen; where at every turn of an alley there is something exciting or beautiful, perhaps to be translated into terms of the Theatre.

The same year brought to Gordon Craig a truly astonishing tribute.

It had apparently dawned on some person of more than ordinary discrimination that some honour was due to an Englishman whose services to the Theatre appeared to be conspicuous, according to what one read in the papers. Gordon Craig was offered and accepted a Companionship of Honour, which pleased him inordinately. Recognition had indeed been slow in coming; one can imagine with what Terry graciousness he acknowledged it.

It was the third honour to be conferred upon Terrys: Ellen Terry first, with her Dameship, John Gielgud had been created Knight Bachelor, and at last, Gordon Craig, Companion of Honour.

Let him speak the tag—a quotation from his own writings:

'Bless your heart, we had so much genius in the House of Terry that we all took that as a matter of course.'

CURTAIN

FAMILY TREE

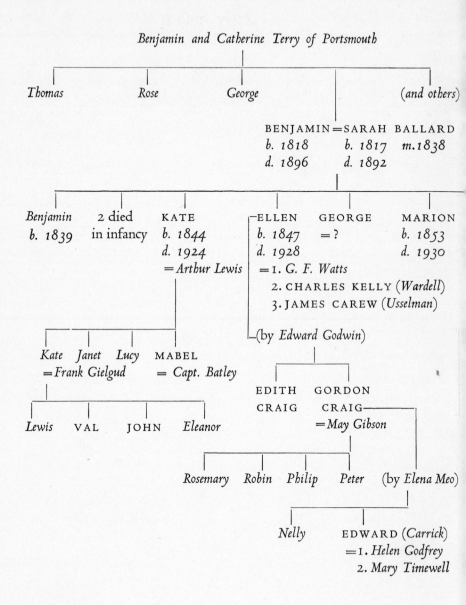

Benjamin and Catherine Terry of Portsmouth

| *Thomas* | *Rose* | *George* | | *(and others)* |

BENJAMIN = SARAH BALLARD
b. 1818   b. 1817   m.1838
d. 1896   d. 1892

Benjamin   2 died   KATE   ┌ELLEN   GEORGE   MARION
b. 1839   in infancy   b. 1844   b. 1847   = ?   b. 1853
                       d. 1924   d. 1928   d. 1930
                       = *Arthur Lewis*   = 1. *G. F. Watts*
                                  2. CHARLES KELLY (*Wardell*)
                                  3. JAMES CAREW (*Usselman*)

                                  └(by *Edward Godwin*)

Kate   Janet   Lucy   MABEL
= *Frank Gielgud*   = *Capt. Batley*   EDITH   GORDON
                                                CRAIG   CRAIG
Lewis   VAL   JOHN   *Eleanor*   = *May Gibson*

                                        Rosemary   Robin   Philip   Peter   (by *Elena Meo*)

                                                Nelly   EDWARD (*Carrick*)
                                                          = 1. *Helen Godfrey*
                                                            2. *Mary Timewell*

*Names in capital letters indicate members of
the family on, or connected with, the stage.*

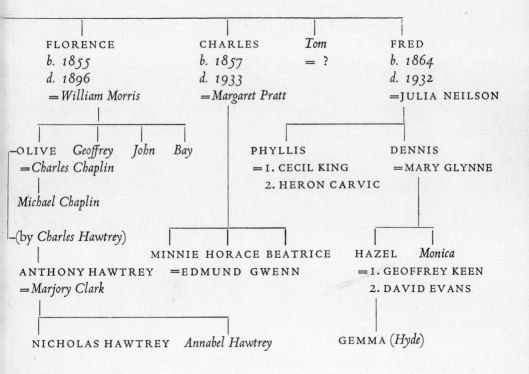

FLORENCE   CHARLES   *Tom*   FRED
b. 1855   *b. 1857*   = ?   *b. 1864*
d. 1896   *d. 1933*   *d. 1932*
= *William Morris*   = *Margaret Pratt*   = JULIA NEILSON

—OLIVE   *Geoffrey*   *John*   *Bay*   PHYLLIS   DENNIS
= *Charles Chaplin*   = I. CECIL KING   = MARY GLYNNE
                                       2. HERON CARVIC
Michael Chaplin

—(*by Charles Hawtrey*)   MINNIE HORACE BEATRICE   HAZEL   *Monica*
ANTHONY HAWTREY   = EDMUND GWENN   = I. GEOFFREY KEEN
= *Marjory Clark*   2. DAVID EVANS

NICHOLAS HAWTREY   *Annabel Hawtrey*   GEMMA (*Hyde*)

INDEX

Adlard, Eleanor, 385
Aidé, Hamilton: *Doctor Bill*, 211
Archer, Fred, 122, 198-9
Aria, Eliza, 186, 297
Ashcroft, (Dame) Peggy, 378
Atwood, Clare, 325-6, 386

Ballard, Peter, 10
Ballard, Sarah. *See* Terry, Sarah
Bancroft, Lady (*née* Marie Wilton), 156
Bancroft, (Sir) Squire, 160, 259-60
Barnes, Hilda, 343-4
Barrie, (Sir) James Matthew, 219, 293:
  Alice-Sit-by-the-Fire, 293; *Quality
  Street*, 281; *Walker, London*, 218
Barrymore, Maurice: *Nadjesda*, 199
Batley, Ralph, 287
Benson, Constance (Lady), 327
Benson, (Sir) Frank, 24, 246, 319
Bernhardt, Sarah, 261-2
Blattner, Ludwig, 336
Bourchier, Arthur, 156
Boucicault, Dion, 22-3, 37: *Hunted
  Down*, 107
Brough, William and Robert: *Endymion*,
  84
Bruckner, Johannes: *Elizabeth of England*,
  361-2
Buchanan, Robert: *A Man's Shadow*, 208
Bulwer-Lytton, Edward: *The Lady of
  Lyons*, 243
Butterworth, Clara, 302
Byron, Lord: *Sardanapalus*, 53

Carew (*né* Usselman), James, 299-300,
  307-10, 349
Carr, J. W. Comyns: *Far From the
  Madding Crowd* (adaptation), 171; *Frou-
  Frou*, 178
Carrick, Edward, 258, 299, 310, 324,
  348-50
Carroll, Lewis, 105-7

Carroll, Sydney, 316n., 320
Carvic, Heron, 215, 368-74, 383
Chaplin, Anthony, 313
Chaplin, Charles, 313
Chaplin, Michael, 313, 351
Chute, J. H., 78, 79, 80-1
Clarke, Marjory, 388
Cochran, C. B., 203, 310
Coghlan, Charles, 140, 142
Coward, Noël, 341
Craig, Edith: birth, 125; childhood,
  127, 136-9 *pass.*; 186, 188-91, 192;
  and her mother's relationship with
  Irving, 186; looks and personality,
  189-90, 210-11, 357; musical career
  in Germany, 197, 204; musical
  career cut short, 209; and her mother,
  210, 250, 251-2, 254-5, 305-6; acting, 248-9; dresses *Robespierre* for the
  Independent Theatre, 249; becomes
  a theatrical costumier, 249; marriage
  opportunities, 250; and Christopher
  St John, 250-2, 324-6; and Gordon
  Craig, 254-5; 'director manqué',
  324-5, 356-7, and Clare Atwood
  and the *ménage à trois*, 325-6; old age,
  356-8; and the Barn Theatre, 357,
  385; death, 385; achievements,
  385-6
Craig, (Edward) Gordon; birth, 126;
  childhood, 127, 136-9 *pass.*; 188-9,
  190, 197; early stage appearances,
  202, 209, 218, 252; talent, 202-4,
  218-19, 253, 310, 323, 394; acting
  ability, 218-19; marries, 224; pro-
  duces *Dido and Aeneas*, 252; and his
  mother, 254-6, 309, 311-12; and
  Elena Meo, 258, 299, 310, 311; pro-
  duces *The Vikings*, 291-2; fame on
  the Continent, 297-9, 310-11; marriage ends, 298; and Isadora Duncan
  and Eleanora Duse, 299; in London,
  311-12; on the Continent during the

Craig, (Edward) Gordon—*cont.*
First World War, 322-4; exhibition at the V. & A., 336-7; aged eighty-nine, 391-2; dislike of Mussolini, 394; during the Second World War, 395-6; in Paris, 396-9; a visit from the author, 397-9; in the South of France, 399-400; honoured, 399-400; *The Actor and the Uber-Marionette*, 323; *The Art of the Theatre*, 297; *The Artists of the Theatre of the Future*, 323; *Ellen Terry and her Secret Self*, 255-6; *Index to the Story of My Days*, 393; *A Living Theatre*, 323; *The Mask* (Journal), 310; *The Page* (Journal), 253, 291; *Towards a New Theatre*, 323
Craig, Edward (II). *See* Carrick, Edward
Craig ('Little Nelly'), 258, 299, 310, 324
Craig, Helen Paula, 350
Craig, Helen Ruskin (*née* Godfrey), 350
Craig, John, 350
Craig, Mary, 254, 298
Craig, Peter, 254, 298
Craig, Philip, 254
Craig, Robin, 254, 298
Craig, Rosemary, 254, 298

Davenport, Miss, 13-14
Dean, Basil, 378-9
Denvil, Clara, 37
Dickens, Charles, 17, 89; *Martin Chuzzlewit* (adaptation), 25; *Nicholas Nickleby* (adaptation), 16; *The Old Curiosity Shop* (adaptation), 131; *The Pickwick Papers* (adaptation), 17
Dubourg, A. W.: *New Men and Old Acres* (with Tom Taylor), 181
Dukes, Ashley: *Vintage Wine* (with Seymour Hicks), 367-8
Dumas (*fils*), Alexandre: *La Dame aux Camélias*, 261n
Du Maurier, George, 103, 104
Du Maurier, (Sir) Gerald, 270
Duncan, Dierdre, 299
Duncan, Isadora, 299
Duncan, Patrick, 299
Duse, Eleanora, 262, 299

Ellen Terry Museum, 366-8
Evans, David, 384

Fagin, J. B.: *The Wheel*, 360
Farebrother, Violet, 341
Fechter, Charles Albert, 88-9
Fernandez, James, 213
Feval, Paul: *The Duke's Motto*, 88-9
Forbes-Robertson, (Sir) Johnston, 143, 144-5

Gibson, May, 224
Gielgud, (Sir) (Arthur) John, 143, 242, 288, 313-15, 326-8, 346, 353-5, 360-1, 388-90: *Early Stages*, 234, 314, 355
Gielgud, Eleanor, 313
Gielgud, Frank, 222-3, 389
Gielgud, Kate. *See* Lewis, Kate
Gielgud, Lewis, 248, 288, 315, 326, 328
Gielgud, Val, 288, 314, 315, 352-3
Gilbert, (Sir) William Schwenck, 205n., 207: *Brantinghame Hall*, 207-8; *Comedy and Tragedy*, 208-9; *Dan'l Druce, Blacksmith*, 143-4; *Engaged*, 146; *Gretchen*, 159; *Pygmalion and Galatea*, 206-7
Ginner, Ruby, 327
Glynne, Mary, 319, 321, 362-4, 384
Godfrey, Helen, 350
Godwin, Edward William, 81-6, 98-101, 113-14, 123-6, 134-41, 198; *The Architecture and Costume of Shakespeare's Plays*, 139
Godwin, Sarah, 82, 98-9
Grantham, Wilfrid: *Mary Tudor*, 368-9
Granville-Barker, Harley, 218
Grein, J. T., 248-9
Gwenn, Edmund, 248

Halliday, Andrew: *Little Nell*, 131
Hardy, Thomas: *Far From the Madding Crowd* (adaptation), 171
Hare, (Sir) John, 239-40
Hawtrey, Annabel, 388
Hawtrey, Anthony, 350-1, 388-9

Hawtrey, (Sir) Charles, 270, 301, 312
Hawtrey, Marjory, 388
Hawtrey, Nicholas, 388
Heath, Caroline, 37
Heijermans, Herman: *The Good Hope*, 292-3
Hicks, (Sir) Seymour, 270, 366-8: *Vintage Wine* (with Ashley Dukes), 367-8
Hodson, Henrietta, 84, 110n.
Hyde, Gemma, 377

Ibsen, Henrik, 159; *Rosmersholm*, 310; *The Vikings*, 291-2
Irving, (Sir) Henry: *Hunted Down*, 107; early parts, 142-3; *Hamlet*, 143; at the Lyceum, 147 *et seq.*; first meets Ellen Terry, 148-9; use of stage lighting, 156; as an actor and producer, 160-2, 183, 196-7, 244-6; relationship with Ellen Terry, 184-8, 226, 243-5; *Twelfth Night*, 193-6; *Faust*, 196-8; second American tour, 202; *Macbeth*, *The Corsican Brothers* and *Henry VIII*, 217-19; and his sons' acting ability, 217-18, 246-7; *Becket*, 224-5; on *Godefroi and Yolande*, 230; ill health, 242-3; death, 294; financial affairs, 295-6
Irving, Laurence, 218-19, 230, 246-7, 319-20: *Godefroi and Yolande*, 230; *Peter the Great*, 246-7; *Typhoon*, 320

Jones, Henry Arthur, 159; *The Dancing Girl*, 213-14; *Hard Hit*, 208

Kean, Charles, 32-8, 45-71 *pass.*
Kean, Edmund, 28
Kean, Ellen, 11, 34-8, 45-71 *pass.*
Keane, Doris, 263-4, 332-3
Keeley, Annie, 32, 36, 37, 38
Keeley, Robert, 32, 36, 37, 38
Keen, Geoffrey, 377
Kelly (*né* Wardell), Charles, 144-8, 182, 184-5, 198, 308

Kendal (*née* Robertson), Madge, 289-90
Kester, Paul: *Sweet Nell of Old Drury*, 257
King, Cecil, 318
Kingsley, Charles: *Hypatia*, 227
Knowles, Sheridan: *The Hunchback*, 108

Lewis, Arthur, 103-5, 109-10, 221-3, 233, 238-42 *pass.*
Lewis, Janet, 170, 192, 199-200, 239, 315
Lewis, Kate, 143-4, 170, 199-200, 221-3, 234, 242, 287-8, 314, 315, 326-7
Lewis, Leopold: *The Bells*, 296
Lewis, Lucy Maud, 126, 170, 199-200, 216, 221-2, 239, 315
Lewis, Mabel. *See* Terry-Lewis, Mabel
Lowther, Aimée, 206
Lytton Bulwer, Edward, 4

Mackay, W. G.: *Doctor Wake's Patient* (with Robert Ord), 300
Macready, William, 11, 28-9, 33, 172
Marshall, Christabel. *See* St John, Christopher
Maugham, W. Somerset: *Our Betters*, 337-8
Meo, Elena, 258, 310, 311, 323-4
Meo, Gaetano, 258
Moore, Edward: *The Gamester*, 142
Morley, Malcolm, 70
Morris, Bay, 235, 248, 313, 315
Morris, Geoffrey, 201, 223, 313, 316
Morris, Gertrude, 207, 214, 236-7, 242
Morris, Hugh, 201, 216-17
Morris, John, 201, 223, 313, 315
Morris, Olive, 223-4, 234-7, 248, 297, 300-1, 312-13, 386-7
Morris, William, 151-3, 193, 198, 223, 233-7, 283-4, 313
Moss, Hugh: *Bootle's Baby*, 199

Naylor, Sydney, 71, 74-5
Neilson, Gertrude, 207, 214, 236-7, 242

Neilson, Julia: *Pygmalion and Galatea*, 206, 207; looks and acting ability, 206-7, 245, 339; background, 207; *Brantinghame Hall*, 207-8; *The Dancing Girl*, 213-14, 227; marries, 214; birth of Phyllis, 227; *Hypatia*, 227; *A Woman of No Importance*, 228-9; *An Ideal Husband*, 229; decides to tour America, 229; *King John*, 245; *Sweet Nell of Old Drury*, 257, 283, 285; management, 257 *et seq.*; marital difficulties, 283-4, 363; *Much Ado About Nothing*, 285; expensive tastes, 285; *The Scarlet Pimpernel*, 286-7, 315; during the First World War, 315-16; *The Borderer*, 339-40; retirement, 341, 366-7, 375-8; and her son's death, 365; and her husband's death, 366; *Vintage Wine*, 366-8; and Heron Carvic, 371, 382; during the Second World War, 375; 'dominant old lady', 381-3; death, 383

Neilson-Terry, Dennis, 229, 248, 302-3, 315-21 pass.

Neilson-Terry, Phyllis, 215, 224, 229, 235, 248, 297, 301-3, 317-18, 340, 360-2, 365-6, 368-74, 382

Neville, Henry, 91, 129-30, 132-3

Nicholson, (Sir) William, 161, 252-3

Offenbach, Jacques: *Geneviève de Brabant*, 157

Ogilvie, Stuart: *Hypatia*, 227; *The Master*, 240

Opera, bouffe, 157-8

Orczy, Baroness: *The Scarlet Pimpernel*, 286, 315-16

Ord, Robert: *Doctor Wake's Patient* (with W. G. Mackay), 300

Parker, Louis N.: *The Aristocrat*, 319

Pemberton, Edgar, 70, 159: *Ellen Terry and Her Sisters*, 82-3, 128-9

Pettitt, Henry: *In the Ranks* (with G. R. Sims), 182

Philips, Beatrice, 138, 141

Pinero, (Sir) Arthur Wing, 159: *The Gay Lord Quex*, 241

Poole, Miss, 37, 66

Pratt, Margaret, 176-8

Prinsep, Mrs Thoby, 91-7 pass.

Prinsep, Val, 97

Pryde, James, 161, 252-3

Purcell, Henry: *The Fairie Queene*, 203

Reade, Charles, 61-2, 89-90, 111-12, 135-8, 141, 198: *Dora*, 107, 111-12; *A Double Marriage*, 110; *It's Never Too Late To Mend*, 138; *Masks and Faces*, 61; *Nance Oldfield*, 218; *The Wandering Heir*, 135, 137-8, 139

Réjane, Gabrielle, 261, 262

Rhona, Mme Albina de, 76-9

Royde, Frank, 339, 341

Ryan, T. F. W., 298n.

St John Christopher, 218, 250-1, 292, 324, 325, 326, 386: *Hungerheart*, 251

Sardou, Victorien: *Dante*, 247, 257, 258; *Nos Intimes*, 77; *Robespierre*, 244, 247

Seymour, Sir Albert, 307-8

Seymour, Laura, 62

Shalders family, the, 15-17 pass.

Shakespeare, William*: *Coriolanus*, 257; *Cymbeline*, 231; *Hamlet*, 28-9, 89, 128-9, 143, 183, 346; *Julius Caesar*, 33; *King Henry V*, 70; *King Henry VIII*, 70-1, 219; *King John*, 46, 69, 245; *King Lear*, 37, 66-8, 225; *King Richard II*, 33-4; *Macbeth*, 69, 205-6, 300; *The Merry Wives of Windsor*, 289-90; *The Merchant of Venice*, 69, 140, 151; *A Midsummer Night's Dream*, 55, 56; *Much Ado About Nothing*, 132-3, 285; *Othello*, 241; *Romeo and Juliet*, 171; *The Tempest*, 61; *Twelfth Night*, 107, 193-4, 361, 364; *The Winter's Tale*, 53-4

Shaw, Mrs Alexander, 188

Shaw, George Bernard, 159, 218, 219-20, 231-3, 244, 326: *Captain Brassbound's Conversion*, 232, 244, 265, 293, 300, 307; *Pygmalion*, 282-3; *Widowers' Houses*, 159, 219

Shaw, Martin, 250

*including some mutilated versions

Siddons, Sarah, 34-5

Sims, G. R.: *In the Ranks* (with Henry Pettitt), 182

Stoker, Bram, 182, 224-5, 245, 296

Taylor, Tom, 61-2, 77, 89-95 *pass.*, 129: *The Hidden Hand*, 108; *The Ticket of Leave Man*, 129-30, 141-2; *New Men and Old Acres* (with A. W. Dubourg), 181

Tennyson, Alfred, Lord, 96, 224-5: *Becket*, 224-5, 294; *The Cup*, 183; *Dora*, 107

Ternan, Fanny, 37

Terriss, William, 129, 182

Terry, Beatrice, 177

Terry, Benjamin (I), 11

Terry, Benjamin (II): voice, 10-11; in Portsmouth, 11 *et seq.*; 'roistering character', 11-13; and the Portsmouth Theatre, 15-17; marries, 18-19; 'on the road', 19 *et seq.*; acting ability, 24-5, 43, 173; in Liverpool, 38-43 *pass.*; encourages Kate, 39-46; in London, 46 *et seq.*; appearances at the Princess's Theatre, 46, 53, 54, 69, 70; 'the Terry heart', 55; coaches his children, 55-6, 146-7; in Stanhope Street, Kentish Town, 56 *et seq.*; summer season at Ryde, 59-61; difficulties with the Kean management, 63-7; first attempt at management, 68; inheritance, 71; 'Entertainment' at the Royal Colosseum, Regent's Park, 71-2; touring with the 'Entertainment', 72; infidelity, 73, 74-6; and his daughters' careers, 76-7, 121, 131; at the Theatre Royal, Bristol, 79-86 *pass.*; letter from Benjy, 86-7; and Ellen's first marriage, 95; and Kate's marriage, 113; and Ellen's disappearance, 114; preference for Charlie, 119; marital difficulties, 120-1; and Ellen's second marriage, 145-6; in Cathcart Road, Earls Court, 152 *et seq.*; financial difficulties, 173-4; letter to Polly, 180n.; 'flu, 212; after his wife's death, 215-16; death, 230-1

Terry, Benjamin (III): childhood; 25-7, 39, 41, 44-5, 52, 60-1; 'a rakish son', 73-4, 86; in Australia, 86-7; in 'the wine and spirits trade', 117-18; in India, 147, 174-5, 217, 288

Terry, Catherine, 11, 18, 60-1, 71

Terry, Charles, 73, 119, 132, 146-7, 176-9, 288, 328-9

Terry, Dennis. *See* Neilson-Terry, Dennis

Terry, Edward, 11

Terry, Ellen (Nelly): birth, 30; on Kean, 33-4; in Liverpool, 38-44 *pass.*; looks and acting ability, 40, 76, 81, 149-50, 184, 219-20, 260-5; to London, 48; at rehearsals at the Princess's Theatre, 51-2; Mamillius in *The Winter's Tale*, 53-5; Puck, 55-6; at the house in Kentish Town, 56 *et seq*; summer at Ryde, 59-61; *Boots at the Swan*, 59; to London, 61; *White Cat* and *Faust* (burlesque), 61; taken up by Reade and Taylor, 61-2; on Ryder, 63; 'removed from the theatre', 64-5; one-night entertainment, 68; and the Keans' Farewell Season, 69-71; Prince Arthur in *King John*, 69; Fleance in *Macbeth*, 69; 'Drawing-room Entertainment', 71-6 *pass.*; *Home for the Holidays*, 72; love of the country, 75; audition with Mme de Rhona, 76; melodrama at the Royalty, 77-9; in Bristol, 79-86 *pass.*; 'besieged by youths', 82-3, 84-5; entertained by the Godwins, 83-4, 85; Cupid in *Endymion*, 84; Titania, 85-6; returns to London, 86; at the Haymarket, 89; visits to the Taylors, 89-90; painted by Watts, 92, 97; marries him, 93-6; difficult married life, 96-101; meets Edward Godwin again, 98-100; compromised with him, 101; returns to her parents, 102; in the family group photographed by Lewis Carroll, 106-7; on tour, 107-8; letter to her mother, 108; Helen in

Terry, Ellen (Nelly)—*cont.*

The Hunchback, 108-9; riding in the Row, 110; small parts at the Queen's, 110-11, 113, 114; accompanies Kate to Manchester, 111; feelings for Edward Godwin, 114-15; disappears, 114-15; life in the country as Godwin's mistress, 122 *et seq.*; birth of Edith, 124; birth of Edward, 125-6; a holiday in France, 126; and her children, 127; financial difficulties, 134; stage offer from Charles Reade, 135-6; returns to London, 136; at the house in Taviton Street, 136 *et seq.*; Philippa Chester in *The Wandering Heir*, 137-8; at the Prince of Wales, 139-42; Portia, 139-40; affair with Godwin finishes, 141; received by her family, 141; on Irving as an actor, 142-3; at the Court, 143-7; *Olivia*, 143, 147-8; divorced, 143; marries Charles Kelly (Wardell), 144-5; meets Irving, 148-9; engaged by him for Ophelia, 149; at the Lyceum, 150 *et seq.*; and amateurs, 162-3; financial and marital difficulties, 170-1; with Fred in *New Men and Old Acres*, 181; relationship with Irving, 183-8, 226; various parts at the Lyceum, 183; separates from Kelly, 184-5; and her children's surname, 188-9; relationship with them at this time, 189-91; Viola in *Twelfth Night*, 193-5; Marguerite in *Faust* (adaptation), 196-8; taste in clothes, 198; death of three friends, 198-9; and Kate, 200-1; portraits of her at this time, 204-5; Lady Macbeth, 205-6; and Oscar Wilde, 206; a Command Performance at Sandringham, 209; in a French Revolution drama, 209; and her mother's death, 215; and her father at this time, 215-16; Henrietta Maria in *Charles I*, 218; *Nance Oldfield*, 218; Katherine in *Henry VIII*, 219; Cordelia, 225; and Irving's waning interest, 226; American tour, 230; Imogen, 231; and George Bernard Shaw, 231-3, 256; difficulties with Irving, 242-5; Lady Waynflete in *Captain Brassbound's Conversion*, 244, 307; friendship with Laurence Irving, 246-7; and Edith, 250-1, 254-5, 305-6; and Gordon Craig, 254-5; Volumnia, 257; Olivia again, 257-8; letter to Fred, 258; and Marion, 259-60; her marriages, personality and acting ability, 260-5; appearance when middle-aged, 263; plays Olivia again, 264-5; buys Smallhythe Place, 265; appeals for the abolition of the 'paper' tax, 268; and 'humble' Terrys, 283; Katherine in *Henry VIII* again, 289; Mistress Page, 289-90; stage dress, 290; takes Imperial Theatre for Gordon Craig, 290-2; Hiordis in *The Vikings*, 291-2; Kniertje in *The Good Hope*, 292-3; *Alice-Sit-by-the-Fire*, 293; and Irving's death, 296; at 215 King's Road, 303 *et seq.*; Jubilee, 306-7; and James Carew (Usselman), 307-10; friendship with Sir Albert Seymour, 307; marries James Carew, 309; during the First World War, 321-2; the Nurse in *Romeo and Juliet*, 332-3; at Burleigh Mansions, 333 *et seq.*; financial difficulties, 333-5; appears for a week at the Gaiety Theatre, Manchester, 335-6; death, 342-5; *Memoirs*, 46, 54, 55-6, 62, 101, 107, 142, 143, 183, 195, 204, 244n., 251, 344; *The Story of My Life, see Memoirs*

Terry, Fred: childhood, 95, 102, 119-20, 145, 179-80; in the Lewis Carroll family group, 119-20; and Ellen's second marriage, 145; education, 179-80; looks, 180; early stage parts, 181-2; *New Men and Old Acres*, 181; meets Irving, 182; *Twelfth Night*, 194-5; as a producer, 196; *Olivia*, 198; *Comedy and Tragedy*, 208-9; *Doctor Bill*, 211; *The Dancing Girl*, 213-14, 227; marries, 214; *Hamlet*, 227; *Hypatia*, 227; *A Woman of No Importance*, 228-9; decides to tour America,

Terry, Fred—*cont.*

229; personality, 229-30, 245, 285; the turn of the century, 245-6; and Ellen's career, 257-8; management, 257 *et seq.*; *Sweet Nell of Old Drury,* 257, 283, 285; *The Heel of Achilles,* 257, 283; *Mistress Wilful,* 257; acting ability, 257, 284-5; *For Sword or Song,* 258, 283, 284; marital difficulties, 283-4, 363; *Much Ado About Nothing,* 285; expensive tastes, 285; ill health, 285, 338-40, 365; *The Scarlet Pimpernel,* 286-7, 315; letter from Ben (III), 288; and Irving's death, 296; during the First World War, 315-16; and Dennis, 316-17, 321; and Charles, 328-9; *The Borderer,* 339-40; retires, 341; and Dennis's death, 365; death, 366; will, 371-2

Terry, Florence (Floss): childhood, 73, 87-8, 105, 107, 116-17; acting ability, 121, 130; early parts, 130-1; clothes, 131-2; understudies Marion, 132-3; on tour, 150; at the Lyceum, 150-1; amateur theatricals, 151; social life, 151-2; marries, 152-3; in Campden Hill Road, 153 *et seq.*; children, 170, 191, 201; personality, 192-3, 201-2; and her mother's death, 215; death of baby Hugh, 216-17; a visit to Brighton, 217; at the house in Harpenden, 223; ill health and death, 233-5

Terry, George, 39-42 *pass.,* 52, 73, 74, 87, 113, 118, 132, 147, 175

Terry, Hazel, 319, 329-30, 364, 377-8, 384-5

Terry, Horace, 177-8, 315

Terry, James, 11

Terry, Kate: birth, 28; in Liverpool, 38-44 *pass.*; very early stage training, 39-40; offered audition by Charles Kean, 42-3; to London, 44-5; audition with Charles Kean, 46; engaged by him to appear at the Princess's Theatre, 46; various pantomimes, 46; Prince Arthur in *King John,* 46-7; Command Performance at Windsor, 47-8; rehearsals and training at the Princess's, 51-2; various parts there, 53; *The Winter's Tale,* 53-4; *A Midsummer Night's Dream,* 55-6; at the house in Kentish Town, 56 *et seq.*; summer at Ryde, 59-61; returns to London and Ariel at the Princess's, 61; aged fourteen, 61; taken up by Taylor and Reade, 61-2; letters to Mrs Kean, 63, 64, 65; Cordelia, 66-7; letter to Charles Kean, 66; one night entertainment, 68; and the Kean's farewell, season, 69-71; Blanche of Spain in *King John,* 69; Titania, 69-70; *Henry V,* 70; 'Drawingroom Entertainment', 71-6 *pass.*; *Home for the Holidays,* 72; booked for the St. James's, 72; at the St. James's, 77-8; looks at this time, 76; *Friends or Foes (Peril),* 77; at the Bristol Theatre Royal, 78-86 *pass.*; 'besieged by youths', 82-3, 84-5; entertained by the Godwins, 83-4, 85; *Endymion,* 84; leading lady at the Lyceum, 88-9; *The Duke's Motto,* 88-9; Ophelia 89; and Arthur Montagu, 90-1; at the Olympic, 91, 102, 107-9 *pass.*; looks at this time, 91; painted by Watts, 91-2; and the plot to marry her to him, 93-4; and Arthur Lewis, 104-5; in the Lewis Carroll family group, 106-7; *Twelfth Night,* 107; with Irving in *Hunted Down,* 107; at the Adelphi, 107, 110-12; *Dora,* 107, 111-12; Julia in *The Hunchback,* 108-9; engaged to Arthur Lewis, 109; riding in the Row, 110; final stage appearances, 110-11; Juliet, 110; *Plot and Passion,* 110, 111; acting ability, 111-12; marries, 113; married life at Moray Lodge, 115, 120-3, 126-7, 191-2, 199-201, 233, 238; birth of Katie, 115; pays for Polly's and Floss's school, 116; birth of Janet, 124; and her children's upbringing, 126-7, 199-200; and Ellen, 200-1; summer at Englefield

Terry, Kate—*cont.*

Green, 222; and Frank Gielgud, 222-3; silver wedding, 223; financial difficulties, 233, 238-42; in West Cromwell Road, 238-42; returns to the stage in *The Master*, 240; old age and death, 331-2

Terry, Margaret, 176-8

Terry, Marion (Polly): childhood, 52, 73, 105, 107-8, 116-17; acting ability and personality, 119, 121, 130, 146, 149-50, 171-2, 191, 195-6, 205, 220-1, 259-60, 281-3, 338; Ophelia, 128-9; *Love in Humble Life* and early small parts, 130-1; clothes, 131-2, 198; *Much Ado About Nothing*, 132-3; *Dan'l Druce, Blacksmith*, 143-4; social life, 151-2; *Far From the Madding Crowd*, 171; and Fred's education, 179; and money, 180; at the Lyceum, 195-6, 198; *Hard Hit*, 208; and her mother's death, 215; *Lady Windermere's Fan*, 220-1; and Florence, 233, 234; and William Morris, 235-6; at Buckingham Palace Mansions, 242 *et seq.*; and Ellen, 259; possible love affairs, 259-60; at Stratford-on-Avon, and on tour, 281; final parts, 337-8, death, 346-7; on John Gielgud, 346

Terry, Minnie, 177-9, 199, 208, 217-18, 248

Terry, Monica, 319, 384

Terry, Nelly. *See* Terry, Ellen

Terry, Polly. *See* Terry, Marion

Terry, Rose, 12, 15

Terry, Sarah: in Portsmouth, 10-19 *pass.*; appearance and voice, 10-11, 72, 169; marries Ben Terry, 18-19; 'on the road', 19 *et seq.*; and child-bearing, 24-31 *pass.*; birth of Kate, 28; and Macready's *Hamlet*, 28-9, 172; birth of Ellen, 30; in Liverpool, 38-44 *pass.*; to London, 44-5; ward-robe mistress at the Princess's Theatre, 49 *et seq.*; in Stanhope Street, Kentish Town, 56 *et seq.*; summer at Ryde, 59-61; marital difficulties, 73, 120; on tour again, 74-6; in Bristol

79-86 *pass.*; concern for Kate's and Ellen's future, 82-5, 90; birth of Tom, 86; and Ellen's first marriage, 94; birth of Fred, 95; letter from Nelly and Polly on tour, 107-8; at Kate's wedding, 113; and Polly's and Floss's education, 116; play-reading, 121; 'comparative afflu-ence', 137; and her actress girls, 143-4; 'fireside coachings', 146-7; at Cathcart Road, Earls Court, 152 *et seq.*; old age, 172 *et seq.*; and Tom, 175; 'flu, 212; death, 214-5, 217

Terry, Tom, 31, 74, 86, 117, 118-19, 132, 152, 175-6, 217, 315

Terry-Lewis, Mabel, 126, 170, 199-200, 239-41, 246, 287, 331, 359-60

Tree, Ellen, 11, 34-8, 45-71 *pass.*

Tree, (Sir) Herbert Beerbohm, 156, 207-8, 213, 227-9, 289-90

Usselman, James. *See* Carew, James

Waller, Lewis, 229, 271

Ward, (Dame) Genevieve, 344-5

Wardell, Charles. *See* Kelly, Charles

Wardell, Edith. *See* Craig, Edith

Wardell, Edward Gordon. *See* Craig, Edward Gordon

Watts, George Frederick, 91-101, 143

Wilbraham, Edward, 316n.

Wilde, Oscar, 206, 228-9, 281-2: *An Ideal Husband*, 229; *The Importance of Being Ernest*, 159, 358; *Lady Winder-mere's Fan*, 220-1; *A Woman of No Importance*, 228

Williams, Harcourt, 306

Wills, William Gorman, 218; *Charles I*, 213-18; *Eugene Aram*, 202; *Faust* (adaptation), 196, 197; *Olivia* (adaptation of *The Vicar of Wake-field*), 147, 148, 198, 218, 257

Wilton, Marie (Lady Bancroft), 139, 156

Wolfit, (Sir) Donald, 341-2

Wood, Mrs John, 135-6

Wyndham, (Sir) Charles, 111

Yerret, Miss. *See* Terry, Sarah